Alan Ramsey began his 56 years in journalism as a £3-a-week, less ninepence tax, copy boy on Frank Packer's Sydney *Daily Telegraph* in 1953, the year Stalin died and Hillary climbed Everest. In 1987, by now a hardened lifer, he wrote the first of 2273 columns from the granite quarry of national politics, Canberra, for *The Sydney Morning Herald*; same time, same place, most every Saturday for 22 years until he was pardoned on December 20, 2008.

# Alan Ramsey

## A MATTER OF OPINION

### Informed, insightful, unafraid...

from over two decades of political writing for
*The Sydney Morning Herald*

**With illustrations by Ward O'Neill**

ALLEN&UNWIN

First published in 2009



Allen & Unwin
83 Alexander Street
Crows Nest NSW 2065
Australia
Phone:  (61 2) 8425 0100
Fax:      (61 2) 9906 2218
Email:   info@allenandunwin.com
Web:      www.allenandunwin.com

Cataloguing-in-Publication details are available
from the National Library of Australia
www.librariesaustralia.nla.gov.au

ISBN 978 1 74237 158 0

Set in 11/12.8 pt Minion Pro by Bookhouse, Sydney
Printed by Griffin Press, Adelaide

10 9 8 7 6 5 4 3 2 1

To Laura and our gorgeous girl, Tosca.
And Steven and Susan, with a father's love.
And to 22 years of *Herald* colleagues and *Herald* readers.

# Contents

*'I'll tell you what I'm tired of; I'm (expletive) tired of gallery deadbeats.'*—Paul Keating, in a phone call on Saturday morning, February 10, 1996, three weeks out from the March 2 election that ended his prime ministership, his political career and 13 years of Hawke/Keating rule, the longest continuous period of national Labor government since Federation. In that morning's *Herald* I'd written, in part: 'Sooner or later in this campaign, the Prime Minister will have to come to terms with the fact that simply jetting about the country, promising a bucket of money here and there, and putting the boot into his opponent whenever he has anything to say, isn't going to work after 13 years. Most people, I think, stopped listening long ago. They're tired of arrogant smarties and tap dancers and excuses and cronyism and, most of all, irrespective of Labor's achievements and its energy of earlier years, they're tired of the Prime Minister's formidable mouth.'

# Preface

## The Week
David Marr

DECEMBER 20, 2008

## Ramsey Saw Things as They Were and Walked a tightrope Without a Safety Net

FOR A man who was absolutely right so often, Alan Ramsey could be magnificently wrong. Not weasel wrong in the political fashion he so deplored, but no wiggle room, up on the high wire without a net, entirely wrong. 'Latham?' he asked himself on the morning of the 2004 poll. 'I think he can get there.'

He was rough on himself; he ran risks; and every time he came a cropper he picked his battered body up again and was back on the field next Saturday laying into the players, the ref, the crowd, the press, the linesman—everyone in sight down to the kid with the oranges at half-time.

This week is the last time Ramsey stakes out his familiar territory in the middle of the Saturday *Herald*. After 21 years, four prime ministers, eight federal elections and God knows how many hundreds of thousands of furious words, he's hanging up his columnist's hat.

Bad temper is hard to sustain. Mere rage isn't particularly attractive. In this trade we're schooled to keep our tempers and pretend detachment. Not Ramsey. And his readers loved him for breaking the rules. They loved his naked anger—and his subjects had little choice but to respect it—because Ramsey was one of the few in the Canberra press gallery who wrote from his heart.

So he was right passionately, wrong passionately and patronised at times by his hardboiled colleagues for taking a stand in their shifting world. He was a moralist—still is, of course, and will be to his dying day—and as an unflinching moralist he did the work over the last decade that mattered most to his readers: seeing John Howard for exactly who he was.

The old Prime Minister was not among the walking dead who came to Ramsey's farewell dinner at Old Parliament House a few weeks ago. What an extraordinary gathering. Ramsey, it seemed, had wandered into Madame Tussaud's and offered the waxworks one last outing in the capital.

Andrew Peacock was looking trim, suspiciously trim. Bill Hayden had misplaced his equerry. Tony Eggleton represented the Pleistocene. Keating picked the eyes out of the room. Still busy. Max Walsh had the satisfied look of a man caught up in a financial catastrophe more appalling than any of the disasters he's spent his life predicting.

And Ramsey was king of them all for the night: subjects, sources, victims and colleagues. The breadth of his friendships on display was astonishing. One of the silliest men in Parliament, Bill Heffernan, was in the same room as one of the sanest, John Faulkner. The senators had nothing to say to each other on this occasion, but each has spoken eloquently over the years through Ramsey.

In an age addicted to the grab, Ramsey never lost faith in the big speech. His head was full of Hansard. Yes, he quoted in slabs, but through great speeches he brought Parliament and its arcane drama alive. And he did what commentators rarely do these days: he allowed his subjects their own voice. Not infrequently, they had the privilege of speaking from the grave.

As time went on, Ramsey lived with legions of the dead in his imagination. Perhaps because he had explored the territory too often himself, the border between this life and the next became rather hazy for him. He honoured the known and the unknown dead in his columns. History was alive in his analysis. One of Ramsey's signature lines is: 'Nothing changes.'

So the fact that he was out the back working frantically on his own speech that night—even while the video tribute was playing—surprised none of his many editors in the room. Ramsey is a chronic late filer. He is loved by his colleagues for this alone: that he is the worst of us, the one that's always last to finish.

If once or twice in the last couple of decades you weren't woken by the satisfying thump of the Herald on your doormat on Saturday morning, know that all the official excuses—the talk of paper breaks at the Chullora printing plant—were only ever a cover. Ramsey was to blame.

On the night of his farewell dinner he was coping with a late final version of an elegant speech of thanks to most of the people in the room. Ramsey was always a generous acknowledger of his debts. Perhaps it was the scribble over the typing read in dim light that led him to call Laura Tingle his 'lovely wife Lorrie'.

A coward would have surged forward at that point hoping to leave the gaffe behind. Ramsey paused deliberately. His face registered swiftly disbelief, despair, confusion and then, as the room erupted in ridicule, huge amusement at himself. Ramsey had done it again.

I never thought he got native title. Somehow refugees didn't engage his heart. These were quirks loyal readers like me bore for the satisfaction of finding Ramsey next week, say, spewing lava over the Howard Government for its servility to Washington and neglect of the Guantanamo prisoner David Hicks.

Every election was Howard's last in Ramsey's mind. Then came 2007 and on the morning of the poll his readers found him at his scornful and triumphant best. Celebration calls for a slab of his own words. There is no one now, and no one coming along, who can write like this:

'The end of the line. Remember that heading in the *Herald* a few weeks back, after one of the opinion polls bumped up the Government's lousy standing a point or two? "Lazarus stirs", it said optimistically of John Howard. Wrong. It was just the flies moving.

'Yesterday, in the nation's Parliament, with hardly a politician to be seen anywhere, we got some election realism. Three rows of recycling bins, whacking big green ones with yellow lids. More than 300 of them.

'Where? In the basement corridor of the ministerial wing. The bins seemed a more apt commentary than all the desperate, last-minute Coalition windbaggery going on around the nation on what is about to descend on the Prime Minister after 33 years in public life and almost 12 years remaking Australia in his own miserable, disfigured image. They arrived two days ago and whoever they're for, 48 hours before a single vote is cast today, you felt somebody, somewhere, finally got it right.

'The end of the line.'

It's said all political careers end unhappily. That's where journalists enjoy a distinct advantage over their raw material. Ramsey is not defeated. He's going simply because it's time. He will be missed.

# The Career
Alan Ramsey

**DECEMBER 2, 1997**

THE FIRST journalist I ever knew was Randy Stone. He covered the night beat in one of those old radio serials and he lit up my small world once a week in the mid- to late 1940s in a way only Mo McCacky sometimes could but Jack Davey and First Light Frazer and Mrs 'obbs and the Yes What classroom never quite managed.

Years later, long after Frank Packer's *Daily Telegraph* freed me from school with an offer of £3 a week, less ninepence tax, to become a copy boy, the year Stalin died and Hillary climbed Everest, I became Randy Stone from midnight to 8am, five nights a week, for seven months on Fairfax's afternoon shrieker, *The Sun*, and competed furiously against other obscure Randy Stones covering police rounds for Ezra Norton's *Daily Mirror*, among them Max Walsh.

That was the year after the Melbourne Olympics and the same year Peter Costello was born and Paul Keating became a teenager, a time when a copy of the *Herald* cost fivepence and the press was still the press and not the media, and television was a gauche infant and when journalism was graced by editors like J.D. Pringle and Lindsay Clinch and names like Tom Farrell, Merton Woods, Tom Fitzgerald, Ian Fitchett and a young Gavin Souter; when the *Herald*'s Column 8 was still signed Granny and was still edited by Sid Deamer, and when the *Telegraph* was unashamedly one of the very pillars in sustaining Menzies' Liberal Party, and when the *Herald*, in all its then 126 years of existence had still not once enjoined its readers to vote anything but conservative.

It was a very different Australia, an insular and still very white Australia proud of the atom bombs the Brits were testing at Woomera and still uncomfortable with the strangeness and mid-European accents of New Australians, a term by then as derogatory as the 'reffos' my father insisted on calling any but pommy migrants; and 19-year-old Randy Stones like me knew nothing about anything except outrunning the opposition and obeying the news editor and the basic rules of our craft: who, what, where, when and how, but almost never why.

Why was rarely our business. Why suggested value judgments, even comment, and such independence was the province only of editors and 'special correspondents' and big name gossip columnists like David McNicoll and Jim McDougall. Reporters remained anonymous gatherers and presenters of fact, faceless artisans in a business that taught us to write with clarity and brevity in formula journalese and to leave the prose to the poets, and readers almost never knew who we were, even if some of us thought we were truly Randy Stone.

It was a time, before the newspaper chains began swallowing everything, when you could learn your craft in the bush on small independents like the once-a-week *Mt Isa Mail* and Darwin's twice-a-week *Northern Territory News*, with their flat-bed presses and hot-metal technology and housewives who came on publishing night to fold and cut and bundle; and then, when you went back to the city to try the deep end, there were seven employers and 15 mainland metropolitan dailies with which to find work, even if Melbourne's Herald and Weekly Times group and Sydney's Fairfax controlled most of it. Now there are just two employers, excluding Perth, in those same capital cities, and only nine newspapers, and if Fairfax and Murdoch won't have you, then you don't swim at all, not in the big pool.

The newspaper families have gone too, though Rupert founded his own dynasty and made the Murdoch name bigger than his father ever did and Kerry Packer still wants what his father could never get. But Norton sold Mirror Newspapers to Fairfax who on-sold to Murdoch, the Symes sold *The Age* in Melbourne to Fairfax, Frank Packer sold the *Telegraph* to Murdoch who later swallowed the whole of the Herald and Weekly Times too, and young Warwick collapsed what his family took 150 years to build so that all that remains, in the hands of the mutuals and the money men, is the Fairfax name. Up in the penthouses, where the real sharks are, newspaper ownership has always been an incestuous business.

What about the rest of us below stairs?

Television changed everything, just as it changed forever the political process and continues to Americanise our culture. It killed the afternoon shriekers and personalised journalism. Readers now get names, even faces, with the news and the opinion. Writers as elegant as Robert Haupt, Lenore Nicklin, David Marr, Peter Bowers, Peter Smark, Janet Hawley, Adele Horin, Les Carlyon and Ross Gittins illuminated *The Sydney Morning Herald* just as they liberated its anonymous and staid columns of yesteryear.

And television did it. It turned the Randy Stones into divas. It forced newspapers to compete by acknowledging their own. The anonymous written word was no longer enough, however elegant or incisive or dramatic. *Herald* journalism is now a highly bylined hybrid of the nightly television bulletins and the ABC's *Four Corners,* complete with graphs, colour, self-promotion, shorter news stories, longer features, more analysis and great dollops of lifestyle. It took 103 years for the *Herald* to put news on its front page and 130 years to start recognising its reporters in print. Now Granny wouldn't recognise herself.

It is 40 years since this Randy Stone covered the night beat and the better part of 11 of them since he arrived (on May 9, 1987) on the *Herald's* Saturday pages to a different beat altogether. Still, the basics remain the same. Only now the story is usually the why. Politics is all about why.

Ian Fitchett, for years the *Herald's* political correspondent and a great walrus of a man with as acerbic a tongue as I ever heard, once told me I was a 'bloody fool' after I'd shouted at John Gorton from up in the press gallery of Parliament the day before Gorton lost his prime ministership to Billy McMahon in 1971. Fitch was right, of course, but it made me aware how easy it can be for politicians to make idiots of themselves in a single mad moment. It's the ones who keep doing it you don't spare.

Yet political writers come and go, just like politicians. The one constant for many more years than our national Parliament itself has been the *Herald*, one of the great newspapers and still recognised as such. And politicians, for all their feigned indifference, understand its influence. Wran loathed the paper, Hawke and Keating often despised, even feared it, and John Howard, too, thought it lived among his enemies. Clearly we must be doing something right, but political leaders listen only for applause.

There are exceptions. A postcard arrived from Europe this week of a painting of a 1930s young woman. 'Dear Al,' it said. 'Not many old comrades left in Barcelona, but I managed to track down this picture of her, painted specially for me the day the bedraggled remnants of the International Brigade marched out of the city. It was the last time the earth moved for me in Spain. Paris is different, a timeless city. I had an aperitif or two at 'Les Deux Magots', but too many tourists asking for autographs, so I moved to 'Le Select', an artists' haunt at the turn of the century. Had an aperitif or two and thought I saw Toulouse Lautrec at a nearby table. I gave him a friendly wave, then realised I was gazing into one of those long mirrors. C'est la vie. John Button.'

Button would remember Randy Stone, and I miss him and so does politics.

# The Colleague
Alan Ramsey

**MAY 11, 2005**

EVERYONE WHO knows him has a Peter Bowers story. It was Bowers who gave Malcolm Fraser his 'Easter Island face', a magical figure of speech later pinched by everyone and never surpassed in political commentary in this country. A favourite Bowers moment of mine came during Fraser's losing 1983 election campaign.

Interviewed on television, Fraser acknowledged Australians' liking for a bet but asserted they would never gamble on Australia's future by voting Labor. Bowers waited until Fraser had sat back, looking pleased with himself, then he lent across and said knowingly: 'You wouldn't want to bet on it, would you?' It was one of those great moments.

Fraser's face said it all. A few weeks later he was gone from politics, his career killed off by yet another messiah, just as Fraser had been in 1975.

'Daffy' Bowers, a truly authentic Australian character, was a Sydney journalist all his working life, first for Frank Packer's *Daily Telegraph* and then, from the late 1950s onwards, for the *Herald*, from which he couldn't be shifted until he 'retired' in the early 1990s, a process he began in 1987. Peter had more farewells than Melba, and deserved them all.

I don't know who tagged him 'Daffy', but it had everything to do with his manic persona, particularly when the heat of a good story was on him, and nothing to do with the way his head worked. I've known him all my working life, since 1953 when I started as a copy boy at the *Telegraph*, just as he had done six years earlier. Thirty-four years later, when he first 'retired' in May 1987, I was given his job filling the top half of the *Herald*'s Saturday opinion page.

I've been doing it ever since.

Peter Bowers never lost his touch, just his passion for politics. He was a superbly original storyteller, and a month after he 'quit' the *Herald* all those years ago and went off to a South Coast caravan park to forget about politicians, he wrote: 'A quarrelsome caucus of pelicans and seagulls scrambling for fish gut made me think of Canberra. Every time I look at a pelican I think of a lot of politicians. There's more to a pelican than a big beak, just as there's more to a politician than a big mouth.'

A few months later he was back writing tennis and Olympics sport and every now and then, when an election rolled around, he'd keep his hand in on politics with campaign sketches. He once told of Labor's Gareth Evans pelting him with a lounge cushion—to which Evans replied, in a letter to the *Herald,* 'He who has never wished to pelt a cushion at Bowers doesn't know him'—just as in late 1986 he wrote of John Howard, far more prescient than most: 'Will you all please start taking John seriously?'

John Button never took Bowers too seriously.

Bowers once told, in print, a lovely story likening Button's political dexterity as a Hawke and Keating minister to his ability to 'dodge raindrops'. Button responded by sending him an illiterate letter under the pseudonym 'Norman Cartwright', which said: 'I have given up reading the *Herald* becorse of your lies about Senator Butten and have also written to Mr Fairfax. The Fairfax yeller press plays the man too much, I told him, and your the leader of the push. Anyway, I found the latest tripe of yours in the dunny at the Broken Hill races, all torn up, which is the way it ort to be. This bit says senator butten told you to piss orf. Well, I hope he did becorse I know the same is a gentlemen and takes things very serieesly. So why do you tell all these lies? I know, its becorse you want to tear down short poppies becaus your a bit sick in the head, same as your poofy fetich about senator Butten dodging raindrops. Why don't you pull your finga out?'

Bowers published the letter. Like Fraser's 'Easter Island face', Button's ability to 'dodge raindrops' went into political folklore.

'Daffy' Bowers long ago pulled his 'finga' out. Now 75, he was admitted to hospital with a ruptured bowel last week. The details are much too much information, as my six-year-old would say. They tried to send him home at the weekend but the bleeding resumed. I visited him two days ago. His bum was much better, he's a long way from carking it, but the spirits were down. Send him a message at Canberra's National Capital Private Hospital.

This newspaper will not see his like again.

**Postscript:** *When Bowers went home a few days later, letters, cards and flowers by the cartload had preceded him. Four years further on and his bum is holding up but not his head.*

# Prologue

BILL HAYDEN rang me at home 31 years ago. We'd known each other as politician and journalist since the mid-1960s. He'd come to Canberra in November 1961 at age 28. I came to Canberra in February, 1966 at age 28. He was down on the floor of Parliament and I was up in the press gallery. Three days before Christmas 1977, Hayden's colleagues elected him Federal Labor leader when Gough Whitlam resigned after Labor's second electoral thrashing in two years. Two days after New Year's Day, 1978, Hayden offered me a job. I know the precise date because I turned 40 the same day. Hayden turned 45 three weeks later. Paul Keating turned 34 in between. 'This is Bill Hayden, politician,' he bantered when I answered the phone that night. 'This is Alan Ramsey, journalist,' I replied. I joined his staff three weeks later.

I stayed five years—as his press secretary and one of two speech writers—the entire period Hayden was Labor leader. I never regretted it, though I stayed too long. You can't make a career out of being a political staffer unless you're serious about getting into politics, otherwise you're too easily swept up by the adrenalin of the lifestyle and you end up just another too-comfortable, ten-a-penny hack periodically shopped around or shunted. I worked for Hayden because I liked him, difficult and all as he could be (and impossible at times as I was). But journalism was my life, and five years in his office taught me I'd known bugger all about politics until I got there, despite 10 of the previous 12 years in the Canberra press gallery.

You can't know how little you know about everyday professional politics until you're on the inside. Across five years, working for its federal leader, I met or dealt with most of the people worth knowing in the Labor Party, parliamentary and organisational. And from May 1983, when I joined the Fairfax newspaper group, these were the same people involved, one way or another, in running the country for the next 13 years. Five years with Hayden established contacts, friends and a broad understanding of the essential self-serving nature of political behaviour that sustained me in political journalism for the ensuing 25 years.

Brian Toohey, editor in 1983 of the then Fairfax weekly, *The National Times*, was my door back into newspapers. He gave me a job in the Canberra gallery. Three years later, before the *Times* hit the wall, I switched to *Time* magazine for a year—still writing politics—after Fairfax bought 50 per cent of *Time*'s Australian edition. Then in April 1987, John Alexander, editor of

*The Sydney Morning Herald*, took me to lunch and offered me Peter Bowers' job as the paper's national columnist. Peter had had enough. He wanted a change. He wanted out from under the tyranny of the opinion page deadline of 2300 words on national politics every Saturday. And, with Alexander's help, Bowers escaped to the glorious international frippery of grand slam tennis and the Olympics.

It was as if he'd been let out of gaol. At age 49, I took my place in his cell on May 4, 1987, a hardened lifer, until I was pardoned on December 20, 2008, a fortnight before my 71st birthday. Same time, same place, most every Saturday, for 22 years (less five months) in the granite quarry of national politics. In all, I wrote some 2273 columns with an aggregate 2.3 million words. Now you know how I got there. And, as acknowledged in my last column on that last Saturday before Christmas 2008, it had been a 'pleasure and a privilege'.

Well, I fibbed. Always a privilege, not 'always' a pleasure. Writing is never easy, whatever anyone says. At times, for me, getting the right words down in order and on time really was choking chooks. And it was only when I got either of my Saturday pieces to sing that it genuinely *was* a pleasure, all too rare near the end. However, for many years I was cocooned by knowing that, no matter how grim the outlook at, say, 2pm any given Friday, with a deadline of supposedly 5.30 (which I almost never met), when I opened the *Herald* next morning, there'd be something I'd written in its usual place instead of a whacking great blank space. In time, things did not always turn out like that.

A few other things you should know.

When Peter Bowers had to deal with the space, what he had to fill was a precise half-page above the fold, with the half below the fold taken up by employment ads. And he would fill it, always, with a single article, whether the piece could carry the necessary 2300 words or not. Like me, Peter always wrote on a Friday. Unlike me, he'd have a bag of jelly beans at one elbow, for the sugar hit rather than the nicotine of the cigarettes he once smoked, and he'd tear his hair, pray, curse, cackle, fart, stamp around, yell at people, generally carry on, until, with one eye always on the time, he'd teased out enough words to fill the half page, minus the fixed space for an artist's illustration. And he did this, for seven years, in a shitty little over-crowded office on the roof of Old Parliament House which he shared with five or six *Herald* colleagues. It was like working on the main platform of Sydney's Central Railway at peak hour. A nightmare.

I bypassed the mayhem of the general *Herald* office. I'd got myself a press gallery cubby hole—next to what had been Jack Fingleton's office—in a smaller office I shared with *The Sun*, Fairfax's Sydney afternoon newspaper (its two reporters were always gone by early afternoon), and there I toiled, in solitary, for 15 months until we all moved up the hill to the Big House in August 1988 where I wangled my own office for the next 20 years. First, though, before taking over from Bowers, I got rid of his single article format as too rigid for a broadsheet half page. Too big a space, at times needing too much 'padding' to fill it. Couldn't the page be more flexible, with a second article if necessary? A counterpoint to the main piece, perhaps? The editor agreed but insisted he wouldn't tolerate a national political column of 'bitty' pieces on the opinion page of *The Sydney Morning Herald* in what was—and still is—the paper's biggest-selling issue of the week.

My first *Herald* column was published on Saturday, May 9, 1987. It was a piece about John Elliott and his fantasy of maybe coming into federal politics on the fast track, not as Prime Minister, as much silliness speculated, but as John Howard's Treasurer should the Coalition defeat the Hawke Government in that year's election. The piece ran to 1500 words and I'd written it by the Thursday night of that first week. Ian Hicks, the page editor, came up with a new page design around a 1500-word lead, with illustration, across five expanded columns, and a wide-measure single column 'sidebar' of 500 words down the righthand side. By mid-afternoon I'd written the 'bar' and filled the space. Never again, in all the years that followed, would my Saturday column be so early.

And the design worked. The page was clean, elegant and easy to read. And the six-column design across the usual 8 columns of a broadsheet page gave it a different look from the *Herald*'s week-day opinion page. From then on, for the ensuing 22 years, the Hicks format remained the Saturday page standard, every bit as inflexible as the single article format during the Bowers era.

Over time, the ads vanished from below the fold, replaced by three 'boxy' articles by different writers, then by two articles, and lastly one bottom-of-the-page column. There were other variations and aberrations as editors came and went, some as bizarre as they were ugly (the editors as well as the page). But nothing disturbed the basic Hicks format, even though my lead space had pushed down the page to a maximum 1650 words, the illustration had grown, and the sidebar stretched to 700 words by the time I signed off on December 20, 2008. Now the Hicks design has gone, with the Saturday page absorbed into the mire of the bland sameness of the weekday Opinion page. Nothing good lasts.

Vale Ian Hicks, long retired to Tasmania.

Something else about that first column in May, 1987. The sidebar began (no groans, thank you):

'You cannot escape the almost daily anguish of John Howard and the turbulence which plagues his house [as Opposition leader]. Sackings, resignations, coalition splits, ambitious rivals, public policy disagreements, voting defections, whatever; you name it, John Howard gets whacked by it. The constant crises seem never-ending. And they are all out there, in full public view, every dot and comma in all their destructive and corrosive detail. The intensity is as remorseless as the assault on Howard's nerve and Liberal morale. These days you rarely hear . . .'

And the piece went on to relate some factional bastardry about to break out within the Hawke Government over Labor pre-selection for a safe Brisbane seat.

You see the point. Across the years, and all those *Herald* opinion pieces—including 12 years of an additional 750 words each Wednesday, from 1994 to 2006—the one constant was the Earlwood garage owner's youngest son with the equally ambitious wife. John Howard was there from start to finish (well, almost). Nobody else. And I do mean there in public life, not just there as rant fodder. Howard got his share of space, and earned every line, but so did a lot of others. I was newspaper archivist to a good many across 43 years in Canberra, among the more significant during my time with Fairfax: Keating (1969–1996), Hawke (1980–1992), Button (1974–1993), Peacock (1966–1994), Howard (1974–2007), Hayden (1961–1996), Dawkins (1974–1975 and 1977–1993), Richardson (1983–1994), Walsh (1974–1993), Beazley (1980–2007), Hewson (1987–1995), Evans (1978–1999), Faulkner (1989–), Ray (1981–2007), Kernot (1990–2001) and Latham (1994–2005). Only John Faulkner is still there. Plus the current mob and a legion of also-rans.

I survived ten *Herald* editors. John Alexander was the only one appointed three separate times as editor or editor-in-chief as various owners and their teams of management suits came and went after young Warwick Fairfax bankrupted the company in 1988. In the end, Alexander was sacked in a piece of malevolent stupidity in 1998 and he went off to become a millionaire executive in Kerry Packer's organisation. The other nine: Max Prisk, Milton Cockburn, David Hickey, Greg Hywood, Paul McGeough, John Lyons, Robert Whitehead, Mark Scott and Alan Oakley. Only two still work for the company. All ten never once, in 22 years, instructed me in what I could or should write about anything or anyone. None ever knew what I was writing each Wednesday or Saturday until I briefed the page editor the day before publication. None ever saw my copy until deadline.

And only one editor ever 'spiked' something I'd written. On the morning of Wednesday, March 7, 2007, an Indonesian domestic flight crashed and burned while landing at Yogyakarta airport. Twenty-two people died, including two Australian police, two Australian embassy staff and an Australian journalist. I wrote a 700-word sidebar for the following Saturday's column. It said:

The Howard Government's week crashed and burned, too. Think of it: the Federal police raids on the Brisbane offices of those three Liberal Party MPs under fraud investigation; the sham sacking of the Government's Ian Campbell for a 20-minute meeting with the dreaded Brian Burke eight months ago; the fifth consecutive opinion poll whoopee for Labor's Kevin Rudd in three months, despite the Government's shrill Burke and Grill sludge campaign; and the Federal Court ruling last Friday which threw out the Howard Government's best efforts to block the David Hicks legal team's latest court action to get him brought home.

So much so that when news of the Indonesian air disaster broke late Wednesday morning, with its uncertain casualty toll, Australians among them, it took our Prime Minister no time at all to don sackcloth and ashes as chief mourner and get out in front of the television cameras. 'Well Ladies and gentleman', Howard announced in Melbourne that afternoon, 'I have called this press conference to provide as much information as I properly can regarding the tragedy which has occurred in Yogyakarta.'

Which was no information at all, really, over and above what was already known to the media. What Howard was really doing is what he does best: exploiting an opportunity to get his face, suitably grave, on that night's television news bulletins. Sporting victories, air disasters, military commemorations, mass death and mayhem of any kind involving Australian voters—anything unconnected with the raw business of politics. They are all electoral meat and drink to Howard's self-absorbed role as the Government's chief public relations huckster.

'It's obviously a great tragedy for all concerned, including of course the many Indonesians on board the aircraft who appear to have lost their lives', Howard told reporters. 'Our immediate focus, of course, is to properly confirm and identify the situation regarding the Australians on board. We must prepare ourselves for some bad news in relation to our countrymen and women. Are there any questions?'

The one question nobody asked was what were two Australian cabinet ministers doing tooling up to Indonesia in two VIP aircraft—yes, two—with their retinues of staff and bureaucratic hangers on, as well as an ABC television crew making a documentary on Alexander Downer for the *Australian Story* series. Downer, as Foreign Minister, had one aircraft for himself and his staff, and Philip Ruddock, the Attorney-General, had one for himself and his people, even though both were going to the same two-day conference in Jakarta.

Downer's office had been spruiking for press gallery journalists to go with them. Three were invited, plus a 'pool' TV crew. All but one of the journalists pulled out when they were told they would have to travel on local commercial flights within Indonesia. So did the proposed 'pool' crew. The one journalist who accepted and was on Downer's plane when it left Adelaide for Jakarta late last Sunday morning was the *Herald*'s Cynthia Banham.

The two-day conference in Jakarta produced bugger-all news, as most journalists knew it wouldn't, and Tuesday afternoon saw the Australian press contingent bussed way out to a school on Jakarta's outskirts as they tagged along with Downer and his ABC crew to a school financed by Australian aid money.

But the trip took longer than expected and the reporters who were flying that night to Yogyakarta on a local flight, to be on hand when Downer arrived there on his VIP plane next morning, had to scramble to change planes and catch the first (6am) commercial flight out of Jakarta on Wednesday morning.

Banham, and Morgan Mellish of *The Australian Financial Review*, were on this plane. It was, of course, the plane that crashed. Mellish died, along with four other Australians, all of them involved in Downer's proposed half-day visit to Yogyakarta. Banham is alive but badly injured. All in the name of Downer's public relations junket and a VIP plane that had no room for the workers.

Think of this when you see the ABC's *Australian Story*.

Many Australians likely thought a great many things when the *Australian Story* episode on Downer and his wife, Nicky, went to air seven weeks later, but not because of anything I'd written. That never got past the editor, Alan Oakley. I was told by one of his deputies on the Friday night that the piece, on Oakley's instructions, was being canned, and in an exchange of emails two days later Oakley told me he'd thought the article 'inappropriate', its first sentence 'insensitive' and 'the piece generally upsetting' to *Herald* staff.

**From:** Alan Ramsey
**Sent:** Monday, 12 March 2007 2.18pm
**To:** Alan Oakley

Alan, I would appreciate being told by the editor why he did not publish Saturday's sidebar?

**From:** Alan Oakley
**Sent:** Monday,12 March 2007 2.39pm
**To:** Alan Ramsey

Hi Alan. It was inappropriate. The intro was insensitive and the piece generally upsetting for staff, for whom I have a broader responsibility. I am not disputing the central theme, but there is a time and a place—and Saturday, so soon after the crash, was not the time to be trying to score political points. The issue of transport on these trips will be taken up with the PM as soon as I can. Alan, I don't like editing writers, particularly commentators. But I could not bring myself to publish it. I believe I made the right decision.

It was Oakley's right to not publish. It was my right to disagree. I felt the circumstances of why those five dead Australians and the *Herald's* Cynthia Banham had come to be on that Indonesian commercial flight should be made public. Oakley did not. I thought he was wrong. I also thought I was working for adults, not adolescents. Newspapers daily publish a variety of happenings and opinion 'upsetting' and/or 'insensitive' and/or 'inappropriate' to many people—immediate family, relatives, vested interest groups, sections of the wider community, even politicians. The nature of a newspaper's business is everybody else's business. And the press can be—and is—hugely intrusive when it suits, which is often. It defends vigorously its right to be so on the grounds of freedom of the press and/or the public's right to know. The double standard is obvious when one of its own is involved. This myopia can be stultifying—or be seen to be so—if a senior political figure's self-serving behaviour is at issue.

So there you have the broad detail of the only time in 22 years a *Herald* editor refused to publish a column of mine. On another occasion I withdrew one rather than agree to the deletion of a paragraph.

In late August 2005 a page editor wanted to expunge a paragraph of a mid-week column, on the grounds of 'taste', which referred to the NSW Liberal Party's 'gutless' John Brogden as a 'coward' after Brogden had resigned as State leader in grubby circumstances and then supposedly sought to commit suicide (unsuccessfully) with a letter opener. I said no and insisted on withdrawing the article if the page editor insisted on the deletion. He did, and so I did.

The *Herald*'s editor-in-chief at the time, Mark Scott, a once Greiner Government political staffer whom John Howard's ABC board nine months later (in May, 2006) would appoint managing director of the national broadcaster, was 'relaxed' about the page editor's decision. I'd have felt more relaxed if a senior Fairfax executive at Sydney head office had not been Brogden's brother-in-law. Three days later I rewrote the column for the Saturday page on the broader issue of political leadership, using a 'spineless' Brogden who'd 'trashed his leadership' by 'sheer stupidity' and an impatient, undisciplined Peter Costello desperate to get hold of John Howard's leadership as parallel examples of why both were political cot cases (see page 326). Nobody at the *Herald* said boo this time.

There were occasional flurries about specific words. For instance, in 2003, when Simon Crean's Labor leadership was a corpse still walking around, I wrote about the ABC's Maxine McKew and her 'Ladies who Lunch' interviews with politicians for *The Bulletin*. In a piece where McKew ramped up Kim Beazley for yet another crack at the top job, I made an ironic reference to 'that ain't no Lady, that's that bitch from *The Bulletin*'. I amended it to 'that woman' after yet another editor, Robert Whitehead, had a brief shriek that I didn't need a phone to hear in Canberra. And during the life of the Hawke Government I wrote in passing about John Kerin, one of Labor's wonderfully droll (and most commonsense) ministers, coming back from talks with the New Zealand Government with a very blokey joke in which Shirl tells Bruce she's pregnant and she's going to jump off the Harbour Bridge if he doesn't marry her, and Bruce replies, 'Gee Shirl, you're not only a good root, you're a good sport, too.'

Kerin thought it a wonderful take on Australian male attitudes but Ian Hicks, my flint-hearted page editor ever mindful of Granny's morals and her responsibility to 'the family', wouldn't have a bar of it, 'not in *The Sydney Morning Herald*', and the offending colloquialism was changed to read 'You're not only good in the cot but you're a good sport, too.' A very Australian joke, however sexist, lost something in translation.

The *Herald's* artists never got lost. They 'never ever' got to see, at any time, what I was writing, either. They had to illustrate the column without ever actually being able to read it. Instead, they'd phone on a Friday morning and I'd brief whoever with as much detail as possible. Sometimes, though, I'd be sitting there, not a thought, and I'd have to tell the unfortunate to call back later. Not often, but often enough. Sometimes I'd even forget what I'd told the artist. Thus some background 'bits', so much a part of these illustrations, would turn up in the published drawing next day totally unconnected to the story because I'd not included the relevant incidents/people.

Across the years it was the melancholy lot of a number of artists to have to 'ring Ramsey' on a Friday. Among them: Michael Fitzjames, Bill Leak, Rocco Fazzari, Andrew Ireland, Michael Mucci, Ed Aragon, John Shakespeare, Amanda Upton, Suzanne White, Reg Lynch, Rod Clement, Jock Alexander and Paul Newman. The most long-suffering was the inestimable Ward O'Neill. John Alexander recruited him in 1987 from *The Bulletin*. He's been with Fairfax ever since and my irregular Friday soul mate from the time of my second *Herald* Saturday page on May 16, 1987, with an O'Neill drawing of Paul Keating. There would be many Keating 'illos' in the years following, none better, in my book, than an October, 1988 O'Neill drawing of Keating as a tattooed, long-booted bikey in dark glasses which, before Annita got him into Italian suits, said everything about his in-your-face, fuck-you attitude to life as well as to politics, at least as a younger man. That drawing, obviously, is here in the book (see page 29) along with 62 others, all of them Ward's work.

That brings us to *A Matter of Opinion*. Richard Smart, the commissioning publisher, first approached me in 1994. Allen & Unwin's Patrick Gallagher did some urging at Paul Kelly's 50th birthday party in 1997 and came to Canberra to chat me up yet again in 1998. But in the 14 years from 1994 until I called it quits last year, I never had the urge or the time to sit down to the simple business of putting together a collection of my *Herald* work.

Now I have done. The *Herald* last December made available, on disc, everything I'd written for the paper. For two months, from the end of February, I culled 150 pieces from the 2273 under my name and grouped them in chapters, chronological and thematic, covering pretty much fifty-fifty the Hawke/Keating years (1987–1996) and the Howard years (1996–2007). They overlap, of course. And there's nothing on the Rudd Government or the bloke who leads it. The Rudd era is for others to chronicle. As it is, I've had to bypass a great heap of material from the Hawke/Keating/Howard period. It was as rich a time as any in this country's brief political history. And the value, I think, of what's here is that it's contemporary. This is not history written in retrospect. It is history as it happened, even if from only one point of view. And that's always the point, of course. It is simply a matter of opinion.

Alan Ramsey
Canberra, June 1, 2009

# Chapter 1

# The Winter Campaign

## Incident in a Country Town

**MAY 16, 1987**

PAUL KEATING never stops running. The other night, after he'd delivered his May 'mini-Budget' speech to Parliament, Bob Hawke put on celebratory drinks in the Cabinet anteroom for officials and advisors. Keating was there with his staff. Sometime later, somebody noticed the Treasurer was missing. They thought he'd gone home. They were wrong. Keating had slipped downstairs to the non-members bar.

He was looking for the journalists on whom public reaction to his quick-footed economic arithmetic the Government depended so much. He wanted to know what they thought, get a smell of what they'd written. Later, he was asked about the incident. 'Just getting the feel,' he said, 'keeping in touch.' As he spoke, he dropped into a fighter's crouch, feinting with both hands. 'You know, just getting the feel.'

Keating has been 'getting the feel' ever since he came to Canberra in 1969 in the first wave of new Labor MPs brought into politics by the Whitlam drive to power. He leaves nothing to chance. He has always worked the parliamentary press gallery as he now works the Cabinet and the Caucus.

As a raw political nobody years ago, he learned quickly his way round the rabbit warren of upstairs press offices in Old Parliament House. He sought out the senior writers, bent their ear ceaselessly. As Treasurer, he has less time these days. But he still does it when it matters. It mattered this week.

The night after Keating's speech to Parliament, John Howard gave his reply. Earlier, just before the House rose for dinner, a journalist asked a Keating staffer what chance of seeing the Treasurer briefly? 'He's going home. He's exhausted,' the reporter was told. Yet two hours later Keating was still in the Parliament. He was still 'getting the feel'.

Upstairs in the press gallery, he stopped to speak to Barrie Cassidy, Hawke's press secretary, about Howard's reply. 'Bloody dreadful, wasn't it?' he chortled. 'Did you see his front-bench? They didn't know what to do when he finished.' Minutes later, Keating was in the office of the Melbourne *Age*, bending ears.

That is the difference between Keating and other ministers. By virtue of his political standing as much as personality, Keating is always news. He just never takes anything for granted. He is always working on somebody. And he has more front than Dolly Parton.

Keating, at 43, is secure as the most dominant figure in the Hawke Government, perhaps in Australian politics. Nobody more consistently manipulates Government policy to his will. Nobody more successfully takes the Government, right or wrong, in the direction he wants to go. Bob Hawke is the electoral figurehead, no mistake. But Keating more than Hawke, more than anyone, drives the show.

The week before his mini-Budget speech Keating appeared before a meeting of the Government's Caucus economic committee. All ministers have such committees. Their function essentially is to keep the backbench involved, the troops happy. A smart minister with a sensitive policy issue always keeps his committee on side, keeps it informed, makes sure its members think they're involved in the policy process even if they're not.

Ministers like Michael Duffy, John Button, and Brian Howe are good at this. To get your Caucus committee behind you is to lessen the risk of a policy proposal hitting the wall somewhere in the political pipeline. Keating, when he sees the need to play, is a master of the game. But he does it differently to others.

In the issues of bank deregulation and the dollar float, which he won, and Tax Option C, the consumption tax which he lost, he simply talked his opponents into submission. Nobody talks, persuasively and remorselessly, like Keating talks. And Keating did not lose his consumption tax in the Government. He lost it in the unions, who in turn nobbled Hawke.

In budget-making, Keating tells his committee only what he wants it to know, which is often very little. He talks in generalities, of economic and political objectives, rarely in specifics. He sticks to the big canvas. Yet the force of his personality and the power of his relentless tongue will almost always overwhelm even the most stroppy party critic.

Such is his confident dominance that Keating attends meetings of the Caucus economic committee only when he judges it necessary. He went before the recent meeting only after members complained. There had been six previous meetings this year. Keating had attended two, the most recent a month earlier. Now, with the mini-Budget only two weeks away, some members were demanding to know what was going on. They passed a resolution insisting Keating come and tell them.

Keating agreed. He chose his own time, two days after that nominated by the committee. The meeting started at 11.30am with 26 Labor MPs present. Keating spoke non-stop for an hour. He answered questions for another 40 minutes. Half-way through the questions only six of the original 26 MPs remained. The others had left. One member said later: 'He simply talked them out the door.'

Those who left did not go unhappy or resentful. 'Keating stroked them like only he can,' the MP said. 'They go away content, sometimes purring. This is as true of the Left as it is of the other factions. Yet they know almost no more when they leave than they did before he started speaking.'

The Government as a whole is in awe of Keating's ability, his mind and his tongue, though not necessarily always in that order. He is feared by some, envied by many, disliked by others, but admired, however grudgingly, by all. It is not just for the influence he wields, inside and outside Cabinet, but for the way he goes about it. He simply never relents.

With Keating's dominance has come super confidence. He has always hustled, confident of his instincts, his objectives and his ultimate success. His confidence is now too often seen as arrogance. Humility is alien to his personality. A colleague remarked: 'He does not know, as well as he used to, when to pull his head in. And he's losing touch'—and he motioned through the window to the real world—'out there.'

Keating would argue vigorously he is more in touch with political reality than any of the doubters. His career, along with the Government's electoral future, depends on his being right. Keating almost solely has determined economic strategy throughout the four years the Hawke Government has been in power.

It is Keating who has insisted, often against strong resistance when the indicators have faltered, that the Government cannot lose its nerve. He has pulled Hawke, the Cabinet and Caucus in behind him and kept them there. 'He has asserted himself as the head guru,' a

backbench MP said this week. 'If he is wrong, he goes, but we all go with him.'

That is the real extent of Keating's political authority and power in this administration. He is the key to Bob Hawke's pursuit of a historic third term.

Caucus is fairly fatalistic. A Labor MP described it: 'There is now a necessary element of economic faith in that Caucus knows Keating is in absolute charge of economic policy. They know he has the prestige to maintain that authority. They also know the political destiny of this Government and their own personal political futures are synonymous with Keating's success.'

In the full Cabinet discussions that approved each mini-Budget decision of Keating's razor gang recently, the abolition of unemployment benefits for 16- and 17-year-olds is a case in point of Keating's authority. Cabinet, in endorsing the decision, replaced the $50-a-week dole payment with a universal $50-a-week so-called 'job search' allowance, means-tested down to a minimum $25.

Keating is supposed to unilaterally have turned the emphasis around for presentational impact. His speech this week announced a universal $25-a-week job search allowance would replace the dole for 16- and 17-year-olds and would be means-tested up to a maximum $50.

The result in both cases is the same. Only the political emphasis is different. In one, the emphasis is in line with the rhetoric of Hawke's 'fairness with equity' approach to social welfare in hard times. In the other, the Keating approach, the impact, aimed at impressing the financial markets, is on the Government's determination to get tough on welfare spending.

There is a lovely story concerning Keating's supposed loss of touch with voters and his colleagues' attitude to it. It occurred during a recent Cabinet meeting in Bathurst, held as a public relations stunt to impress country people—in a marginal Labor seat—of the Government's concern for their welfare. The truth may well have grown in the telling but the story delights other ministers.

Keating and John Button, Hawke's Senate leader, are kindred souls. They are the true policy innovators of this Government. Apparently they were out walking in Bathurst when they passed a supermarket. Button suggested Keating go inside and talk to some shoppers, some real voters. Keating demurred. Further on they came to a pub. A woman rushed out and asked Keating to shake her hand. Keating did so, and as they walked on, he said to Button: 'See, that woman recognised me and she was friendly.'

'Yes', said Button, 'but she was pissed.'

Alan Ramsey

# Chasing History

**MAY 29, 1987**

FOR THE first time in our history, a prime minister is going to the polls in the dead of winter. In 38 previous Federal elections, four of them Senate only, none has been held in July. The coincidence fits the personality of a man with a long reputation for defying convention, mostly social. Bob Hawke, our 25th Prime Minister, likes setting precedents. He is a man who runs with one eye always on the history books.

Now he seeks a mandate for a historic third term, with an election on Gough Whitlam's 71st birthday. No Labor Prime Minister has ever led his party to three successive election victories. Whitlam was the first to achieve two. Hawke duplicated the feat in 1984. The irony that Hawke should now seek to make it three on Whitlam's birthday will delight him.

One is a Labor leader firmly established in history for the way he lost office. The other is seeking to rewrite it by his electoral deeds in staying there. They are not friends. Yet Hawke's choice of July 11 links the party's greatest loser with the man who hopes to become its greatest winner in what would be the ALP's finest electoral hour.

The coincidence will seem fitting to staunch Labor supporters. What would appear more fitting to Bob Hawke is the historical parallel between what he is now attempting and that achieved by John Curtin, Australia's fifth Labor Prime Minister and still its most venerated. Until Hawke's decision yesterday, Curtin was the only Prime Minister to go to the polls in winter, though a month later. Curtin took his Government to an election on August 21 of wartime 1943. He won in a landslide, Labor's greatest win ever.

Hawke would see no parallel with Whitlam. He did not know July 11 was Whitlam's birthday until told just before he walked into the House of Representatives late yesterday to announce the election date. It would have annoyed him enormously. Yet Hawke would like to see many similarities between him and Curtin, the one Labor leader he has sought in public life to identify with in the public mind.

Both came from Western Australia, one by adoption, the other by birth. One is seen as one of our greatest prime ministers. The other seeks, almost desperately, to assume the same mantle. Curtin was a reformed alcoholic who led Labor into its most sustained period of continuous office (eight years) in the 1940s under three separate leaders—Curtin, Forde and Chifley.

Hawke had to beat the booze before he beat Bill Hayden and then Malcolm Fraser. His turbulent drinking habits almost ended his political career before it started. He has not touched a drop in eight years. Hawke has now served as Prime Minister longer than Curtin. If he wins on July 11, he will overtake Chifley and Andrew Fisher as the longest serving of Australia's nine Labor prime ministers in 86 years. But first he has to match Curtin's feat of winning in winter.

Curtin blitzed both Houses, doubling non-Labor's numbers in the Lower House and sweeping all 19 Senate seats. No Labor leader has ever had an election win of such magnitude. Curtin not only won in winter, he died in winter. Polling day on July 11 falls just six days after the 42nd anniversary of Curtin's death in 1945. Hawke will hope to celebrate it in the most appropriate way.

Alan Ramsey

# Learning to Tell the Time

**MAY 30, 1987**

IT WAS late Wednesday afternoon. Bob Hawke had been to Government House. He had secured the election. In 20 minutes he would walk into the Parliament and formally announce the date. Now he had called his ministers together in the Cabinet room to tell them what he expected of them in the crucial six weeks ahead. He surprised them by what he had to say. He delighted them by the way he said it.

Hawke spoke for perhaps 15 minutes. He is not a modest man. When you think of Hawke you think of ego, a strutting bantam cock who looks on the world as his personal chookyard. A man of great appetites and capacities, of great flaws, of charm and loyalty and vulnerability, a political leader who often thinks he knows it all and just as often behaves like he knows nothing. Now, as he talked to his colleagues, without bravado, one remark stood out.

It fitted the high mood of the moment. It helps explain Hawke's authority in a Cabinet more able than its leadership in all but public appeal. It shows why Hawke, despite the flaws, despite everything, constantly delights his friends and supporters and confuses his critics.

Hawke was talking about discipline. 'Over the next six weeks, we have to be disciplined,' said the most undisciplined member of the Government. 'There can be no arrogance, none at all.' He paused. 'And that remark is directed to no-one in this room more than me.'

It disarmed everyone. One minister said later: 'He had us all with that remark. It threw everybody. You felt a great rush of warmth for him, and that is not a word I usually associate with feelings about Hawke. I'm sure others felt it, too. He's an extraordinary man.'

This is the paradox of Hawke. His personal popularity is his Government's best electoral asset. His arrogant and undisciplined personality is its most exploitable defect. More than anyone, Hawke is the key to the election. He is the Government's front man, its salesman, still the most popular political figure in the country. He is also its Achilles heel.

The economy is the issue, unquestionably. But leadership perceptions and how the economic debate is sold by either side will decide the outcome. Hawke the smug smart alec would be a disaster. And if Hawke goes bad, so does the Government. Yet at his best, Labor will win. The political climate of the moment says so, irrespective of what John Howard might do.

In this context, Hawke's quiet pep talk about discipline was recognised by all who heard it as nothing but sheer commonsense. The surprise was that Hawke was prepared to acknowledge his own failings. He could not have made a more appropriate gesture to his colleagues. Now all he has to do is take his own advice. On past performance, that is the hard bit.

Pumped up by confidence, and with the applause washing over him, Hawke is hard to contain. He thrives on the adrenalin of adulation. And that's when he makes mistakes. He gets arrogant and says too much. He talks himself into trouble. His election re-think all but went sour because he could not hold his tongue when it mattered most. His incautious mouth got the better of his judgment.

There is nothing very mystical about Hawke's early election conversion. Three months ago, when the May election option began running in public, only two people were urging Hawke to seize it. One was Bob Sorby, his staff political adviser. The other was Richard Farmer, a political fringe dweller who sells wine for a living.

Sorby had been pushing Hawke since February. Farmer, whose political instincts are as sharp as his business acumen, worked for Hawke in the 1983 campaign and for Bill Hayden in 1980. When Hawke asked him in March what he thought about May, Farmer had no doubts. Hawke should not hesitate. Get in before the harsh economic decisions later in the year. Exploit the turmoil of the Coalition. Go now.

Nobody else agreed. The Cabinet, the ministry, the backbench, the party, all said no, don't be a fool. The risks were too great. The economic news was not good enough. Paul Keating more than anyone argued passionately to wait. Sorby and Farmer were shouted down. Hawke listened. On April 1, he publicly killed the May option.

However, in one of the many bull sessions in Hawke's office while he was sifting opinions in March, Keating argued that he was convinced his May mini-Budget would create the maximum economic and political climate for an election in the months before the main August Budget. Everyone else present ridiculed him. Hawke and others openly laughed.

Besides, who'd ever heard of a winter election? Keating stuck firm. The gap, he insisted, between the Government and the Opposition would be greatest in July/August.

Keating then decided to move the bulk of the Budget forward from August into his May statement. He cancelled a planned Easter visit to Washington and set about, as chairman of Cabinet's razor gang, looking not for $2 billion in spending cuts, as planned, but $4 billion. His plan: to create the economic climate to fit his instincts of the political climate in winter.

Keating already was appalled by Hawke's April 1 statement pledging an election 'towards the end of the year or early next year'. He urged Hawke to keep his options open, to shut up about an election later rather than sooner. In the last week of April, when the Coalition formally split, Keating felt sure he would be proved right. But nobody, Hawke included, felt an election would be possible once the May cuts were announced.

About this time Hawke and Keating had a falling out. The day the brittle Coalition agreement between John Howard and Ian Sinclair collapsed, Keating pushed Hawke to move in hard to exploit it. He wanted Question Time cancelled immediately the House met and a debating motion moved to kick the daylights out of the ex-Coalition partners. Mick Young disagreed. Hawke listened to Young.

Keating was furious. He felt the Government was allowing the worst internal split in the non-Labor parties to slide by without squeezing it for every drop of political advantage where it would hurt Howard and Sinclair most: in front of their own troops on the floor of the Parliament.

Young thought otherwise. He felt the Opposition was doing itself enough damage without the Government needing to give it too big a shove. When the House met and Question Time drifted on, Keating, his speech still in his hand, got up and left in disgust. He went home and stayed there. He was still angry when he returned the next day.

A few days later, a brief press report appeared saying Keating was urging a July election. The same report carried a denial of any interest whatever from Hawke's office. Keating was annoyed. He felt a backbencher was responsible for the leak. He also thought Hawke was pushing himself into a corner by his persistent denial of election speculation.

And then strong public and market response to the May mini-Budget turned all no-election attitudes within the Government on their head. Two instant converts were Young, the ALP's national president, and Bob McMullan, its national secretary. They immediately started hammering on Hawke's door to have an election yesterday. No date would be too soon. Go!

Rod Cameron, Labor's pollster, was next to line-up. He polled mini-Budget reaction in 10 selected marginal seats the weekend after Keating's statement to Parliament. By Tuesday or Wednesday of last week, with the whole of the Government getting caught up in the post-mini-Budget euphoria, Cameron had the poll results with Hawke. They showed Labor in front for the first time in a year and rising.

The trend in all Cameron's polling since last September had been up. Not spectacularly, but moving up steadily. Now, based on marginal seats in all parts of the country, the Government had hit the front. Cameron was convinced the trend was strong enough and steady enough to hold through a campaign. His advice matched Young's and McMullan's: for God's sake, go! Go tomorrow!

Hawke's public election musings, already tentative, hardened. Now he had moved away from his earlier categorical no-July election denial which so upset Keating. Now the adrenalin was pumping. Hawke was charged-up and responding accordingly. So was the party. Keating had been right.

Bob Sorby had been amused by all those who bagged him so unmercifully in March now leaping aboard in late May. Initially, after the mini-Budget, Sorby had remained cautious. Then he too caught the infection, along with Barrie Cassidy, Hawke's press secretary. All five—Young, McMullan, Cameron, Sorby and Cassidy—were now—in the last 10 days of May—pushing Hawke as hard as they could. They are the five closest to him on political advice.

They were convinced the time was right.

Throughout Monday, during the Premiers' conference, the mood went on snowballing. Hawke sounded out all four Labor premiers. All said the same—go! By early Monday night, after another meeting in Hawke's office, the political decision had been made: a winter election was on. But what specific date? The talking went on until midnight.

The next day Gareth Evans, Hawke's Senate deputy leader, was called into the group. Evans' advice was sought on constitutional procedures. Early in the afternoon, Keating saw Hawke again. He wanted polling day on August 8. He argued his case. He told Hawke no announcement of a double dissolution would be possible before July 1 unless the next Parliament was to be shortened again to little more than two years. Another early election!

Keating's argument was wrongly based. His reading of the Constitution was in error. After seeing Hawke on Tuesday he flew to Sydney for a speaking engagement. Seamus Dawes, his senior staff adviser, later phoned to tell him of his mistake. He told him a July election was certain.

Others say Keating's real reason for an August 8 polling day was more personal: he'd been due to leave with Annita for a fortnight in Europe this coming week. A July election would kill his trip. He only cancelled it two days ago—24 hours after Hawke announced the July 11 date. He was not pleased.

But first, At 8.30pm four nights ago, four people sat down in Hawke's office: Bob McMullan, Bob Sorby, Richard Farmer and Hawke. McMullan was arguing for July 4, the earliest possible date. Sorby, Young—who later joined the group—and Hawke wanted July 25. Farmer, a new entrant called in only earlier that day, wanted the first possible date, whatever it was. Cassidy supported July 25 when he joined the group.

Gareth Evans was phoned and asked to join them. Jean Sinclair, Hawke's personal secretary who came to politics with him from the ACTU, was there too. Other staff members drifted in and out as the discussion went on, back and forth, for four hours. Gradually the organisational problems were worked through. Hawke phoned the Chief Electoral Commissioner, only to find him on holidays.

His deputy cleared away one problem that had made it seem July 25 was the earliest practical date: school holidays from July 3 to 20 in some States would not upset polling booth arrangements at schools around the country, so long as the electoral commission was alerted early enough.

That swung unanimous support in the group to July 11, the date most favoured initially but thought to be impractical. Other issues were canvassed in detail: how to explain Hawke's change of mind, the timing of the announcement, the rationale of the election, the dissolution of Parliament, and so on.

At one point, Jean Sinclair asked if anyone knew whether the Governor-General, Ninian Stephen, whose formal approval of an election would be necessary, was in Canberra. Nobody did. It had been overlooked. A discreet phone call ensured he was not away travelling.

Gareth Evans was detailed to liaise with the Democrats next morning (Wednesday) to ensure their co-operation in getting the supply bills passed within a week. Normally it takes three to four weeks. Nobody felt the Democrats would be a problem: their delight at a double dissolution would dissolve any hesitancy about co-operation.

But that meant Hawke would have to announce the election next day. The group had wanted to delay until after Hawke's return from his South Pacific talks the following Tuesday. Thursday or Friday was the choice. They wanted campaign notice reduced to the minimum. But bringing the Democrats into the secret next morning killed any delay. It would have to be announced immediately.

The group broke up at 12.30am. Everything was set. And, as events unfolded, nothing went wrong. Everybody co-operated, including the Governor-General. At 5.06 that same afternoon Hawke announced the July 11 double dissolution election in Parliament. By then, of course, everyone knew. What they didn't know was how Paul Keating had got all he wanted, except his European holiday.

Alan Ramsey

# An Honest Trier

JUNE 29, 1987

SIX WEEKS ago Bill Snedden telephoned Andrew Peacock to ask if he could intervene to try to heal the damaging rift between ex-Liberal leader Peacock and his successor, John Howard. Snedden and Peacock were old Melbourne friends. The day Peacock came into Parliament in April 1966 in Menzies' former seat of Kooyong, Snedden was one of the two Liberals who ritually bring a new member before the Bar of the House of Representatives.

Eight years later, when Snedden was trying to save his leadership of the Liberal Party from the driving ambition of Malcolm Fraser, Peacock was one of the few senior Liberals who aligned himself with Snedden. For days Peacock had been warning Snedden a new challenge by Fraser was imminent. Snedden refused to believe it. He told Peacock and others that Fraser had given him his word.

Peacock warned Snedden he was being 'played for a sucker'. Ten days later the Liberal party room ousted Snedden and seven months later Fraser was Prime Minister. Now, 13 years on, with Fraser gone and Labor in power, Snedden was trying to find a role in bringing Howard and Peacock together on the eve of another election he felt crucial to the Liberal cause.

If Snedden went ahead with his peace moves they came to nothing. He saw Peacock at Howard's policy launch in Sydney two nights ago but they did not discuss the matter. Snedden asked Peacock to join him for a drink that night but Peacock had campaign commitments in Melbourne. Snedden went off by himself.

Sometime overnight, after drinking with a small group of casual friends in a Sydney hotel, Snedden died in his motel room. [Police would confirm later he did not die alone. The woman with him was never identified, despite intense gossip.]

Billy Mackie Snedden was the perennial loser. He gave almost 40 years of his life to politics, 27 of them in the national Parliament. In return, politics dismissed him in humiliation as a temporary leader of little substance, destroyed his marriage and his family life, and left him in his last days still seeking an illusory role in the party he had served since his early 20s.

John Howard in a weekend tribute called Snedden a 'very decent and honourable' Liberal leader. He was both, but, with the greatest of goodwill, not much else, except naive politically and far too trusting for his own good. His leadership will be remembered more for the manner in which he lost it to Fraser than anything he did while he had it, except perhaps his 1974 defeat by Whitlam.

Even in this, he made a hash of things. Had Snedden not forced Labor to a double dissolution in May 1974, by threatening to use the Senate to block Supply, he might well have survived as leader to become Prime Minister after the usual three-year term. And in losing to Whitlam he parodied himself with his 'I didn't win, but I didn't lose' declaration.

The remark was quoted for months after to ridicule him, just as his judgment about his colleagues betrayed him mere weeks before Fraser dispossessed him. In a speech to Melbourne businessmen, he boasted his party would go through 'the valley of death, over hot coals' in its support for him. By the end of the month his colleagues had dumped him.

As Speaker of the House, a political payoff from Fraser in 1976 that brought with it an imperial knighthood, Snedden found his niche in politics. It gave him status but no power, parliamentary standing but no political eminence. He tried hard but in the end it made him very pompous. He enjoyed the ritual of wiggery and black robes and fought throughout the seven years of his speakership to enhance its role in parliamentary life. Like most things he did, he failed. But he tried.

Snedden was always a trier, an honest journeyman whose ability never matched his ambition. Yet he never gave up on loyalty to his party, and at John Howard's policy launch he was the only ex-leader there, apart from Peacock. Fraser was nowhere to be seen. Perhaps the unkindest cut came in Howard's weekend tribute. Snedden never ran away from the simplicity of his given name. In this final tribute from his party Howard spelt his name wrongly ('William').

Still a loser, even in death.

Alan Ramsey

# On the Road with John

**JUNE 20, 1987**

JOHN BUTTON was sitting in a $40-a-night motel room watching Clint Eastwood do what he does best and waiting for the electric blanket to warm his bed. Button was feeling a bit like one of Eastwood's victims. The noisy violence of the big semis charging through the night just outside his door didn't help.

John Button's campaign trail this night was the Hume Highway.

Bob Hawke flies VIP and stays in $250 hotel suites in the big cities mostly. John Howard does it in only slightly less style but with greater stoicism. The rest do it any way they can.

John Button this day had travelled 400 km by car, from Melbourne to Wangaratta in northern Victoria, stopping for three hours at a Labor Party barbecue at Macedon, east of Ballarat, and arriving at 8.15pm for a buy-your-own dinner of steak and eggs and two 90-cent glasses of cask Riesling with six ALP branch members in a Wangaratta pub 70 km south of Albury.

He didn't get back to Melbourne until 48 hours later after a round trip of 1,000 km, back through the marginal Labor seats of Bendigo and Ballarat, via six factories, two dinners, two lunches, and six radio, TV and newspaper interviews. A day later, after a morning's filming for TV advertising, he was in the suburbs of Adelaide doing it all again.

Hawke and Howard are the leaders, the front men, the public focus of the election. They travel with their wives, political advisers, staff members, security police and big press teams. Their daily schedules are marked off in carefully-planned media events. They campaign for the 6pm bulletins on commercial TV. They are the campaign.

Behind the high profiles of Hawke and Howard are the others. You rarely hear of them unless they make goats of themselves. The press isn't interested unless they do. Ian Sinclair gets lots of attention because of the Joh factor. Sinclair is the son of a deceased undertaker and his campaign has the mesmerising fascination of a funeral. The press adores big funerals as much as it does conflict. Sinclair and Joh between them promise both.

Paul Keating is noticed because he's Paul Keating and because of the economy, the real issue, and tax, which John Howard wants you to think is the real issue—or he did when he started. For the same reason, some of the Liberal extras, like Jim Carlton and Michael Baume, flit on and off screen with their one-liners. But they are just bit players. In the end, Howard carries the Liberals' campaign just as Hawke carries the Government's. It is the nature of the chase.

Button, like the others, knows his place: mostly unsighted, unwanted by the national media, out on the road, going through the grind of lunches, dinners, party fundraisers, factory visits, shopping centres, local interviews. Anything to spread the word, to get a local candidate noticed. They campaign up to 10 and 12 hours a day, five and six days a week. It is the reality of elections.

In 1984, in Hawke's Long March election, Button told an audience in Launceston he felt like Burke and Wills wandering across Australia and every now and then being told to dig. It was that sort of aimless, never-ending campaign. The effect on ministers was profound. They did not forgive Hawke his complacency nor his error of judgment in making the formal campaign an eight-week test of endurance. They forgave him even less the shock of the Government's relatively narrow win in political circumstances in which it should have bolted in.

Button believes the Government now relies less and less on Hawke's electoral authority for its public support. He doesn't dismiss Hawke's public standing; he simply thinks the Government is recognised more in its own right for its competence. He isn't concerned about saying so. 'I think this has not been a bad government,' he says. 'It's made some awful mistakes, but all governments do. We've learnt. And I think there's a strong suspicion out there that it's a reasonably capable government now.'

Button's understated candour makes him one of the Government's more attractive figures. His success in the difficult industry portfolio has made him one of its most respected. The chief executive of a big Australian company referred to him recently as the 'best minister of any government' he'd had to deal with. Many manufacturers would, and do, agree.

'The Whitlam Government were amateurs,' Button says over breakfast in Bendigo next day. 'Not this lot, not now. I always draw football analogies. And just as I can see young players turning into professionals, so I can see some of this Government turning into professionals, much more than they were. Much tougher now, more adept at taking hard decisions.'

And Hawke: 'There is always concern within the Government about Hawkie's morale and so on, because he's the front man, and he's certainly a bonus in the electoral context . . . (long pause) . . . if he goes well.' And is he going well? Another pause. 'He seems to be.' The qualified response reflects a party holding its breath and still unsure Hawke will not make some appalling mistake at some stage of the campaign.

The point is confirmed when someone remarks about the engine trouble of Hawke's VIP jet on an aborted flight to Perth from Melbourne. 'Better the engine should blow up than Hawkie,' says Button. His wry humour underscores a view unanimous in the Government. Labor goes in dread of a Hawke campaign outburst of arrogance or petulant anger.

Like most of his colleagues, Button is glad John Howard and not Andrew Peacock is leading the charge against them. 'Peacock would be a more dangerous opponent, yes. He really doesn't stand for anything in particular so he picks up everybody. I mean, Howard essentially is about an ideological experiment, and experiments are very risky. Andrew's a politician. He's not about experiments, he's about winning.'

Button went to Wangaratta for two reasons: he wanted to honour a promise some thought he mightn't keep, and he wanted to settle a score. Not unpleasantly, for that isn't Button's way, but just so those involved know he knows the score is settled. Just being there, at this time, did it.

In August last year, with Australia's textile, clothing and footwear industries spending tens of thousands of dollars in a campaign to whip up fear and loathing of lower tariff protection, Button's name was mud in Wangaratta. The city of 16,500 has three textile and clothing mills. They are its biggest private employers. Button thought they were going to tar and feather him. He told them they were wrong and he would be back to prove he was right.

Button's seven-year TCF scheme to make Australian industry more competitive is now endorsed by the industry. The climate of fear among its workers has gone. This time, on Button's return, John Laidlaw, the million-aire chairman of the family group of Yakka companies, drove up from Melbourne in his Mercedes to welcome Button at his Wangaratta plant. He was not expected.

Laidlaw's Australia-wide Yakka operations employ 2,000 people. Its annual turnover is $160 million. Laidlaw's personal wealth is reputedly $40 million. At his Wangaratta plant, Laidlaw was there to shake Button's hand and to stop his factory so Button could speak to its 250 women workers.

He went further than the courtesy of allowing Button to make a political speech to his employees in company time. In intro-ducing Button, Laidlaw endorsed the Hawke Government. Their jobs, he told the women, would be more secure under the Govern-ment's policies. Laidlaw even made a point of criticising the Nationals' policy on tariffs. It was a remarkable turnaround from the mood of a year earlier.

Later, at the Wangaratta Woollen Mills, Button looked at the raft of senior manag-ement behaving suitably deferentially and said quietly: 'This is all about guilt.' Button

was guest of honour at a lunch to mark the 10th anniversary of the takeover of the mills by the Liberman JGL group. Leon Liberman, too, had come up from Melbourne.

At the lunch, Liberman introduced Button to assembled local dignitaries and mill workers as a 'dedicated man of vision'. A year ago, they had worn black armbands and booed him. This time, after the speeches and the birthday cake, Button remarked out of the side of his mouth: 'You know, last election these people were putting slips into pay envelopes saying, "Vote Labor and you'll lose your job".'

Wangaratta is in the seat of Indi, which Labor can't win unless the earth really moves. Button seemed unconcerned. The day had been a good one. Later, as he drove to Bendigo, his mood matched his inner satisfaction. The talk, on a day of crisp sunshine in a cloudless sky, was about river banks and green fields and picnic hampers.

Button was ahead of schedule. He wanted to find some such place to stop and sleep. The day was too good to waste on politics. The fantasy never materialised, but he mused out loud about a children's song he used to sing at Sunday school in Ballarat, where his father was a Presbyterian minister.

'I'm H-A-P-P-Y, I'm H-A-P-P-Y

'I know I am, I'm sure I am,

'I'm H-A-P-P-Y.'

Happiness is a government minister three weeks from polling day.

Alan Ramsey

**Postscript:** *The Laidlaw family sold the Yakka companies to Pacific Brands, an Austral-ian clothing and hosiery group, in February 2007. Pacific Brands, set up in 2004, owns the Berlei, Bonds and King Gee brands, and in February 2009 announced it was shedding 1850 local jobs and moving its clothing opera-tions to China.*

# It's Howard, by a Whisper

**JULY 25, 1987**

THEY ARE still counting votes in the latest Federal election. That might not excite too many people, given there are no polling day mysteries left to unravel. Besides, most Australians are numbed by numbers. But a remarkable statistic has been accumulating quietly in the computers of the Electoral Commission. John Howard won!

Not in seats, but in votes. More Australians actually voted for Howard and the Coalition parties on July 11 than they did for Bob Hawke and the Labor Party. Not many more, but certainly more. A bare Coalition majority—a bit under 23,000 primary votes in a national turnout of more than 9.7 million, or a bit more than two tenths of 1 per cent. But still a majority of popular votes.

Bit staggering, isn't it? The Government takes six seats off its opponents, loses only two of its own, increases its parliamentary majority by eight (to 24), actually widens the voting gap (from 2.3 per cent to 3 per cent) in the 13 most marginal seats the Coalition must win next time to win office, yet polls fewer votes over the country as a whole than did the Opposition.

How? Well, that's the story of how Labor won.

As recounted many times since polling day, it won the votes where it had to win them: in the marginal seats. And it lost votes everywhere it could afford to lose them. A breakdown of national voting patterns emphasises just how disciplined was the Government's win.

Labor's overall vote went down in its heartland—in all capital cities except Brisbane, Hobart and Canberra. Its worst result was in NSW where 44 of the State's 51 seats recorded swings against the Government. Yet Labor lost only one NSW seat, while four of its five most marginal NSW seats actually increased their majority, this despite the fact the anti-Labor swing in the Sydney metropolitan area (3.5 per cent) was a thumping 2 1/2 times the national anti-Labor swing (1.38 per cent).

The same happened in Melbourne. Victoria, with a huge swag of marginal seats, was one of the election's two key States. Yet, again, although 23 of the State's 39 seats swung against Labor, five of Labor's eight most marginal seats picked up votes and two barely moved. It lost the eighth seat. By contrast, in Queensland, the election's second key State, 22 of Labor's 24 seats recorded swings to the Government. Labor won everywhere—the city, the bush and the provincial towns. And the only two Queensland seats in which its popular vote fell were both safe Labor seats.

The evidence supports the theory: the professionalism of Labor's exquisitely targeted campaign strategy stole the election on preference votes in a climate in which Johannes Bjelke-Petersen, in his home State, was thoroughly on the nose.

Alan Ramsey

**Postscript:** *John Howard's Coalition Opposition polled 4,255,289 primary votes (46.1 per cent) to Labor's 4,232,563 (45.8 per cent), sweeping up majorities in Queensland, South Australia, Western Australia, Tasmania and the Northern Territory, halving the popular vote with Labor in NSW and gaining a minority only in Victoria and the ACT. Yet the preference votes of 557,000 Democrats and 186,600 'others' comfortably won the election for Labor by 86 seats to 62 in a 148-seat House of Representatives.*

# Chapter 2

# The Historic Third Term

## Thank You, Voters

OCTOBER 10, 1987

NINETEEN YEARS ago, when John Gorton first visited the United States as Prime Minister of Australia, he took with him his wife, three staff and two departmental advisers. They travelled Qantas and two journalists went along to cover the trip. Total bodies: nine.

Yesterday, when Bob Hawke left Australia on his 16th trip abroad as PM, he was accompanied by his wife Hazel, 11 personal staff, three security guards, his Melbourne doctor, eight departmental advisers, 17 journalists, four TV crew and an official photographer. They travelled on a 707 VIP aircraft which, during the 19 days Hawke circles the world, will be manned in relays by 19 RAAF flight crew, maintenance staff and cabin stewards. Total bodies: 66.

The cost to taxpayers of the Gorton trip, in present-day dollars, would not have exceeded $40,000. The cost of the Hawke trip, based on the known cost of similar earlier travels, will not be less than $600,000, though more likely a great deal more. (In June, 1983, Hawke's first prime ministerial foray abroad, a 20-day trip to Papua New Guinea, Indonesia, Europe and North America, cost $663,300. In February, 1985, a 10-day trip to Belgium and the United States cost $534,745.)

The justification for much of the additional expense of overseas prime ministerial travel these days—the use of a VIP aircraft—is security and convenience. The justification for the massive growth in the official baggage trains which tag along is far less credible. People talk about greater pressures, increased demands, the need for a PM to be well briefed, and so on. Mostly it is self-serving humbug.

I doubt even Bob Hawke could look you in the eye and adequately explain why he must have 19 staff and departmental advisers on a trip in which, despite four days of ceremony with Commonwealth leaders in Canada, the highlights for him are a weekend's golf with George Shultz in San Francisco and Monterey, a football match in Dublin, and visits to two Irish horse studs. The rest, really, is just respectable padding.

Gough Whitlam is most to blame. He began the trend in big overseas caravans in 1973. Fraser and Hawke in the years since have followed his precedent unblinkingly. Malcolm Fraser in Opposition had no compunction in exploiting public resentment of Whitlam's flamboyant junketeering. Yet in Government Fraser was no more frugal of the public purse than he was of his own sense of importance.

Hawke is no different. Like Whitlam and Fraser, he accepts as his due the indulgent right to go abroad in great style, cosseted by a horde of supernumeraries and hangers-on. Restraint is a word which stays at home.

So does political prudence. Hawke is not the only senior member of the Government off overseas this weekend. Senate leader John Button leaves tomorrow with his wife and a more modest party of six staff and advisers for three weeks. Like Hawke, Button is also going first to the United States, later to Europe. There were no spare seats apparently on Hawke's VIP plane. So 48 hours after Hawke departs the country, Button and his group leave for Los Angeles on a commercial flight just about the time Hawke will be relaxing in San Francisco after his first 18 holes of golf with George Shultz.

The 'historic third term' is doing well.

Alan Ramsey

# The Jam Man Cometh

**NOVEMBER 14, 1987**

*'All three are pragmatists and they all want to win. Certainly John Howard, like other politicians, has always been a bit uncertain about John Elliott. But Elliott's never been uncertain about him. And I think all three of them, including Andrew, realise that while we might have managed this time to deal with our third loss in a row—and deal with it effectively and resiliently—I wouldn't feel too confident about a fourth loss. There's a limit to people's patience. I certainly think everyone will expect us to win next time. Really, we have to. And those three leaders are very well aware of that. It will be foremost in their minds in the next two years.' – Tony Eggleton*

TONY EGGLETON is the great survivor. He's been in the business of national politics for 23 years with a party which rarely tolerates losers. While Eggleton has been involved with more wins than losses, he and the Liberal Party lately have been losing consistently. He now has $2 million a year to spend to get back on a winning streak. John Elliott is the difference, The Jam Man cometh.

Until the 1984 election, after which Elliott became party treasurer, the Liberals' national headquarters had operated on a budget of about $500,000 a year. Elliott's aggressive influence doubled that to $1 million. Now, as the Liberals' new Federal president, he has doubled it again. Elliott did not join the team to be a loser.

Eggleton, the Liberals' Federal director, makes the point. 'John Elliott's whole philosophy is to win,' he says. 'And, despite his personality, he is a team player. I mean, it was very interesting at that famous dinner a few weeks ago when the parliamentary party wanted reassurance about the way he would play the role of president.

'Elliott really had no problem with that. His view was, "Look, as from tomorrow, I'll be playing in a different place on the field. Tomorrow, all being well, I'll be Federal president. And I know my role as president. This is a team game and I'm going to have to play the game, and I'll play it properly because only as a team can we win. And I'm not coming into this to lose!"

Eggleton and Elliott go back a lot of years.

In 1974, a struggling Bill Snedden, then Opposition leader, persuaded Eggleton to

return from London where he'd gone to work from John Gorton's staff for the Common-wealth Secretariat. Snedden, desperately short of experienced staff, wanted Eggleton as his political adviser. Three Melbourne business-men funded Eggleton's salary. Elliott was one of them.

After the recent (1987) election loss, some people, particularly among the defeated politi-cians, thought Eggleton should be asked to go from head office. John Elliott wasn't one of them. He flew to Sydney on polling night and next morning was at Eggleton's hotel, phoning him from downstairs.

'He rang me early in the morning and said, "Tony, I'm in the hotel, let's get together". He and I had a session starting at 8.30, we were joined by John Valder an hour later, then by John Howard. By the end of that day, we had hammered out a number of objectives. One was a much closer relationship between the parliamentary wing and the party organisa-tion, a much more cohesive interlocking.

'Another was a strong desire to see peace restored in the parliamentary party and a sen-sible relationship involving Andrew Peacock. That's why, within 48 hours of that meeting, Andrew was in Sydney.'

Perhaps. But that Sunday meeting did more than just set organisational objectives. The Liberals had just lost another election. Howard, Eggleton and Valder were highly vulnerable. Valder had decided already to quit as president. Now Howard and Eggleton, con-sciously or otherwise, were locking themselves into Elliott to survive.

It was, in every sense, a pre-emptive strike against the challenge Howard knew was coming from Peacock, who was no close friend of Elliott's. And it worked. Within three weeks, Howard was re-endorsed as leader, Eggleton's safety as Federal director was assured, and

Elliott was all but guaranteed the presidency. Peacock, fossicking hard, picked up the bone of the deputy leadership.

'Three defeats in a row do focus the mind of a party which likes to be winners. Giving that a whole new momentum has been Elliott. The great thing about John Elliott has been a capacity to get rid of cobwebs and conventions and be very pragmatic about the way ahead. Through him, and the changes agreed to by the party, I'm getting backing and resources I've never had before. By the time I've restructured this place, it will be potentially the strongest political centre we've ever had.'

After the July defeat, there was a severe shake-out at head office. Eggleton's staff was halved to 10. The Liberals rarely sack indians, only chiefs, and Eggleton insists no-one was asked to go. But go they did, among them the head of the national policy unit, David Trebeck. Now Eggleton is recruiting a new team. By the time he's finished he'll have more staff than ever—24 people. Three of them, each paid about $50,000 a year, will head separate new units on strategy and campaigning, communications and marketing, and party policy.

Two of the key appointments are being finalised. All will be operating by the New Year. And Eggleton has more authority. 'At the first federal executive meeting after the elections, I put forward two lots of plans,' he says.

'One was a new approach to election campaigns which would give the Federal campaign director real control of the campaign, not just its Federal elements such as advertising and Federal campaign headquarters, but actual operational responsibility for everything, including the leader's staff.

'I made it pretty clear I didn't know what people might want me to do in the future, but that I certainly wouldn't be prepared again to be Federal campaign director unless I got that authority. If you have the authority, and things go wrong, then you put up with the kicks. But it's a bit irritating if you get the blame for matters you have no control over.

'That was totally endorsed. The other important decision was a much stronger hands-on role for the party organisation, including the controversial stuff about discipline, because both Valder and Elliott were quite determined to demonstrate an organisational concern on that front. Twelve months earlier that would have run into a lot of problems with the State branches. This time, in the changed climate, it went through.

'I've never had parliamentary aspirations. Nor have I ever got involved in internal politics. I've tried to always serve whoever was the leader in a totally objective and loyal fashion. I think that's been well recognised. You know that Tony won't let you down, he won't play politics around you, and he'll do his damnedest for you.'

In 23 years Tony Eggleton has served eight Liberal leaders, five of them prime ministers. His first election was the 1964 Senate election, on the staff of one of Menzies' ministers. The next year he became Menzies' last press secretary. Ten elections and seven leaders later, Eggleton is still there, doing what he does best. Surviving. It takes great skill to run the gauntlet from Menzies to Howard and still remain in the game. The range of personalities was enormous.

Yet Eggleton managed it with style. He is the perfect hand servant. Always there but never in the way, the discreet chameleon who adapts instantly. A superb bureaucrat. A team player. And as Harold Holt once said: 'If I have a few drinks at night, I can always be sure Tony will get me home.'

The only election Eggleton has missed in the past quarter-century was Whitlam's winning 1972 poll which ended the Coalition's record 23-year run. When John Gorton's prime ministership ended abruptly and destructively in March 1971, and McMahon took over, Eggleton had decided already to leave Gorton's staff for London. He agrees it was one of his better moves. He missed the McMahon circus and the stigma of ultimate defeat.

In 1974, after Snedden recruited him back, Eggleton stepped off the plane just in time to join the May double dissolution campaign. It was his first loser. A year later, he was working for Malcolm Fraser.

'Malcolm was a totally different personality again,' he says. 'I'd already known him a long time. He became a minister the day Holt became Prime Minister in January, 1966. After the crisis with Gorton in 1971, and Fraser was out on the backbenches again, we were talking one day, just before I went to London, and I said to him, I don't know why, but I said, "You shouldn't be depressed. You're going to be PM one day. I still think you're the man with the most prospects".

'He looked a bit shocked and said, "Oh, I thought I ought to go back to the farm", and I said, "No, hang in there". Later, of course, I worked for him after he replaced Snedden. We got along well. I understood him in a way few people got to understand him. We had a mutual bond. And yes, we keep up the contact. I hear from him a lot. He rings often. I call him my Big Adviser. It always gets a giggle in the parliamentary party when I say, 'Well, my big adviser tells me . . .'

'The night of the last election, I was doing a lot of TV, and suddenly I found myself talking to a panel which included Don Chipp. He's never been very well disposed towards me, and he said, "Tony, isn't it about bloody time you went? You're a disaster!" I said that was for others to decide, but I knew that would be a mood. It was in 1983. The point I always make to people is you never fight an ideal election campaign, you fight it on the landscape you're given. You're the bunny. Perhaps the last thing you want is an election, but suddenly that's where you are, you're the campaign director, and it's all uphill'.

Eggleton runs his working life with the same efficiency he has lasted the highs and lows of the past 23 years. Each day he gets up at 5.20am precisely, goes jogging on a nearby golf course until 6, showers and breakfasts and is in the office at exactly 6.40am. On his desk waiting is a press summary and newspaper cuttings prepared by a staffer who already has been at work an hour.

By 7 o'clock he is ready for anyone who wants to ring, mainly John Howard. If an issue is running, they'll compare notes, discuss tactics. When Parliament is sitting, Eggleton each day walks the kilometre across to Parliament House for an 8.30 meeting with the Liberal leadership group. The routine rarely varies. Tony Eggleton is always there.

He is well paid but, like other financial matters, won't say how much. John Elliott, now the party's organisational patron, ensures the Federal staff is properly looked after. It's part of his style. But will it all work? 'Look,' says Eggleton, 'Elliott thought this was a role he could play at a time when the party obviously could do with some new blood, some revitalisation. He's not in the business of making waves or difficulty for the Liberal Party. He's come into this job because he's damned determined we're going to win.

'Obviously there are many conservative and conventional types that support our party, but I think even they would see in John Elliott a man of great vitality and vigour and success. And while some people in the parliamentary wing are still apprehensive, he's a very successful man who's prepared to hitch his star to the party at a point in its history when it can do with all the success it can get.

'Make or break? Oh I think so, yes, I really do. We're inclined to say that a lot in politics, you know, talk of watersheds and so on, but I guess one can be fairly sure of one thing. And that is, that if the Liberals don't win next time, the Liberal Party after that will be a very different sort of party to the one it is today. Very different. I think we all realise that.'

Alan Ramsey

# End of Year Blues

**DECEMBER 19, 1987**

FOUR YEARS ago, John Button looked back on the Hawke Government's first year and remembered the cockatoo he had saved. I forget the detail and so does he . . . It involved a departing Indonesian diplomat who wanted to take it home, something like that. At the time, though, Button recalled that cockatoo with great affection. Saving it, he said, had been his most satisfying ministerial decision in that first year.

This week, four years on, the Government's Industry Minister and Senate leader tried to regurgitate another year and couldn't. It had been too long, too hard, he said. Grindingly long. He apologised. 'I'm stuffed,' he said, and looked it. 'I'm sorry. Too tired. Everybody'll be glad to get out of here. I will.' Yes, he remembered the cockatoo.

'That's probably still the most influential thing I've done. (Pause.) Although I suppose there's been a few other parrots since then. (Longer pause.) I get my kicks not here, out there, seeing good things that happen. (Many good things?) Oh, yes. I wish it could be better, but I think it's all happening now. There are vast cultural changes taking place in industry, vast attitudinal changes. Yes, good things are happening.'

And politics? 'Well, Joh [Bjelke Petersen] occupied the first part of the year, didn't he? (Long pause.) Joh occupied most of the year. (Longer pause.) Joh's year, we could say. We're all going to miss him, particularly the Labor Party in Queensland. And what are the comedians going to do? I mean, half of them have made fortunes out of him.'

The interview was going nowhere. Typical quirky Button humour, but tidbits. 'I can't even think of anything entertaining that's happened. Perhaps that's a bad sign.' Then he did. If he couldn't say profound things about the year, he said, he could tell of his 'two most miserable experiences overseas'.

'I was in New York, and we were having a cup of coffee in a little shop one morning and I said to the waitress, 'Can I have a sandwich?' And she looked at me very quizzically, said nothing, so I said, "You know what a sandwich is?" And she said (he affected a Brooklyn accent), "Of course I know what a sandwich is. You just gotta learn to be descriptive." Talk about put you down! I was in decline for the rest of the day.'

His second 'major indignity' occurred in London. 'We went to a pub in the East End, which apparently was a bit of a gay pub, or becoming one, and had a few drinks, and after a while I was busting for a pee. They had this little stage up front and the toilet door was right next to it.

'So I pushed through the crowd towards the toilet, and this compere on the stage says (this time a Cockney accent), "Oh, it's no good goin' in there, guv. You won't do any good f'r yeself. There's nobody in there!" The place roared, and I got in there, then I thought, Christ, what am I going to do, I've got to go out again! I finally screwed up my courage and go out, and he looks round and says, "There y'ar, I tol' you. See, not a hair out of place".'

Alan Ramsey

# The Big Picture Show Man

**DECEMBER 26, 1987**

PAUL KEATING is a Big Picture man, always has been. He watches the economic detail, all of it, but is forever absorbed by the symmetry of the whole, how it must all fit together. On Christmas Eve, with not another minister in sight at Parliament House, Keating was still at work at his canvas in his basement office. 'Just knocking the last of the paper over,' he called it. He stayed six hours before going home.

Before he went, Keating showed how he does it, his game plan for the Australian economy: where he says he is, where he's been since 1983, where the economy is going if he gets his way in Cabinet, which he usually does. After another long, hard year, his authority remains immense.

He insists it's all there in the key figures, in the Big Picture. You have to keep the Big Picture in focus all the time, he says. He makes it sound simple, which he knows it isn't.

But that is Paul Keating. Utterly confident, always very sure of himself. A Treasurer on a mission, doing God's work as well as Bob's, refusing to be deflected by those he dismisses as pissants and know-nothings. He is very convincing, as all his colleagues know. He gives up nothing.

To explain it all, Keating takes an hour, mixing jargon and hard language in his tour of the economy. What started as an interview to look back at four years and ahead for one, ends with a hand-written note, later delivered by one of his staff, which begins: 'Just in case you balls it up!' A scribbled list of figures follows, the very core of the Keating Big Picture.

That is pure Keating, too.

He thinks nothing of telephoning an editor and paying out on some pundit he believes doesn't know a Budget forecast from a bull's foot. A few years ago, after an article that annoyed him a lot, a note arrived on my desk the same day bearing very explicit language and the concluding paragraph: 'Journalists are supposed to think as well as write. Some old-fashioned cerebral activity would do you no harm at all.'

This time, on Christmas Eve, Paul Keating left out nothing in explaining his case. He not only talked—which he does remorselessly and without effort, like a Sherman tank on the move—he scribbled as well.

In a corner of his office is an easel, and with it some 12 to 15 large pasteboard illustrations, all of them coloured graphs of one kind or another on key economic indicators. Keating keeps them as props to convince Caucus, and anyone else who might doubt his economic management.

Now he turned two of the graphs to the wall, propped them against the back of a settee, and began drawing furiously—figures, arrows, additions and subtractions, squiggles, bumps, curves, circled sweeps, hard underlines, his pen rarely pausing, the Van Gogh of Treasurers.

The theme is simple: Australia must trade its way out of its straightened circumstances. The Government has induced structural change in the economy to ensure this happens, to make us more competitive. And it is working. Export growth is overcoming imports. But we must do more.

The commentary overwhelms. 'Look,' he says, 'when net exports come through, they tend to come through like this. (He draws what looks like a very fat tadpole.) It starts off as an appreciation. Prices shift. Importers hang on, cut their margins, because they think it might be temporary, right? Later, they realise that's hopeless, give up market share, and what happens is you get this (the tadpole bulge). So, 1 per cent net exports here (scribble), then 2 1/2 per cent (scribble), then one (scribble), right?

'Now, a coupla other points. When exports really start to flow, it comes through in a blob (scribble). That's the 2 1/2 per cent we got last year, this bit here (scribble) is the 1 per cent we got the year before. We'll get another 1 per cent this year. But up here (scribble), we need more, another 2 per cent of GDP, a thicker tail.' (He scrawls a heavy strap from the head of the tadpole.)

He deflects briefly. 'If the US could do this, they'd wet themselves. And they will do it, because the depreciation of their dollar is just as deep. But they're not tightening up fiscal policy the same as we've done. I mean, this here (scribble, scribble) is a text-book change.

'But when the blob comes through, that's about all you get. You then have a whole lot of other handstands to do to get this last bit (scribble), the thicker tail (heavy underlining). It's like driving a car to 100 mph from 90; it can do it at 90, but at 100 it's got everything blatting full-out, all the (expletive) valves are jumping, you know what I mean?

'In other words, to make it do THAT (scribble), so that in HERE (scribble) we get, say, another 2 per cent of GDP, which would get THIS (scribble), we got to pick up another two times 2,800 (scribble), that's 5,600 million off the current account. Well, roughly $5 billion, right, to get that 2 per cent of GDP.

'Now, the only way we can do that is by high levels of investment and less demand. In other words, pulling demand off. You know, cutting consumption, lifting savings. And one of the ways of continuing to do this is by further public sector dis-savings. (He repeats this, slowly, like speaking to a retarded child.)

'That means the Commonwealth Budget will go further into surplus and we'll start cutting those deficits of the States, right? In other words, the public sector can cut demand and add to savings by further fiscal action, you with me?'

No, not really. But over the next hour, as Keating fills first the back of one pasteboard graph, and then a second, with his frenetic scribbling, explaining bit by bit as he goes, he makes his point and rams it home. It is, broadly, that if the Hawke Government had just 'sat on its bum and done nothing', our foreign debt, through an expanding current account deficit, would be growing now at an underlying rate of $25 billion a year.

It isn't. It's growing at less than half this rate, or $11.5 billion this year. Still high, but much better. And it's continuing to slow, to turn around, as investment builds up and Australia begins to trade its way out of trouble.

The reason, says Keating, is the profound and permanent structural changes, including financial deregulation, forced by Government policy. Those changes have helped slice some $13.5 billion off the yearly growth in international debt, now approaching $100 billion in total.

Exports are overtaking imports. This is the fat tadpole. It represents 4 1/2 per cent

net growth in exports in three years. It means the current account deficit has been cut from an underlying rate of 8 1/2 per cent a year, including the 1985/86 slump in world trade prices, to 4 per cent. You with me?

That is what Keating's extraordinary artistic performance is all about: explaining how this has been achieved, what was responsible, and what is needed to cut further and get Australia moving more quickly towards the black instead of deeper into the red.

On the way through, he makes it clear he has no intention of easing the brakes. The squeeze of the last four years will stay, despite his Christmas bonus of a projected Budget surplus of $580 million by the end of next June. Federal spending, or outlays, will again be cut in the coming year. The next Keating Budget will go much further into surplus. And the States will be hit even harder.

The lesson continues: 'We had a nice graph here the other day, our indebtedness graph line (he shuffles around in the cards behind the easel). Yes, here it is. That's another thing people don't understand. People say, oh, you shouldn't let Bondy and Elliott and all these blokes go offshore, that's offshore investment.

'Yet if Bond ends up building up a massive equity in US breweries, and Elliott does the same in English breweries, and you get Boral and all the others; well, let's say they end up with $20 billion in gross assets abroad, our net debt abroad is reduced by $20 billion. So all this stuff about their offshore investment not coming back as dividends, and so on, it's just bullshit.

'Our net debt as a percentage of GDP is rising, yes. But we've got the rise slowing. And we've got to win the current account game to win the debt game. And the biggest addition to the current account is not Alan Bond borrowing to buy a brewery. It's this (scribble), our trade performance.'

So does Paul Keating ever wake up in the middle of the night and think, maybe he might be wrong? 'Oh no,' he says. 'This is all pretty simple. No, you can't be wrong about THAT (scribble), and THAT (scribble). You don't have to be a genius to work that out. The hard bit is getting to it, getting the higher export growth rate, the investment.

'The hard bit is keeping all the balls in the air to keep this structural change coming through. What I've got to do now is the Houdini trick; instead of having the blob finish, I've got to get a long tail on it, this bit(scribble). We've got to get that other 2 per cent.

'That's the really hard bit, the last grunt. It's very hard. Look, by not importing things like, say, clothes pegs, by selling just a bit more steel, by doing a few ordinary things, you can get the easy bit of it just by getting off your bum. Well, we've already done that.

'But this next bit takes a real national effort. Now I reckon the investment is coming through, we've got these lower interest rates (scribble), investment follows, THAT (scribble) pulls THIS (scribble) through, and if we do that, well, we win the next election, I mean it.

'Look, all the performance goals have been met by this Government. People who say we won in July because Joh kicked hell out of Howard, that's nonsense. Leadership was the issue. That's why we got back. We might have been helped by a bit of spanging on the other side, but we got re-elected because in the end the mob trusted us, not them.

'That's the main game. You ask me what we've done, what lies ahead, that's it. The economy's the main game, and this (scribble, jab) is what it's about. This is the Big Picture. And if we can cut demand a bit longer, sit on demand a bit longer, we can get there.'

Keating is eloquent about tax. He believes, that in Labor winning re-election last July, the new tax regime he introduced in 1986 cannot be dislodged. 'All those things like FBT, capital gains tax, substantiation, and the rest, they're all fixed in the system now,' he says. 'They're there, locked in.

'That's why I was so desperate to win that election. I mean, the tax office now has the best background in law they've ever had. And for the first time in our history we've got a revenue operation of some world standing.

'That's why revenue's coming up. All the compliance is coming back, which is why refunds are down to buggery. Refunds reflect claims, and claims are not down just because of substantiation. They're down because people are no longer game to put in a bodgy claim. They're not doing it. The game's got better.

'So compliance is back, the revenue bases are up, substantiation's running multiples of our Budget forecasts. The FBT is running at twice our forecast, an extra billion, capital gains will continue to be an enormous boon over time. That all lets you run a decent fiscal policy. It lets you end up with these lower interest rates.

'That's where we're winning this, you know. People are not going to let a Coalition Government come along and wreck it all.'

And next year? Will it be harder? 'No, not harder. Nothing could be harder than 1986/87. That was a shocking year. All those problems, the collapse of our trade, and then smoothing in the new tax regime. No, it couldn't be harder. And this year never stopped!'

Keating goes back to his makeshift blackboard.

'Overlaying all this (scribble, scribble) next year will be the business tax review and the structural adjustment review—telecommunications, shipping, and so on. We've got to clear all the bloody crap out of the pipes. You know, like when the gas man came and blew the pipes out. That's what we're doing. We're blowing the pipes out.

'And I've got the economics of all that to marry into the Budget and the Premiers' Conference. Some more tax things changed, the Budget a bit tighter, fiscal policy better, some of these big structural issues out of the road. It's going to make it another pretty gigantic year. But not harder.'

And no, of course the Government has nothing to apologise for, not to anyone. 'The thing is, this Government is running way ahead of the Labor Party. That's a bit of a shame, but if we're around long enough, they'll catch up. Then they'll see this Government for its real substance.

'Sending people down to the social security office is not looking after them. By the end of next year we'll have created a million new jobs since 1983. That's looking after the people we're supposed to look after. That's what I think keeping the faith's all about.'

He puts his pen away and returns his graphs to their place behind the easel. 'Yes, I'll continue doing this job,' he says easily. 'I still like it. I'm tired by it, but I like it. I like the achievement.' One day Paul Keating will be Prime Minister, and deservedly. But not yet. For the moment he must stay where he is. 'Anyway,' he says, 'there it is.'

The lesson, like the year, is over.

Alan Ramsey

# Chapter 3

# Turmoil in the Castle

## Watch it Bob, Here Comes Paul

**AUGUST 8, 1987**

THE BEST story in politics is often the story behind the story. Mostly it's the story you never hear. Some years ago, the Labor Party in opposition pulled off the coup of getting hold of the entire detail of the revenue measures in the Fraser Government's 1978 Budget a week before it was announced. That was John Howard's first of five budgets as Fraser's Treasurer.

The leak must rate as the worst breach ever of Budget security. Had it been known at the time, the repercussions would have been extreme, even in a town where the extraordinary is often the norm. The story did not get out. Bill Hayden's Labor Opposition kept the secret tightly to itself. Even within its ranks very few people knew. And their knowledge proved more secure than the Budget's. No word of it became public until eight years later.

What Labor did with its leaked knowledge was two things. First, it allowed Hayden, as

Opposition leader, to be better prepared to respond on Budget night to a budget that was a real stinker. And why wouldn't he? He knew in advance everything John Howard was going to say.

More significantly, it allowed the Opposition to create the most exploitable political climate it could create by selectively leaking, during the three days before Budget night, its worst decisions. Two senior journalists had the detail fed to them, bit by bit, for a series of exclusive front page revelations. This meant that instead of the Budget's bad news arriving in one big chunk, the Opposition's manipulation generated a succession of bad news headlines over several days, all accurate. The political objective was to heighten, to Labor's advantage, the Budget's thumping impact on voters.

There was a second spin-off. What was happening would have badly shaken Howard and Fraser. They had no idea where the leaks were coming from. Their Government was held up to public ridicule as the most leak-prone in history. One fanciful analysis even theorised Fraser had leaked his own Budget. Hayden's office sat back and enjoyed the turmoil.

The Budget story that year was a good one, but the story behind the story was better. The story behind that wasn't bad either. The original leak to the Opposition came from the Treasury itself, a fact which known nine years later will assist no-one. The trail is now too cold.

The two journalists, Peter Bowers and Brian Toohey, were locked into silence by the journalistic ethic of neither disclosing nor jeopardising their sources. Thus, while everyone else was having a field day blaming the Government, and Fraser and Howard were conducting witchhunts among their own, Bowers and Toohey knew the real culprits were the Opposition but could not make their knowledge public. Nor could they pursue the even bigger story of who was leaking the Government's Budget secrets to its opponents.

There are two points to be made from all this, neither startlingly new. One, nobody leaks anything in politics without a motive. And two, journalists are always captives of their sources. A third point is made obvious by the first two: politicians, if they can get away it, will shamelessly manipulate journalists for their own advantage, just as journalists feed off the same process.

That brings us to what will be the real story behind the story in Federal politics for the next two years. That story is not going to be management of the economy, or the great sell-off of public assets and deregulation of the labour market that can be expected from a confident Government re-elected for the third time. Or even how the renewed Coalition refashions itself as a political force amid the competing pressures of its longest period in opposition for 40 years.

All of these will be constants this term. Yet for sheer drama and conflict of wills, however subterranean, the real story of the next two years is going to be how successful Paul Keating is in his ambition to become Prime Minister during the life of this new Parliament. There is a revealing anecdote of how just how real this is.

On the morning of the day Bob Hawke announced the 1987 election, Keating burst into Hawke's office to complain about the proposed July 11 date. The previous night, in talks in Hawke's office, the date had come down to July 11 or 18. Keating wasn't there. Earlier, he'd argued strongly for early August. A July date would kill Keating's imminent visit to Europe. He already had his tickets. Hawke's staff joked about it later in unflattering terms.

But next morning, when Keating fronted Hawke in his office, he was upset about something else altogether. Lionel Bowen, the deputy Prime Minister, had told him that any double dissolution called before July 1 would mean another half-Senate election within two years. Keating was utterly opposed. What he is recalled as saying to Hawke is: 'I don't want to have to be fighting a Senate election in 18 months time', or words very similar. Bowen's advice was wrong, but Keating had nailed himself.

The remark registered with Hawke and others who later recalled it. Keating's use of the personal pronoun suggested he expected to be Prime Minister by mid-1989 and he didn't want Hawke circumscribing his election options. Keating might have meant something else. He might simply have been talking in the general sense of the Government. Or as a Treasurer whose chief concern was political decisions impinging on economic management.

But others don't think so. They include people close to Hawke who are convinced of the primacy of Keating's prime ministerial ambitions.

Keating is not a patient man. Among Hawke's staff, there is a sensitivity to Keating's nakedly overt ambition that at times comes close to paranoia. They resent the massive publicity Keating gets as the chief architect of Government policy. They are critical of what they see as his direct role in influencing some of the more senior opinion makers among political journalists.

Hawke's staff are good at news management. But Keating is better. Recently, I asked to see him about a particular issue. His office called back to say come down. When I arrived I was told I'd have to wait. Someone had jumped the queue. The wait lasted one hour and 20 minutes. It ended when Paul Kelly of *The Australian* walked out of Keating's inner office. An off-the-record talk lasting 80 minutes with the nation's Treasurer is powerful stuff.

Keating has always stayed well plugged in wherever he sees his own best interests. The press is one such area. He is the politician who's made a career out of Jack Lang's great line that you should always back self-interest because you know it's a goer. And earlier this year, during a strained exchange over parliamentary tactics, Keating told Hawke with some heat: 'If you want to wear the belt, you've got to have the fights. And if you won't have the fights, you'll have the belt taken off you'.

Strong words from an impatient challenger.

Alan Ramsey

# Whack 'em in the Mouth

**NOVEMBER 7, 1987**

THERE IS a dangerously sour mood in the Hawke Government's ranks at the moment. At a private meeting one night this week, a Labor backbencher told Paul Keating in very explicit language he thought the Government was much too arrogant and losing touch with its base support. Keating replied in kind. He used a great many four-letter words imaginatively in telling anyone who felt they qualified what they could do with themselves and their grumbles. Keating is not one for delicacy.

What the backbencher, Sydney's Russ Gorman, actually said to provoke the Treasurer was equally frank. In a broad verbal sweep of the Cabinet, Gorman insisted: 'If youse blokes would stop stroking your stalks and get out there in the electorate, you'll find out what the people really think of you.' There were several similarly colourful remarks.

The issue which provoked the exchange had little to do with the economy. The October stockmarket crash and the uncertain dollar stirs no heat in the rank and file of the Hawke Government. In Parliament, yes, there is a public contest in rhetoric between Government and Opposition. But not within the Government itself. There it strikes no chord at all as yet.

What unsettles Labor MPs is more basic, more personal.

A whole set of circumstances is responsible, involving diminished self-esteem, their sense of impotence, the long, hard year behind them, the relaxed discipline which always follows an election, Bob Hawke's heightened love affair with his own place in history, even MPs' niggled frustration now that they know they are not going to get anything like the 11.7 per cent pay rise they believe is their right.

It is one irritant after another, all rubbing together and generating an ill temper right across Government which is testing the authority of what Gorman calls 'youse blokes'. What he means is the small group of senior ministers who hold the real power in the Hawke administration. In the end, of course, he means the Prime Minister.

Whatever your perspective of the health of the Government's unity, Hawke created an intense climate of ill-will in his parliamentary party by his unilateral behaviour immediately after the election. He not only angered ministers by the way he went about reconstructing the Government. He annoyed everyone else by launching into the proposed sell off of government assets without talking to this party. Things have only become worse since. Hawke's proposed aborigine pact did not help.

It is the assets sell-off, the so-called privatisation debate, that saw Gorman and Keating mixing four letter words this week. Senator Peter Cook, the organisational heavy of the party moderates, or Centre Left, has a motion before the Caucus to effectively lock Hawke and the privatisation debate into control by the parliamentary party. Cook's proposal has strong support in the Left faction. Even Hawke's own faction, the Right Wing Centre Unity group, is split on the issue.

Caucus was due to debate Cook's motion on Tuesday. The previous night, the Centre Unity group met to discuss how to deal with it. Gareth Evans, Hawke's Senate deputy leader, proposed an amendment at the Monday night meeting which, if adopted, would neuter the Cook proposal. Yet the group could not agree even among themselves.

In the flow of words, which quickly tapped the range of sour feelings pervading the Government, Gorman did his thing. Keating does not often attend factional meetings, but helped make this one memorable. He told all present the critics could go stuff themselves. The Government, he said, would do what it had to do, whatever way the Caucus might eventually vote on privatisation.

Keating insisted he had no fears about taking the issue to Labor's national policy making conference in Hobart next June. This caused Senator Robert Ray, a key factional leader, to observe: 'You'd be a dope, Paul, if you thought you could get more than 30 votes'. Darwin's Senator Bob Collins interjected: 'No, 20 votes!' Keating apparently was unruffled.

Later, MPs present said there had been no anger, no rancor, in the tribal exchanges, despite the hard language. They are used to Paul Keating. This was the macho Right talking as they always do to each other. Hairy chests at ten paces. Get a serve, whack it back with interest. But no heat. Keating summed up his feelings, perhaps his political philosophy as the meeting broke up and he left, still talking to a group of MPs walking out with him. 'It's often necessary just to stand in the middle of the street and hit the first (expletive) that

goes past right in the mouth' he told them. 'It settles a lot of political problems'.

It didn't settle this one, though Keating's uncompromising attitude might have caused some people to rethink rebellion. Then again, it might have hardened attitudes, too. The next day, when Caucus met, debate on the Cook proposal was deferred a fortnight. Yet the cross-factional militancy of the backbench was evident in the Caucus reaction to a virtuouso performance by Lionel Bowen, the deputy Prime Minister, who stood in as leader for Hawke, still absent in his sick bed.

Some people are working hard behind the scenes to ensure that whatever ultimately happens to Cook's motion does not humiliate the Prime Minister publicly. In the meantime, everyone is happy to let off some of their frustration at matters in general by making Hawke the butt of Bowen's private joking. Keating, meanwhile, is immersing himself in defence of the Government's wait-and-see attitude to the upheaval in the financial markets.

Privatisation is an issue still months away. Publicly, at least, he will not get involved. The economy is where the action remains. Parliament has been sitting throughout the three weeks since Wall Street went sour and took the rest of the world's stock markets with it. The falling dollar added a further dimension. Yet Keating, as confident as ever, remains convinced the Government has the political ascendancy.

'Pressure?', he echoed in his office yesterday. 'No, no pressure. To put pressure on a government an opposition has to fight from a framework of substance. This Opposition doesn't have an economic framework. John Howard's in a very weak position in trying to put pressure on us about anything fundamental at all. He hasn't touched first base.

'Howard's trying to run this phoney line the Government has left Australia unprepared for external shocks and that we are taking a risky or gradualist approach. Well, any policy of a Government which takes the budget deficit from 3 per cent of GDP to zero in 18 months is entirely activist. There's no other government anywhere which has done this.

'Everything we've done since 1983 has been about trying to insulate Australia from external shocks. Before the stockmarket fall, we were being hailed around the world as Australia pointing the way. People were saying in New York things ought to be done in the United States the Australian way.

'Now, to be told by John Howard and Andrew Peacock, who 12 weeks ago were running around the country with a $6 billion unfunded tax cut, that we're not adjusting the place rapidly enough, after we spent nearly five years cutting their deficit legacy to zero, is really pretty hard to take'.

Like Hawke, Keating is anything but modest. And he insists the Government will not be stampeded into quick decisions just to appease newspaper critics. 'It's a matter of the Government keeping its nerve and being able to make fine adjustments about if and when to shift, and to shift in what way, by what order and how. It's for the Government to make the judgements. We were the ones that had to make the changes. We're the ones that'll have to live with the outcomes. We make the judgments.

'Our best judgment at the moment is we should see what the fallout is and, if adjustments are necessary, make them. I said a week ago the Government should stand ready to do whatever has to be done, whatever that might be. But we're not going to run around, rapidly changing policy settings on some mythical view of well, look we don't know what you should do but do something! This Government doesn't work like that'.

So what will happen?

'The markets everywhere are very uncertain. What we all need is a circuit breaker, is a major shift in US fiscal policy. There's no easy way out. Either, governments face up to structural changes, as we did last year, or the markets will take the initiative and force the changes, but more harshly and more bitterly'. Keating well understands the choice. It's a bit like doing as you're told or being whacked right in the mouth.

The philosophy is universal.

Alan Ramsey

# Public Enemy No. 1

**FEBRUARY 27, 1988**

TWO YEARS ago, almost to the day, Paul Keating arrived at the front steps of Old Parliament House and announced he would destroy John Howard. 'From this day onward,' he told journalists, each word delivered like the crack of doom, 'Mr Howard will wear his leadership like a crown of thorns, and in the Parliament I will do everything I can to crucify him.' Keating is not usually a man to make idle threats.

That day, the venomous mood he was in, you'd have thought Howard was already last night's dinner. Keating's cold anger was truly chilling. Had Al Capone, icepick in hand, stepped out of the Treasurer's car that morning, the waiting press pack could not have been more impressed. What happened after that is now folklore. Having excited the press, Keating, still seething, strode inside to his office where he telephoned Howard a dozen doors away.

The ensuing conversation was very threatening and very abusive. And very loud. Keating's anger was white hot again. So was his imaginative language. The Opposition leader, it is said, did not really need the phone to hear what Keating had to say from one floor down. It was that sort of call.

Outside the occasional insult on the floor of the House and the formalities of political debate, they have not spoken to each other since. Previously, there had been mutual regard and respect. You would often see Keating and Howard, heads together, in the lobbies or at the occasional office party. But no more. The cause of the one-sided exchange of views that morning ended a political friendship which had transcended party politics for ten years.

Even now, two years later, you can't mention Howard's name to Keating without those hooded eyes hardening as he looses off a burst of expletives. It's the same in Cabinet. His colleagues say reference to Howard in any Cabinet discussion is enough to have the Treasurer go off the deep end. The Bankstown boy is a good hater with a long memory.

And John Howard, what of him?

Well, whatever you think of him, Howard, for all his owlish, Little Johnny image, has proved surprisingly durable, a better survivor than we thought. Keating has not crucified him nor 'obliterated' him, as the elegant iceman promised. Neither has the electorate or anyone else. Not yet. Two years on, against, you'd have to say, all odds, Howard is still hanging in there, still Liberal Party leader, still defying the opinion polls and the rest of us who argue well, yes, a decent bloke, and sure, he's not all ego and no substance, but really, he isn't worth a cracker as an electoral asset, not where it matters: the ballot box.

Maybe. But the longer Howard stays there, the more secure he tends to look. He has an inner toughness which, in the early, more kindly light of a new political year, seemingly is more evident after the blast furnace of recent turmoil and lost causes. Perhaps, in the end, this stoic resolve will overcome all those prejudices and negative perceptions which so killingly jump into view every time he appears on TV. You know, the imagery of the gauche adolescent in king's clothes.

In the meantime, Howard is winning where he always does best, on the floor of the Parliament. That would get a sneering dismissal from Bob Hawke, but it's true. In the last fortnight, the first of the new Parliament, Howard has flogged Hawke every which way and back again: in tactics, aggression and sheer debating skill. And luck, too.

Never dismiss luck in politics. For once, everything has fallen the right way up for the Opposition. The Government's Adelaide by-election defeat in February, the resignations of Mick Young and John Brown, both cabinet ministers, two police investigations of ministerial sloppiness, the savagely ominous climate in NSW; you name it, it's all come together, melding one into the other. The Government has not been off the defensive since before Christmas.

In its own way, Parliament is as harsh and unforgiving a test of a party leader as television. It might not be the great shaper of public opinion. But what happens there influences the politicians. And, of course, the press. It's a gladiatorial contest, all theatre, but it's also a contest of judgment and competing wills.

That brings us back to Paul Keating and his rage of two years ago. The cause of all the heat at the time was the Liberals' dreaded Wilson Tuckey—he of the iron waddy—and an old Keating affair of the heart. Tuckey used his knowledge of it to taunt Keating one day at question time. The effect was devastating. Keating lost his composure completely.

'You stupid foul-mouthed grub,' he flung at Tuckey. 'You piece of criminal garbage!' Tuckey in reply inflamed Keating even more. Murder most violent could well have been done there and then on the floor of the House. Later, Keating phoned Howard to ask for the exchange to be expunged from Hansard. Howard talked to Tuckey who refused. Keating was ropeable. He blamed Howard for encouraging Tuckey. He fumed overnight and delivered his crucifixion threat the next day.

Now it's history. But it will never be forgotten, not by Keating, not by anyone in the Government. All his Labor opponents have since treated Tuckey with caution and not a little fear. He has proved the thickness of his hide and the potency of his waddy. He is to be messed with only at your peril.

With this impression of a government at odds with itself and the electorate has come a new, very personal bitterness by Hawke towards Howard. It's as if Hawke now mirrors Keating of two years ago. Hawke these days almost never speaks about Howard without putting him down in the most contemptuous manner.

Question Hawke about any one of the problems besetting his Government and you get the most awful harangue about what a no-hoper of a failed, repudiated, pathetic leader John Howard is. Pathetic is a word Hawke uses a lot about his opponent. So is repudiated, despicable and stupid. In Parliament, Hawke railed on about how the Australian people had 'thunderously confirmed' him as Prime Minister over Howard at last year's elections.

Later, when Howard raised Mick Young's shock resignation in February for 'family reasons', Hawke spent much of his answer sneering at Howard for 'the smallness of his mind matched only by the meanness of his spirit'. It went on like that, day after day, as the Government stonewalled its way through its worst session in ages.

Two days ago, Hawke turned a question from Howard on Health Minister, Neal Blewett, into a rhetorical bucket on Howard being pursued by John Elliott and 'the sooner it happens the better. Anyone would be better than you'. Howard should be chuffed. Hawke could pay him no greater political compliment.

Alan Ramsey

# The View from St Ita's

**JULY 30, 1988**

*'If you allow for my background from infancy at South Brisbane, where we never saw the Governor-General and rarely saw a politician, let alone ever expected that someone from that area would ever assume such a respected office, then the more I look at it, the more I find it a very exciting role . . . I think there's a case for very ordinary Australians to have a share of the action.'*— Bill Hayden, on ABC TV's *7.30 Report*, July 26, 1988.

BILL HAYDEN, by his own lights, is a very ordinary Australian who's been looking for his share of the action for 40 years or more. His first school was St Ita's Convent, not far from where his parents lived in a rented, five-room weatherboard cottage on stilts in Mabel Street, Highgate Hill, with its corrugated iron roof, its outside cold water bathroom and its chooks and loquat tree in the 12-metre square backyard.

St Ita's was a small, depressed parish school in a big, depressed area of South Brisbane. Bill Hayden Snr, a drunk and an itinerant piano tuner, sent his four kids there because he tuned the school piano. When the school took its business away, Hayden Snr, after a blazing row, took his children away from St Ita's and put them in the local state school, with Boggo Road gaol on one side and a VD clinic opposite.

The point about St Ita's was that from there, looking across the Brisbane River, you could see the new Queensland University site. Years later, long after Hayden Jnr had escaped the poverty of his background, he recalled St Ita's, in a rare moment of revealed introspection, and that childhood view of the university.

By then Hayden was a successful politician, his party's Federal leader. A few years earlier, when the heady years of the Whitlam Government disintegrated in chaos and great drama, Hayden had opted out, first declining Gough Whitlam's overtures to seek to become his successor and then refusing to serve on Labor's front bench in opposition. Instead, Hayden, despite much criticism, retreated to the back bench and the indulgence of a part-time university law course.

Now, as Labor leader, one night 10 years ago, he was seeking to explain why. Yes, there'd been the considerations of his family and the burden of his wife Dallas being mother, father, housekeeper and general dogsbody in far away Ipswich while he pursued his political career in Canberra. But there were other factors, too.

One was the frightening realisation, the morning he woke after the 1975 election debacle, that he was the only Labor MP in Queensland who'd survived the Fraser landslide. The only one! And survived by a bare few hundred votes. What if he'd lost? What could he, an ex-policeman, have done for a living after 14 years in politics? How could he, cut adrift from the financial security of his parliamentary seat, support his family, let alone give them the advantages he'd never had?

Hayden said the thought, as he lay in bed, had been one of the worst of his life. He determined then and there to do something more to secure his future. His other reason was even more revealing of the inner forces that drive Bill Hayden. It was that view across the river from St Ita's.

He used to sit, said Hayden, in school, or in St Ita's Church, both of which stirred nothing inside him, and look at the university site across the river and know that, for him, it was as far distant as the other side of the universe, another world altogether. It was the world of other people, wealthy people, of doctors and lawyers and others, but not him. Not the children at St Ita's or the parents who sent them there.

So, in 1976, with Labor back in Opposition, Hayden determined he would join that other world and get a law degree, however long it might take. He already had a degree in economics, gained in 1969 after eight years of part-time study and, before that, five years of correspondence courses for his matriculation.

Bill Hayden never did get his law degree. That surge of panic felt the morning after polling day in 1975 dimmed in time and, by the end of 1976, he was back on Labor's front bench, totally involved in politics. The law course was postponed. It has not been resumed. There has been no time.

Hayden, in middling middle-age, almost 27 years in politics, is no longer pursued by quite the same demons of 13 years ago. His grip on a quid has always been as firm as his grip on political life has proved. It is a mark of his background. Now, in 1988, there are more quids to grip. Hayden's financial future is secure, whatever he does. So is his family's.

Yet the recollection of Hayden's words on the view from St Ita's, and the obvious deep feelings it stirred, came surging back from 10 years ago as he defended himself and Dallas on ABC television last Tuesday night against those who insist there is no room for them at Yarralumla. So did the memory of a later, similar incident.

Early in his leadership, Hayden addressed a group of academics at Melbourne's Monash University one night about his thoughts on education. John Button, then Labor's education spokesman, had organised it. Although a relatively informal affair, held in the university staff canteen, Hayden insisted on a written speech. Button spent perhaps 10 minutes introducing Hayden as only Button can: with wit and easy charm.

By the time Hayden spoke, his audience could not have been more responsive. What followed was deadening. Hayden rarely reads a speech well and this was not one of the exceptions. He stumbled over the words, the phrasing, even the pronunciation. Afterwards, answering audience questions, he was far more at ease.

Back in the privacy of his motel later, over a drink, he asked for an opinion on how he'd gone. He already knew the answer. Question time had been fine, he was told. But not the speech. He'd looked and sounded so nervous. 'I couldn't avoid the impression you felt they were all better than you.' Hayden, showing no emotion, replied: 'Was it that obvious?'

It says as much about Hayden as did his feelings about the view across the Brisbane River all those years earlier. Another 10 years on, the same sense of insecurity, the same carefully-sheltered feeling of social and intellectual inferiority, was there again last Tuesday night, at least to this pair of ears.

So was the sense that Hayden, once denied the prime ministership, wants public acknowledgment of his worth as someone deserving to be this country's head of State. His chip-on-the-shoulder attitude to the system, to that other world of privilege he first glimpsed from St Ita's, remains as much a part of him as it ever did. Maybe not as strong as when he was hauling himself up out of the educational and economic trough of his early life, trusting no-one, self-taught, doing it all himself.

But still there, just the same.

'It (the Governor-Generalship) is an office of public respect and esteem and it has its importance,' Hayden told Paul Lyneham's ABC viewers. 'I suppose if I indulge myself in my selfishness it would allow, I hope, my wife and more particularly our children, and maybe one day our grandchildren, the opportunity for them to say, 'Well, the old chap came from South Brisbane without much hope, and look where he ended up'. That may be some small reward for them, if I decided to do it.'

There's no chance the Old Chap won't 'do it'.

Hayden has locked himself into the appointment, just as his extraordinary interview locked Bob Hawke into making sure he couldn't withdraw the offer Hawke only hours earlier was maintaining he still hadn't made. And in committing himself on national television Hayden made it crystal clear that while he might want the appointment for his family, for South Brisbane, for St Ita's, for all 'ordinary Australians', he very much wants it for himself, too. It's his ultimate share of the action.

Bill Hayden's two fingers to the system.

Alan Ramsey

# First Class All the Way

**AUGUST 18, 1988**

FINALLY, IT'S official. The silly word games are over. Now Bill Hayden has only to pack up and move out of Parliament, go through the long round of farewells the Labor Party will heap on him in the months ahead, and return home with Dallas to Ipswich to await Sir Ninian Stephen's departure in February.

Then plain Bill Hayden, ex-copper and tired politician, becomes His Excellency, the Queen's Man. For Hayden, it's the end of 26 years and eight months in politics and the beginning, after a six-month interregnum, of another five-year stint on the public purse. Only the pomp and magnitude of it will change.

Many years ago, Hayden's father, an American seaman who arrived in this country by jumping ship as an illegal immigrant, gave his son a piece of advice William Jnr never forgot. Work for the Government, young Bill was told; it's secure. Bill Hayden has never worked for anyone else. All his working life, 40 years of it, has been spent on the public payroll: a clerk in the State Public Service in Queensland, national service in the Navy, nine years as a policeman, and finally, a politician.

A lot of pap will be written and read about Hayden today and in the months to come. His life of hard knocks is the exploitable stuff of epics. Most will ignore one simple fact: Hayden has always grabbed the main chance. He won a seat in Parliament by defeating a Cabinet minister in an election in which he was given no chance. He became leader of his party when almost nobody wanted it after two of the worst thrashings Federal Labor has ever received.

And he got so close to the prime ministership, after being hounded for two years by a rival who cared mostly for self, that he broke down and wept when he was forced, by the conspiracy of his impatient colleagues, to abandon the chase with the prize just beyond arm's length.

In 27 years, Hayden never lost an election at the ballot box and only one in the Labor Caucus: in May 1977, when he ran Gough Whitlam to a margin of only two votes for the leadership. How different things might have been if he'd not lost that, either. Later, he beat Sydney's Lionel Bowen in December 1977 and Melbourne's Bob Hawke in August 1982. But he couldn't beat the enormous party pressure in January 1983.

Hayden was 8 1/2 years a minister and five years his party's leader. And, in March 1983, when Labor swept to office, he determined to remain a first-class passenger on the Hawke steamroller.

And that's what he's been ever since. Effective, able, sincere, decent, yes. But still a first-class passenger enjoying the ride and the perks and the pay.

Nothing changes next February.

Alan Ramsey

# Tiberius Hangs Up

APRIL 2, 1988

CARTOONIST BRUCE Petty got Billy McMahon right. So did speechwriter Graham Freudenberg. In the late 1960s and early 1970s, when Petty was the foremost political cartoonist in the country, he would draw McMahon as a small, frenetic stick figure with big ears forever involved in some Looney Tunes escapade or other, or conspiring against John McEwen or John Gorton.

And Freudenberg was the man who gave Gough Whitlam his famous 1971 line caricaturing McMahon as Tiberius with a telephone. These are the images that stick. Sir William McMahon was an original, a great political survivor, an irrepressible man of vast energy. Unfortunately for others he expended much of that energy on self-interest. It made him one of the most distrusted and scheming individuals in Australian politics.

Do not expect any of his former colleagues to be so crass as to say so at this time. Yet those who doubt the truth need only read Peter Howson's diaries, *The Life of Politics*, published in 1984. Howson was a junior minister promoted by Menzies, nurtured by Holt, sacked by Gorton and reinstated by McMahon. His diaries tell you more about the essential McMahon, the politician, than anything likely to be said now that he's dead.

To the Canberra press gallery, McMahon was a delight: he leaked like a sieve. He flattered journalists by telephoning at any time of the day or night, usually at weekends, to chat about some alleged outrage or other committed by McEwen or Gorton in Cabinet, then left you with the problem of sorting fact from fantasy.

Yet he was unforgiving of personal criticism. In late 1971, with 23 years of Coalition Government dying under him, I wrote an article in *The Australian* about his sacking of Les Bury as Foreign Minister in which I said McMahon had behaved like a 'nasty little twerp'. He rang at 7.30am, demanded to know if Rupert Murdoch had put me up to it, and ended the call with the words, 'Well, if that's the way it's going to be . . .'. He never spoke to me again.

Every Canberra journalist of the period has a favourite McMahon atrocity. Mine concerns his first and only trip to the United States as Prime Minister in 1971.

McMahon stayed in New York two days before launching himself on Richard Nixon in Washington. The day after he arrived he ordered Australia's three most senior diplomats in America to give him a breakfast briefing on his White House speech. They arrived at his Waldorf Tower suite to be greeted by McMahon, fresh from the shower, wearing only a large white towel. Inside, McMahon flopped into an even larger lounge chair and waved the suited diplomats to three straight-backed chairs he'd lined up in the centre of the room in front of him.

And there they sat, like three wise monkeys, while they briefed the Prime Minister of Australia, wrapped in his bath towel, on what he should say to the President of the United States. The briefing was interrupted three times. Once by the arrival on a trolley with McMahon's breakfast. And twice by Sonia McMahon wafting in and out of the room in an impromptu fashion show of dresses she'd brought from Australia to wear at the White House.

The diplomats never forgot the experience. I never forgot the story. It encapsulates the madcap quality of McMahon's personality, life and times.

Alan Ramsey

# Chapter 4

# The Keating Ascension

## A Question of Leadership

MAY 28, 1988

IT WAS truly awful. A dead speech in a dying Parliament. The previous night had seen Paul Keating strutting his stuff. Now it was John Howard's turn. He should have called in sick. Howard is nothing if not competent, often forceful, on the floor of Parliament. This night he was nothing. It was the content. There was no spark, no life. Worst of all, no substance.

The words limped out flat and tired and meaningless, half an hour of flummery. Not a single new thought, not one new idea. It was like hearing all the old press statements of John Howard's leadership after they'd been boiled down in the Liberal Party's knackery of dead rhetoric.

The newspapers the next day reflected the worth of what he'd said. The Howard reply to Paul Keating's latest May mini-Budget was no more than a sidelight, a political footnote. The real news, the substance, was still Keating's speech. That was predictable, of course. Governments make news. Oppositions rarely can unless they're cutting themselves to pieces. And Keating's speech was news on the grand scale.

Yet this was one of those occasions an opposition can make people take notice. Howard declined the invitation. He opted instead for the safety of criticism. Oppose rather than propose. Attack the Government, appeal to prejudice. Generalise rather than specify. The superficial instead of the substantial. Sound tough, talk puff.

It is two years and eight months since John Howard became Opposition leader and the alternative Prime Minister. At no time has it been easy. Often his own colleagues, his own allies, have made it harder. Still, Howard has survived. His resilience has been enormous. Yet all the killing political perceptions that make life so difficult for Howard came flooding back on Thursday night. This was not the speech of a confident, aggressive leader of ideas and purpose. This was the speech of a leader who had nothing to say.

Too harsh? Then you didn't hear his speech. Nor have you read it. I mean, really read it. All of it. Howard has not done such a bad night's work on his own behalf since he became leader. There were more long faces among his own colleagues afterwards than we've seen since last year's election.

Earlier in the day, in another speech that attracted almost no attention except in the Parliament itself, Paul Keating sought to suggest why the Opposition under John Howard can't be taken seriously. His speech was neither gentle nor gentlemanly. It was Keating aroused, Keating passionate. Keating utterly contemptuous of his opponents. A slam-bam, whack 'em in the ear speech that only Keating these days can deliver so effectively as a piece of stirring political theatre.

It touched more than a few raw nerves opposite. Andrew Peacock had just sat down after speaking on taxation. In reply, after a slow beginning, Keating's emotions took over. His voice lifting, his finger constantly stabbing at the Opposition benches, he let go.

'You were in office from 1949 to 1983, bar three years. You had the place for nearly 30 years, for all that time. And you left everything the way you found it. The place got old and tired and worn out, just like you are. JUST LIKE YOU ARE. Now you're saying to us, change things . . .

'For 30 years, all we had was Black Jack McEwen trowelling on the tariff protection while he was kidding farmers he was representing them. And Liberal Party treasurers sitting up, like slugs, while they were handed speeches by Treasury officials. Like SLUGS.

'They couldn't even read the speeches, let alone comprehend the stuff. That's how you ran the Commonwealth. The mandarins ran things. You got given the speeches. You didn't bother with the detail, that was for the public servants. Oh, you wouldn't worry about the detail. Because you NEVER ran the policy. You never RAN the place!

'Well, let me tell you this. WE run the place. WE run the departments, WE run the policy. WE comprehend. WE know. And that's the difference between this Government and you lot over there . . .

'That's why the public service holds you in such contempt. Because they know what you did to the place. They were hard-working, committed, earnest Australians working in the public sector for some decent altruistic outcomes, relying on BUMS in ministerial jobs for 40 years to try and change the place.

Well, WE've changed it. And now you're up saying to us, 'Oh, you've not touched the micro-economy, you've not touched the craft union structure'.

'I mean, really! I mean, you can just imagine how switched on they are, how concerned they are, at the blue-rinse set meetings of the Liberal Party in Toorak, about the craft union structure. Oh yes, they're worried about it down there, all right . . .

'And we bring in these vast changes, floating the exchange rate, opening up the economy, cutting the budget deficits, changing the tax system, dropping the tariffs, and you say, 'Oh, you haven't made any changes.' I mean, you've got no concept of nation, no concept of structure in government. You've got no policy, you've got no leadership, you've got no heart, you've got no guts, you've got no courage. And you've got no ideas . . .

'Is it any wonder you've got [John] Elliott and [Ian] McLachlan, all these other people outside, saying, 'God, what can we do with this parliamentary party of ours? What can we do to put something back into it?' I mean, where are the people that gave the Liberal Party some form, some structure?

'They're gone. But here you are, wandering around here, playing parliamentarian, picking up the salary, asking a few questions. Not saying, 'Well, look, we're not born to rule any more, we've got to actually earn our way back, so let's do a bit of thinking'. Oh, no no. No no. 'We're the born to rule mob, we've been out for five years, and, basically, we'll be back one day. But we can go on as we usually did because we're the chosen few, born to rule', etcetera.

'Well, where you all come a gutser is, over here, we think we're born to rule YOU. And we're going to keep on doing it. And let me tell you this: it's been ingrained in me from childhood, I think MY mission in life is to run YOU. And the Prime Minister thinks his mission in life is to run YOU. And let me say, the Labor movement thinks its mission in life is to run Australia. That's what's producing the changes, that's what's modernising the Australian state, that's what's putting us back up there . . .'

That's Paul Keating.

As rough as bags when he chooses, his language stunning. A parliamentary bearpit speech, delighting those behind, goading the forces opposite. A leader's speech. Everyone who heard it knew it. Neither Bob Hawke nor anyone else has the same ability to rouse the troops or humiliate the opponents. Now perhaps you understand why the leadership tensions these days are beginning to focus more on the Government and less on the Opposition.

John Howard may well have more to worry about. But the Keating/Hawke story is only just stirring. It has a long way to run. Hawke is still the Government's most popular figure. But his standing is not what it was. It's why Hawke has become more subdued, less abrasive in public. It's why we hear less about his golf these days and more about the work he puts in as Prime Minister. In a series of radio and TV interviews this week, Hawke was at pains to point out how he had chaired all the Budget meetings, and how this really wasn't the Keating economic statement but the 'statement by Mr Keating on behalf of the Government'.

Of course, Prime Minister.

Alan Ramsey

# The Great Love Affair

**MARCH 25, 1989**

ON TUESDAY night, Bob Hawke got to bed at 2.30 the next morning. Just over five hours later, he was strapped in his seat in an RAAF BAC-11 as it took off from Canberra for Melbourne. At 11.30 that night, after 16 hours and 1,600 kilometres in the air and on the road, Hawke climed out of C-1, his white prime ministerial car, driven up from Canberra, to bed down in a motel far up the NSW Hunter Valley. He was still awake at midnight, reading.

All day Bob Hawke had been selling himself. It is what, throughout his life, Hawke has always done best. Now, in his 60th year—and his seventh as head of Government—it's what he still does best. Hawke rouses people, seduces them. Public adulation makes his sun rise each day. Bob Hawke is a vain and vulnerable man who cannot survive without the esteem of an audience.

Hawke, in turn, gives all of himself. Three nights ago, having been on the move all day after little more than four hours' sleep, there he was in the Maitland leagues club at 10pm, signing autographs for a queue of people— men and women, but mostly women—that could have capsized a Manly ferry. In the adjoining bar, among the beer and the poker machines, the rest of us, dead on our feet and short-tempered to boot, were urging a member of Hawke's staff to get him out so we could go home.

Yet for 15, maybe 20, minutes, Hawke just stood there at his table, still animated and smiling, as the people shuffled past with their bits of paper and their expectant faces, to exchange a few words and get his signature. I do not admire his prime ministeship or his personality; he is a sheep in wolf's clothing.

But I cannot but admire the patience and good humour of his love affair with the Australian community.

The infidelity of his marriage to Hazel does not yet extend to the electorate.

The next day, at a little school in a green and tranquil placed called Denman, Hawke was as tolerant and attentive with several hundred primary schoolchildren as he had been the previous night with the adults. The common bond was their enthusiasm. Hawke was late arriving, and the children had been waiting in their rows and rows of chairs out in the hot sun. So did the mothers, old and young, down the back in the shade, with their strollers and pre-schoolers.

In his talk to them, Hawke was mercifully short. He simply told them school was important but they should enjoy it too and have fun, and he was glad to be there, and the way he said it you felt he meant it. For the rest, he just went up and down the rows of chairs, not like a political fireman rushing through but like someone as interested in them as they were in him. It took ages to get through them all, but he never quickened his pace and not once gave the impression it was a chore to be borne stoically.

There were small hands thrust at him from all sides, as well as letters; even Easter eggs. I have no idea if they really cared he had come to their school, but they knew he was Bob Hawke and they knew he was the Prime Minister, and no prime minister had ever been there before. It was a bit like a day at the fair, with royalty in attendance.

You could not help but notice the mothers, either.

Throughout his prime ministership, Hawke has always attracted huge numbers of women wherever he has gone. In the early years, they were forever wanting to touch him. In one campaign, I remember a woman obsessed with getting her hands in his hair. Three years ago, on a non-election visit to Melbourne much like this one, where he was just out and about, I watched Hawke walk around a shopping mall and saw the crowd of women who drifted out of shops to follow him, like mice after the Pied Piper, just get bigger and bigger.

They were mesmerised by him.

On that same two-day trawl through Melbourne's suburbs I also saw the near hysteria of nubile schoolgirls and the unconsious body language of a Prime Minister totally aware of his sexuality. His visit to one girls' high school was like nothing else I've seen in Australian politics. It was like a pop concert, not a prime ministerial call.

There was nothing similar on this visit. Yet at all stops, in a two-day schedule, I was very conscious of women's rekindled interest in Hawke. I don't think I was kidding myself.

It started in Melbourne when he arrived at radio 3UZ for an interview with John Jost. Three young women, their eyes shining, were absolutely transfixed as Hawke bustled out of his car and crossed the footpath. On the way out, a well-dressed woman attracted by the waiting TV cameras stood off to one side while Hawke emerged and gave a quick interview. She had the fascinated look of a spider watching a fly.

At the next stop, the formal opening of a new union head office, Hawke was waylaid on arrival by a group of women who wanted their photo taken with him. Hawke obliged with great charm, as he did all day long with anyone who wanted to get near him. Hours later, in far-off Cessnock, it was the same.

There was a civic reception at the Town Hall there, with a school band and the senior citizens' choir. All of 500 to 600 people turned up. The band played the anthem, the choir sang *I Still Call Australia Home*, and Hawke spoke for 20 minutes about togetherness. 'We've come a long way together,' he told

them with great theatricality. 'Together we can meet the challenges of the last decade of the century.'

Everyone cheered and applauded. It was that sort of occasion. Later that night, at the Maitland leagues club, I counted the word 'together' 14 times in Hawke's off-the-cuff speech to a dinner audience of 390 who had paid $25 a head (they turned people away because there was no more room).

Out in the Cessnock audience, I saw a host of women, young and not so young, who I felt were watching their visitor in a way that suggested they regarded togetherness with the Prime Minister in a much more personal sense. They were listening to him, but they were hearing his TV interview with Clive Robertson the previous night, I'm sure.

It had nothing to do with their voting preferences.

That morning, on 3UZ, Hawke had tried to put to rest his true confessions to Robertson. 'I don't want to go on and on essentially about private matters,' he responded to John Jost's squeezing of the lemon. 'Questions were asked, there was no point in avoiding them. I did want to take the opportunity, really, at that time, of paying a tribute to my wife. And I did that. But I had no feeling that it would be offensive, or that Australians wouldn't expect me, if asked, to talk about these things. It was nothing more complex than that.'

Hawke's people hope that will be the end of it. We shall see. In the meantime, it seemed to be fate that, after flying into Cessnock, there on the roadside, as we sped past in our small convoy of white cars led by a police escort, was a huge billboard for a motel chain which read: 'Spend the night with someone friendly.' It's been that sort of week.

It even ended with Hawke opening a re-foaled Hunter Valled horse breeding stud. As the mother of a well-known Sydney racing writer told her son, when she learned he was to be a guest at the gala function, who more appropriate than the Prime Minister to open it? And, on the day, there were the obvious tacky jokes, too, among the moneyed throng, about the five stallions at the stud and the sixth at the you-know-where.

Still, Hawke has to expect that. He gave the issue life.

For the rest, the two days on the road with Hawke achieved two things: it killed off the silly speculation about a July election; and it confirmed, at least for me, that despite Hawke's still formidable personal support, the mood of the people, even in a hard-core Labor region like the Hunter Valley, is bad news for the Government.

The seat of Hunter, though vastly changed over the years, has voted Labor for 78 years. It's that sort of seat. Yet population changes have pushed it further and further up the valley away from its working-class heartland. It is now marginal, with a safety buffer of just 3.6 per cent. And its people want more than sweet talk and a sexy Prime Minister.

On five separate occasions, at three quite different places, people I'd never met before quietly asked what had gone wrong with the Government. Four of the five said they had never voted anything but Labor in their lives. Three of the five said they were thinking of changing next time. They are losing patience. They are being hurt, particularly by housing prices and interest rates. They worry about the future. They want reassurance.

The election is still a long way off. A year away, is my guess. The Government has a lot of damange control to do. None of it is going to be easy.

Alan Ramsey

# Goodbye, Old Parliament House

**JULY 2, 1988**

SLOWLY, OLD Parliament House is emptying. Walk around the lobbies and there are stripped offices, bare walls, appearing everywhere. A lot of the public servants have already gone, up the hill to the Big House. So, too, has the Opposition. John Howard moved into his 717 square metres of new office suite a fortnight ago. Your average three-bedroom home is 120 square metres. Howard will not be cramped, at least for room.

Neither will anyone else.

On Thursday night, back in the old House, we knew, finally, it was all coming to an end. The bar closed for the last time. Normally, with Parliament not sitting, the non-members' bar shuts down each day at 3.45pm. Two days ago, in a nostalgic wake, it stayed open until 8.30pm. There were a lot of tired and emotional people about. Senator Peter Walsh, his shoes still on, was among them.

The new bar up the hill opens on Monday.

But space, not booze, is what the new Parliament is all about. Space and light. And money. $1.1 billion's worth. In all, 250,000 square metres, gross, of floor space. Or 152,000 square metres, net, of functional space. Some 4,500 rooms. Nobody knows exactly, but the construction people say yes, something around that. You may wonder why we need 4,500 rooms for 224 politicians.

Do your sums. Total net floor space divided by three-bedroomed house. Answer: 1,260, approximately. Then divide $1.1 billion by 1,260. Answer: $873,000, approximately. So for the same taxpayers' money that built the new Parliament the politicians could have built and furnished 1,260 three-bedroomed homes—average size, mind you—for $873,000 each!

Unfair maybe, but it puts into a perspective we understand the degree of money-no-object magnificence invested, by public funds, in the workplace of our elected representatives. WE have a unique building. THEY have some-where to sit and think and speak in splendid comfort for less than a third of the year. Happy Bicentenary, everyone.

Happy birthday, too, to executive government, particularly our Prime Minister. They—and he—will need it. The ministry has its own exclusive piece of the new Parliament, approximately 17 per cent of it. Its own walled city within a walled city. And the wonder-ful acronym of PHEW—Parliament House Executive Wing: that bit that sits inside the top half of those huge intersecting concrete arms, the ones with the grass on the roof.

It's the building's backside, the bit that faces south across Canberra, to the grand homes and wide, leafy streets of the national capital's most expensive real estate, the suburbs of For-rest and Deakin, the top people's greenbelt, and right into the front yard of The Lodge, half a kilometre distant. Sadly, for them, very few ministers will be able to see it.

You see, everybody associated with the working of Parliament, all of us—politicians, public servants, even the press—do very well in the new building. Very well.

Some, however, do better than others. The very best office suites—those with the magnificent views, the sunniest aspects, the most relaxing outlooks—have gone to the senior backbenchers and public servants. The executive, as a group, has done by far the worst. All ministers have space, oodles of it. But most are shut in, cut off, more remote than ever. Most are condemned to views that look out on concrete walls, concrete courtyards and someone else's windows. The sky is just a blue strip here and there. And the trees and distant hills have vanished.

John Button, Hawke's Senate leader, couldn't believe his office the first time he saw it. It's the strangest shape, like a bit left over when all the rest had been divided up. All angles and plate glass, like a deformed finger. And it looks smack across a wedge of barren courtyard at a soaring concrete wall. Button was in a bleak mood for days.

Bill Hayden, on PHEW's eastern side, doesn't do a lot better. He's got a horribly shut-in view, bounded by more soaring walls. No sun, ever. But then, Bill won't be here much longer, anyhow. Paul Keating looks into the executive courtyard, again all concrete and sculptured knobs. He, like Button and Hayden, is on PHEW's ground floor. He can just see the sky if he crooks his neck at the right angle.

But Keating can, by bending forward a bit, look straight into Bob Hawke's office down the courtyard. That's the sort of view Paul thinks about these days, not trees and hills.

Between Keating and Hawke is Lionel Bowen, the quiet man of the Government. Our deputy Prime Minister. His office looks across into Hawke's press office. Like his public face, Lionel's ambition these days is subdued. He thinks more of retirement and going home to the grandchildren at Kingsford. In the meantime, he'll enjoy what he's got without complaint. That leaves Bob Hawke.

The Prime Minister's office, so far as aspect is concerned, is almost the worst there is. Not in terms of space, of which his official suite has 874 square metres. More than seven of those three-bedroomed houses we were talking about. Sitting room, dressing room, dining room, reception hall, bathroom, the lot. A real presidential suite. But the view!

From the desk in his working office, Hawke can't see anything outside. And unless he keeps his curtains closed, everyone up on the first and second floors around the courtyard, can see straight in and see him and his visitors. Even when he looks squarely out his window, it's like looking on to the exercise area of a prison.

It's an impression heightened by the huge grilled doors at the far end, through which Hawke can drive each morning, depositing him right outside his office door, or through which his official visitors can arrive by car. Except that everyone with a courtyard window upstairs will know who's coming and going. No privacy. None at all. No cosy courtyard strolls.

And no grass, no trees. The only green Hawke sees is far away through the bars of the two courtyard doors: one entry, one exit. Even then it's just the merest sliver. And Canberra's sky is a neck-craning two stories up, a tantalising strip when the curtains are open.

Hawke's dining room, two along from his office, has no windows. It's as claustrophobic as you get. Beautifully furnished, like everything else in the prime ministerial suite and much of the rest of the building. But shut in and shut off, remote from the real world.

Why? Why is the head of government in our new billion-dollar Parliament hidden away, out of sight, away from reality? Why does he come and go, his visitors too, through what is Parliament's back door, whisked in and out like unwanted relatives?

Security, apparently. Malcolm Fraser was paranoid about security. He was the one who wanted a bomb-shelter deep under the Parliament. That was scrapped somewhere along the line. But not the siting of the prime ministerial suite. A long line of future leaders are going to curse Fraser.

Particularly when they see some of the outside top-floor suites that have gone to backbenchers. Four senators have the best offices in the building. Magnificent. Afternoon sun, superb 180 degree views north, west and south. All very big. Seniority determined their choice. The Parliament's four longest-serving senators.

The Cabinet room is windowless. Deep inside the building, surrounded by a security vacuum. And inside, it has just the most provocative cabinet table. A rounded, bulging oblong with a wide split running halfway down the middle. Design gone mad. It's already the butt of all the obvious ribald jokes. Even to the blowfly painted on the overhead mural.

Finally, there's the Federal parliamentary press gallery. The media has been allocated 2,800 square feet of office space to house a press corps of two to three hundred. It used to be free, totally subsidised by taxpayers, but not anymore.

Happy Bicentenary.

Alan Ramsey

# Carcass in the Wind

**OCTOBER 22, 1988**

NOBODY ASKED a better question all week. 'It's a bad taste question but I'll try and put it tactfully,' prefaced Laurie Oakes, political editor of the Nine television network. 'Good on you, Laurie,' replied Bob Hawke. 'I'll try and reciprocate in the same spirit.'

And he did. It was Tuesday morning, in the small conference room opposite the Prime Minister's suite in Parliament House. Bob Hawke was in his presidential mode, at his new presidential lectern. He was talking to the press gallery. Paul Keating was nowhere to be seen, not in Canberra. Keating was up in Sydney, at the Bankstown Sports Club, launching a biography of himself and talking to the press, too.

Nobody was getting very far at either place, and nobody did.

In Canberra, at Hawke's press conference, it took 17 questions before the issue was even raised. 'Prime Minister,' a journalist finally asked, 'can I ask about your friend and colleague, the Treasurer?' Hawke was relaxed. He had known the question would come, sooner or later. It had to. He was ready. Today, there were to be no snarls, no petulance, no intimidating putdowns. Hawke had left his unpleasant face at home. 'Yes,' he said politely.

Two questions later everyone was still being polite.

Yes, Hawke said, he 'believed' Paul Keating would stay in politics as Treasurer. Had Keating told him that? Well, they'd had a 'lengthy discussion' the previous day on a 'number of issues', but he was not going to go into 'what I talk about with Paul, or with any other minister'. Of course not. We could draw our own conclusions.

Then Laurie Oakes asked his question.

'For two weeks in Parliament,' said Oakes, 'the Government looked lousy. Paul Keating came back yesterday [from overseas], and you were on top. Has that got any leadership implications?' Bingo.

Hawke refused to be provoked.

'As usual,' he responded quietly, 'Paul performed very well. We had, back in the portfolio, in the key portfolio, the Treasurer—the man to sell that portfolio for five-and-a-half years. And who, as I have said on many occasions, is the best Treasurer in the world. I expected a good performance. We certainly weren't let down.'

The answer ignored the question but was exactly the right one. To have been any fuller in his praise would have been too obvious, too much like a prime minister under threat perhaps. Yet anything less generous would surely have rekindled the bad news interpretations Hawke and everyone else in the Government were now trying so hard to put behind them.

Two further questions and that was it. The issue was dropped. Not, however, before Hawke had the last word, if only for now. '(Paul Keating and I) are both pretty intelligent, mature people,' he said, 'who have a deep commitment to the success of the Labor Party. I think it's recognised that it's been a unique and remarkably successful combination.

'I don't think either of us would allow any considerations to come in the way of a continuation of that success. Because it's not just Hawke, and it's not just Keating. It is about changing this country. And we don't have to rely on Keating statements or Hawke statements about the success that we've achieved. That's something that's recognised internationally, and we intend to ensure (that continues). Those sorts of considerations are very, very much bigger than any question of individual personalities.'

It was a nice exit line. It's also one the Labor Party would like fervently to believe. For now, it was enough that it was being said and not contradicted.

Yet the substance of the Oakes question went begging, despite Hawke's generous acknowledgment of Keating's ability. And the analysis was right: with Keating away, the Government had looked dreadful in Parliament. With Keating back, it behaved like a different team altogether. A single day had proved it.

The previous day, on Monday, only one parliamentary question to Keating had been necessary to turn around an issue which, the previous week, had left Hawke and the hapless John Dawkins and everyone else in the Government floundering on the defensive. That issue was the public disclosure [by Paul Kelly in *The Australian*] of advice Dawkins gave Hawke late in August to 'get out of politics' and 'make way' for Keating as Prime Minister.

Now, half an hour into Question Time on Monday, the Liberals' Wilson Tuckey, who'd had a wonderful time with Dawkins, tried to embarrass Keating the same way. He misjudged badly. Keating is not Dawkins. Keating is Keating. Tuckey should have left well alone.

Those people who do not watch the every-day theatre of Parliament think some of us get carried away by Keating's political artistry on the floor of the House. They do not compre-hend the man's absolute authority there, his extraordinary parliamentary presence. They should see for themselves. Maybe then they would understand why, in this Parliament, Paul Keating owns the place.

This time, Keating's performance not only closed off Dawkins's rash if brave behaviour

as a continuing source of embarrassment at Question Time. He also gave John Howard's leadership such brutal stick the Opposition lost all interest in pursuing John Dawkins.

'He (Howard) has now got his sheepish grin back on again,' Keating said at one point. 'I know he is embarrassed. I noticed that one of his comments was that I ought to get out of public life. Well,'—Keating leaned across the table toward Howard a few feet away—'I bet he wishes I would! Because, brother'—looking directly at Howard—'as I said a couple of years ago, whenever you look behind you, I will be there. I have stuck to that. And I will be there.'

John Howard's smile had gone.

And as Keating went on, ridiculing Howard's leadership as a 'dead carcass swinging in the breeze, but nobody will cut it down because there is no-one to take its place', there were no grins left on Howard's front bench, either. The Opposition did not raise the issue again. Wilson Tuckey's question was the first—and last—of the week.

There was something else few seemed to notice.

When Keating got the question, rising to his feet and, by arrangement, accepting it after the Acting Speaker had sought to rule it out of order, Bob Hawke was an absolute study in body language. Hawke sat there, hunched down at the centre table, his arms hugging himself, one hand on his face, looking up at Keating over the top of his hand as the Treasurer started to speak.

He looked wound as tight as a drum, as if unsure exactly what Keating was going to say. In those first tense moments, Hawke could not help himself. 'Mr Acting Speaker,' began Keating, 'the only leadership problem in this Parliament is on the other side of the House. 'The position in our party is quite clear. My friend and colleague, the Prime Minister, will remain Prime Minister for as long as he chooses. But that is not the case on the other side . . .'

The instant Keating spoke these words—the same careful form of words John Dawkins had used in the House the previous week—the spring inside Hawke unwound. He straightened in his chair, leaned back, and dropped his arms—an instinctive gesture of tension eased, like a huge sigh of relief. I could almost imagine the muttered words, 'Thank Christ!'

The next day, at his press conference, Hawke had only kind words for his 'friend and colleague, Paul'. Now, of course, there was every reason to be relaxed and affable, even with the press. Two Hawke press conferences in five days is a very rare event. By yesterday, this had become an unprecedented three in eight days. Our Prime Minister is a changed man.

Paul Keating is not.

On Tuesday, at the Bankstown Sports Club, the press was there in droves to see Paul's mate, the ACTU secretary, Bill Kelty, formally launch Edna Carew's biography of the Treasurer. It was a family affair, with old friends and supporters. Kelty spoke generously of Keating's optimism, persuasiveness and courage. No hint of controversy, just a wry conclusion: 'I assure you there's a lot more to be said, a lot more to be read, and a lot more to be written about Paul Keating.'

It sounded like a political slogan for the future. And so it is. We just have to wait.

With the press, Keating is saying nothing, except all the right things. On Wednesday, back in Canberra, he was sweeping aside all suggestions he and Bob were not the closest of mates. Talk of strained relations was 'figments of your imagination', he told journalists with a smile. It was the smile we remember.

Our problem was, he told us, that, in viewing this Government and some of its key members, we'd all become used to being fed a continuous diet of change. 'You now think if we can't turn in a triple somersault with pike once a week there is something wrong with the Government. There isn't.' Of course not. Everything's just fine again. Ask Bob Hawke.

Ask him anything, except about leadership.

Alan Ramsey

# One Last Grunt

**AUGUST 17, 1991**

EARLY THIS year Bob Hawke had what he later described as 'a good yarn' with Paul Keating. The day after their talk, which lasted three hours, Hawke remarked in a radio interview: 'It was a very civilised, I think, basically friendly discussion. I intimated I would be staying (as Prime Minister) and he understands and accepts that.'

This was a piece of fiction.

A staff spokesman for Paul Keating made similar soothing noises the same day. Referring to the Hawke meeting, the spokesman commented: 'Bob said he'd continue till the next election and beyond, and Paul's more than happy with that. Paul said he's happy to continue as Treasurer.'

That was a piece of fiction, too.

Four months later we learned the supposed 'good yarn' on January 31 was the one where Hawke finally told Keating he was reneging on his promise to him two years earlier. That promise was the so-called Kirribilli pledge of

November, 1988—the promise by Hawke to step down as Labor leader and Prime Minister after the 1990 election . . .

At Keating's insistence, because he didn't trust Hawke, the commitment had been given in the presence of Sir Peter Abeles and the ACTU's Bill Kelty. Now, two years later, Hawke was telling Keating he'd changed his mind, despite his unconditional promise. He now intended staying as Prime Minister at least until after the 1993 election . . .

Unsurprisingly, Keating did not react generously. Far from being a 'basically friendly' discussion in which Keating was 'more than happy' to learn he was being shafted, the atmosphere of their meeting was more in keeping with the following exchange:

Keating: 'If you hang around, you'll hang around for a punch on the nose.'

Hawke: 'I'll take my chances, my friend.'

What politicians say and do, and what they say they say and do, is part and parcel of the political game, just as are self-justification, rationalisation, hyperbole, revisionism, rhetoric, downright lies and dishonoured promises, private or public. It's whatever they're skilled enough to get away with.

Out in public the political imperative is always to keep the voters anaesthetised, if not blissfully ignorant. Hawke has always possessed this skill because the artfully matey nature of how he presents himself fits comfortably around his knockabout version of the Good Bloke image. Keating can be just as accommodating of self-interested circumstance.

So it is that the very personal power struggle between them, inexorably becoming ever more bitter and destructive, has been going on for a full three years, yet always behind a public facade of denial, ridicule, scorn, deceit and, when necessary, gushing togetherness.

This too, of course, is endemic to politics.

Alan Ramsey

# The Power and the Enmity

**MAY 29, 1993**

THE TALL, elegant figure of Paul Keating came round the corner and down the long corridor in Parliament House. It was Friday, December 20, 1991. Early the previous night, by 56 votes to 51, his colleagues had ended the public agony of Labor's leadership turmoil by ousting Bob Hawke and installing Keating as Prime Minister. Now it was the next afternoon and Keating was coming to claim his inheritance.

He had phoned ahead, and now he was approaching the Prime Minister's suite where the emotionally drained Hawke and his staff, some of whom had partied all night, were packing up to leave after nine years. Keating was alone and deep in thought. So deep he didn't notice, in the corridor gloom, the ABC television crew until he was right on top of it.

The crew had flown in from Melbourne that morning to film Hawke's last hours in office. In mid afternoon, learning that Keating was on his way to talk to Hawke about moving in, they'd immediately set up their camera outside in the corridor.

They were filming Keating walking towards them, out of the darkness, when, like a door banging, he was suddenly aware they were there.

'I'm behind the crew and watching Keating as he comes round the corner and down the corridor,' ABC-TV producer Phillip Chubb later recounted. 'He was totally lost in thought and doesn't see the camera until he's virtually on it. And really, he's quite startled. He didn't have a clue we'd be there.

'So he veers off into the Cabinet room which is opposite the PM's suite. Then he re-emerges, completely thrown, and sticks his hand over the camera lens and says, "What are you blokes doing here?" or something like that. He's not hostile, just bewildered.

'We were shooting on the run and there hadn't been time to line Keating up to talk to him. So I explain we're filming Hawke's last day and how I wanted a shot of him, Keating, first time into his new office, and he says, "Oh, right. Well, I really f . . . ked it up, didn't I? Do you want me to do it again?" So he goes back down the corridor and repeats it. And it's this second shot, with the indistinct, shadowy figure coming gradually into focus as Keating emerges from the gloom, that you see in the opening sequences of the series.'

The symbolism is obvious.

Over the past 18 months, on a budget of $800,000, Chubb and a special ABC unit have been making a five-hour television series on Labor's 10 years in power based on a mountain of material gathered in 450 hours of background and on-camera interviews with some 120 Government ministers, Labor MPs, staff advisers, party officials and senior public servants.

And while the series is a remarkable inside account of the exercise of power by the most electorally successful Labor Government to win office federally, its most revealing theme is the intensity of the personal power struggle that went on between its two dominant personalities for all of 11 years. That is, from the

moment Hawke and Keating first discussed the Labor leadership at an arranged meeting in Sydney's Boulevard Hotel some time in 1980, until Keating walked out of the corridor darkness on December 20, 1991, to claim the Prime Minister's suite as his own.

Apart from some extraordinary detail of various Cabinet meetings involving a number of landmark policy decisions during the Hawke years, most of them highly contentious at the time, the series' most potent revelation is the disclosure of how longstanding and poisonous was the power struggle between Hawke and Keating. The antagonism, deep and growing ever more bitter, was always there, just below the surface, making a farce of the mythology fed to voters of their closeness as a partnership, from as far back as two full years before Bill Hayden resigned his leadership in favour of Hawke on the eve of the 1983 election that brought Labor to power.

And the details come not from anonymous sources or political bystanders but from the participants themselves. This is the real impact of the series. All the key figures tell their own stories, give their versions, from Hawke and Keating down through the Cabinet, the ministry, the Labor Party and into the top ranks of the bureaucracy.

And they do so with a candour at times devastating and, now that Labor has been re-elected, politically embarrassing at least for some. Most would have rated Labor's 1993 election chances zilch or they'd never have been so frank.

Keating on Hawke (referring to leadership discussions in 1980): 'I had meetings with him at the request of, in the first case, his colleagues in the ACTU from NSW. I'd not had other than pleasantries with him before that. I'd never had a meal with him, for instance. I was then president of the NSW ALP and I think he understood the old Labor political adage that where goes NSW so goes Australia.

'And he said, "Look, let's try and do something together, because I think I can beat the Coalition and we would be a successful team . . ." I think it's fair to say he proposed he should be given priority. The fact that he would be there a couple of terms was to give me some interest in seeing him take the leadership before me.'

Hawke on Keating, in response: 'I think at one point I made the observation—about two terms—that I would hope that in two terms we would have done the substantial work of laying the basis of Labor reform. But at no point was there any unequivocal undertaking, to Paul or anyone else, that two terms was it and then I would leave it to him.'

Keating on Hawke: 'He thought my role in life was to sort of basically keep him looking like a, you know, alert, alive Prime Minister. Well, for many years it was. But then it became a joke. It went too long.'

Hawke on Keating: 'He was brusque, there were lots of things about his approach which used to grate with me but I used to swallow, because the importance of change was paramount. And it could be argued in hindsight that perhaps I was too accommodating, that I should have seen him as a greater danger to my own position that was going to ultimately spill over in the way, in fact, that it did.'

Keating on Hawke (relating an incident during the 1984 election campaign after they'd both addressed a business dinner at Sydney's Regent hotel): 'I got up and gave an extemporaneous performance. At that stage the economy was picking up, and we had a good story to tell. So I told it, enthusiastically, colourfully, and got a big reception, a big ovation. And I'd mentioned him (Hawke) appropriately and graciously on the way through.

'But, as we left, I said, "Well, it didn't go too bad." And he said, "Look, my friend, I'll tell you this. You can have this job when I'm good and ready to give it to you. And," he said, "that'll be about, at the earliest, about 1990." And I thought, "God, what I have said?" You know, "What have I done to deserve this sort of rebuke?"'

Keating on Hawke (referring to Hawke's prime ministership in 1985): 'A leader's job is to nourish his party with ideas, zest, leadership, zing; call it what you like. That happened with Bob with the economic summit, with the reconciliation theme, with the bringing together of the Cabinet and getting the best out of it, and taking the big changes in economic policy. All that happened in '83 and through '84. And what I say is, he stopped nourishing us. And you can't be a leader and stop doing that. But he lived to tell the story, that's Bob. He's a very lucky guy. He always ends up with a group of people who will look after him when he's in strife.'

Hawke on Keating, in response: 'Of course it was a nonsense that in any sense I stopped being Prime Minister. It may have been that he made a decision then of proceeding to deceive me. That may be true. I don't know. But the fact that I was in a very depressed emotional state because of my daughter (and her heroin addiction), and to go from that and (say) I showed that was when I ceased being Prime Minister, is, I would suggest, a comment not upon me but upon him.'

Senator Stephen Loosley, a Keating supporter (referring to an attempt by Graham Richardson in May 1991 to persuade Hawke to stand down): 'I was sitting in the Senate, and Graham came in and just tapped me on the shoulder. And I said to him, "How did you go?" And he replied, "No good. We'll have to go to war."'

Hawke on Keating (after Keating failed in his challenge against Hawke in June 1991, and exiled himself to the back bench): 'Keating and his forces had not given up. They regarded the political imperatives then as not doing the best for the Government, not doing the best to defeat the Opposition, but doing the best to advance the leadership aspirations of Paul Keating.

'And so anything that could destabilise the Government—but most particularly, that could give John Kerin (the new Treasurer) a feeling of insecurity—that was the imperative. And, as I was told, the pro-Keating forces were ceaselessly up in the press gallery offices undermining Kerin, and even, as it was reported to me, providing actual ammunition for attacking Kerin. So that was part of, as I say, what was a very, very destabilising situation. It was hopeless.'

Robert Ray, Cabinet minister and Hawke supporter: 'What sort of adjectives could you use to describe the role of the media from June to December 1991? Craven, blood-lusting, incompetent, biased, bigoted? None of them adequately describe the way Hawke was treated by nearly all the press gallery.'

Keating on Hawke: 'When John Hewson released Fightback (in November 1991), the Government was struck dumb. It didn't know what to say to a highly political, ideological document. It was trying to run around and count the sums and do an arithmetic reply. The thing to do was an immediate political reply. I mean, in the end, Fightback finished Bob off, not me.'

Bill Kelty, ACTU secretary and Keating supporter, on Hawke: 'John Kerin and Ralph Willis, they buried him. Not out of any malice, not because they didn't like him, but because they set this country on a different economic strategy (in 1991) when they had the chance to do something a bit better, a bit smarter. And you took Paul out of the team and there was one glaring, glaring hole. And that was Paul Keating. And when he replaced Paul with John Kerin, Bob Hawke was not going to be Prime Minister for long.'

Michael Duffy, Cabinet minister and Hawke supporter, on Keating (after the first challenge): 'In his own colourful way, he said to me one day that he was in the coffin and we forgot to put the nails in the lid. And, in a sense, I think he's right. But he got out of that coffin and was able to fight another battle.'

Keating on Hawke: 'So leading another life (as ACTU president), and then dashing in (to Parliament) later on in life, in his case in 1980, I did regard as a low entry price, which entitled you to a modest but reasonable run. And I've said as much, you know. But the idea that we were saddled with leaders forever because of their innate glory and capacities was not a concept he would try to, I don't think, weary me with.'

Gareth Evans, Foreign Minister and Hawke supporter: 'Neither of them had much to be proud of, I guess, in terms of the way the whole issue (of the leadership) was conducted. In terms of the electorate, I mean, and their reaction, it was pretty much a choice between arsenic and strychnine, I guess.'

It's gritty stuff, and the television series is full of it. The Government was paralysed by the leadership warfare throughout 1991. The extent of this paralysis, with unemployment soaring and the economy in deep recession, is openly admitted by ministers. But who was to blame, Hawke or Keating, depends on who was supporting whom.

Bob Collins (Keating supporter): '. . . we threw away an entire year due to this leadership stuff. Unforgivable . . . As far as the Prime Minister was concerned—and it's a hard thing to say—I think it was true his shelf life had expired. I mean, there was just nothing happening.'

Michael Duffy (Hawke supporter): 'It was a bit similar to a campaign that would be run by schoolyard bullies. Not nearly as much happened in that 12 months as should have, no doubt about that. But it's a very easy criticism to make of Bob Hawke when you look at what was going on within that government.'

Robert Ray (Hawke supporter): 'Constantly carping, at every meeting and every social occasion; constantly bagging Hawke, constantly leaking to the press gallery, trolling upstairs with the latest story to hurt Hawke. That is destabilisation of the worst and most disloyal kind.'

Yet the most damning criticism of Keating and his close ally John Dawkins, now Keating's Treasurer, comes from the Left's Brian Howe, now Keating's deputy Prime Minister. Howe supports John Kerin in his contention that the Budget brought down by Kerin as Treasurer in August 1991, and later so discredited, was a Budget strategy framed by Keating before he resigned as Treasurer.

Kerin: 'We were bound to put in place the Keating Budget which was agreed on May 22 (1991); the whole budget strategy. We knew we couldn't divert from that (even though) I didn't think that was really appropriate . . .'

Hawke: 'What stuck in John Kerin's craw was the fact the basic framework and strategy of the Budget was formulated by Paul himself . . .'

But Brian Howe, in his only comment included in the series, has the harshest words for Keating and his allies. 'When you took decisions, you expected, particularly if people were part of those decisions, to back you. And when they walked away from those decisions, then you felt you were being betrayed. It's one thing to stand outside (the Budget process) and fight it out, as I did in 1987—and I think

I gave as much as I got. It's another, having become part of a group that necessarily must make difficult decisions and must try to make the numbers add up, to be betrayed by people who are, and were really, your former comrades.'

But Bill Kelty attributes most blame to Kerin and Ralph Willis for the Government's mishandling of the economy during 1991. Kerin he dismisses as being out of his depth. Willis, he felt, as Finance Minister, should have known better. 'I was very disappointed with all the economic statements of that year,' says Kelty.

'I thought the March economic statement (by Hawke) got the timing wrong. The budget was pathetic. And Bob's mini-economic statement at Christmas was so meaningless he could have forgotten about giving it. And I thought, "Well, this shouldn't happen." And I'd argued strongly with Kerin, but more importantly with Ralph Willis, over all that period.

'And the faith I'd had with Ralph. I had always supported him, and liked him, and actually believed in him for a great number of years. (Yet) I found him and John Kerin leading Australia's economic performance into a hole. I just thought it was terrible.'

The candour is no less remarkable across a range of policy and political issues that engulfed the Hawke Government. In 1985, after Hawke abandoned Keating's proposed consumption tax at the national Tax Summit, Keating vented his spleen on Hawke's two staff political advisers, Bob Hogg and Peter Barron, the so-called 'Manchu Court' in Hawke's office.

Hawke on Keating, referring to the tax decision: 'When I exercised the judgment that not only had I the right to but the responsibility to exercise as Prime Minister, he was terribly upset about it, and he said some harsh things. I mean, he's given to invective and lashing out.'

Hogg, later ALP national secretary, on Keating: 'The following week I had to go in and interrupt a meeting in the Prime Minister's office, and Paul turned on me. He turned around to Hawke and said, "If you had any f . . . king guts, you'd sack the bastard," da-da da-dum. "And you're gutless." It was that sort of stuff.' A year later, in 1986, with Hawke in China, Keating gave his infamous 'banana republic' warning after new trade figures showed a dramatic surge in Australia's trade deficit.

David Morgan, then a Treasury official: 'When I saw the April balance of payments figure, my reaction was, "We're stuffed." In China, Hawke's staff warned him that Keating, without consultation, was taking too much on himself in Hawke's absence.

Bob Hogg: 'Our advice (to Hawke) was, essentially, to get on to Paul and get him to pull his head in. He didn't act on that. He acted to find out what was happening, and he didn't do anything definitive . . . I put it to him, in the harshest terms possible, that Paul had been sitting underneath (on the floor below Hawke's office in Old Parliament House) for the past year, pointing upwards and saying, "That silly so-and-so thinks he runs the f . . . king country, when it's run from this office." And I said, "You've done nothing about it, and now it's got to this . . ."'

Two months later, after more bad trade figures sapped international confidence in the Australian economy, the dollar plummeted below the 60-US-cents mark. Peter Walsh, then Minister for Finance: 'I was closer to despair than I'd ever been in politics . . . We'd been hit with this, and we really didn't deserve it, and how the hell were we ever going to get out of it?'

Don Russell, Keating's senior adviser: 'This was one of those cataclysmic-type situations which governments normally don't get faced with, when the governor of the Reserve Bank is on the phone to the Treasurer, and I think the Prime Minister, and the governor says, "I don't know what to do."'

And so it goes on, for five one-hour slabs of the most revealing detail of the inner workings of government, a lot of it quite stunning in the myths and the flaws and the frailties it exposes about the political and bureaucratic system and the people who somehow run it. John Clarke and Max Gillies wouldn't believe how close to the truth they get.

Alan Ramsey

# Chapter 5

# The Hindenberg

## To Voters, with Love

**DECEMBER 3, 1988**

JOHN HOWARD lives in a house that was built in 1906. He bought it in Wollstonecraft the year he was elected to Parliament, in 1974, and as you would expect of someone like Howard, it's not trendy flash, despite the swimming pool out back he added this year. Solid, safe and conservative, you'd call it. Old-fashioned even, but quality old-fashioned. Very sound. Exactly the sort of values John Howard likes to project.

When John and Janette first moved in, from a unit up round the corner where they lived their first three years of married life after crossing the Harbour Bridge from far off Earlwood, the house was very run-down. Over the years they've renovated extensively without altering its essential character; inside big and comfortable, outside the same turn-of-the-century, middle-class stodginess you find all over Wollstonecraft.

Again, the analogy is obvious.

Howard seems, as a politician, to have been around forever, even though he post-dates the glitzy Andrew Peacock by eight years. And while, as Liberal Party leader, he's been constantly buffed up in that elusive search for a more positive and sharper public image, the essential John Howard remains intact. The teeth have been capped, the eyebrows made bushier, the glasses changed—the frames are larger, more substantial—even his ears bored out to help a hearing defect.

He now speaks more gravely, too. Howard and his minders, Janette included, have done what they can, short of a head transplant. Yet, underneath, nothing has changed. Nothing has changed with the voters, either.

Two months ago, on the third anniversary of Howard's accession as Opposition leader, two market research surveys of political leadership perceptions rated Howard the most unappealing leader his party's ever had. The Quantum organisation surveyed an equal number of Liberal and Labor voters in Sydney and Melbourne only. The Morgan Gallup survey was national.

Quantum concluded: 'John Howard appears to be a leader without any kind of voter mandate. He is neither liked nor respected. Reflections on Howard are almost entirely negative. We can only question the potential inherent in a leader whose strongest perception is that he's boring.'

Gary Morgan was just as brutal. Morgan observed on October 26: 'Mr Howard is the most unwanted leader of the Liberal Party since my father began polling in the early 1940s.' In September 1985, when Howard became leader, his standing in Morgan Gallup's survey of 'preferred' Liberal leaders was 42 per cent. Now it was 14 per cent.

This week the news was no better. Morgan Gallup's latest poll in *The Bulletin* had two in every three voters saying Howard is a dunce as an Opposition leader. Their view of him as a preferred Prime Minister over Bob Hawke was worse: less than one in five voters, or 18 per cent. Hawke's preference rating was 68 per cent. The gap between the two has never been so wide.

And this on the very eve of a $500,000 exercise in sophisticated political marketing that has John Howard, from tomorrow, trying to sell a new/old you-beaut Liberal Party to the Australian people. Tarantara, tarantara. Have we got a deal for you. In reality, it's the reverse: the Liberal Party is trying to sell John Howard. Same product, new package. Yet the real sales crunch remains: their most 'boring' and 'unwanted' leader ever still has to sell himself.

Whatever Howard lacks, it isn't courage.

Before we go further, there's something else you should know about John Howard and his house; it says much about the man and the inner forces that drive him.

In the downstairs front, looking out down the hill towards the Harbour, is his study. It's an extraordinary room, less a study than a museum. There's the compulsory big desk and two phones, but what makes the room different is the memorabilia. Everywhere you look—the walls, the bookcases, the cabinet, even the old coat stand—are pieces of John Howard's life. And I mean, all the pieces. None of it just heaped anywhere, either.

Everything has its place, all of it arranged meticulously, even lovingly—from the Howard family tree portraits to his framed commissions as a Cabinet minister in the Fraser Government, to the myriad bric-a-brac of his life at school, university, law and in politics. Even down to the horned Viking headpiece of a distant school play, his school cricket cap, and his rolled scarf, woggle and badges from the Boy Scouts. Everything.

You wouldn't credit just how much of one man's life is in that room. All of it proudly out on display, like showcases in an exhibition. And that's what it is, an exhibition. For most everything there, in some way or other, represents individual achievement, however ephemeral or fleeting at times.

It means John Howard can sit at his desk in his own personal museum surrounded by the security of his success. Everywhere he looks he would see something that says, I have achieved, I have not failed. John Howard, this is your life.

Even the overflow—the jumble of flotsam that comes to political leaders as mementos of their trade in opening and closing and gladhanding, from inscribed plaques to penholders to paperweights to autographed photos, from the gauche to the ghastly—litters his city office. I doubt he has ever thrown a thing away.

To achieve means everything to John Howard.

He does not quit.

That brings us back to the selling of John Howard, by John Howard. The latest road show has its premiere at midday tomorrow at Parramatta's Masonic Centre, hosted by Nick Greiner as MC and with that old trouper and well-known political undertaker, Ian Sinclair, scripted to warm up the audience. It will be just like an election campaign launch, and just as staged and stooged.

For the following two days Howard will do the usual round of TV current affairs shows and radio talkback in Sydney before moving interstate. Everyone who will have him gets to hear him: Melbourne, Adelaide, back to Sydney, over to Perth, up to Brisbane, down to Hobart. All in 10 days. John Howard's Christmas message, sponsored by the Liberal Party. A Merry Little Johnny and a happy Future Directions to you all.

The re-run comes in the New Year. That's when the paid advertising takes over, with the commercials and the jingles moving on to television, radio and into the newspapers. You won't be able to avoid them. By the end, you'll have John Howard and his Future Directions coming out your ears. And that is just what the Liberals want. Anything and everything that gets people to take notice, any notice, of Howard and his manifesto for the future. Only the truly faithful will read the whole document, an eye-glazing 151 pages.

Every Federal Coalition MP gets their three copies today, specially delivered by air and road courier. That's for security reasons. Howard was insistent the detail should not leak beforehand. The precautions say much about the Coalition's prevailing climate of trust. It is not a happy ship.

Yet the Future Directions manifesto has no hard policy detail, no new specifics. It's not that sort of document. It's more like John Howard's study at Wollstonecraft: an exercise in nostalgia, in old memories and past achievements. An exercise in feeling good.

Good about ourselves, good about Australia. In particular, good about the Liberal Party and about John Howard. It reaches back to the supposed good old days, to the old values of the past, to evoke the future and what may be. Like a favourite family story with a happy ending.

If only it could be so simple.

Alan Ramsey

# Play is Getting Desperate

**APRIL 29, 1989**

JOHN ELLIOTT is Federal president of the Liberal Party and president of the Carlton VFL football team. Both used to be big winners. Now it's hard to tell which is doing worst. Five days ago, on Monday, Elliott arrived home in Melbourne from a business trip to London and landed right in the middle of Ian Macphee's troubles. The next day Carlton lost again.

The day before he got back, Malcolm Fraser had verbally thumped, by implication, his old vice-captain, John Howard. John Elliott retaliated on behalf of his little mate. A day later, on the football field, Carlton was thrashed by Essendon, Andrew Peacock's team. For an unfashionable player, Peacock, an old pro, has been making some subtle moves lately.

Everything in Victoria tends to revolve around football. John Elliott is one of those people who likes everything to revolve around him. Everything except defeat.

Elliott doesn't like losers. So far, this year, his football team has lost its first four games. A loss today to last year's premiers, Hawthorn, will mean Carlton's worst start to a season this century. Malcolm Fraser will have his fingers crossed. Fraser cares little about football and less about John Elliott. Malcolm would like Elliott to stick to the beer business and company tax minimisation. Unlike politics, Elliott knows and understands both.

Elliott's political party isn't doing any better than his football team. In Victoria, the Liberals haven't had a State win since 1979 or a Federal win since 1980. Like Carlton, they used to win everything. Menzies, Bolte and the DLP made sure of it. Now they win nothing.

A week before Elliott got back, the Liberal Party lost again. This time it was a State by-election. Labor's Premier, John Cain, was supposed to lose it. Everyone said so until the final quarter. Instead, the voters blew the whistle on the Liberals yet again. Victoria's Jeff Kennett now has the longest losing sequence of any Liberal leader in the country. Kennett hasn't kicked a goal in seven years. That's even worse than Carlton's record.

Yet it's still not as bad as the Victorian branch of the Liberal Party. It has remained goal-less and win-less for nine years. You'd think, surely, someone down there would wake up, would realise that maybe they're doing it wrong. That maybe, despite all John Elliott's money and hustle and Michael Kroger's youthful enthusiasm, they still don't know it all.

If the legs of the body politic are working feverishly in the Victorian Liberal Party—taking it helter-skelter in ever-diminishing circles until one day it may well vanish up its own backside—the party as an organisation continues to behave as if it's dead from the neck up. The ongoing electoral malaise of the past nine years says so.

So do Ian Macphee's troubles in trying to hang on to Liberal endorsemernt for his safe Melbourne seat of Goldstein. What the Macphee turmoil points up, as much as anything, is the sheer lack of professionalism that now exists in the Victorian Liberal organisation. This, after all, is the party that held State office in Melbourne for 27 uninterrupted years. Victoria is where it all began for the Liberals under Menzies, almost half a century ago. Now look what's happening.

Not only can the Liberal Party not win elections, irrespective of the local climate or the national mood or the state of its opponents; it can't even conduct its own affairs without so mismanaging and/or misreading the political imperatives that a single domestic preselection ballot is allowed to become a source of national ridicule of both the party's credibility and John Howard's authority as Federal leader. The whole affair has been a disaster for all but the Labor Party.

And how does the Liberal Party respond?

For two weeks now, its Victorian president, Michael Kroger, has hardly been off television or out of the newspapers. He and Macphee have publicly been at each other's throat virtually from day one. Macphee needs the publicity. It is the route he has chosen to try to save himself. But Kroger doesn't need publicity, nor does his party.

The public dogfight only compounds the gross error of judgment that dismissed or refused to see the political insanity of a challenge to Macphee's Liberal endorsement in the first place. Until two days ago, Kroger and his State director, Petro Georgiou, were still out there in public, slanging with Macphee. And for what?

Discipline should have shut him up. Kroger's lack of political judgment wouldn't let him. Yet Kroger is supposed to be the engine of the new, let's-go-get-'em political saviours of the Victorian Liberal Party. In 1987 he replaced Eda Ritchie, Malcolm Fraser's sister-in-law, who was an undistinguished State president for four years. In winning the post, Kroger, a partner in a Melbourne law firm, beat Alan Castleman, a BHP executive and 30-year Liberal Party member.

Among Kroger's supporters was John Elliott. Kroger, in turn, recruited David Kemp from Monash University as the Liberals' State director. To get Kemp, Kroger paid him a six-figure annual salary. Between them they ran the party. They have been personal and political friends since long before Kemp worked as a senior adviser in the Fraser Government and Kroger was a Fraser disciple.

Kemp was in the job only a year. While there, he and Kroger drafted the Liberals' submission on the new Victorian electoral boundaries for the next Federal election. This happy coincidence has now become part of the 'pattern of behaviour' that Ian Macphee alleges was behind deliberate moves to steal his seat. And it is David Kemp, of course, who is now Macphee's challenger.

When Kemp finished as State director last December, Petro Georgiou, another ex-Fraser staffer, moved in. Georgiou had worked for both Peacock and Fraser and, in more recent times, for Jeff Kennett in a policy research unit set up and funded by John Elliott. In Victoria they tend to keep it in the family. And always, somewhere, is Elliott.

Elliott isn't as close as he used to be to Kroger, who has become the key influence in the Victorian branch. Unlike Kroger, David Kemp now stays in the background and says very little—except 'no' to those who urged him not to contest the seat of Goldstein against Macphee.

Kemp knows what he wants; he intends to get it [and he did; and seven years later, in 1996, when the Liberals swept into office in Canberra, Kemp would become a cabinet minister in John Howard's first administration] . . .

And that is the true pattern of behaviour in the Liberal Party down south these days—self-interest. Everybody, it seems, from Ian Macphee down, is intent on looking after number one. The corporate interest of the party, unwittingly or otherwise, has tended to be pushed into the background. That is Michael Kroger's essential flaw: he has allowed the Macphee serial to become personal. He is an amateur in a pro's business. But that is his party's flaw, too.

It has lost sight of its real opponent.

Alan Ramsey

# A Dreadful End Awaits—Who?

MAY 6, 1989

TODAY IS the 52nd anniversary of the death of the Hindenburg. On May 6, 1937, the great German airship, full of passengers, burst into a vast fireball as it was docking near New York and fell onto a lot of people. Ian Macphee is John Howard's Hindenburg. Today we see if Ian Macphee immolates and who he may fall on.

Only in the past few days has an alarmed Howard come to realise, with shocking and mind-wrenching clarity, that what a burning Macphee may fall on is him.

Suddenly, John Howard is no longer the aloof, self-righteous leader wringing his hands on the sidelines, hearing and seeing no evil in Melbourne, saying little and doing less. Now Howard is there underneath, aghast at what is happening above and around him. Like that radio broadcaster who, 52 years ago ,witnessed the first Hindenburg's fiery plunge and told the world, sobbing: 'Oh, this is dreadful. Oh, people are running . . . Oh, my God, oh, oh, this is terrible . . .'

In the Liberal Party of 1989, people are running, too. Everywhere and in all directions. And yes, it is terrible.

Some, like the party's Victorian State president, Michael Kroger, and its State director, Petro Georgiou, and other assorted enthusiasts who should know better, are silly enough to be running into the flames. Others, like the Liberals' Federal director, Tony Eggleton, are running full tilt away from the disaster already raining down on them.

Others, like John Elliott, aren't quite sure which way to run. Still more, like Andrew Peacock and Malcolm Fraser and Peter Baume, are well back, out of danger, saying quietly:

'I told you so. Pass the hose.' John Howard is running up and down on the same spot.

Until now Howard has been blind and deaf to reality. Not any more. The blind man has opened his eyes. The deaf man has begun to listen. Yet his sudden return of political sight and sound has come too late. Ian Macphee has been alight for three months and ablaze for three weeks.

John Howard sees and hears again just in time to, perhaps, be fried. His paralysis of leadership deserves nothing less.

Further south, across Bass Strait, another impending Liberal Party calamity is drifting around in the political heavens, waiting to happen. Robin Gray's State election in Tasmania was not due until next February. Instead, Gray has jumped early and very quickly. Polling day is next Saturday. Like Howard, Robin Gray looks as if he could have misjudged appallingly. And as is the case with Howard, something very unpleasant may well be about to fall on him.

The Tasmania election, in national terms, is significant for no reason other than as a barometer of electoral feeling on the greening of politics and for what it might say about the continuing litany of Liberal Party disasters which seem to have been going on forever.

Robin Gray has been in power for seven years. In early 1982, when Liberal governments everywhere on the mainland were beginning to fall like shattered green bottles, the Liberals under Gray in Tasmania were defying the national trend. Gray that year ousted the ugly, brawling nest of snakes the Holgate Labor Government had become.

He's been there ever since.

For a long time, from late 1983 until Nick Greiner gave the Liberals and John Howard something to cheer about in NSW early last year, Robin Gray's Government was the Liberal Party's only hold on political power anywhere in Australia. Gray is—or was—a shrewd populist. He cleverly exploited Tasmanians' acute parochialism and State Labor's atrocious image. He was the noble warrior doing battle with the alien hordes across the water as well as those within.

All that is now starting to run down. No longer can Robin Gray glibly explain away his State's unemployment, the worst in the country. No longer can he continue to rationalise Tasmania's quite appalling economic stagnation as the fault of Canberra socialists and interfering environmentalists. His Government is getting old and tired and soft, and looks it.

So does Robin Gray.

Labor's new leader, Michael Field, is well placed. Like the Hawke Government in Canberra, Field is playing sweet music in the concert halls of Tasmanian green politics. Federal Labor is taking Tasmania seriously. Three Hawke ministers were campaigning in the State yesterday. Bob Hawke flies to Launceston and Hobart for a day of sport and gladhanding today. Paul Keating will be there next week. And the Liberals?

Well, don't say it out loud, but nothing has been seen nor heard of John Howard. Robin Gray doesn't want him. In the recent WA and Victorian State elections, Howard at least made a formal appearance before he was sent back to Sydney. But not in Tasmania. The Liberals have ignored him. That says all that needs to be said for the electoral impact of Howard's leadership and the appeal of his frontbench. What has been happening in Melbourne lately will not have made them any more welcome.

It is not a happy party. Events of the next seven days are likely only to make it much less happy. The Hindenburg disaster in 1937 marked the end of airship travel. Who, or what, you wonder, besides Ian Macphee, will be ended today?

Alan Ramsey

# Ambushed by Ignorance

**MAY 10, 1989**

AT 9.30 on Sunday night, John Howard sat in his office in Parliament House with his deputy, Andrew Peacock, and his Senate leader Fred Chaney. Peacock had just flown to Canberra from Melbourne, Chaney from Perth. Howard had called them to his office to discuss the fallout of the weekend's turbulent party events in Melbourne, notably the defeat of Ian Macphee.

They talked for almost an hour. Not once, at any stage, did Peacock and Chaney give Howard a hint of what they had planned for him next day. Yet by Sunday night, John Howard's leadership of the Liberal Party was hung, drawn and quartered. The numbers had been canvassed, counted and recounted. They were locked up tight as a drum for Andrew Peacock.

Howard was dead in the political water. And he didn't have a clue what was happening to him.

In the end, that's what did John Howard in: his blissful ignorance of events going on around him. That, and his poor judgment. He was utterly out of touch, both with the mood of the electorate and the mood of his own party. His leadership was evaporating and he didn't know it. Or he simply wouldn't believe it.

On Sunday night, after Peacock and Chaney left the unsuspecting Howard's office and drove away from Parliament, they didn't go to their hotels. Instead, they went to a flat in trendy Kingston, a nearby suburb where Bob Hawke used to live and plot against Bill Hayden when he first came to Canberra in 1981. Now the Liberals were doing the same. Waiting there for them were Peter Shack and John Moore, the two senior Liberals who are

Andrew Peacock's closest advisers and political lieutenants. Shack is a West Australian, Moore a Queenslander.

It was Shack who first approached Fred Chaney just two days earlier, on Friday, to recruit him into the Peacock push. It was Moore who organised in the north and owned the flat. The four men talked until after midnight. When the meeting broke up, every last detail had been talked through. Each of them left convinced the group had an absolute minimum 40 votes out of 71—and a maximum 44—to dump John Howard in 36 hours time. They were spot on.

The numbers stuck. Their plan was simple. They would go to Howard at 8.30 the next night—Monday—and formally let him know they were moving against him. They would ask for a special party meeting to decide the leadership at 9 o'clock the next morning.

If Howard tried to resist, they would have a petition already signed by at least 25 Liberal MPs—a full third of the parliamentary party. Until then, Peacock insisted security should remain absolutely tight.

He didn't want to ambush Howard without warning, and neither did Fred Chaney—but they didn't want Howard to know too early, either. They didn't want to give him time to organise.

John Howard's ignorance was now their best friend.

Peacock would replace Howard as leader, and Chaney, although in the Senate, would become deputy leader. Shack and Moore, both with ambitions as deputy, agreed to stand aside for Chaney. They would not contest the position. Shack had agreed to this in Perth that morning when he called around at

Chaney's home. There, as the two men talked over breakfast, Chaney made his decision to give his 'unconditional support' to a Peacock challenge.

But, he said, he was interested in the deputy's job. Chaney immediately rang Andrew Peacock in Melbourne. The previous night, in their first long phone conversation, Peacock had brought Chaney into what he was planning the following Tuesday. Now, after thinking it through overnight and talking with Shack, Chaney committed himself. He told Peacock he was on board.

That night, at John Moore's flat, not everything went without a hitch.

There were some strained words between Moore and Chaney over the deputy leadership before Moore, like Shack, agreed to stand aside. Peacock wanted Chaney as his deputy, and he got him. The Liberal Party in turn got the best leadership team available.

Nobody should be surprised Howard was dumped. That was inevitable sooner or later, given the way the Liberals have lurched from one electoral loss to another under the unwanted leadership of the dogged Howard for almost four years. He was a loser with no authority. The big surprise was the efficiency of the way his opponents got rid of him. It was, in the end, almost a military operation. Each of the key Peacock players even had a typewritten script covering their respective areas of responsibility, marked off in terms of D minus 3, D minus 2, and so on.

And D-Day was set for yesterday.

There were five in Peacock's Army: Shack and Moore as the generals, and Wilson Tuckey (WA), David Jull (Qld) and Senator Chris Puplick (NSW) as the troops. For months they have been quietly sounding out the party mood as internal frustration with, and alienation by, Howard's leadership grew in intensity. They didn't lobby votes. They just waited and channelled them in their man's direction as they fell away from Howard.

Peacock always planned to challenge before the end of the current Autumn parliamentary session on June 8. Last Thursday, the Gang of Five met in Canberra and agreed everything— the numbers, the mood, the timing—was right for yesterday. The turmoil of the past three weeks around Ian Macphee was the perfect background.

The last phase of the operation—the recruitment of Fred Chaney—was completed Sunday night. The next day, with Parliament meeting, Shack went round the lobbies quietly gathering signatures on his petition. By 2 o'clock he already had enough names. John Howard, sitting just a few offices from where it was happening, was still in the dark. He stayed there, uncomprehending, until the Hindenburg fell on him.

Alan Ramsey

**Postscript:** *Peacock regained the Liberal Party leadership, in a landslide vote against Howard. Fred Chaney was endorsed as deputy leader. The following Saturday, Robin Gray's State Liberals lost office in Tasmania and a minority Labor Government was elected with the support of the Tasmanian Greens, one of whose new State MPs, Christine Milne, would be elected to the Senate 18 years later in the Federal poll that brought Labor's Kevin Rudd to power.*

# Chapter 6

# A Year of Carnage

## Game, Set and Match

**MARCH 26, 1990**

ANDREW PEACOCK is still looking for the elusive miracle to make him Prime Minister. He isn't going to find it. Amid all the confusion, the ignorance and the guesses yesterday about who won and lost Saturday's election, Andrew Peacock still couldn't distinguish reality from self-delusion. All he has going for him now is wishful thinking.

It sustained him throughout the Election '90 campaign. And last night, as Peacock went through his fantasies with Richard Carleton on the Nine Network's *60 Minutes*, wishful thinking still had him hanging in there. The Liberal Party has made an art form of wishful thinking. It infects the policies Andrew the salesman couldn't sell and it befuddles their view of what it really takes to win.

And the Liberal Party still can't count.

The reality of what happened on Saturday is that there won't be a Peacock Government and there won't be a hung Parliament. The Labor Party has won the election, however narrowly. It's only a question of by how much. In a 148-seat House of Representatives, either side needs 75 seats for a bare majority. The Hawke Government will get no less than 75 seats. It might get as many as 78. Whatever, Labor has won. That is reality.

This was another election the Liberal Party butchered.

You have only to look at what happened— what really happened, not what Andrew Peacock or Bob Hawke would like you to think happened—to see that the Coalition should have bolted home on Saturday. Labor's primary vote, right across the country, fell in a huge hole. In one State after another, almost everywhere you looked, voter disenchantment with the Hawke Government was so great the result should have been a Coalition landslide.

Labor voters deserted in the tens of thousands. But only in one State—Victoria—did this massive disillusion with Labor translate into net gains by the Coalition parties. Elsewhere, the overwhelming majority of alienated Labor supporters gave their first vote to minor party candidates, notably the Democrats. Then, more often than not, their preference vote reluctantly flowed back to Labor. They simply wouldn't vote for Andrew Peacock.

Even in Victoria, Peacock's home State where nine Labor seats have fallen to the Liberals, Peacock couldn't sweep up all the Labor votes on offer. Labor's primary vote in Victoria collapsed by 10 percentage points, or one in every four Victorians who voted Labor in 1987. The Liberals got just 2 per cent of it. What was different in Victoria was that the Liberals gained the bigger flow of preferences. They didn't do this anywhere else.

In Western Australia, where the lost Labor primary vote in individual seats ranged as high as a massive 19 per cent—in Cabinet minister John Dawkins's seat of Fremantle—the Liberals will win only one Labor seat. And yet the State-wide collapse of Labor's primary vote in WA was greater than in Victoria—a huge 12.4 per cent. Again, the Liberals got only slightly more than 2 per cent of it. It was the same sorry story right across Australia.

Voters did not want to vote Labor. But they wanted even less to vote for Andrew Peacock and the Coalition. Even in Queensland, where Labor has taken two seats off the Coalition, Labor's State-wide primary vote fell by 3.5 per cent.

Saturday's poll was not so much one Federal election as six separate State elections. In each case, localised State perceptions seem to have had an enormous influence on how people cast their votes, especially their second preferences. Voters everywhere were ready to buy, but too many in marginal seats were leery of what Peacock had to sell.

Alan Ramsey

**Postscript:** *Bob Hawke's unprecedented fourth and last election victory as Labor leader. Yet the Coalition parties again out-polled Labor, this time by almost 400,000 primary votes (43.4 per cent of 10.2 million formal votes to Labor's 39.4 per cent). The difference was the surge in popular support for Janine Haines' Democrats who polled a record 1.1 million votes without winning a single seat in the House of Representatives but whose preferences ensured Labor retained office with a significantly reduced majority (78 seats to the Coalition's 69 with one Independent).*

# Another Premier Quits

AUGUST 8, 1990

VICTORIA'S JOHN Cain gave up yesterday and walked out on his Government. His Labor colleagues, State and Federal, deserved no less. They'd all but abandoned him as terminal months ago, despite his record as being far and away his State's longest-serving Labor Premier in the 135 years Victorians have tended to their own affairs.

But Cain's party deserved more than capitulation. Despite all that's happened in Victoria in the last two years—the errors of judgment, the careless management, the lost millions of public money and Labor's result-ant appalling image—Cain still represented Labor's best chance, however small, of pulling the Government together. Now all he's pulled is the plug.

Two months ago, at his State Labor conference, Cain was decisive about staying. He refused to be driven out by a few political hoons around him who saw their chance in exploiting the turmoil besieging his Government. Yesterday, Cain surprised everybody by being even more decisive about going. He was tired of what he saw as the disloyalty eating away at his leadership and his authority from the inside.

'I've tried now for four-and-a-half months to get that loyalty and get back the corporate spirit that made this Government a great government,' was how Cain explained his decision in Melbourne.

'For governments to be effective, they have to have a united party behind the leader. That's what I had for eight years. In recent months (there) has been something else.'

He didn't say what this 'something else' was. He didn't have to. Everybody knows the job that was being done on John Cain from within his own Government. And almost no-one with any clout, in Melbourne or Canberra, tried to stop it.

It is a melancholy end to his leadership. It's also a sad end to the Cain name in Victorian politics.

The first Labor Government in Victoria came to power in 1913. It lasted just 13 days. Victoria has had six Labor governments since and there's been a John Cain in all of them. John Cain's father, John Snr, served as a minister in the Prendergast Labor Government in 1924 and the 1927/28 Government under Edmund Hogan.

Each of the subsequent four Labor governments were all Cain Governments. The first of these, in 1943, lasted four days. John Cain Snr returned as Premier in 1945/47 and 1952/55. His son's continuous premiership of eight years four months, from April 1982, comfortably exceeds the total period served not only by his father but all of Victoria's previous Labor administrations.

Now it's all over.

Alan Ramsey

# Small Financial Mishaps

**SEPTEMBER 1, 1990**

EARLIER THIS year, the West Australian Labor Government under Peter Dowding sacrificed its Premier, its deputy Premier and its Agriculture Minister. They lost their political heads because the Labor stench was so overwhelming in the West that it seriously threatened not only the State Government but the electoral prospects of Bob Hawke's fourth election campaign.

Their sin was simple.

They were perceived to be the three ministers most visibly culpable, politically, in the WA Government's gross financial mismanagement in various sordid business deals which had blown away a minimum $320 million of taxpayers' money. Just how sordid we now know from this week's 400-page special report tabled in State Parliament.

The arithmetic of the earlier sacrificial offerings is as simple as the sin. Vanished public money equals three ministerial resignations equals roughly $100 million a head. It isn't much of a bargain. Even with a Premier's resignation included, taxpayers got a poor return for their dead $320 million. The WA Government did far better—it's still there.

And it still has more than two years to clean up the mess and pray that voters forget, unless the Opposition majority in the State Upper House finds the courage to force an earlier election. Sounds familiar, doesn't it? Across the continent, in Melbourne, another Labor Government has lost a Premier, a deputy Premier, a Treasurer and, for good measure, a leader of its Upper House, in circumstances similar but different.

Similar, in that many millions of taxpayers' dollars have been lost by official incompetence, poor judgment and/or mismanagement; different, in that the political agony embraced a series of misbegotten ventures while the resignations, loosely connected, dribbled through over 18 months. What really sets the two governments apart is the scale of the losses.

The smell might have been greater in Perth, and the circumstances sleazier, but when it came to the real business of losing money by the truckload, the Victorians made their Perth colleagues look like kindergarten tots. The Burke/Dowding Government in WA lost 'only' $320 million that we can be sure of. The Cain Government in Victoria lost something like $3000 million.

Around $2.8 billion of the $3 billion has gone. None of it can be retrieved. Some $100 million went down the enthusiastic plughole of the Victorian Economic Development Corporation (VEDC). Another $2.2 billion vanished in ill-judged business loans through Tricontinental, the merchant-banking arm of the State Bank of Victoria. The SBV itself blew $500 million in 'non-performing loans' and bad debts.

Victorians learned about the VEDC's $100 million calamity 18 months ago. That cost the grudging Government its deputy Premier. Taxpayers were told the full extent of the Tricontinental/SBV's $2.7 billion disaster last Monday. By then a Premier, a Treasurer, an Upper House leader and the entire board of the SBV had gone, too.

Between times, in circumstances that did nothing for perceptions of the Government's appalling judgment, the Farrow group of building societies, including Pyramid, collapsed. Amid the political turmoil created by the shrieks and screams accompanying that disaster, the Government committed itself to an open-ended guarantee on the return of $1.3 billion in unsecured Pyramid deposits held by 200,000 small investors.

The Victorian Government cannot be blamed for Pyramid's management. Where the Government failed was in proper financial supervision of the Farrow group's operations. Such supervision is a State responsibility, not a Federal one. And Victoria clearly defaulted on its responsibility.

So not only do Victorians now have to bear the ongoing Budget fallout of the $2.8 billion in cumulative losses racked up by the defunct Development Corporation (a Labor creation), the Tricontinental fiasco and the SBV, but, because of a government impelled by panic, taxpayers will foot the bill for any shortfall in the $1.3 billion owed Pyramid's small investors.

That may be anything—or nothing. Anguished investors won't know for some time yet. But you can be sure nobody expects it to be nothing.

What all this means is as simple as the sums. It means that, over the past four to five years, two of the country's longest established State Labor governments have somehow managed between them to lose about $3.5 billion by ignorance, naivety or sheer bone-headed incompetence.

And why? Because, basically, both governments thought they could play the financial market and the entrepreneurs at their own game. Instead, like some of the freewheelers, they were caught short and taken to the cleaners. Yet this fundamental fact of so much public money having been lost tended to get obscured this week by the relative red herring of whether or not Australia should keep the Commonwealth Bank as a wholly publicly-owned asset.

Paul Keating bedazzled everyone by buying a bank with someone else's money and making the Labor Party accept it. What the ideologues seemed to forget was why he was being allowed to do so.

It was the ultimate irony that Labor should be indulging in so much breast-beating on behalf of the public purity of the so-called People's Bank—the Commonwealth—when the very reason 30 per cent of it was being flogged to private investors was to finance the rescue of a smaller People's Bank—the State Bank Victoria—which had been run into insolvency under the strongest left-wing government in the country, guided by the same naivety that now inflamed its defenders.

This seemed to get lost, too.

Yet Keating had made Victoria's new Socialist Left Premier, Joan Kirner, an offer she couldn't refuse. Her State parliamentary colleagues knew it, even if it pained many of them. What choice was there? Their own Government's flaws had dropped them in the financial sinkhole. Keating was offering them a way out that would replace $2 billion of the $2.7 billion they'd lost. The Victorian ALP, spiritual home of the Left, could only blame itself. It should have watched the shop more diligently.

So of course they accepted it.

They had to. Keating would allow the Commonwealth Bank to join the bidding for the SBV only if it could sell 30 per cent of itself to pay for the deal. This element was non-negotiable. A clear majority of the Hawke Cabinet, though not all, backed the Treasurer. (One heated opponent, himself a Victorian, insisted his State colleagues had got themselves into the mess 'and they can f---ing get themselves out of it'.)

It was the same in the Federal Caucus on Tuesday after State Labor had accepted the inevitable in Melbourne two days earlier. Keating talked everyone to a standstill. He demolished the arguments against him, point by point. Yet the debate was meaningless. Members of the Left faction already had agreed among themselves to oppose any partial sell-off of the Commonwealth Bank, irrespective of the decision of their Melbourne colleagues.

And they did so knowing they were going to lose. At no stage did the Left have the numbers. The Centre was solid in support of Keating and the Right. Everything that followed was shadow boxing, not street fighting. And Keating was still unchallenged king of the block.

Later, at a press conference, the Treasurer was not in the least coy about placing the blame for Victoria's financial mess squarely with the State Labor Government he'd just helped rescue. No, of course his policy of deregulation was in no way to blame, he insisted. And neither was he.

'No federally supervised bank is in any difficulties whatsoever. It's not deregulation that's caused this; it's inadequate supervision—inadequate supervision by the State Bank Board of Tricontinental, and inadequate supervision by the State Government of Pyramid. These were the causes of Victoria's problems, not deregulation of the financial system.'

'Problems' seemed an overly polite way to describe losing $3 billion, but that's our Treasurer. He wasn't too polite about the departed John Cain ('the Government in the last weeks of Mr Cain's premiership was divided, lacking in cohesion, and did not know how to respond to the problem at all') but very enthusiastic about what beaut, decisive, resolute new brooms Joan Kirner and her 'new' Government really are.

'New' Government?

Of course not. It's the same old mob, with two new ministers, and a Premier who was there in the ruck as part of the old Cain Government for years. But we'll hear a lot about the 'new' Kirner Labor Government in Victoria in the months ahead, just as we've heard a lot in months past about the 'new' Carmen Lawrence Labor Government in Western Australia.

Paul Keating is merely spring cleaning.

Alan Ramsey

**Postscript:** *The men who run politics only turn to women when the blokes have all but buggered the show. So it was in Melbourne and Perth as the profligate 1980s ended. Voters liked Joan Kirner and Carmen Lawrence, Australia's first female State premiers, but they weren't silly enough to cop what Labor was up to when it drafted both women into the top job to try to save the blokes' political hides. The Kirner Government was routed at the polls in 1992 and the Lawrence Government was swept out a few months later, in February, 1993. It would be another 16 years before Queensland's Anna Bligh would become Australia's first woman Premier in her own right, in May 2009.*

# The Recession We had to Have

DECEMBER 1, 1990

PAUL KEATING was getting his lumps everywhere yesterday. The newspaper headlines kicked him black and blue. The Opposition's new leader, John Hewson, and his deputy, Peter Reith, were telling everyone they'd told us so, without trying to sound like the country's bad news is their good news. Then there was the Cabinet minister who delighted in recounting the joke about Gaddafi, Hussein and Paul Keating. If the three are together and you have only two bullets, whom do you shoot? Answer: Keating, twice.

The Treasurer's Cabinet colleague likes the joke almost as much as he doesn't like Keating. He is a Hawke man. Late on Thursday, he was seen telling two journalists the joke in the press gallery. 'Don't source it to me,' he concluded between guffaws. He was still telling the joke outside the parliamentary coffee shop yesterday morning. And he was still insisting: 'Don't source it to me.'

The traffic wasn't all one way. A Keating man phoned to ask if I knew why the election of Britain's John Major to replace Maggie Thatcher would strengthen Anglo-Australian relations? Because the Poms now had a prime minister whose father used to make garden gnomes, while we had a prime minister who was one. Fear and loathing is alive and well in Canberra.

So too, throughout the country, is the recession.

Early on Thursday afternoon, as we waited in Committee Room 7 for the arrival of the Treasurer to explain why he's been walking around nude for so long and he's only just noticed it, somebody opened a book on how long it would take him to actually use the dread word. You paid your dollar and you made your guess. The winner would collect the pot. One stoic nominated never.

Eventually Keating arrived, 27 minutes late. The pot was $26. He walked in, looking as cool as ever, sat down, ignored the fact we'd all been twiddling our thumbs for half an hour, and began: 'Well, I'll just give you a few comments on the National Accounts. And the first thing to say is, the Accounts do show that Australia is in recession (Bong!). The most important thing about that is, this is a recession Australia had to have . . .'

Bong, bong!

By the pot-holder's count, the first came in seven seconds, with the bonus of two inside 10 seconds. Radio 2UE's Julie Flynn and the ABC's Matt Peacock shared the money with 10 seconds. We should have run another book on how often he would use 'the word'. And still another on when he'd stop using it and fall back into more comfortable economic-speak.

I counted six recessions before we got a 'slowdown'. In a press conference that lasted just on an hour, the first slowdown came after 5 1/2 minutes. We then got one more recession and two more slowdowns before we had our first 'correction'. That was at the 9-minute mark. After that, there were five more recessions, all in the abstract.

Twelve minutes into the press conference and the recession was fading fast. We zipped past 'a bad patch' and, at 15 minutes, we were into the 'next upturn'. A lot wasn't said about upturns, past or future. As for recession, well, it had vanished by the 25-minute mark. By then we were back to correction.

Somebody asked: 'Are you concerned about the all-time low the Government has reached in the polls? And how do you think these figures will affect that?' And Keating replied: 'Well, I think when the numbers go with you, up goes your popularity. When they go down, down you go. Of course I'm concerned about it. I'd like us to be doing better. But again, this is less than nine months after an election. And, as I've said, this is a correction the economy had to have.'

So there you are. That's how the recession we had to have became a correction we had to have. Even, finally, a 'slowing' we had to have. And all in 25 minutes. If only the economy could be fixed as simply.

Right at the end, after 56 minutes of impenetrable defence, we even tried an underarm donkey drop. 'Mr Keating,' somebody asked

rather desperately, 'does this recession mark today as the most disappointing day for you as Treasurer?' He couldn't be goaded. 'Oh no,' he said. 'This had to happen. This slowing in the economy had to happen. This is a necessary change in the economy's behaviour.'

What was worse?

'What was worse? I think what was worse was losing the 3 per cent to 4 per cent inflation rate in the boom of 1988/89. That was worse, because it meant that a well-laid plan, including the huge tax cuts that were there to pull inflation down in a trend way, and probably for the first time in 20 years, was lost by that boom, as was the turnaround in the current account. I mean, that was far worse for me. Worse in terms of disappointment. Not in terms of wear and tear. We all have to suffer that.'

A few minutes later, Keating left the crease, his calm and his confidence as undisturbed as his wicket. We hadn't come even close to getting one past him. One of my colleagues complained it was simply because the Treasurer is such an artful batsman: he keeps moving the stumps.

Maybe. But there isn't another like him in the Parliament. He is the master with both ball and bat. You had to sit through his hour-long innings on Thursday to appreciate the complete political player. No replay highlights would do him justice. Out there, in the real world, you might think he's a fink and you might be right. But here, up close, he plays us all off a break. That's the thing about Keating. We're no match for him.

Not the Cabinet, the Labor Caucus, the Opposition, or the press gallery, singularly or collectively. Anyone who gets within earshot is either clobbered or seduced. The quality of his mind is as formidable as his political footwork. He really is the Bradman of politics, however much that offends the purists. Hate him all you like. But don't ever think he couldn't or shouldn't—or won't—be Captain.

We saw another innings on Thursday on an adjacent pitch.

Half an hour before Keating was due to appear in Committee Room 7, the Opposition's Peter Reith took strike in Committee Room 5. Reith made it as John Hewson's deputy because he's a Victorian, because the Howard push obliterated Perth's Fred Chaney, and because Reith went on the offensive while the rest of the contenders dithered. But oh, an economic spokesman he is not. Not now and, on performance to date, not ever. Listening to Reith trying to sound plausible about economics is like listening to Andrew Peacock. Press a button and out it comes.

But understanding? Not a shred! Hewson had better do something about his salesman. What is desperately needed is what Paul Keating would call a correction.

Alan Ramsey

# Grim Xmas Fare

**DECEMBER 12, 1990**

POLITICS IS pretty grim Christmas fare. After the year Australia has just had, only masochists could want more of what Bob and Paul and John are doing to each other and what, collectively, they're doing to the rest of us. The real news [the disintegration of the Soviet Union, the collapse of the Berlin Wall, and the first Gulf War] is happening on the other side of the world, as it was a year ago. The Christmas message from Canberra is no more joyful than from Moscow or the Gulf.

It is simply less relevant. So, unfortunately, is the Opposition, which is something John Hewson will have to think about over the holidays. If next Tuesday were polling day, instead of Christmas Day, Hewson would be Prime Minister by New Year's Day. No government as old and as besieged as this one can survive electoral retribution for the recession we had to have and the dreadful state Labor has got itself into just about everywhere except Queensland.

Yet Hewson would be Prime Minister by default, not by merit.

The Government deserves to lose, but the Opposition does not yet deserve to win. From the moment he replaced Andrew Peacock eight months ago, Hewson had seemed like the best thing to happen to the Liberal Party since Malcolm Fraser ousted Bill Snedden 15 years ago. His was a new face, untainted by past excesses or electoral defeats. He carried none of the corrosive imagery that was the sorry lot of Peacock and John Howard.

In a remarkably short time, for someone so new to politics, Hewson was able to erase the doubts he might only be a stop-gap leader. His public profile is high for so untried a leader, and his standing, in all polls monitoring leadership perceptions, much higher than Bob Hawke's.

Two months ago, Hewson's defensive, chip-on-the-shoulder speech to the Liberal Party's annual Federal Council in Brisbane struck the first discordant note. He offered nothing more inspirational than supposed working-class credentials and the same generalised rhetoric Peacock had been flogging a few months earlier. This week's censure debate was worse.

While Parliament is essentially political theatre and always will be, a censure motion used to be the most extreme form an opposition could take to seek to force a government to account for itself under the parliamentary system. Now, in this expensive farce we call a Parliament, it's just another device to drum up an easy headline.

The Government is as much to blame as the Coalition's opportunism. If ministers were serious about their responsibility to Parliament, the Opposition's constant resort to censure motions to make itself heard would be far less credible. As it is, Question Time each day is just a bit of rollicking sport that ministers treat either with contempt or buffoonery.

Gerry Hand, Hawke's knockabout Minister for Immigration and a lifelong supporter of Melbourne's Richmond football team, once confided he always found it hard, as ministers lined up on the front bench each day for Question Time, not to bellow, 'C'arn the Tigers!' Hand's attitude is endemic. Ministers view Question Time either as a daily dose of heavy body contact or a meaningless frivolity. Question Time has nothing to do with

accountability. It has everything to do with a smug government manipulating procedure to suit its own political ends.

All governments are culpable. This Government has made it an art form. The next one, now on the receiving end, will take its revenge by treating Question Time no less contemptuously. Repeated censures have no currency. Kim Beazley reminded the House that when Margaret Thatcher resigned as Britain's Prime Minister this year, the Labor Opposition moved the first censure motion in the House of Commons in five years. The motion Hewson moved against Hawke this week was the sixth by his Opposition in seven months.

This time, the tactic was sound enough and the grounds plausible. With the Government in no better shape than the economy, the Opposition had every reason to exploit the leadership tensions between Hawke and Keating. Where Hewson and Reith failed was in content. Their speeches were dreadful.

Hewson spent 20 minutes asserting how bad things are and what an awful Government we've had for eight years. It sounded like a speech he'd pulled off the top of his head as he walked into the House. It had no substance, no focus and very few specifics. It had no credibility.

This isn't the worst Government we've had, and Hewson knows it. For much of its time, it's been as good a Government as we can reasonably expect and much better than we're used to. Its achievements over eight years outnumber its failures. It is a better Government than the one it replaced.

Now it's failing for the same reasons the Fraser Government failed: its mistakes are catching up with it. It is tired and aging and its rhetoric is far ahead of performance. Hewson had only to recite the detail of the past eight months to make his point. He chose instead a generalised thrash at the past eight years. He chose badly.

Neither Hawke nor Keating was much better. Hawke delivered the usual rant which passes for one of his parliamentary speeches. Keating seemed bored by it all. So did everybody else, who were very few. They play this game in these debates which says more clearly than anything what political play-acting it all is. As the Opposition leader begins speaking, all the Government MPs yawn, stretch, get up and walk out. Then, when it's the Prime Minister's turn to speak, they file back in and the Opposition MPs walk out. It's as juvenile as it sounds.

The television news that night insisted Keating 'strongly defended' Hawke's leadership. So did the newspapers next day. I must have been listening to the wrong debate. I heard Keating mention Hawke's leadership once. He also recited a brief list of rhetorical questions about the Government's leadership. It was a token defence at best.

Darwin's Bob Collins, a jolly senator with an irreverent sense of humour, seemed more attuned to reality. Collins is one of the Government's junior ministers. On Thursday morning he sauntered along Parliament's central ground floor lobby, past the Qantas travel centre and the Westpac bank, to Aussie's coffee shop. Aussie is an Italian-born entrepreneur who used to work on Hawke's domestic staff at The Lodge. Now he runs the cappuccino concession in the big house.

Aussie's latest gimmick to attract custom and profit is a VCR among the tables and pot plants outside his shopfront. On Thursday morning the video playing was the ABC's cassette of the Domingo/Carreras/Pavarotti concert from this year's World Cup spectacular. Bob Collins arrived among the pot plants just as Placido Domingo appeared on screen.

'There's our Treasurer!' he exclaimed, theatrically. And flinging his arms wide, he launched, sotto voce, into an aria of his own: 'The economy is fuuuuu--ed, We are up sh--creeeeeeek.' Then, trillingly falsetto, Collins switched to what he called the Cabinet chorus. 'Oh yes, Paul! Oh yes, Paul! We want you for our leaaa-eee-derrrr.'

At least he made us laugh.

Alan Ramsey

# Chapter 7

# The Sweetest Victory of All

## The Change Labor had to Have

**DECEMBER 21, 1991**

SO THEY buried Caesar. Later, despite the emotion, the cant, the repressed bitterness and the misplaced sympathy which usually attend political deaths, only Bob Collins got it right in explaining why. 'Politics is a shitty and uncompromising business,' he said, slumped in his office, utterly exhausted, just hours after the Caucus ballot that dumped Bob Hawke for Paul Keating. 'It pays on results. So it should, and I hope it always does. And the political reality is that the Government has been performing badly ever since the first leadership vote six months ago. If it hadn't, Paul Keating wouldn't have had a dog's chance today.

'The price for that has now been paid.'

Collins is one of the 13 Labor MPs who changed allegiance between June and December to make Keating Prime Minister. In June he voted for Bob Hawke. This time he didn't. Collins is not an insensitive man. Nor is he a political amateur. In June, with the Government in deep trouble, Hawke got another chance. Caucus rejected Keating. Instead of seizing the chance, Hawke wasted it. And because he wasted it—foolishly, self-indulgently and unseeingly—Collins and the others behaved like professional politicians by refusing Hawke yet another chance and giving Keating his only chance.

They had no choice. You pay on results.

Mesmerised by her own perception of herself, Margaret Thatcher, too, thought she had a mortgage on the leadership of her party because of her remarkable electoral record and because, so she thought and behaved, only she knew best. A year ago, her colleagues taught her different. Hawke never saw a lesson in the British experience. He sneered at the parallel and those who drew it. He, too, now knows differently.

Late on Thursday night, while Bob Collins shut the door of his office and tried, with Mozart, to shut out what was left of the day, one floor down, John Button, Collins' Senate leader, was looking and sounding just as dog-tired, just as flat, but no less realistic. Button didn't change between June and December. He voted for Keating both times.

Now he was trying to put into words, that wouldn't offend his colleagues, why he thought it had been such a dreadful year and why Hawke's fantasising with himself had made his defeat inevitable. 'Big changes, aren't they?' Button said by way of greeting, his face crinkling. 'Conrad Black and Paul Keating arriving together.' For all his care with words, his broader message was no less pointed.

'It's been a bad year because those members of the Government and the Labor Party who were most in touch with the community were,

I think, very conscious of a deteriorating situation in the economy. I think there was less consciousness of that in Canberra, and that creates a sort of tension which means people who are out and about in the cities and towns come back here and find there doesn't seem much response or sensitivity.

'That occurs, of course, because as always in economic management, the forecasts, the figures, are always lagged, the projections are based largely on past figures, and there are all sorts of assumptions which are not necessarily correct. That was the major tension in the Government.

'And that, of course, was exacerbated by the tensions over the leadership which began some time ago and reached a head in early June when Keating, quite unannounced, in quite an unplanned way, no reference to any of his colleagues, announced his challenge based on a sort of accumulated resentment of the (secret) Kirribilli House (leadership) agreement (which Hawke later disowned and) which was subsequently revealed to everybody.

'That challenge took everybody by surprise, really. Since then, the fortunes of the Government have continued to decline, and as they declined, the leadership tensions began to rise again. So you had in the parliamentary party more uncertainty about the directions of the Government and more concern about the leadership. That reached the point where it was quite disabling to the Cabinet in responding to the economy.

'I mean, as one minister said to me, "You can't conduct an interview about anything, you can't announce anything, without being asked about the leadership. You can't do anything. Politics is about projecting what you're doing. If you try to do that, you're immediately asked about the leadership because they're not interested in what you're doing."

'I understand what that minister was saying. I think it was very largely true. The leadership issue overshadowed everything. Another minister, a senior one, said to me the Cabinet just hasn't functioned at a time when the Cabinet most needed to function. That's the sort of year it's been.'

Button's explanation is about as candid a public assessment of what sank Bob Hawke as you're likely to get from anyone in the Government concerned with reality and not self-serving excuses. There was a divided and frustrated Cabinet, an ego-tripping Prime Minister who wouldn't listen, a determined pretender, and an aging, half-dead Government. The outcome was inevitable.

And Keating's 'political terrorists'? What about the argument they destabilised Hawke to the point of destroying his prime ministership? 'Look, I don't think the majority of people in the ministry or in the Government were conscious of acute destabilising by anyone. I mean, there was one issue, a fairly crucial one, in which Keating had a very strongly-held different view to Hawke. That was the issue of (delegating) taxing powers to the States. That was certainly destabilising of Hawke's genuine attempts to get a new relationship between the States and [Canberra].

'But that could only be destabilising because so many people in the party had different views about it and probably felt the process of consultation and discussion hadn't been thorough enough. Apart from that, I think any destabilisation was very much at the margin. I think the overwhelming issue that concerned Cabinet ministers was the grave sense of being, well, powerless.'

Does Button accept that Hawke's future was always in his own hands? 'Yes. And it always has been, because that's the style of person he is. That's the way he saw it, and he was largely right.' But in the end he was wrong?

'The decline in the Government's performance and public support suggest yes, he was.' Was there any alternative?

'No, I don't think so. There was certainly no alternative candidate. I mean, after the last ballot, the one in early June, I believed the Government may have been able to get on with the job. I thought for some time there were signs that it could.

'But the parliamentary party, itself very concerned about the Government's fortunes, about unemployment and so on, started again to be concerned about the leadership. And once that started to emerge again, I thought there was no alternative but to make a change. I mean, you have to ask yourself: what if Bob had won by two votes today? What would have happened then? The Labor Party, in my opinion, would have been totally (pause), totally (longer pause), totally disabled. In an impossible position. That became the only realistic alternative. And that's no alternative.'

Button agrees Keating couldn't have become Prime Minister in worse circumstances.

He regrets that Hawke forced Caucus to vote him out. He knows the Liberals are looking better. He knows Keating will wear the label of Mr Recession. But he knows there was still no other choice. 'Look, Keating has enormous political skills. And yes, it will be tough, of course. At the moment, people would say the Liberal Party for the first time has a reasonably credible [tax reform] package about which they're all very excited.

'But I assure you we'll peg out the ground much better in the next few months about what the real issues are for an election still 18 months away. So the Liberal Party is not, to me, the issue. The worry issue is the one which has to be confronted by any government. And that is the economy.'

Alan Ramsey

# The Last of the Suits

SEPTEMBER 2, 1992

JOHN BANNON was the last of The Suits. Queensland's Wayne Goss is still there, but Goss came so late in the piece he doesn't count. Back in 1979, a full 10 years before Goss, Bannon was a founding member of that small group of political illusionists who middle-classed the Labor Party and made the 1980s their own.

NSW's Neville Wran, of course, was first—first in (1976) and first out (1986). Then Victoria's John Cain (March, 1982), SA's Bannon (November, 1982), WA's Brian Burke (February, 1983) and Federal Labor's Bob Hawke (March, 1983). In between, briefly, was Peter Dowding (February, 1989), another Suit. Now, like the decade of politics they dominated, they're all gone.

Only Wran survived a full 10 years as Premier. Only Burke in Perth left at the peak of his power. Only Hawke in Canberra refused to go and had to be voted out by his party in 1991. Cain in Melbourne jumped in 1990 before he was pushed. Dowding, after barely a year, got an offer from his West Australian colleagues he couldn't refuse.

John Bannon completes the cycle.

Like Adelaide's State Bank, the last of The Suits has taken himself to the cleaners. Given his Government's dreadful standing, the State Bank debacle, and the levels of State debt and unemployment he leaves behind, Bannon has denied the voters of South Australia the satisfaction of doing it for him. Very prudent, too.

This way he goes with some dignity, however tatty, while still sounding like a hero in accepting ultimate responsibility for the $3.2 billion of taxpayers' money lost in propping up the profligate State Bank. That he accepts none of the blame, too, will surprise nobody. Political leaders on their death beds rarely do.

Thirteen years ago, when Bannon became State leader, at 37, after SA's Corcoran Labor Government was wiped out in the 1979 election, he was eulogised as the boy wonder for taking Labour back into office a mere three years later.

A protege of Clyde Cameron, for whom he worked in the Whitlam Government for two years, Bannon went from obscurity to Premier in five years. It was a remarkable rise to power for a leader who made a career out of being as cautious and conservative as he was invisible.

Just as remarkable was the fact he stayed Premier for almost 10 years. That says as much for the quality of the Opposition as it does for the quality of his Government. Bannon gave his State stability, a car race and a big share in the contract to build Australia's new submarine fleet.

There may have been more, but you'd have to be stretching generosity to name it. Long after he's gone, South Australians will remember John Bannon much more for what his Government cost the State than for what it gave it.

In Canberra, there'll be few tears apart from the ritual farewells, although another domino gone will do nothing for public perceptions of Labor's disintegrating corporate image. John Bannon's demise, self-inflicted or otherwise, means nothing in the great scheme of politics.

That in itself says all that needs saying about the last of The Suits.

Alan Ramsey

# UnButtoned, One Last Time

**MARCH 13, 1993**

JOHN BUTTON was into his second drink and his 15th answer by the time we got to the hard bit. Up until then, at the end of a day's electioneering in Adelaide for a Government he is leaving, win or lose, it had been mostly nostalgia and gentle reflections, almost something of a wake. But the question that wouldn't go away kept sneaking up, demanding an answer. It didn't get one.

What had gone wrong?

'Look,' he said, 'I do think people forget that, prior to 1983, what a closed and cosseted country Australia was. And we set about opening all that up. I mean, in some ways it's captured by one of Keating's phrases, in that we've been getting the cobwebs out of the place. And we have been. In a major way, although we've got all sorts of other problems at the moment, Australia is now much stronger in its capacity to stand on its own feet. Much stronger. And I think you'll see that in the '90s. I mean, Keating said the other day he wanted to be around in the '90s, and I understand that. I think the '90s will reap the rewards of a rather difficult '80s.

'There's a whole range of companies doing better things. And that had to happen. And I like to think that through all of this we've kept the notion of the social safety net. You know, the good things, like Medicare and so on.'

So what had gone wrong?

'Well, I don't want to talk about what went wrong. It's not the time to talk about what went wrong. But I'd just like to make the point that basically what went wrong is, in slightly different circumstances here, what went wrong in most Western democracies, for different reasons and with different degrees of intensity.'

OK, but the Labor Party's changed, hasn't it?

'Yes, hugely. There's been a big change of thinking which has moved the party away from the shibboleths of the past, where certain things were sacred. But a Labor Party doesn't exist in my view, it just dies, unless it sees employment as its major goal. I mean, we can't allow this country to fall into the sort of models espoused in other countries of efficiency at all costs.'

Hey, hang on! Australia has a million unemployed! 'Yes, well, that's a big problem. A big problem.' Surely, after 10 years, that's a failure of Labor government? 'Well, our opponents say that.'

What does John Button say?

'You keep coming back to the same question.' (Pause.) 'And I'm buggered if I'm going to answer it.' (Longer pause.) 'I'd sooner pay for my own drinks at this stage.' He didn't, but that's where we dropped the subject of what had gone wrong. Yet in his own way he'd answered it.

Times haven't always been hard, and 10 years of Federal Labor produced more than its share of good government. John Button was a big part of the better times. He came into politics in 1974 in the election that also gave us Peter Walsh, Fred Chaney, John Howard,

Don Grimes, John Dawkins and Peter Baume. It was a quality year. Grimes and Baume are long gone.

Now Walsh and Chaney and Button are going too. After 19 years a senator and 10 years a senior minister, Button has had enough. He retires as the only minister to see out Labor's entire 10 years in the same job. Most of his constituency think he's far and away the best Industry Minister we've ever had. Does he leave disillusioned?

'No, just sick of it, I suppose. I mean, there's a limited period in which you can be effective. What I always found was that between the making of a decision and its actual effects flowing through to the community is a hugely long time. And there's nothing any government can do about that.

'Really, there isn't. When I first came to Canberra, I had all the idealistic convictions that people in politics could make changes. I really believed it. I still do, but only at the margin. The process is so dreadfully slow. Much more frustrating than I thought possible. There really are no magic wands. But there is a built-in inertia in the system which is exhausting to try and overcome.

'Look, put it this way. I think as Industry Minister I've been very hands-on. And there's a limit to making the same sort of exhorting speeches to people to do things better. You can't do that forever, not with conviction. And if you're hard-working, which I think I've been, though I'm not claiming that as a great virtue, then, apart from everything else you have to do in Canberra, all those days and nights away talking to groups and things, particularly in Australia, with its vast distances, all that sort of stuff is not a good life, you know.'

It was two years ago Button decided enough was more than enough, that he wouldn't contest this election. He turns 60 in June, barely time enough for another life beyond politics.

And while politics has been good to him its nomadic and absentee lifestyle extracted a terrible personal price. Not only did his first marriage fail, a familiar Canberra story, but he lost one son to drugs.

These aren't things he ever talks about. As for his resignation, 'I was asked after the 1990 election if I wanted to go earlier, if I wanted a post overseas, but I said no. I mean, if you're going to be an ambassador somewhere, really all you're doing is an extension of the glad-handing life you're in now. And I didn't want that, God save me. It's not a very creative thing.

'And look, politics and the administrative system is a pall on creativity. You know that. And everybody likes to do creative things, even in politics. And that's difficult, very difficult.' He made it sound impossible.

So what does another life mean for John Button?

'Well, a more balanced sort of life. I mean, the other day I was up in the country in Victoria and I drove past a farm that I used to have a bit of years ago. And I stopped, and walked over the paddocks and things, and I thought, 'For God's sake, why did I ever give this up?' They were the happiest days of my life; I really loved it. What did I give it up for?'

It was another question that went unanswered. Those sorts of questions that people ask out loud of themselves always do. I wished I could have told him what he wanted to hear. Yet, for an instant, the silence that hung on his words seemed to say everything you never wanted to know about politics.

'Anyhow,' he went on, 'I'm not saying you can recapture those things. But it was the nice, leisurely, healthy pace of it all, you know. And what will I do now? Well, all I'm saying is that I hope to have two or three jobs to use a few of the skills I may have, creatively. I'm interested in businesses in this country. Good

businesses, not dull, lethargic businesses. And there's some very smart businesses around the place now, and I think perhaps I'll get the opportunity to work with some of them.'

You can bet on it.

Back in 1973, before he came to Canberra, Button could have become a judge of the old Arbitration Commission but turned the offer down. The thought of the next 30 years on an industrial bench horrified him. Instead he became a Labor senator. Then, when he got to Canberra, the Whitlam Government, close up, horrified him almost as much.

'I came into Parliament very naive. It was the last year or so of the Whitlam Government, and I was stung by what was going on, because I thought, "If my Labor branch operated as badly as this place does we wouldn't have any members." That period was a revelation.'

So was John Wheeldon.

Wheeldon was a disaffected Whitlam minister with a black sense of humour whom, after Labor lost office in 1975, Button asked one day, 'What do you think we should do about so-and-so?' Wheeldon replied, 'What do you mean, "we"? Don't you call me "we". I'm a swinging voter now.' He then told Button about a Labor branch meeting in Perth. 'They were pretty angry and kept saying, "People don't understand what the Labor Party stands for any more." And I said, "Well, you're very lucky, because if people did understand what the Labor Party stood for, you'd have no Labor MPs at all".'

'That was my initiation to Canberra,' said Button. 'We went into Opposition, a lot of us, in 1975, with the feeling, "Well, we've got to get it better than that." And in the late '70s a group of us, with Bill Hayden, worked very hard to make the Labor Party more modern if you like, more realistic about economic issues. It wasn't easy.'

Of course not. But given what's happened since, did they make Labor too 'modern', too 'realistic' about economic issues? 'Oh, look, I think the answer is "no". As I said before, with a number of things we kept the faith. Social security, health, those policy areas. But I guess those of us who came out of the Whitlam period were very conscious you can't succeed in social policy unless you have a strong, wealth-creating capacity; you know, the ability to pay for these things.

'And I still say the country is now in better shape, in terms of that capacity, as a result of our period of government. Our early years were probably the best, that's all.'

Indeed they were. Now it's all coming to an end, for Labor as well as John Button. Somewhere along the way, in the turmoil of the 1980s, the pace of events overwhelmed the Government. Employment as the 'major goal' got lost in a million unemployed. For that it will be held accountable today. The Huns are inside the castle.

Alan Ramsey

# For Bronwyn and Jessica

MARCH 13, 1993

DESPITE ALL the silly hats John Hewson insisted on wearing whenever there was a camera about, the [1993] election campaign was a pretty sour and humourless trudge for five weeks. The only light relief was Tim Fischer, the strange man who leads the National Party, but everything about Tim is light relief. He's that sort of politician.

There is, though, the story of John Button's postcards to Bronwyn Bishop. It has nothing to do with the election, but it will cheer you to know that, despite most evidence to the contrary, not everything in politics is confrontation. While most politicians usually behave as if the world is always coming to an end, there are those who don't. There used to be more of them. These days, sadly, there aren't so many. A genuine sense of humour is rare in Canberra.

It will be rarer now that Button is leaving.

Part of the joy of being a minister is the overseas trips. Part of the joy of going overseas for Button was being able to send postcards back to the NSW Liberals' excruciatingly formidable Senator Bishop. As Button tells it: 'I was staying in this place in South China, at the Golden Dragon Hotel, and they had these postcards in the room with the Golden Dragon motif on them. So I sent one to Bronwyn, and said, "I don't know why, but this reminds me of you".'

'And then I said, "Look, you really ought to come here, there's a big job for somebody like you. They've been protecting all sorts of over-manning in the Chinese public service, and there's a lot of corruption in bicycles among middle-level bureaucrats. I'm told some are even getting free air. Really, there's a big investigative job to be done."'

'Another time we went to Korea, and I sent her a postcard from the demilitarised zone. I said, "Bronwyn, you ought to come here and have a look at this. There's a two-kilometre no-person's land between the antagonists, and if they meet they meet in this hut in the middle. Maybe there's something to be said for this, so maybe you ought to come and see for yourself."'

'In politics, you have to be able to see the funny side, to be able to send people up a bit. You know, postcards to Bronwyn, and so on. Things like that kept you sane.'

What they did for Bronwyn we can't be sure. She ignored the postcards and John Button, too. He was very disappointed. Somebody who didn't ignore him was Jessica.

'Jessica is this little girl from a place near Young, in NSW. She wrote me this letter about 18 months ago saying, "Dear Senator Button, I love you Senator Button because I watch Sesame Street and then I watch Question Time in the Senate, and Question Time is much funnier." Jessica became an instant soul mate and they correspond regularly.

Finally, a postscript. Perhaps the wisest thing written about national politics last year came from the pen of Geoffrey Barker of *The Age*. It said: 'There is good news and bad news from Canberra this week. The good news is the Government seems hellbent on destroying itself. The bad news is it may be replaced by the Opposition.'

Alan Ramsey

# Hewson Loses the Unloseable

**MARCH 15, 1993**

IT WOULD be easy to say John Hewson has an absolute hide. Here was a political leader who, both wilfully and very deliberately, and with all the self-righteous fervour of an American television evangelist, created the circumstances for his party to lose, yet again, an election it should have only had to remain on its feet to win.

In a political climate of the worst recession in 60 years, and with a million Australians out of work—as Hewson never tired of telling us—he set out three years ago, almost from the very day he became leader, to construct a set of policies even more odious and divisive to a majority of Australians than the hardship and dislocation of a 10-year-old government's persistent mistakes and misjudgments in the management of the economy.

Having somehow achieved all this, climaxed by his party's most severe repudiation since it lost office 10 years earlier, what does Hewson then do? He appears, as he did yesterday, stark naked, and without shame or apology, and says he's ready to start all over again. His GST clothes are gone, he says, and presumably The Plan with it. But Hewson is still here, ready, willing and able to continue leading the party which, single-handedly, he has just led into another three years of opposition, if not many more.

Most of us pundits, with one or two honourable exceptions, not only thought he would succeed in this brilliant strategy of defeat but, to some extent, encouraged him to persist by our complete lack of perception that enough Australians usually recognise a fraud when they see one. We thought 10 years and a million unemployed would overcome even the GST and its associated Fightback assaults on existing health and industrial relations structures.

We were wrong. Some were 'wronger' than others. The Huns never even made it up the walls, let alone into the castle. Only the 'True

Believers', and the passion and conviction of Paul Keating, thought otherwise. The magnitude of Keating's extraordinary victory—and it is Keating's victory, almost wholly and solely—is now likely to shape political life in this country to a depth and an extent well beyond the usual implications of a single election win.

What, you might ask, has Labor got to do to lose?

Well, the first thing its opponents have to do is to get a sensible leadership team. Hewson and his dogged deputy, Peter Reith, who was seemingly struck dumb by Saturday's debacle, are now tainted as the pig-headed ideologues who thought they could pull the country in behind them by dividing it with the most radical economic and industrial surgery ever put forward in an election campaign. The Plan is now dead.

So, by all accounts, should be Hewson and Reith, its creators and most devout proselytisers. The Liberals, still in shock, will probably accede to Hewson remaining alive, if only because there is simply nobody else, so barren are the alternatives. Peter Reith may not be so fortunate.

Meanwhile, Paul Keating probably has not made a more memorable election speech than his victory acceptance late Saturday night. It had everything except a cheerio to Bob Hawke.

The 'sweetest victory of all' indeed.

Alan Ramsey

# Chapter 8

# True Believers

## Lies, Damned Lies and Election Stats

**MARCH 20, 1993**

JOHN HOWARD would have you believe the Liberals' defeat last Saturday was the worst in the party's 47-year history. Paul Keating would have you believe it was Labor's most sweeping victory since the Government came to office 10 years ago. It is neither, though we can understand why they should say so.

Howard has a vested interest in making John Hewson look worse than he already does. Keating has a vested interest in making his mandate as Prime Minister seem more resounding than it is. However, before too much history is rewritten, the result should be kept in perspective.

In a formal vote of 10.6 million, Labor polled 4,751,390 votes, or 44.93 per cent of the Australia-wide primary (or popular) vote. This far exceeds Labor's popular vote in Bob Hawke's fourth winning election in 1990 (39.4 per cent) but is less than Labor polled in each of Hawke's first three victories in 1983 (49.5), 1984 (47.5) and 1987 (45.8).

At the same time, in a 148-member House of Representatives, Labor this election will win fewer seats than it did in either 1984 (82) or 1987 (86) and proportionately many fewer than the 75 it gained in a 125-seat House in 1983. Even Labor under Evatt, in losing in 1954 (50.1 per cent), won more primary votes than did Labor last Saturday. Gough Whitlam's first three elections as leader saw Labor exceed the Keating vote each time—47 per cent in 1969, 49.6 in 1972 and 49.3 in 1974. Even Labor under Bill Hayden polled more primary votes (45.2 per cent) in losing in 1980 than Labor under Keating did in winning this time.

Keating's victory, in the circumstances, was as stunning as it was unexpected. It just wasn't as decisive as some like to think and others like to pretend. Similarly, the Liberal defeat, at least in terms of votes, wasn't the disaster it has been depicted.

The Liberal Party primary vote (3,923,786), at 37.1 per cent, is its strongest since Malcolm Fraser (37.4 per cent) won for the last time in 1980. In 1983, '84 and '87 the Liberal vote did not exceed 34.5 per cent while three years ago it was a bare 35 per cent. It was also more than John Gorton got in winning in 1969 (34.8) or McMahon (32) and Snedden (34.9) each got in losing in 1972 and 1974 respectively.

The National Party's effort, on the other hand, was a shocker. Its overall gain of two seats—after losing five sitting members three years earlier—only obscures what in every other respect was its worst result in a Federal poll. Never in its history, going back to the

formation of the Nationals' predecessor, the Country Party, in January 1920, had Tim Fischer's party polled so poorly as it did this election.

In 28 Federal elections, over 68 years, from 1922 to 1990, the Country Party/National Party percentage share of the popular vote only ever fell below 8 per cent in one election—in 1955 when it slipped to 7.9 per cent. In all other elections it ranged between a high of 15.6 per cent in 1937 to a low of 8.4 per cent in 1990. In this latest election, the Nationals' total primary vote across Australia slumped even further—to 7.2 per cent, a fall of 1.2 percentage points.

On 1990 figures, an extra 800,000 Australians voted this time for Paul Keating's Government than did for Bob Hawke's Government in 1990. John Hewson's Liberals got an extra 400,000 votes, a Labor gain of two to one. But although 600,000 more Australians voted this election than did three years earlier, the Nationals gained none of them nor any of the massive 700,000 votes the Democrats dropped.

Indeed, the Nationals lost 75,500 voters. Not only did their relative share of the vote go down but so did their absolute support in an expanded electorate—from 833,557 voters in 1990 to 758,000 this time. The Nationals' vote fell in every State. Yet dear old Tim Fischer pretends 'we're on the way back'. Pardon?

One final point: Labor's vote went up in each State with a Liberal Government and down in those States where Labor is in power. That probably says as much as anything about the result.

*Alan Ramsey*

# The Same Old John

**MARCH 24, 1993**

THE TWO most wilful men in Australian public life yesterday showed us the election has changed little in national politics. John Hewson proved that whatever the stoic John Howard might have learned in 19 years in Canberra he still hasn't learned how to count, by blowing Howard away, yet again, in the contest for the leadership of the Liberal Party.

Howard had been insisting for days he would win comfortably. He lost, 30 votes to 47, and immediately announced he would not challenge Hewson again. It seemed a wise decision, which is more than can be said for Hewson's determination to run again and the Liberals' determination to re-elect him. They did not make the same mistake with the hapless Peter Reith.

With seven alternatives as deputy leader, they kicked Reith to bits. He didn't even make it to the final ballot, his colleagues electing Victoria's baby-faced Michael Wooldridge, a moderate, ahead of Peter Costello, an even dryer clone of Hewson. Over on the other side, Paul Keating was no less ruthless in disposing of any pretence his new Government isn't a self-indulgent one-man band by getting just about all he wanted in the make-up of his new ministry.

Among the 11 'new' ministerial faces are nine MPs who voted for Keating in toppling Bob Hawke 15 months ago. Half a dozen can be categorised as political debts and three as factional cronies, including the recycled Graham Richardson. Even the unspeakable ex-Speaker, Sydney's Leo McLeay, who resigned before the election to kill the damaging headlines over his $60,000 payout by taxpayers for falling off his rented bicycle, gets another share of the spoils, this time as Government Whip.

All that upset the transition was some angst one of the ministerial cast-offs, Melbourne's Peter Staples, delivered to Keating in the supposed privacy of the Government party room. Staples was the only one who refused to go quietly, thus disturbing the illusion the Government, now 10 years old, is truly a happy band of regenerated Vegemites.

That illusion is as brittle as the one being fostered in the Liberal Party that Hewson's leadership is secure for the next three years now that John Howard has been denied yet again. Keating has yet to explain his ministry. In contrast, Hewson appeared for 45 minutes before the assembled press with his new/old leadership team. It would have been better had he stayed away and kept his mouth shut.

Like Keating, Hewson is not one for public contrition or humility. He still wants us to believe the only reason he isn't Prime Minister is because the nasty Labor Party told a lot of lies about his policies and voters were gullible enough to believe them. Listening to him still trying to justify his defeat was excrutiating. The policies had been sound, the campaign 'outstanding', and everyone involved had turned in 'phenomenal' performances.

All that had gone wrong was they'd lost!

'Where I failed was in terms, I guess, of party development—spending time, not only with my backbench but with the party organisation, building the organisation to be consistent with what is required these days to win,' Hewson told us. He probably even believes it.

Alan Ramsey

# On the Burning Deck

PAUL KEATING'S admiration for things French empire runs to more than clocks and sculpture. In 1835, Felicia Hemans,a gentle Englishwoman, wrote *Casabianca* as a eulogy to Nelson's epic victory over Napoleon's Mediterranean fleet in the Battle of the Nile in 1798. Last weekend, Paul Keating, a not-so-gentle politician, plagiarised the poem's most famous line to eulogise himself in his epic victory over John Hewson almost 160 years later.

Hemans celebrated her eulogy in 372 stanzas. Keating celebrated his on Kerry Packer's obliging *Sunday* program. 'There wasn't a lot of consultation with me in the three weeks coming up to the election,' Keating complained, under questioning, to *Sunday*'s political editor, Laurie Oakes, 'when (Labor) people were walking, with the old head bowed down, towards the guillotine. There wasn't any consultation then. When I was on the burning deck, alone, there wasn't much consultation.'

On the burning deck, alone?

It is this heroic view of himself that is the absolute despair of his colleagues and the core of most of Keating's political problems lately. Yet if Keating sees himself alongside Nelson and Napoleon, take your pick, then Bob Hogg, an old, world-weary party general, has a more realistic view.

Two nights ago, at an invited gathering of the Labor tribe in a Canberra restaurant, Hogg told the 130 guests, Paul and Annita Keating included: 'A few days ago, when I was thinking about tonight, what I was going to do was get hold of a copy, a full copy, of Felicia Hemans's *Casabianca*. Which is, of course, "The boy stood on the burning deck/whence all but him had fled"'.

'I won't get through the rest of it. But the scatological version of it when I was a kid, was, "The boy stood on the burning deck/his pocket full of crackers/some silly bastard lit a match/and badly singed his knackers".' Everybody roared, Government ministers among them. Some applauded with even greater appreciation when Hogg added, after an appropriate pause: 'You're never on your own, Paul.'

The remark brought the house down.

Hogg's rebuke was good-humoured. Like the occasion, so was the audience. The unsmiling faces of two Keating staff members were the exception. But underneath all the jollity was a hard edge Keating would be foolish to ignore. To do otherwise, to persist as the arrogant Emperor, is to invite getting more than singed. Everyone from the ministry down has just about had enough.

People are tired of being doormats.

A few months ago Hogg stepped down as Labor's national secretary and went off to work for John Singleton's advertising agency. He took with him 27 years' distinguished service to the Labor Party. He also took a lifetime of political experience and knowledge. No party official anywhere had more gongs or more clout. Hogg went with eight winning elections on his CV. He was, for the last 15 years, one of the most significant political figures in the country.

And he walked away without regret. He'd had enough. He was the last of Bob Hawke's old Manchu Court, his 1983 staff originals. The other two, Peter Barron and Geoff Walsh, were at Hogg's testimonial dinner two nights ago. Barron now works for Kerry Packer and remains a significant influence with Keating and NSW Labor. Walsh is a senior bureaucrat in Foreign Affairs.

It is Paul Keating's loss that he has nobody like the Manchu Court on his staff. It is the nature of the beast that even if he did he might only listen to them when he felt like it. Keating's most effective staff member ever was Barbara Ward, now a senior executive with the TNT empire.

Ward talked to him—and in the same language—the way Keating talks to most everyone else. She wouldn't take his rubbish. She was with him for five years. When Ward left in 1985 she created a vacuum Keating has never filled, even with Don Russell, now Australia's Ambassador in Washington. Russell was too much the loyal Lothar to Keating's Mandrake. He needs somebody he can't intimidate.

It was in these circumstances, and against the background of the Government's recent turmoil and the worst few weeks of Keating's leadership, that Bob Hogg returned to Canberra on Thursday night to be farewelled by his peers and friends.

Keating was one of the speakers, throwing away his prepared text and matching the occasion with a more appropriate extemporaneous performance. There were others, too, Barry Jones and Gerry Hand among them.

Hand told a riotous story of his first day working for Hogg as an organiser in the Victorian State ALP office in the late 1970s, a story which included the detail of a municipal ballot in which a party member was hung upside down from a second-floor window until he agreed to vote the faction ticket. It was that sort of nostalgic night.

But Hogg was the star turn, even with Keating on the speakers' list. The reason why was that Hogg, in his own dry way, decided to give the Prime Minister some advice, wanted or otherwise.

It was there right through his speech, like the burning deck parody. In essence he told him, gently but pointedly, that Keating cannot and never should behave like a one-man band marching only to a tune he alone can hear.

His message was unmistakable.

'You have by definition the loneliest job in the country,' Hogg said, speaking directly to Keating sitting at the head table in front of him. 'And that's as it should be, because you have to act with probity, rigour, not favour, but what you believe are the correct decisions. Even so, you're not alone.

'The whole pack may be saying you're wrong. Or asking what are you doing. But you're not alone. We're all out there, giving you a free kick, like we do in a campaign. We all do our jobs and we do them with one objective. And that is to maintain (Labor in) Government so we can do something to improve the quality of life in this country.

'I mean, sometimes I used to go home and make notes about how I felt. That's what got me depressed, I think. But ultimately, you're not alone. You've got the whole movement there. They'll appreciate you when you're gone, but you've still got them while you're there. Critical, nagging, annoying, all that. But that's all important. Very important. It keeps us sharp and thinking. So even though it feels lonely sometimes, in a perverse way—and the Labor Party is very perverse—you have the friendship of the movement, and that should sustain you . . .'

There was more.

'Everyone's written the Government off already. Jesus, they wrote it off (every year) from '84! They wrote it off three times in 1990. It was written off even on election night in '93. Well, we're not written off. There's a long way to go. I think Paul's speech tonight shows his determination. It's like playing footie. Maintain your balance, get your feet back on the ground, maintain your balance. It's a long way to the next election, and there's a lot to be done. And that other lot can never, ever do it . . .

'Paul's right in what he's saying (about the High Court's Mabo decision on Aboriginal land rights). The tactics, perhaps, are not brilliant; the methodology could be improved. But the principle is correct. So get your feet back, get your balance, and work it out strategically how you get there. That requires a bit of subtlety and incorporating people and bringing them into it.

'You've been one of the great educators. And what I've missed, as an observer, over the last three months, or whatever it is since I left, is the need for you to be back out there educating. It's important. It's what politics is about.'

I couldn't see Keating's face from where I sat, so I couldn't see how he was taking all this advice about what he should be doing and the way he should be doing it. He isn't good at listening. But everyone else was enjoying it hugely. They enjoyed, too, the unsubtle warning about Peter Reith, the Opposition's reinstated Mabo Man.

There was even advice for Keating's staff to 'hang in there—you do survive it all, ultimately. It's all your fault, you know. It's your fault Paul won't talk to anybody. The fact he's a dreadful grumpy bugger early in the morning, doesn't want to talk to anybody; that's your fault, right? So just hang in, with your mates.'

Finally, there was the ultimate advice, dressed in all the Irish sentimentality of Labor rhetoric and struggle which would so appeal to Keating at the same time as he would hate being lectured so publicly before his peers.

'Never give up,' said Hogg, insisting this was his last lecture. 'Never, ever give up. That's what the labour movement's about—its perfections and imperfections. Let's not be arrogant about it, but the views we have, the ideas we have, relate to the broad community and matter to them.

'In a sense, what the Government is trying to do in some of the really difficult issues in this country, which have to be faced at some point—like its identity, like its relationship to an exploited minority that's been dreadfully treated—they're important, because the morality of this society is always important. So just never give up. It's always worth it. Always.'

It wasn't your ritual farewell speech, but Bob Hogg isn't your ritual party official, either. Paul Keating stayed to the end. Whether he really understands that the burning deck is still burning is another matter.

Alan Ramsey

# 'You Gotta Have Someone to Hate'

SEPTEMBER 11, 1993

HAVE YOU heard the story about Bill Hayden and Rod Cameron, the Labor Party's former pollster to whom Hayden hasn't spoken in more than 10 years? Bob Hogg told it at his testimonial dinner this week. The Governor-General from Ipswich mightn't appreciate the story but Hogg's audience loved it.

You should share it. The story is instructive about the depth of the passions unleashed by the Hawke/Hayden leadership struggle all those years ago. Some people never forget or forgive.

'Very recently,' said Hogg, 'Bill Hayden rang me. He said, "I need some research, I'm writing a book." Everyone's writing a book, I'm not. Graham Richardson and Bob (Hawke) have sucked the market. Neither has produced yet, but they got a lot of money for not producing, not yet anyhow. And when (the publishers) got to me it was a pittance that wouldn't have paid for the typing. So I'm not writing a book.

'But Bill is, and when he rang me he said, "I need some particular research." And I said, "Well, Rod Cameron's got it." And he said, "I can't talk to him," and I said, "Why not? You've talked to me. You've even had me over there for dinner." He had a spare seat at the table one night. So I said, "Ring Rod." And he said,

"I can't. For Christ's sake, Hogg, you've got to have someone left to hate." He said, "I'm now talking to you. If I ring Rod, who the hell do I hate?"

'I said, "Can't you find someone else? I mean, Christ, Bill, you've been in this new job five years now!" And he said, "You don't offend anyone in this job."

'Anyhow, to get back at me, he invited me to Government House to play tennis one Sunday morning, and this Machiavellian bastard, you know what he does? He partners me with Alexander Downer! So Bill had his way, in his own perverse manner.' So did Hogg. At one point in the tennis match, he drilled Downer right between the shoulder blades with a tennis ball Hogg swears 'made Boris Becker look tame'. He says he had a score to settle.

'It was a top serve.'

Something the dinner audience didn't hear was a letter of apology from the former Victorian Labor MP, Peter Steedman, one of the wild men of politics. Steedman wanted Gary Gray, Hogg's successor as national ALP secretary, to read his letter to the dinner. Gray wouldn't because the press was present. It's easy to understand why.

'Bob,' the letter said. 'I hope all goes well for your farewell dinner, but I fear for you a bit, comrade, in the midst of some of the jackals who are glad to see you go. Many, of course, do not remember the years of struggle to turn Victoria around after 26 years, and the flow-on from the Cain victory that brought Hawke to office. Since that time we have had to witness a long line of our pre-selected candidates "betraying the revolution", or at least becoming arrogant and insufferable little pricks.

'Those of us who worked with you in the hard years of Opposition in the '70s and early '80s, while acknowledging your total lack of social skills and occasional delusions of omnipotence, will always appreciate your hard-headed approach to the political agenda, even if it meant assassinating a few of our mates on the way to the "greater cause". Many, of course, these days wonder if "the cause" was worth it. At your dinner tonight, among the new heroes, the time-servers and the would-be-if-they-could-bes, always remember the Labor Party owes you a lot more for your contribution to our rise to power than a thousand present Cabinet ministers.

'Good luck, Pete Steedman.'

Alan Ramsey

# Chapter 9

# Hello and Goodbye

## The Rise of Baby Alex

**MAY 24, 1994**

IN THE end, John Hewson's only chance proved no chance and his party, pushed to a choice it didn't want to have to make, reluctantly told him no thank you. The self-doubt is borne out by the slim margin of Alexander Downer's victory, a mere four votes in 79.

For months now, as Hewson has been bleeding to death, even if most people, including Hewson, refused to recognise it, you sensed that what his despairing colleagues most wanted was for Hewson to end it for them. That is, that he'd just get up one day and, finally realising it was all too hard and too terrible, simply go home to Carolyn, never to return.

That way, in a party paralysed for 10 years by poisonous personality divisions and leadership rivalry, nobody would have to dirty his/

her hands or conscience getting rid of him and nobody would have to create an alternative where no clear alternative existed.

You'd be surprised how spineless most politicians are, but even the Liberal Party, forced to a vote it didn't want to confront because of the paucity of the choice, opted for the unknown of Baby Alex rather than the known of Terminal John, though only barely. That so many MPs, in the end, stuck with Hewson says far more about their reservations about Downer than it does for blind loyalty to the Liberal's latest leadership corpse. Three such walking dead will now sit behind the new man, a melancholy legacy of 11 years' opposition sure to delight Paul Keating.

In changing the guard yet again, the baptism of Downer and the last rites for Hewson produced two contrasting performances. Downer promised a 'fresh start', a 'bright future' and a 'united team', in that order, along with a 'directional document' in the months ahead.

He was most keen on a fresh start.

The Liberal Party has made many fresh starts since it was last in government but Downer's is clearly the freshest. He promised a fresh start four times, along with a 'new start', before he thanked his wife and four children and handed over to Peter Costello, the new deputy, who thanked his wife and two children and told us what 'integrity, energy and determination' Downer possessed and what 'a great leader' he would be.

It was all very jolly.

It was less jolly in the room next door, where John Hewson was saying his goodbyes as leader. He did so with a grace and strength rarely shown in the four years he led his party. Hewson talked about a 'fresh start' too, but the word he used most was 'loyalty'. We all knew what he meant.

One of the casualties of the past week's turmoil has been seven years trust and friendship between Hewson and Andrew Peacock, who Hewson, by Thursday, felt had deserted him. Hewson in turn abandoned Peacock. He wouldn't take his phone calls. And he ensured Peacock was told nothing about Hewson's decision to pull on a snap partyroom ballot yesterday to try to save his leadership.

When Peacock again rang Hewson from Melbourne late Friday, it was Richard Alston, Hewson's Senate leader, who finally came to the phone and told him what had been decided. Peacock was angry Hewson had turned his back on him. They talked, finally, by phone on Saturday night, but the relationship will never be the same. Yesterday, Peacock declared for Downer, though reluctantly. He did not lobby at the weekend against his former friend.

The Liberals have agonised about Hewson's leadership for months.

One option was to go back to John Howard, who has more capacity than any of his colleagues. He also has more baggage. He is yesterday's man. And, within the parliamentary party he's hugely divisive. Yet at worst Howard would lose well next election. He could even surprise. But after five defeats on the trot the Liberal Party isn't interested in losing well with anyone. It wants to win, badly. The alternative was to go straight to the next generation of Costello and Downer, however inexperienced and untested.

The last time the Liberal Party made a leap into the unknown they got John Hewson. Nobody wanted to repeat the mistake. Hewson is an honest man but he is no politician. The great pity is he didn't walk away after the last election 14 months ago. Instead he chose to stay and shred himself.

Now we'll see what Heckle and Jeckle can do.

Alan Ramsey

# The Politics of Gentlemen

**MAY 28, 1994**

LAST SUNDAY, amid some furious leadership lobbying across the country, Tony Staley phoned a colleague. He wanted to talk to him, Staley said, about a 'sensitive matter'. Staley, once a member of the Labor Party and now, ironically, the Liberal Party's Federal president, was one of those involved in the Victorian push to get South Australia's Alexander Downer up as party leader.

The previous day Staley had publicly declared for Downer. Two nights earlier, while John Hewson in Sydney was planning how to save himself, Staley and Downer had met privately for two hours at the Melbourne Club, the second oldest and most prestigious of Australia's so-called gentlemen's clubs, before they left by slipping out the back door.

Now Staley was phoning to tell of his 'concern' about the 155-year-old club being drawn into political controversy because of media speculation about the clandestine nature of his meeting with Downer. The friend he rang told him he shouldn't waste their time. Events had moved on. There were other more important things to concern them now that Hewson had called a special party meeting in Canberra the next day.

'But what about the club?' Staley protested.

'F--- the club!' he was told. 'We've got a ballot to win tomorrow.'

Anthony Lejeune, an Englishman, would have recoiled at such colonial language. In 1979 Lejeune wrote in his book, *The Gentlemen's Clubs of London*: 'The gentleman's club, like the gentleman inside the club, is a peculiarly English institution. Others have copied it. The Travellers' in Paris, the Melbourne Club, the Metropolitan in Washington, the Knickerbocker in New York, are almost indistinguishable from their English originals, except that nowadays they tend to be rather more luxurious and exclusive . . .'

Certainly the Melbourne Club has always mattered to people like Tony Staley, a member for more than 25 years. And the club, despite Staley's delicate feelings, has always been a place of power and influence, gossip and intrigue. It's the way the club plays the politics of gentlemen.

Peter Howson told us how 10 years ago.

Howson, English-born and Cambridge-educated, entered Federal politics for the Liberal Party in 1955, the same year as Malcolm Fraser. He was a young contemporary, of wealth and good breeding, of Downer's father, Sir Alexander, a Cabinet minister under Menzies, and, although a parody of a politician, Howson became a junior minister in the mid-1960s and early 1970s. In 1972 Howson lost his Melbourne seat in the Whitlam sweep that brought Labor to office after 23 years, and Canberra never saw him again.

In 1984, however, Howson published his diaries, *The Life of Politics*. Edited by Don Aitkin, now Vice-Chancellor of Canberra University, the Howson diaries were a remarkable if self-serving account of a minor insider's observations, from a Melbourne Club perspective, of the disintegration of the Menzies legacy.

Howson was 17 years in politics. He was never in Opposition and his diaries cover the last nine years, from 1963 to 1972, of that extraordinary 23-year sequence of Coalition power that began in November 1949. The diaries spanned four prime ministers and remain a window into establishment attitudes and political mores of their time such as we rarely see in Australia.

They also say much about The Club.

Aitkin wrote of Howson: 'He was an Englishman of the upper middle class who had been to a great public school as well as to Cambridge's wealthiest and most illustrious college, and he looked and sounded the part. He had inherited money and he would inherit more. Though not a member of the Melbourne establishment, he was well regarded by it and had been elected to its meeting place, the Melbourne Club . . .

'In Melbourne he moved around the little world at the top of Collins Street bounded by the Melbourne Club, the Victorian Parliament and Treasury Place, where he had his ministerial office. The Melbourne Club was important to him not just as a place at which to lunch, though he did that frequently, but as a source of opinion, a sounding board, a place for comfort. The club's conventions assisted him in this respect . . .'

There are 116 references to the Melbourne Club in Howson's diaries. Many are inconsequential, others less so as a barometer of the times and the rarefied world in which Howson moved. Some examples:

January 23, 1963: 'Melbourne Club for Lunch. Malcolm Fraser sat next to me and was just as rude and difficult as always.'

March 30, 1967: 'Lunched at the Melbourne Club where General Clyne, head of the Army Medical Service, attacked me again on this wretched medical evacuation problem (of Australian wounded from Vietnam). I told him he might at least have had the decency to acquaint us of the details before the article appeared (in the newspapers) . . .'

April 24, 1967: 'At the Melbourne Club we were talking about Anzac Day. One interesting comment: it was often those who performed least well in the war who take the greatest part in the marches . . .'

August 3, 1967: 'On to lunch at the Melbourne Club with Bob Southey (then the Liberals' Federal president). We had a number of matters to talk about (including) the feud between Bill McMahon and Jack McEwen and the dangers that has for us all in the political future . . .'

November 27, 1967: 'Lunching at the Club, I find there is a lot of antipathy to McMahon. I'm told he is a trouble-maker and is stirring up trouble not only between the Liberal and the Country Party but also within the Liberal ministry itself.'

March 31, 1969: 'Lunched at the Club, where there was some talk on (Prime Minister) John Gorton's behaviour, and the comment that, if one behaves oddly with people in the establishment, there's not much trouble. If, on the other hand, one conducts the same sort of behaviour with people outside the establishment, such as Miss Willesee, then the world gets to know and nothing can be done to prevent trouble . . .'

February 13, 1970: 'Lunch today in the Club with David Fairbairn (former Cabinet minister) and Ranald Macdonald (then chief executive of *The Age*). David used the opportunity to tell Ranald why he had taken the steps he did last November (to destabilise Gorton's leadership) and what future moves he was proposing. I think it was useful Ranald was able to meet David and have an opportunity to size him up as a future leader . . .'

March 11, 1971 (The day after McMahon replaced Gorton as Prime Minister): 'Caught the early plane to Melbourne. Lunched at the State House and found that yesterday there had been a tremendous roar of enthusiasm when they heard the news at 1pm. All our State members are thrilled, and there was a similar reaction when I looked in at the Melbourne Club.'

June 18, 1971: 'Lunched at the Club with Tom Hurley and Ainslie Meares and had a long talk about the need for birth control among Aboriginals. Generally I find they are well in agreement with my ideas but see some problems about the way we should handle public relations . . .'

January 19, 1972: 'This evening Kitty and I dined at the Melbourne Club with Dick Casey (former Governor-General) . . . Later he raised the subject of Alick [sic] Downer's successor (as High Commissioner to London) and we wondered if he was trying to sound us out as to whether we wanted the job.'

There are many similar comments from other club lunches, dinners and cocktail parties over the years. Howson was a meticulous diarist. His account of several club meetings in the destabilisation of John Gorton both before and after the Coalition's narrow 1969 election victory makes Tony Staley's support of Alexander Downer seem tame by comparison.

Lord Casey, still, as always, an influential Liberal Party figure since his retirement as Governor-General six months earlier, was up to his ears in the intrigue. Howson records a lunch at the club with Casey five days before the election of October 25, 1969.

'He told me he felt Gorton's performance (in the campaign) was as bad as anything he could recollect and wondered what we were going to do about it . . . He said he wouldn't consider Malcolm Fraser who was far too arrogant and impossible as a team member . . .'

Five days after the election, Howson wrote: 'In the Melbourne Club today I saw Dick Casey lunching with [Deputy Prime Minister] John McEwen, which gave me to believe he was following up on the talk we had last Monday.'

The next day, again over lunch at the club, Howson 'asked the table to analyse the election campaign'. The general view was that 'a change was necessary' if the Coalition was to keep government next time. 'Either Gorton had to change his ways or we had to have a new leader.'

Three years later, with Gorton gone, McMahon proved a poor alternative. Nothing could stop Labor under Gough Whitlam. On November 29, 1972, just three days before the election defeat that brought Labor to power and ended, forever, the Liberals' Born to Rule delusions, Howson wrote of the impending disaster: 'Lunched with Tony Staley today. The air of depression at the club is very marked. It's the most depressing place in Australia at the present time.'

Not this week it wasn't, seven Liberal leaders and 21 years later, despite that anguished Staley telephone call last Sunday.

The politics of gentlemen.

Alan Ramsey

# The Colt with No Regrets

SEPTEMBER 14, 1994

EVEN THE *Times* of London noted he was 'one of the brightest hopes of Australian politics'. That was just short of 25 years ago. It was November 1969 and Andrew Peacock was 30. John Gorton had just made him Minister for the Army, our youngest Federal minister ever. It's a distinction Peacock still holds, five prime ministers and seven Liberal leaders later.

Only now, at 55, a quarter of a century on, it's his only enduring distinction, apart from political survival for 28 years and five months. In the beginning no star shone more brightly. Peacock inherited Menzies' seat and was expected to inherit everything else in due course.

Yet the light went out long before ambition did.

So, gradually, did the hopes and expectations. Somehow, in his unfussed and careless way, he strangled them all over the years. Now, finally, when all his Liberal contemporaries from April 1966 are long gone, Peacock is going too. Enough is enough. He wanted to go at the last election. John Hewson persuaded him to stay. But no more. His mind is made up, his decision irrevocable.

The Liberal Party in Victoria decided earlier than expected to call nominations for the next Federal election. Peacock felt he couldn't defer a decision any longer.

He told four people, including his two closest political friends: Jeff Kennett, the Victorian Premier, and Ron Walker, the Melbourne businessman who is the Liberals' party treasurer and chief fundraiser. He asked all four to respect his confidence until he'd told his own campaign people at a meeting tomorrow night. But if you want to keep something to yourself in politics you don't tell anyone. And by yesterday, despite the very few people Peacock had told, the word was out around and Peacock's phone started ringing yesterday morning.

So what does his decision mean?

Well, there'll be a frenzy of speculation about who might want his prize seat, including Michael Kroger, the former Liberal State president who's more interested for the moment in making money. And while the draft-Kennett-for-Canberra school of thought, bizarre as it sounds, could get a bit of a shove, Kennett kept insisting yesterday:

'There are two things in life you don't want. One is to die a slow death and the other is to go to Canberra.'

Alexander Downer is learning they can be one and the same.

Even if the Coalition had won the last election, Peacock had told Hewson he didn't want to serve another full term, even though Hewson promised to make him Foreign Minister again and later Ambassador to Washington. In short, Peacock really has had enough. He's mostly done it all, through the highs and the lows of one of the more tumultuous periods of Australian politics.

It's time to go. In fact, as Peacock knows, it's well past time. His poisonous relationship with John Howard stunted the Liberal Party throughout the 1980s. In the late '60s and early '70s, when Gorton was Peacock's mentor, the rivalry between Peacock and Malcolm Fraser was just as potent but never as destructive.

After losing government, Fraser, ironically, became Peacock's ally in first denying Howard the leadership and later in taking it from him and keeping him out of it. The Peacock/Howard bloodletting endured for 10 years and beyond. Peacock served eight Liberal leaders, four Liberal prime ministers and twice led the party himself. Politics ended two marriages and, by the time he goes, will have consumed almost 30 years of his life.

Nobody came to non-Labor politics with more advantages.

Few will ever have left it having frittered away so many so thoroughly. Peacock was, in a sense, the ultimate political dilettante, if always an open and honest one. Yet his role and influence in the affairs of the Federal parliamentary Liberal Party over the years, often motivated by his deep personal enmity with Howard, are more responsible than most for much of what has happened to the Coalition in its long winter of discontent. He and Howard have much to answer for.

Peacock said this week he'd been in politics so long elephants had visibly aged. It was a nice line. So was the response from the Adelaide radio announcer who asked if, after 30 years, he was leaving public life with any regrets. Some, said Peacock, but overall he'd enjoyed it all immensely. The colt with no regrets, quipped the announcer.

Alan Ramsey

# The Fall of Baby Alex

**NOVEMBER 11, 1994**

ANDREW PEACOCK is very relaxed about life since he left politics. Two days ago, in Melbourne, he turned up at the formal launch of the Liberal campaign for the Kooyong by-election. He had no choice. Kooyong was his old seat, just as it was Menzies' before that. Peacock simply had to attend, even though politics hadn't seen hide or hair of him since he abruptly quit Parliament almost two months ago. However, there was a problem.

The Liberal launch was being held on the same day the Oaks was being run at Flemington as part of the VRC spring carnival, the most important couple of weeks on the Victorian racing calendar. And Peacock, as everyone knows, is a great racing man. He'd done his dough in the Melbourne Cup two days earlier and was determined not to miss the Oaks. He could not, however, avoid the by-election launch on Thursday.

Downer was there, along with Peter Costello, his deputy, and a stack of Victorian Liberal MPs and party notables. And that night, on the TV news bulletins, Peacock's beaming smile was duly prominent in the throng of outwardly excited and happy faces at the start of this, Downer's first electoral contest as leader. The speechmaking got under way at 10.45am. What the TV cameras didn't show was that Peacock was out the door and gone the instant he could decently do so. The first race at Flemington, on the other side of the city, was timed for 12.10.

He made it with 15 minutes to spare.

And he had to make it—one of his horses was running in that first race, a horse called Pazazamatazz, which sounds more like a Downer speech than the name of a racehorse. Anyhow, it finished second at 33/1. Peacock, against advice, backed it handsomely for a place. He was always luckier with horses than he was with politics.

In Kooyong, where the Liberals' candidate, Petro Georgiou, is almost as impossibly named as Peacock's horse, Downer will have no similar problems backing a winner. Kooyong is one of the country's foundation electorates. Since 1901 it has returned only five MPs, all of them conservatives.

Three were knighted. One was a prime minister for a record term. Another was a foreign minister and later Liberal leader. Yet another went on to become chief justice of the High Court for 17 years. It's that sort of very establishment seat. Menzies held it for 34 years. Peacock was there for 28 years. Kooyong is not used to changing its MP.

And while, after good WASP names such as Knox, Latham, Best, Menzies and Peacock, some of its voters might be a bit sniffy about Georgiou, the Greek-born Liberal candidate with the cockney accent and striped braces now has a job for the rest of his working life if he wants it.

On top of all that, Labor isn't even running a candidate, which is just the sort of election that delights every party leader, particularly if it's his or her first. One-horse races have that appeal, even in politics. With Downer's form, of course, it might be that he gets a Bronwyn Bishop result. That is, a re-run of the Sydney by-election in Mackellar earlier this year where Bishop, even without an endorsed Labor candidate against her, saw, with horror, the Liberal vote go backwards. Good night, Bronwyn, at least so far as the fantasy of her leadership aspirations were concerned.

Something similar isn't likely in Kooyong, but you couldn't be dead sure. And until the votes are actually counted and the dreaded possibility banished you can bet Baby Alex will not sleep well for the next two weeks, with or without comforters. Things are bad enough as it is.

Ever since the bottom fell out of his public standing two months ago, Downer has been looking as insecure as John Hewson ever did in that last terminal year of his leadership. The party now realises it chose a complete dud when it dumped Hewson and, in desperation, replaced him with Downer. What it doesn't know is what to do about it.

Costello doesn't want the leadership yet and is doing nothing to get it. John Howard would do almost anything to get it, except make a move too early that failed. Like Peacock in 1989, when he organised a strike against Howard that surprised everyone, John Howard has only one chance and he can't waste it. The wonder is he has any chance at all.

After Downer defeated Hewson in May, by a margin of four votes in 79, Howard thought his leadership hopes had gone forever. So did most everybody else. Howard wasn't even a candidate. Peacock blackballed him out of the race, just as he blackballed Howard after the 1993 elections and Hewson, very foolishly, recontested and won.

Well, Howard is still there and Peacock has gone. And when somebody asked Peacock a few weeks ago what he thought about maybe Howard getting hold of the leadership now that he'd gone, he replied: 'I couldn't give a f---.'

So Howard, after all, has one move left. And, improbable as it may sound, his prospects of leading the Coalition to the next election are better than they've been for years. He isn't doing anything about it yet, but he doesn't have to. He's there and he's available and, for the moment, that's enough.

Downer, publicly, would regard any such suggestion as ridiculous, and so would his supporters. Well, ignore them. Downer has no option but to ridicule leadership talk and to hope, in doing so, it will go away. It won't. His party knows how vulnerable he is and how little it will take to set off a move against him. So, despite his rhetoric, does Downer. All he can do now is talk up his leadership and hope people are listening. And if he's accomplished at little else, he can certainly talk. The day he goes to his grave the last part of Alexander Downer that ceases working will be that flapping mouth.

If only he could hear himself.

Some weeks ago, when he was blatting away in one of those interminable radio interviews he can't stop giving, Downer was asked about Keating's threat in Parliament to start unloading on the Liberals' personal financial affairs if they didn't stop raking around with their innuendo about his new house. Downer took it to be personal. He insisted, at length, he had nothing to hide. Wasn't he worried at all, he was asked? 'Not even a teensy weensy bit worried,' Downer replied, gushing.

Teensy weensy? Downer is always reverting to the language of the schoolroom, if not the nursery. It's one reason cartoonists around the country draw him as Winnie the Pooh, or depict him as a child dragging his teddy around, or as a schoolboy in short pants. That's how he sounds as well as often behaves. But 'teensy weensy' has to be the ultimate in baby talk, particularly from somebody posturing as the alternative Prime Minister. It's like this week, when he was having a go at somebody for being 'horrid'.

I mean, how can Downer expect ever to be taken seriously if he can't even talk like an adult, let alone say anything sensible. And never, ever is there a single idea about an alternative approach, even a 'teensy weensy' one. Downer and his inner circle have decided most voters don't like the Prime Minister, therefore constantly whack Keating, not the Government. Surely, you'd think, they'd wake up that even Pooh Bear has got to say something positive occasionally.

Will somebody please stand up and rescue this rabble?

Alan Ramsey

**Postscript:** *The Kooyong by-election on November 19, 1994 buried Downer's leadership. The result mirrored Sydney's Mackellar by-election so damaging to Bronwyn Bishop's ambitions in that, even without a Labor candidate, the Liberal vote slumped more than 5 per cent. Over the Christmas holidays, with politics moribund, Downer quietly negotiated with John Howard the terms of his resignation of the leadership. Downer's decision was formally announced on January 26 (Australia Day). His price for going quietly was the same as Bill Hayden's had been in standing down for Bob Hawke 12 years earlier—the Foreign Minister's job for as long as he wanted it. Howard kept his word. When he became Prime Minister a year later, he appointed Downer Foreign Minister for the entire 11 years 7 months the Howard Government was in office, longer than any of Downer's predecessors in the 106 years since Federation.*

# At the Emperor's Pleasure

**DECEMBER 24, 1994**

PAUL KEATING is notorious for being late. Cabinet, Caucus, appointments, everything except perhaps his family. He's always been the same, even long before he became head of government. It seems a matter of honour with him that everybody should await the Emperor's pleasure. Two days ago he sauntered in, late as usual, to address the assembled press. He spoke for seven minutes, took 13 minutes of questions, then he was gone, out of the door, more shouted questions fading behind him as he walked off with his retinue.

Before he went he gave some advice. It came as he tired of being quizzed about the gaping holes in the detail of what he'd just announced. 'Where is the news in this?' he asked rhetorically, cutting off a reporter in mid-question. 'The news—I mean, let me go through my own little incantation—the news is where the weight is, right? For those of you who didn't go through the appropriate formalities of training as journalists, the news is where the weight is. And the weight is a policy change here . . .'

Well, Prime Minister, you were half right.

Yes, the news is where the weight is, as you put it. But the weight in this instance wasn't the policy change at all. The weight was in why you changed policy, and how you did it. And, even more pertinently, if we look at the bigger picture, which is another piece of advice you're fond of giving constantly, the even greater weight was in what the incident says about the self-indulgent way you run this Government.

And that sucks, Prime Minister, it really does.

What's happened in the fiasco of woodchip licences over the last few days is typical of much of what laughingly passes for due process and proper standards. Parliament, Cabinet, the structure of executive government, the parliamentary Caucus, the principle of accountability, even the public service to an increasing degree, have all been debauched, manipulated or traduced to suit the whims and wishes of one man, and one man only.

Remember how Graham Richardson announced in the ABC's *Labor in Power* series 18 months ago that Paul Keating now had more power, since his election win, than any leader in Labor's history? Well, for once, Richardson wasn't gilding the lily. Pretty much everything the Government has done—and not done— this year only emphasised the dominance, the authority and the indulgence of the Prime Minister. We now have a presidential system in just about all but constitutional name.

Yet the Opposition remains as much a joke as is meaningful ministerial accountability in the House of Representatives. Only the Senate, despite its Jekyll-and-Hyde profile of commonsense and zealotry, responsible

behaviour and rank opportunism, acts as any brake on the political excesses the Prime Minister enforces on the rest of the system.

And Keating despises the Senate, less so, I think, for what he calls its unrepresentative character, as for the fact he cannot, as a matter of course, bend it to his will. It denies him. And after 25 years in politics and three years as Prime Minister, that isn't something his personality readily copes with. Dick Warburton of the Business Council, by no means an enemy of the Government, gave substance to the point only this week.

Which brings us back to woodchips.

What Keating tried to get his press conference to accept on Thursday was that, in essence, it didn't matter what had gone wrong in a junior minister, the Right's pro-logging David Beddall, ignoring the advice of a Cabinet minister, the Left's anti-logging John Faulkner, by increasing, by almost a million tonnes, the amount of woodchips our timber industry can export next year—and, of course, how much and what sort of native forest they can chainsaw to harvest those woodchips.

Nor did it matter that Faulkner, on the advice of his department, had advised Beddall, as directed by Cabinet a year ago, that 40 per cent of the proposed new logging areas—or some 1,300 specific sites—should get at least interim protection because of their high con-servation values as wilderness or old-growth forest, but Beddall had ignored this advice in all but a handful of cases.

Nor did it matter if Beddall had defied the views of his Prime Minister, even though Keating declined, several times, to say exactly what those views might have been. We're led to believe Keating wanted a decision more sensitive to the environment and more attuned to Faulkner's advice, as Environment Minister, and that he told Beddall so. But we don't really know. He wouldn't say. His spokesmen were left to whisper it in receptive ears, though even they couldn't get their story straight.

Nor did it matter that ministerial approval of this extra one million tonnes of woodchips flies utterly in the face of the Government's own stated policy of phasing out woodchip exports by 2000, a policy announced in March 1991 but which has not, in any of the four years since, so far been applied to the annual renewal of export licences.

Nor did it matter that everybody in the Government, the industry and the environment lobby knew the licence renewals were a matter of great political sensitivity but, somehow, still the outcome was grievously mishandled. Nor did it matter that Faulkner, the night before Beddall signed the licences on Tuesday, without any Cabinet oversight, had written to Beddall voicing his 'extreme concern' at the 'approach you are reported to be adopting' to the renewals, and then sent copies of the letter to Keating and four senior Cabinet colleagues.

Nor did it matter that Keating took 48 hours before he said or did anything after the Beddall decision became public and then only after it had become a screaming political problem. Nor did it matter that, in Keating's intervention, Cabinet as such was again ignored and the issue dealt with by the Prime Minister phoning a handful of ministers and, essentially, making the decision himself.

None of these things mattered.

Nor should they be pursued, questioned or challenged. What mattered, insisted Keating, was that 'the news is where the weight is', that 'in the end, what's come from this is a very large (policy) change'. That policy change is 1) that, as from a year's time, export woodchip tonnages would be pared back 20 per cent a year every year, and 2) the co-ordinating process of licence renewals will, in future,

be handled by the Prime Minister's own department.

There are qualifications, as there always are. They relate to woodchip operations that process here in Australia, rather than export, and the cutting of plantation timber rather than native forest. The industry however, despite soothing public noises, wants to do neither, because they're costly and it's much easier and more profitable, in a compliant political atmosphere, just to cut and chip native forest.

Why the policy change couldn't have happened a week ago, before the latest licences were renewed and before it was too late to unscramble them, again Keating didn't say. He did get a bit cross and suggest he couldn't do everything, which was an admission in itself, but really he just let the question lie there.

I'll tell you why, though: because until it was botched and needed fixing politically, Keating, in his usual complacent and detached way these days, was quite happy to let the renewal process stooge along the same unsupervised and largely unstructured way it has since 1991. It's just nobody thought Beddall would be dopey enough to increase the tonnage so significantly.

Well, almost nobody.

Now Beddall appears a prize mug; John Faulkner, as Environment Minister, is left looking naked and ineffective after being stood up by a junior colleague he detests; the Government's environment credentials, after a year of significant repair, have gone up the spout again; and Paul Keating presents, just as he did in the third runway uproar, as someone who comes around and cleans up only when the politics fall apart, not the process.

As he told us, in one of the more revealing quotes of the year: 'You know, if I've got enough time, I can strip the tariff barriers out of Australia, open up the financial markets, deal with native title issues, fix the old-growth forest policy problems and then move onto the bigger, broader identity issues into the bargain. I mean, it's all a matter of what one can reasonably do.'

What do the 29 other members of his ministry do?

Two weeks ago, at the last Cabinet meeting of the year, Keating told his colleagues just how strongly things were going for the Government, despite some delicate economic issues ahead; how well all ministers were doing; and how hopeless was the Opposition. He reeled off a list of the year's achievements, notably APEC and the Employment White Paper, and as, the meeting concluded, he gathered up his papers and remarked: 'It's nice to finish the year on a high.'

No, Prime Minister, that isn't where the weight is at all.

Alan Ramsey

# Chapter 10

# Four Blokes and a Lemon

## The Finest Cloth

DECEMBER 14, 1994

FOR MANY years there were these two men in adjoining offices in a far corner of the press gallery in Old Parliament House. One was Jack Fingleton. The other was Stewart Harris. They were very different, but the same. One was as Australian as a meat pie and sauce. The other was a transplanted Pom. They wrote about different things for different papers in far off and different parts of the world. As such, they seemed in 1966, to someone who'd just arrived down the corridor from the war in Vietnam, to belong to another time and place.

Jack Fingleton was the former Test cricketer from the bodyline years, and when he wasn't making his elegant prose sing about cricket for *The Age* in Melbourne, he wrote from Canberra for a group of South African papers. Stewart Harris was for some 20 years the Australian correspondent for *The Times* of London, once one of the great newspapers and truly The Thunderer, as it was known, for what used to be the British Empire.

I was a bit in awe of them both for what I imagined they represented; and their adjoining offices, whose doors always seemed to be shut, as if against the parochial insignificance of Australian politics, were, to me, almost mystical places.

Years later, after I got to know them, I remained in awe of them for themselves.

Jack Fingleton would talk about cricket, good manners, bad politicians and his abhorrence of bad language. Stewart Harris would talk about the world and our individual responsibility to make it better. He never lectured or harangued. I never heard him raise his voice to or about anyone or anything, despite his deep convictions and his remarkable compassion.

I think most people are sods at heart; he wouldn't have it, not out loud. Stewart was the gentlest man I ever knew.

Jack Fingleton died a dozen years ago, and when he did a light went out, just as it did for readers of his cricket symphonies. I missed, above all, his optimism and unfailing good humour and his window into another time. And when they went into his tiny office and tore up the worn lino and removed the old newspaper files going back decades and took away every single bit of evidence he'd ever been there, to make way for a radio correspondent young enough and green enough not even to know who he was, I thought it a truly sad day.

By that time Stewart Harris had gone from the press gallery, but not from Canberra. He was always committed to more than just his bread and butter and, though English-born, pursued passionately, for most of his 40-odd years in Australia, the causes of Aboriginal land rights and social justice, just as he later did Palestinian self-determination, and just as he wrote with great sensitivity about the massive insensitivity of Australian police and politicians during the South African rugby tour of 1971.

I never met anyone more involved in human affairs.

A few weeks ago, after a visit to my home lugging a tape recorder as big as a suitcase, he wrote me a letter. 'It was good to spend some time with you again last month,' he said. 'But something you wrote last Saturday, when dealing with Laurie Brereton, made me determined to write to you, because you touched on the issue of privatisation as it affects air safety.

'Now I would like to see you go much further and deeper, to question the relation between free market forces and unemployment. If you don't raise this issue, then I think you will be missing the biggest story of our time. As you know, I have respected your reporting and analysis for many years. But for a long time I have wanted you to move occasionally from the detail of Australian politics and lift your eyes to the hills and horizons of Australia . . .'

These are now the words of a dead man.

I had put his letter aside and, unlike the man who wrote them, did not lift my eyes to the hills and horizons. Laurie Brereton and the third runway kept me transfixed on the flatlands of today. The bigger picture is always harder. You put off looking for it and then, suddenly, it's too late. The train has gone.

Stewart Harris died eight days ago. They cremated him on Monday. At the overflow funeral service, in the beautiful old St John's Anglican Church just off Canberra's Anzac Parade, I heard a single Scottish piper and then a didgeridoo wail a haunting lament to his passing. My neck really prickled. It was an extraordinary juxtaposition of sound.

Harris was a lovely human being. It takes no courage to eulogise the dead, but he is one of the very few people I've known utterly deserving of all they said about him. Unlike most of us, his eyes rarely left the hills and horizons, and not just of Australia. And now those two offices in Old Parliament House are truly empty of all but the past.

Alan Ramsey

# The Jumbos are Killing George's River

**DECEMBER 21, 1994**

A FEW years ago I went to Cairns to read books and go fishing. When I asked around for where and how to catch barramundi, I was told there was only one bloke to see. That's how I met George. I've been fishing with George every year since. And then, six months ago, sitting in his canopied runabout on a late June day in the estuary of the Barron River, he told me about the hairy caterpillars.

There are some things you should know about George. His full name is George White and he's been fishing the Barron River for 50 years. It's his livelihood and his life. He doesn't go out to the Reef where the fish commit suicide for the tourists. George is a craftsman. He fishes the tidal estuaries with subtlety and skill and he loves the Barron River. To fish with George is to break bread with Mozart, at least for me.

The other thing about George is he detests politicians. He thinks they are, in the main, gutless and stupid and incredibly short-sighted. That doesn't make him unique. It does make him angry. George thinks they're killing his river. Encourage him and he'll tell you why, in passionate detail. That's how I learned about the hairy caterpillars.

The Barron River is one of the great rivers of North Queensland. It rises somewhere up in the Tablelands, comes through the Tinaroo Dam and on past Mareeba and Kuranda, before dropping down through the beautiful Barron Gorge to Lake Placid in the foothills and then meandering 12 kilometres, through canefields and the mangroves of the wetlands, to the sea. It comes out on the coast just north of Cairns airport. And that's where all the trouble is.

The airport used to be little more than a paddock with a runway. Not any more. The developers discovered Cairns just before the tourists did. So they expanded the airport to take the international jumbos that now deliver, in ever increasing numbers, great bins of two-legged tourist dollars every week, mainly from Japan. And in expanding the airport they started killing off the river.

You smell the planes leaving. We were sitting there in George's boat this day when a jumbo took off right over us. That's what started George off. This part of the river, he said, was now called Kerosene Corner. It was the burn-off from the jets as they lumbered into the air, the fuel misting down onto the mangroves. It didn't hurt the mangroves, not yet, but a lot of wetlands plantlife that grew on the mangroves began dying. Plants like golden

orchids and button orchids and pencil orchids and staghorns.

Then the hairy caterpillars disappeared.

The caterpillars used to be there in their thousands, apparently. George says they've all gone now, at least from this lower part of the river. He doesn't know what their role was in the ecology or food chain of the river system, but he does know a lot of the bird life has gone, too. And that isn't all. The jumbos don't just urinate on the mangroves; they also defecate into the river. George reckons about 50 international jets a week now arrive or hub through Cairns, a 24-hour-a-day airport. And every big jet that comes in leaves its sewage behind before returning overseas or flying on to the cities down south.

The jets pump out at Cairns airport. The sewage gets a secondary treatment process, but not full tertiary treatment, before it then goes where? That's right, into the Barron River! And at 50 jumbos a week, for 50 weeks of the year, with each of them carrying up to 450 kilograms of sewage, plus what all the domestic flights leave behind, that's a lot of crap finishing up in George's office.

George is no expert. He's just a fisherman who knows his river. But he sees the wetlands' plants dying in the mangroves, and the hairy caterpillars vanishing, and the birds getting fewer, and the shell life on the river banks and the small crabs from the mud flats disappearing, and the barramundi getting scarcer every year, and he wonders why politicians can't understand what's happening. If all these things go, so will the tourists eventually.

It's like the big-powered catamarans that thunder out to the Reef every day. They carry as many as 400 and 500 tourists. And did you know all their raw sewage goes straight into the sea, flushed out on the way back to port? The Barrier Reef Marine Park Authority allows them to do so. Wonderful, isn't it? What would all those tourists think if they knew they were snorkelling in their own raw waste?

I thought of George and the Barron River and its hairy caterpillars when David Beddall, another Queenslander, authorised the loggers yesterday to cut down more native forest to export another 6.7 million tonnes of woodchips to Japan next year. Slowly killing off the countryside makes no more sense than killing a river.

Alan Ramsey

# That Nagging Noise at 5am

**NOVEMBER 30, 1994**

A RACEHORSE clip-clops past Laurie Brereton's Kensington home before dawn most days. The strapper lives just down the street, apparently, and the stables must be close by. Brereton told me about the horse the other day when we were talking about noise. It was an odd little story. One minute we were talking about jetliners making life a misery for whole new slabs of Sydney, the next about Laurie's horse.

Brereton is like that. He has the sharp, lean look of a ferret and is no less quick on his feet. Ask him about potatoes and he'll give you a long story about pumpkins. I asked about the tens of thousands of Sydney people who've just discovered, rather rudely, what the Third Runway Debate has been all about for 30 years. Brereton told me about the horse.

The first time the horse went past his house was 10 years ago. Laurie remembers because it woke him up. It wasn't a noise he was used to at that time of the day. In fact, it woke him every morning for the first week or so. Ten years later, the same strapper, though presumably not the same horse, still goes by the Brereton home at the same ungodly hour.

Now, however, neither Laurie nor Trish hear it. In fact, they haven't heard it for years. After that first week all those years ago, the clip-clopping of the horse passing their bedroom ceased to wake them. And you know why, of course. Because, as Brereton says, they got used to it. In time, that passing horse was no longer an alien and intrusive sound.

You see what the Minister for Alibis is getting at, don't you? Apparently a succession of jetliners rumbling over your house day and night is really no different from that noisy horse each morning. It's merely a matter of routine. After a while, you're no longer aware it's there; and the aberrant noise simply slips into the background hum of daily life.

An inventive little parable, isn't it?

I thought of that horse when those angry protesters set up outside the Brereton home at sparrow twit the other morning and gave Laurie and Trish, along with their outraged neighbours, a few hundred decibels of amplified jet noise, just to let them know what they're missing out on. I thought surely all Laurie had to do was go out and tell them his horse story and they'd have packed up and meekly gone away, reassured by the Minister's wisdom and deep understanding of such things.

However, I presume in the chaos of the moment he forgot about the horse, for he did no such thing. Instead, while his neighbours, their Saturday morning shattered, charged outside to mix insults with the protesters,

Brereton did no more than courageously peep through the front curtains and stay inside. Somebody should tell him that maybe if the protesters keep going back, he'll get used to it in time.

The third runway has always been a sorry story.

Five years ago, when the Hawke Government reneged on its 1983 promise and decided to build the extra runway it had insisted for six years it would not build, most non-NSW members of the Government largely dismissed it as a parochial Sydney issue exercising only those few MPs, mostly Labor, holding electorates around the airport. They didn't take it all too seriously.

What they did take seriously, though, was the supposed vast amounts of money needed to build a second Sydney airport, something governments of all kinds, State and Federal, had been buck-passing for donkeys' years.

So, to the loud applause of all the vested interests, among them the airlines, the business community generally and the then Greiner Government, the Hawke Cabinet changed its mind and spent $238 million building the runway that tens of thousands of ordinary Sydney residents didn't want, knowing what it would do to their lives, and their real estate, if they did.

Now Brereton has to make the system work, even though it won't. Suddenly whole new areas of Sydney know what aircraft noise is all about. Like his strange little horse story, Laurie wants us to believe that somehow the pilots of huge jetliners have suddenly started flying wherever they like over Sydney and once the Government starts fining them, that will fix the problem and everything will settle down again. This is just expedient tosh.

However, with the politicians blaming each other for an issue that is, suddenly, rampaging out of control, it won't be the last absurdity you hear this side of the next election. Bob Carr, John Fahey, Brereton—all of them want you to believe it's someone else's fault. I think it's quite wonderful they're all wetting their electoral pants.

Just don't blame that horse.

Alan Ramsey

# You Can't Hang up on Sydney, Laurie

**DECEMBER 3, 1994**

LAURIE BRERETON was furious. 'It's Brereton here,' he said, his anger boiling down the line. What followed was not for small children or sensitive grown-ups. The conversation was as brief as its content was explicit. The end was no less abrupt. 'I just want you to know you're a GREAT BIG C!' he concluded, banging the phone down. He hasn't rung back.

Brereton doesn't usually use alphabetic code to say what he means. Maybe he was intimidated by the phone. Maybe he was still shaken by the brick that came crashing through his window overnight. Maybe he was still coming to terms with what a huge political cock-up Sydney's third runway schemozzle has become. Whatever the reason, he made himself understood.

This hasn't been a good week for Paul Keating's Minister for Aircraft Noise. His sense of humour is strained these days. My column in the *Herald* that morning didn't make it any better. I hope the phone call improved his day. That was three days ago. The piece that excited his attention was the one about the noisy horse that passes by his Kensington home before dawn most mornings. He'd told me the story the previous week. He was not impressed by the unflattering way it had been recounted to *Herald* readers.

Brereton insisted he'd been talking about the old east–west runway, not the new north–south runway. I didn't, couldn't, see the difference, given his horse story was related to how people, over time, can get used to intrusive noise, and I said so. That got him only more excited. It was at that point he terminated our frank exchange of views.

Alan Ramsey

# And What About that $20m Lemon?

SEPTEMBER 17, 1994

PAUL KEATING and three Cabinet ministers spent a minimum $20 million in several hours of late night talks on Monday turning a lemon into the end of a national port strike. The four-day strike is reported to have cost the shipping companies $60 million. Ending it by spending $20 million of public money to make the government-owned Australian National Line and its 13 ships attractive enough to sell might seem a reasonable deal.

It might not, too. Nobody will really know until we know the full cost of the taxpayer subsidy or who it is, if anyone, that finishes up buying ANL, a shipping line Laurie Brereton, the Minister for Transport, insisted a few weeks ago 'you couldn't give away'. Well, what the Government is now giving away is the public's $20 million to try to prove Brereton wrong.

The maritime unions are delighted.

In the meantime, Brereton's old mate, Neville Wran, will go on earning his $150,000 fee from the Government as the new chairman of the ANL board that was trying to make the whole loss-making ANL exercise viable before the seamen and the wharfies stepped in with their strike late last week.

If you understand how this has all come about then you're doing well. Very few others do. Even Brereton, when asked to be specific about the cost of the deal worked out with the unions on Monday night, had to admit the next day that he didn't know. Ask the Treasurer, Ralph Willis, or the Finance Minister, Kim Beazley; he said; that was their concern, not his.

A curious way to run a government.

Meanwhile, having appeased the unions and ended the port strike by spending $20 million, Paul Keating flew off to Queensland on Wednesday to try to fix up the drought-stricken farmers by spending we-haven't-the-faintest-idea how much. He talked with a number of rural leaders, visited a couple of the worst-hit properties in the worst-hit drought areas, then flew home again. Farmers are still waiting for rain. The rest of us are waiting for the bill.

Before he left Queensland, Keating had some terse words with the press. Unlike Andrew Peacock, the Prime Minister is rarely good-humoured, specially with the vacuum cleaners of the media. His sense of humour was not sharpened by some of the questions.

The drought had been going for four years, said one intrepid reporter. Shouldn't he have come a bit earlier? Why had it taken so long? 'The reason I'm here now is the drought has not broken,' Keating explained, as if that needed to be explained. The Federal Government already had spent $100 million on drought-relief since 1992. But it still hadn't rained, and so it was back to the drawing board.

The reporters were unconvinced. So the Prime Minister hadn't been 'dithering' on the drought? And had he 'got a big shock' now that he'd finally seen how bad it was? And what about bigger tax concessions? No, said Keating, he didn't think $100 million was dithering, 'even for people who want to trivialise the issue'.

One of these days a leading politician is going to go berserk and strangle a member of the press. When he or she does, you'll know why.

Alan Ramsey

# Chapter 11

# The Gathering Storm

## A Colonial in London

**FEBRUARY 1, 1995**

SOME WEEKS ago I was sitting in a faraway place reading an account in a day-old London newspaper of the Melbourne cricket Test. Australian politics couldn't have been more distant or more irrelevant. Some things, however, you can't escape, even on a dark, cold morning in the middle of a northern hemisphere winter.

The columnist was Roy Hattersley. For God's sake, he was saying, it was only a game, after all; and he was trying to put into perspective the hysteria being written and spoken in Britain of the home team's defeat, yet still explaining why, to the Poms, defeat by Australia is so hard to stomach. Losing to the new Commonwealth, Hattersley wrote, was never pleasant but didn't make English gorges or inferiority complexes ever rise in the same way.

'The Australians remind us we have lost an empire but not found a pair of fast bowlers. We think of West Indians as joyful, Pakistanis industrious and Indians polite. Australians are rude to their elders and betters.' Hattersley is not a cricket writer. He is a Labor MP and former minister who's been in British politics for every bit as long as Ian Sinclair has been in the business here, a good 30 years.

And he went on to amplify his point about Australians with a wonderful anecdote about, of all people, guess who? 'When I was shadow Chancellor of the Exchequer,' he wrote, 'I was visited from time to time by Paul Keating, then Federal Treasurer and aspirant to the leadership of his party. He would walk into my office, removing his teddy bear overcoat as he came through the door, and greet me with such cheery salutations as, 'When are you going to get these extremists under control?' or 'You still haven't sorted out the trade unions.'

'I was usually in agreement with his point of view. And I rarely doubted he would achieve our mutual objective with a success which would be denied to me. But I always wished he could be right more graciously. It is the same with Australian cricketers. They are incapable of winning with reticence.'

Hattersley is right about both.

Regrettably, our cricketers seem to have become as smugly complacent about their opponents as our Prime Minister has about his and, accordingly, have resumed losing again. The analogy is obvious. It's why I thought of Roy Hattersley and his elegant column two days ago as I watched, for the first time in five weeks, Paul Keating return to the Parliament he mostly ignores.

It was the same day John Howard rose again. It was also the same day the loggers and their supporters so jammed the roads to

Parliament that Keating was forced to walk, at least part way, to work. He looked his usual unconcerned, confident self, striding along with his bodyguards, so much so that just before he disappeared into a secure underground car park, thus restricting the intimidation of the loggers' gauntlet to a minimum, he flippantly told a protester who wanted to argue his case to 'write a letter'.

The remark was highlighted on the national news that night. It only reinforced the bad imagery and perceptions so many voters have about the Prime Minister's arrogance. It was unnecessary and silly, for if Keating understands little about being graciously right, he knows no more about being graciously wrong. And he is, quite palpably, wrong in the way he's gone about handling the woodchipping issue.

Not a whit has changed over the Christmas recess.

Somehow Keating has allowed his Government to go on offending both the greens and the loggers, at the same time displaying a level of administrative incompetence and political insensitivity that beggars understanding for a government that's been there 12 years. The responsibility lies entirely with the Prime Minister and his office.

Yet when the Labor Caucus met on Monday for the first time this year, what did it do? The Right got stuck into the Left's Cabinet Minister for the Environment, John Faulkner, the Left got stuck into the Right's junior Minister for Resources, David Beddall, and nobody got stuck into the Prime Minister, heaven forbid. For his part, Keating whinged about the fact everybody was blaming him and not the States, but he was no less venomous about the Greens for not publicly endorsing his attempts at compromise.

Faulkner defended himself and his statutory responsibilities. Beddall kept his mouth shut. Only one Labor MP, NSW's Allan Morris, came even close to pinning the blame where it ultimately belongs. 'Paul,' he said, 'this issue isn't going to go away while David Bedall remains Minister for Resources.' It isn't a point of view the Prime Minister cares to hear, least from his backbench.

Nothing has changed.

There's been a view in the Government for some time that no matter what might go wrong, come election time the Government will get it right. Labor won the 1990 election with 17 per cent interest rates and the 'unwinnable' 1993 election with a million unemployed. Twice in the last three elections—1987 and 1990—the Coalition won more votes but Labor still won more seats.

All these factors sustain a Government contemptuous of its Opposition.

It is, as our cricket team behaved, smug beyond belief. The smugness was compounded by the aberration of Alexander Downer's leadership. Exit Downer, re-enter John Howard. Some things do change. This one was inevitable, however the Liberals now try to rewrite history to sell it.

Howard has his baggage and is no messiah. But he's the best the Liberals have and he is every inch a competitor. It should be an interesting year.

Alan Ramsey

# The Black Knight

O'neill
After Monty Python

IN THE cult film *Monty Python and the Holy Grail* there is a scene where King Arthur, riding an imaginary horse, confronts and defeats the defiant Black Knight, methodically hacking him to pieces, but failing to force him to yield. 'I'm invincible,' boasts the Black Knight, even after losing both arms and a leg. 'The Black Knight always triumphs,' he insists, as Arthur cuts off his other leg. All that's left is mostly mouth. 'Come back here, you coward!' it taunts, as Arthur trots away. 'I'll bite your legs off!'

The Monty Python team made *The Holy Grail* in 1975, the same year yet another Camelot disintegrated. Twenty years later, John Howard, riding his imaginary policies, is closer to his particular holy grail than ever. And Paul Keating, bleeding profusely—though not quite armless or legless—continues to behave like the Black Knight, just as he more often sounds like his mutilated torso.

The grossest absurdity Labor apologists for the Queensland election have sought to cultivate this week is that Wayne Goss was the unintended victim of a protest vote gone wrong.

To call the thumping handed the Goss Government a 'protest' is a travesty of language. Labor's vote collapsed—not just in pockets or specific regions but right across the State. This was no protest by an electorate 'quietly' angry. It was a deliberate slash-and-burn denial of Labor by the entire State—not to rebuke the Government but to get rid of it.

You only have to look at the figures.

Overall, in a State vote of 2 million, Labor's primary vote dropped 6.5 percentage points, to 43 per cent, and its two-party preferred vote was down 5 percentage points, to 47.5 per cent. In the Brisbane metropolitan area, Labor's electoral heart since it regained office in 1989, the collapse was even worse. There its primary vote slumped 8.8 percentage points (to 48.8) and its two-party preferred vote was down 7.9 per cent.

The rot was almost as bad in Queensland's south-east corner, the State's most populous area—made up of Brisbane, the Gold Coast and the Sunshine Coast—where Labor's primary vote was down 7.1 percentage points (to 45.9) and its two-party preferred vote fell 7.3 per cent.

Outside the south-east—that is, across the whole of the rest of Queensland—the Coalition's primary vote increased 4.3 percentage points (to 53.9) and Labor's went down 3.7 percentage points (to 38.6). The two-party preferred swing against Labor was even greater at 5.7 percentage points, emphasising the strength of the minor parties in directing preferences away from the Government in the big regional centres and all up and down the vast coastline.

Yet how did the Black Knight react to this unwelcome news?

In Cairns the morning after polling night, with State Labor in confused turmoil amidst the bodies, yet everyone unsure if there were enough to defeat the Government, Paul Keating found fault with the voters, not the political stupidity of its Premier.

'It is rather disconcerting to see a good government in any way suffering these sorts of problems from a protest vote,' Keating lectured his listeners, ignoring the evidence on both counts. 'It is quite obvious that the Opposition here, without policies and without a program, urging only a protest vote, there could have been no positive vote for them.'

It wasn't obvious at all, only to a Prime Minister trying to make self-interested and ungrammatical excuses. But it got worse. 'There has got to be some appraisal of, again, the point that political parties must stand for something,' his lecture continued. 'And when they don't, there can be no guarantee for the community that they are going to get some value from it—from such a protest or such a change.'

That's democracy, Prime Minister.

It offers no guarantees about anything. After all, Australians used to think they knew what the Labor Party stood for—among other things, public ownership of the Commonwealth Bank, Qantas and the now-subsumed TAA. They were wrong. Certainly they never thought Labor stood for 17 per cent mortgage rates, 1 million unemployed, or the country's worst recession in 60 years.

They were wrong there, too.

And I'm not aware, during any one of Labor's five successful Federal election campaigns since its last loss in 1980, that any of these misconceptions were ever explained to voters to enable them to properly judge if they could expect, as Keating puts it, 'to get some value' from supporting a Labor government.

Voters may not always be sure what they want. Nor can they ever truly know beforehand what they're getting. But they usually know what they don't want, just as they're always very sure what they're voting against. The Prime Minister understands that better than anyone, after what happened to John Hewson and his GST 28 months ago.

It is the only reason he is still Prime Minister.

And when a clear majority of Queenslanders went to the polls last weekend, they, too, knew exactly what they were voting against, and why: a self-satisfied, inward-looking, parsimonious Government which, after six years in office, they felt was taking them for granted.

It was also the case that, having done so, the very last thing voters needed was Paul Keating, of all people, to be telling them they hadn't known what they were doing. Keating wasn't welcome in Queensland at any time during the campaign. Goss wanted no part of him. Yet there he was, appearing in their midst a day later, lecturing voters on what they should have done.

No humility, no acknowledgment that smug and arrogant politicians might have been responsible rather than the foolishness of thoughtless voters.

Just another Keating lecture. It didn't stop with Queensland, either.

'Let people understand this about John Howard,' he said, moving to his favourite subject. 'He is following the same policy (of) running around without a policy. He is saying, "I'll have no policies; just concentrate on them (the Government)." But, in the end, someone has got to run the country (and), as I say, there can be no honesty or credibility without policies.

'So, I think what the media has got to do with John Howard is line him up and say, "OK, John, you want to be Prime Minister, what do you stand for?" Not some vague generalisation . . . If he wants to be Prime Minister, he has got to say where he stands in policy . . . Whether you are talking about (Rob) Borbidge (Queensland's alternative Premier) or Howard, essentially they are free riders on the system. They are to be held accountable for the things they really stand for but want to keep hidden until an election . . .

'They represent nothing. They stand for nothing. Yet they seek to denigrate governments that do things. I think the public ought to say: "Well, hang on, before we leave value behind, before we leave behind governments

that have got quality and substance and value, we have got to know what we are getting in return and not just, basically, the fluff that comes from an advertising agency".

You would have thought Paul Keating would by now understand it's long past the time when it was enough for him just to stand there, like the Black Knight insisting 'None shall Pass!', and harangue us about how he knows best. People are tired of his lectures. They're tired, too, of his indulgences and slipperiness and of him always seeming to be looking down his nose at them.

Keating is a figure of stature, but the 'quality and substance and value', as he puts it, of the Government he leads have been degraded and corrupted, by time as much as by imperious attitudes, in the same way government policy and process are too often corrupted these days by political circumstance for political advantage.

And voters don't punish governments that 'do things'. They punish governments that do the wrong things or which fail to do those things they said they would do. The Goss Government, whether it survives or not, got exactly what it deserved. And unless John Howard, for all his ordinariness and lack of ideas and grey faces behind him, makes a complete hash of the next six months, so will the Keating Government.

Howard doesn't need talent or policies to win. Victoria's Jeff Kennett and WA's Richard Court and South Australia's Dean Brown proved that. Queensland's Rob Borbidge may repeat it. What a political party needs most is voter hostility on its side. John Howard has that in spades.

All the Black Knight has is a formidable mouth.

*Alan Ramsey*

**Postscript:** *The Goss Government survived voters' anger by a single seat. In losing eight seats, its one-seat majority in an 89-seat State Parliament was secured by just 16 votes in 23,000 in the election's last seat declared— the seat of Mundingburra, one of three in the northern coastal city of Townsville. But seven months later, in February 1996, after a National Party legal challenge to the Mundingburra result succeeded, it all came crashing down. Labor lost the resultant by-election, the Goss Government lost its majority and was swept back into Opposition after just six years in office, and Wayne Goss lost the leadership and his political career. The Nationals' Rob Borbidge formed a minority government—with the support of a country independent—that survived , precariously, until July 1998 when Labor regained office under a new messiah, Peter Beattie.*

# The Truth, the Whole Truth . . .

**AUGUST 12, 1995**

JOHN HOWARD'S good mood was obvious. And why not? The Liberals' pesky Noel Crichton-Browne was gone from the morning headlines and Labor's Carmen Lawrence was up to her neck in them. 'Well, ladies and gentlemen,' Howard warmly greeted waiting reporters, as he left a business breakfast at the North Sydney League's Club three days ago, 'I'd just like to say that Paul Keating is charging the Australian taxpayer more than $10,000 a day to protect Carmen Lawrence from the truth. It's about time this stonewalling stopped. Let the truth come out.'

Ahh yes, the truth.

Whenever a politician wants 'the truth' to 'come out' you know it's bad news for somebody. For five months John Howard slithered and weaved and dodged around the truth about Crichton-Browne until, finally, the Perth senator was knee-capped, not by the truth but by his own stupidity. Now truth had joined the Liberals and Howard wanted his full measure from the ailing Dr Lawrence.

'Why is she running from the revelation of truth?' he demanded indignantly in front of the television cameras and the microphones on Wednesday morning. 'Why are we paying for this stonewalling? Why is the Australian taxpayer underwriting this pathetically cowardly attempt to run from the truth?'

Reporter: 'Why can't the Liberal Party get rid of Noel Crichton-Browne?'

It wasn't the answer John Howard wanted, but on the news bulletins that night it was his appeal for 'the truth' from Carmen Lawrence that got the air play, not the annoying questions from the annoying reporters about the dreaded Crichton-Browne, who, despite Howard's insistent assertions 'he's finished', went on proving all week he's harder to kill than Rasputin. Carmen Lawrence is far more vulnerable.

Half an hour after John Howard insisted the 'truth come out', Lawrence walked into 2UE's head office in Sydney and went on John Laws' radio program. It seemed a foolhardy thing to do. Only the previous day, over in Perth, she'd copped a stern serve from the retired Melbourne judge, Kenneth Marks, QC, the royal commissioner investigating the events at the heart of the political crisis that now engulfs Lawrence's career. Marks was angered that Lawrence and her legal team were doing all they could, in challenges to the WA Supreme Court and the High Court, to prevent him 'investigating the truth' inside the commission, while outside it she gave herself total licence to denigrate it as a political 'witch hunt' and to impugn the testimony and credibility of witnesses she wouldn't confront at the commission hearings.

'I find that a remarkable position,' Marks told her lawyers. 'It has to be one thing or the other. Dr Lawrence is aware of the rules about contempt.'

Maybe. But Dr Lawrence is certainly aware of the rules of political survival, even if she doesn't practise them too well. Thus she ignored the warning from Perth and, like the fly being welcomed by the spider, took herself into John Laws' studio to spread 'the truth'

to his listeners. Laws was at his oiliest and beguiling best.

He charmed, massaged, stroked and sympathised. And he winkled out of her admissions that yes, when the whole sordid business started almost three years ago, in November 1992, when Lawrence was Premier in WA and Richard Court was the State Liberal leader, she had known the infamous Easton parliamentary petition and its accusations— later proved to be totally false and which drove a young woman to commit suicide—would damage Court.

Laws: 'But didn't you try and do a job on Richard Court politically?'

Lawrence: 'Well, the petition obviously had that impact. Obviously had that impact. But the suggestion, as I say, that I somehow solicited (it) or was involved in its development or its tabling is clearly wrong . . . There's no suggestion from anybody, except Richard

Court, that this was somehow an elaborate ploy to damage him.'

Laws: 'Yeah, but did you know the thing was going to be tabled?'

Lawrence: 'Yes I did, and I've said that all along. I was briefed beforehand that it was going to be tabled.'

Laws: 'And did it cross your mind this could be politically damaging to Richard Court?'

Lawrence: 'Oh, it was obvious. Yes, of course.'

Laws: 'And you didn't mind that?'

Lawrence: 'Well, you know what politics is like.'

Laws: 'Exactly!'

Exactly, is right. A Labor backbencher, John Halden, now Opposition leader in the State Upper House, tabled the petition on Thursday, November 5, 1992. It accused Penelope Easton and her sister of perjury in a Family Court action stretching back to 1986. It also accused Richard Court of having corruptly provided confidential evidence to Easton in her court fight against her former husband. It was the last day of the parliamentary week.

And that same afternoon the news broke that police were investigating Carmen Lawrence for pocketing $5000 in travel expenses for an overseas trip she never made. She'd been paid the money in February, 1990, and, she later claimed, she 'forgot' about it after the trip was later cancelled. Almost two years later the money was 'discovered' and repaid, on her own initiative, after police began investigating the expenses payments of all ministers in the former Burke and Dowding Labor governments.

The next week, in the Federal Parliament, the Liberals' Wilson Tuckey would claim the two events—the Easton petition 'conspiracy' and disclosure of Lawrence's 'forgotten' $5000 advance expenses—were linked. The petition, primarily to damage Court, had been a 'typical Labor diversion', asserted Tuckey, to take the political heat off disclosure, the same day, that police had investigated Lawrence's 'copping five grand she was not entitled to and forgetting it was in her bank account' for two years.

However, before Tuckey's speech on November 12, and before the resumption of the State Parliament on Tuesday, November 10, real tragedy intervened. Penny Easton killed herself after three days of intense publicity in Perth, even though the WA police commissioner had announced on the Friday, the day after the petition, that its accusations against Easton and Court were false and had been investigated and found to be false two years earlier.

A lawyer, Easton left her partner, a newly-installed Supreme Court judge, at home and went to work on the Monday morning. Then she drove up into the hills that afternoon and gassed herself in her car with its exhaust fumes. In a letter, she wrote in part: 'I have been set up so well that I have no way out but this. I cannot live with the hurt that is being done my family. I know it's all political.'

Three months later the Lawrence Government lost office. Richard Court became Premier. He has pursued Carmen Lawrence ever since. But it wasn't until April this year that Court got what he believed would finally expose 'the truth' and nail Lawrence as a liar.

And it came from one of Lawrence's own former Cabinet colleagues, Keith Wilson, who told Paul McGeough, of this newspaper, on April 7, that Lawrence had known all about the Easton petition and had discussed it in Cabinet beforehand. 'She brought it to Cabinet, saying "We've got this against Richard Court," and talked about how it would do maximum political damage. She threw up her hands and said she had no control over what Halden would do, and she told us to "get real, everyone is doing it, it's too good a chance to miss". It just appeared to be such a blatant, naked act of political expediency and we couldn't believe anybody would be fooled by it.'

A second former Labor minister, Pam Beggs, has since broken silence and supported Wilson. Lawrence has stuck to her story she knew nothing of the petition that caused a woman to take her own life until the day Halden tabled it in State Parliament.

Now, in the royal commission set up by Court, two former Lawrence staff members have repudiated her version of events. Her lawyers, financed by public money authorised by the Keating Cabinet, are fighting in the High Court to close the commission down, having already lost in the State Supreme Court. Lawrence is fighting in the media. Whatever 'the truth' the perception is dreadful. She behaves like someone being dragged kicking and screaming to the witness box. She can no longer win politically even if she does so legally.

She has destroyed herself.

Alan Ramsey

# Adrift on a Lifeless Raft

**AUGUST 26, 1995**

FOUR CABINET ministers have quit the Keating Government in the last 20 months. Alan Griffiths and Ros Kelly went with a smell hanging over their political acumen if not their ministerial behaviour. Graham Richardson went without warning, having been resurrected by the unwinnable 1993 election, only to run smack into an unpleasantness revived by the Hanson inquiry in Brisbane.

Only John Dawkins quit untainted. Although a great Keating loyalist, Dawkins was driven out of the Government, not as a conscious act but because of his refusal to accept what he saw as Keating's disloyalty to him as Treasurer by his heavy-handed interference in his portfolio. And when Dawkins went from the Cabinet in mid-December 1993 and out of politics six weeks later, he went quietly, loyal to the end. And when he went he was allowed to go only because Carmen Lawrence, then State Opposition leader in Western Australia, was persuaded to switch to Federal politics by taking Dawkins' seat of Fremantle in March 1994.

It was Keating who made Dawkins' resignation from Parliament conditional.

Keating at the time was already facing two prospective by-elections. One was for the disaffected John Kerin's safe seat of Werriwa in outer Sydney. The other was coming up because of a Keating deal earlier that year with South Australia's Neal Blewett, a 10-year ministerial original from the first Hawke Government. Blewett had agreed to stand down from the ministry after the 1993 election to make way for another South Australian, Chris Schacht, one of Keating's strongest allies in his long leadership battle with Hawke. Schacht had been on a promise for more than a year.

After Keating was endorsed in his own right as PM, Blewett's agreement to go made it possible for Keating to keep his promise to Schacht. But Blewett only went to the back bench in March 1993 on the strength of another Keating deal: that he would send Blewett to London as Australian High Commissioner within the year. And Keating kept that promise, too.

Thus, when Dawkins quit the Cabinet in December 1993, Keating was already committed to a by-election in Werriwa in January and a prospective by-election in Blewett's relatively safe seat of Bonython, in Adelaide, soon after. The Government was in no position to tolerate a third by-election with just any candidate in a relatively marginal seat such as Fremantle, given the uncertain mood in Western Australia.

So if Carmen Lawrence, one of the most popular politicians in the west, despite the defeat of her Government the previous February, wouldn't resign from State Parliament and run as Labor's candidate, Dawkins would have to cool his heels on the back bench, either until Lawrence changed her mind or until the next general election in 1996.

Keating felt only Lawrence could be guaranteed to retain Fremantle for Labor. Dawkins and the Federal ALP organisation agreed. Their faith wasn't misplaced. When Lawrence gave in to the overtures, she defied the usual anti-government swing at by-elections by increasing Labor's two-party preferred vote by 1 per cent at the subsequent ballot.

By contrast, the Werriwa by-election for John Kerin's seat two months earlier had seen Labor's vote drop 6 per cent. A week after the Fremantle result, the Bonython election for Blewett's seat saw Labor's vote drop 8 per cent. A similar result in Fremantle would have cost the Government the seat. Keating had good reason to thank Carmen Lawrence. So, of course, did John Dawkins.

In fact, Lawrence's transfer to the Federal arena, and the strength of the Fremantle vote she pulled to get there, was about Labor's only ray of sunshine at the time. Starting with Dawkins, Keating lost four Cabinet ministers in a span of three months.

Dawkins resigned on December 17. Alan Griffiths went belly-up from Cabinet on January 22 in the political wreckage of his ill-fated

Melbourne sandwich shop. Five weeks after that, and 16 days before the Fremantle poll, Ros Kelly packed away her whiteboard and quit on February 28. And nine days after Fremantle, Graham Richardson suddenly pulled the plug on himself on March 24 amid much speculation and widespread political shock.

It wasn't Labor's happiest New Year.

These were the circumstances, and against this background, which saw the good Dr Lawrence join the Labor family in Canberra. The transition to the Government's elite was immediate. Yet maybe she should have taken notice of the omens. She'd made it over the bodies of three colleagues. She had Dawkins' seat, Kelly's slot in Cabinet and Richardson's portfolio of Health. The dominoes of their careers couldn't have toppled in more convenient harmony.

And Keating had even bigger plans. He saw Lawrence's gender, image, popularity and ambition all combining in his Government's re-election strategy. From the very day she arrived, Keating and key people in the party organisation saw her great political potential as a softening and reassuring influence on the worn and somewhat discredited public face of the Government. Her future elevation as deputy leader to Keating, in place of the dour Brian Howe, was taken almost as a given, though far from unanimously.

What counted, though, was Keating's support and patronage. And that she had by the truckload. Lawrence was always in the forefront of his election thinking.

And then it all fell apart.

When Howe stood down as Keating's deputy two months ago and announced he was leaving politics at the election, Lawrence never had an earthly of replacing him. She was now tainted goods. All the potential of 15 months earlier had been crunched by the re-emergence of Penny Easton's death in November 1992, and the sordid political opportunism surrounding it, both before and after Easton died. Lawrence didn't even contest Howe's old job.

Keating told her she had no chance. This week, almost five months after the past first leapt out to seize her new career, Carmen Lawrence was alive politically only because the Prime Minister who'd brought her to Canberra 20 months earlier would not abandon her.

Now it isn't just Lawrence's fitness to be a minister, along with her credibility, that is on trial at the Marks Royal Commission in Perth. Now Keating has put his own authority as Prime Minister and the standards he sets for his Government on trial with public opinion. It is dangerous and desperate but these are now the stakes. It might say something for his courage and his loyalty to Carmen Lawrence, as well as for his arrogance. It says nothing for his judgment or the wellbeing of his Government. This is Keating in his best crash-or-crash-through mode. If he listened to majority opinion inside his Government he would insist Lawrence at least stand down.

But Keating listens to nobody when his mind is made up, just as nobody in his party has the balls to confront him and tell him that while his loyalty to Carmen is laudable, his continued stubborn support ignores all commonsense and political prudence and jeopardises a Government in no fit state to wilfully court further erosion of its public standing.

The public record says so.

The charge against Lawrence is that, on the eve of a State election her Government seemed certain to lose, and on the same day as the disclosure of other events damaging to her own public image, she connived, against advice, in a grubby piece of political mischief that went horribly wrong when Penny Easton killed herself. And then Lawrence lied—and went on lying for two years—to conceal her role in the affair.

Her defence is she knew nothing beforehand, connived in nothing with anyone, and has told only the truth, as she knows it, ever since. Eight of her former Cabinet ministers say the opposite, including four in evidence to the Royal Commission. So have three of her former staff. These aren't Liberal Party stooges. These are her own Labor colleagues, her own staff advisers. If it's only a political witch-hunt, then it's her own party and her own people who've tied Lawrence to the stake.

And what does Paul Keating say? In essence, so what! If that remains his opinion, in defiance of everything, he'll find out soon enough.

Alan Ramsey

# Then There was Fred

**AUGUST 23, 1995**

THE PARLIAMENT has always treated its dead with more courtesy and generosity than ever it did its living. So it was yesterday. Even the Prime Minister, who hasn't been seen on the floor of the House on a Tuesday for well over a year, was there to farewell Fred, as was everyone else. Keating did not, however, stay for the witch-burning.

As events turned out it was a very small fire. The real incendiaries are in Perth, not in Canberra, and Carmen Lawrence, as defiant as ever, emerged from Question Time with her credibility no more inflammable than when she entered.

John Howard and his colleagues had their chance yesterday and did remarkably little with it. They won't get another, not this week. Paul Keating doesn't believe in pampering the Opposition, any more than he believes in pushing his luck, and has excused Dr Lawrence from any further parliamentary scrutiny until next week. It seemed a wise move in the circumstances.

However, for a Government that insists its determined shielding of Lawrence from Richard Court's political pursuit is in defence of the principles of the primacy of Parliament and the sanctity of Cabinet, it is in no way shy about doing all and everything it can to hide her from judicial and parliamentary accountability. Yet before Carmen yesterday we got Fred, and given all the hard things expected of the last parliamentary session before the election, and the harder things to come in the nine sitting weeks ahead, it's a blessing we did.

It meant some softer things were said and some courtesies extended. There was even humour, even if only a dead man's remembered humour.

You could count on two hands the number of Parliament's 224 MPs who were actually in the place while Fred Daly was still there. Daly retired 20 years ago and when he died earlier this month the eulogies heaped upon him made him almost unrecognisable. Fred was a shrewd politician and a memorable parliamentarian. But he was a human being, not a saint.

For an hour yesterday the House of which Daly was a member for 32 years paid him its respects, mostly by people who never knew him. They did the same in the Senate, where Gareth Evans, who arrived in Parliament three years after Daly had gone, struck the most realistic and pertinent note of all. Evans said, in part:

'In the introduction of his book, *The Politician Who Laughed*, Fred offered the following account of his personal philosophy, which I think is worth putting on the record—"I was privileged to serve in Parliament with some of the great political performers, masters of the arts of scorn, ridicule, satire and humour, who used them devastatingly to win their point. Humour as practised by the masters of these skills was not for amusement; it was to win an argument, cheerfully yet effectively. Humour to be good should be without malice. It should be good-natured, pertinent, and effective in its application. And you must be able to laugh at yourself."'

Evans went on:

'I think we would all acknowledge these days that that is very good advice. Fred Daly, above all, was a great Australian character, and it is worth saying there are not too many of those left in the Australian Parliament these days. Maybe it is just nostalgia, talking with all the error which we are prone to with nostalgia, but the political process does seem to dry up the juices of the current generation of politicians in a way that never seemed to be the case in earlier years.'

Fred Daly could only agree, just as only Gareth Evans would acknowledge it.

In the Senate, where they conduct the business of Parliament with more civility and good manners than they do in the House, and always have done, the Government's defence of Carmen Lawrence's truthfulness and the Opposition's pursuit of her lack of it, was no more persistent, just a great deal less oafish. The Senate has accommodated itself to the Government's lack of a majority. In the House, where the Government's numbers are enforced ruthlessly, it's a case of never give a mug an even break.

Yet what Paul Keating and Carmen Lawrence needed yesterday, above all, was a Fred Daly, somebody with the qualities and skills to lower the political temperature of a poor political brief with some style and quality, even good humour. Keating simply absented himself, leaving before hostilities began. Sooner or later Carmen Lawrence will surely have to do the same.

Alan Ramsey

**Postscript:** *Lawrence 'survived' far longer than her patron. Keating was gone from public life within seven months, his Government destroyed by the voter firestorm of March 2, 1996. Lawrence stayed a Labor minister until the end and, remarkably, an MP for a further 11 years. Her voters never gave up on her, despite everything. She resigned on the eve of the 2007 election that rid us of yet another messiah who stayed too long. In reality Lawrence's career died by her own hand in the exhaust fumes that killed Penny Easton 15 years earlier.*

# Terminal Decay

AUGUST 30, 1995

TWO DAYS ago Paul Keating made himself available to Parliament, for the first time in two months, to answer questions about his Government's conduct. The last time he'd done so was June 29, the day before Parliament adjourned for its winter recess. And although Parliament resumed eight days ago, Keating aborted his only appearance at Question Time last week by launching a childish censure motion against John Howard.

Rather than answer questions in defence of Carmen Lawrence, Keating took refuge from scrutiny by moving censure of John Howard immediately Question Time was due to begin, and then dumping all over him for two hours before gagging the debate and approving the censure on party lines.The whole thing was a farce, its only point being to deny the Opposition the opportunity to question the Prime Minister.

That was last week. This week, appearing at Question Time on Monday, Keating did the next best thing. He mostly ignored the questions put to him about Dr Lawrence and did exactly what he'd done in the censure debate the previous Thursday—heap vitriol by the truckload on the accursed John Howard who, he told us, was guilty of 'unctuous hypocrisy', was an 'accomplished liar of long-standing', 'someone with the morals of an alley cat', 'the same old shop-soiled, shop-worn political hack he's always been', and 'a joke and an immoral fraud'.

Question Time, as a consequence, was bedlam. It culminated in the incident where the Liberals' Peter Costello, with the words, 'Here, read it', flicked a Lawrence speech, from perhaps a metre away, across the table to land in front of Keating, the speech catching the edge of the table and ending up in Keating's lap. This was later described by the more excitable news reports as Costello 'throwing' the speech, even 'hurling' it, at him.

Costello did neither, even though his action resulted in his suspension for an hour. I can recall several similar incidents over the years and nobody ever got tossed out for them. Gough Whitlam, in a flush of anger, even threw the contents of a glass of water over Paul Hasluck once, and that was back in the days when Parliament was not the castle of contempt its inhabitants treat it like these days. Costello's sin came after the following abridged exchange:

Keating: 'Mr Speaker, I have been in public life here for 26 years. This man (Howard) has left a trail, for 20 of them, slipping and sliding through a criminal evasion of the tax system, Budget deficits undeclared one after the other. As a consequence, having outlived most of his opponents, politically, and seeing them all off the block, he is back here. He has no virtue. He is the same old shop-soiled, shop-worn political hack he's always been.'

Howard: 'I'm supposed to be devastated by that, am I?'

And what question did Howard ask to cop such a blast? Nothing more odious than: 'I ask the Prime Minister—do you accept that the Minister for Human Services and Health (Lawrence) told the truth about the Easton affair when she addressed the National Press Club on 13 April?' Such is Keating's sensitivity in these troubled times.

It was still showing at the usual weekly meeting of Labor's parliamentary Caucus yesterday when Bob Brown (NSW) asked, very gently, what Keating had to say about Labor's national secretary, Gary Gray, telling Lawrence last week she should consider standing down. That was enough for Keating, in defending Gray, to get stuck into Gray's predecessor, Bob Hogg, and into this newspaper.

Hogg's sins live in Keating's paranoia about the conduct of the 1993 election. The *Herald*, a paper Keating likes to despise, was guilty this time of not having published, as the Murdoch papers did, a photo showing Costello 'throwing' the Lawrence speech at him. Worse, there was no comment piece saying what a terrible thing this had been and how the Government had 'won' the Question Time exchange.

Labor is bleeding all over the place, and all our Prime Minister does is kick the tripe out of his opponent, dredge up old, twisted resentments against one of his party's most effective and loyal servants, and rail against a newspaper that doesn't report politics in a way that pleases him.

Last February, in the first opinion polls published after Howard regained his party's leadership, both major polls showed the Coalition nine and 10 percentage points ahead of Labor. Yesterday the same two polls showed Labor trailing by 10 and eight points respectively. Labor and Keating have gained nothing in seven months. It's all beginning to smell like 1975, and so is the Government's behaviour.

Alan Ramsey

# Chapter 12

# An End and a Beginning

## No-one to Blame but Himself

MARCH 2, 1996

THIRTEEN IS Paul Keating's number. In an odd quirk of history, the Government he formed after ousting Bob Hawke in December 1991 was the 13th Federal Labor administration since 1901. Now, four years on, Labor completes 13 years continuous office, almost to the day, during which, against all odds, Keating won his only election on March 13, 1993. And

were he to again defy electoral gravity today it would be only Labor's 13th election victory in 95 years.

It all has a fatalistic symmetry about it.

Andrew Fisher formed three Labor administrations, Hughes two, and Watson, Scullin, Curtin, Forde, Chifley, Whitlam, Hawke and Keating one each. Ten Labor prime ministers in all, yet only seven were legitimised at the ballot box. Watson and Hughes became Labor Prime Minister only by internal turmoil, not by victory at the polls. Frank Forde filled the shoes of a dead man for a single week. The seven others led Labor to 12 election victories between them, with Hawke (4) and Whitlam and Fisher (2 each) the only leaders to succeed in multiples.

And to get this last 13 years into perspective, understand that Labor has governed for only a bit more than a third, or 33 years, of the 95 years Australians have been voting as a nation. The conservatives were there for the other 62 years, winning, in all, 25 of the 37 elections this century which kept or changed various administrations (four other elections involved the Senate only).

So 12 winning Labor elections in 95 years isn't much of a strike rate, particularly when you consider seven of those victories (in 10 elections) have come in the last 23 years. That's a lot of barren Labor years and a lot of lost elections when you realise their opponents won all but five of 27 elections in the first 72 years of Federation.

Now you know why, historically, impending defeat comes hard to Labor.

They learned how to win through the 1970s and 1980s and to go on winning into the 1990s. All but a handful in the present Government know nothing of what it is to lose, just as they know nothing of being in Opposition. They have, for 13 unprecedented years now, taken winning as their due. Yet only twice in that 13 years—and indeed, in their seven winning elections since December 2, 1972—has winning come easily.

Paul Keating understands this better than anyone. He alone of all his colleagues has been there for all of Labor's seven victories in the last quarter-century, plus three defeats as well. He hates to lose at any time to anyone, not least to John Howard.

'When the government changes, the country changes,' he said two days ago, as he sought to explain, in his last major campaign speech, why to him it was unthinkable voters could get rid of Labor. 'When the government changed from McMahon to Whitlam, the country changed. When it changed from Whitlam to Fraser, the country changed. When it changed from Fraser to Hawke, the country changed. But what we've built in these years (since 1983) is, I think, so valuable, to change it and to lose it is just a straight appalling loss for Australia.'

Well, Prime Minister, if so, that's democracy.

It would also be a fair indication that, rightly or wrongly, a majority of voters not only don't share Keating's view but fervently want change, whatever 'change' might mean. After all, that's usually why people get rid of one government and replace it with another, surely? And if this time, in changing, Labor's defeat means 'an appalling loss to Australia', whose fault is that? The media's? Ralph Willis's? Dopy voters? No. Only the prejudiced and the self-serving will look for scapegoats other than where the blame truly lies.

The reality is Labor lost the last election everywhere but in the counting of the votes. Only Paul Keating and his mythical True Believers didn't recognise it. They wouldn't accept Labor had been reprieved only because of their opponents' political idiocy. They got lost in their self-indulgence, their contempt for disbelievers and the mirage of their own infallibility.

And yet, on election night three years ago, when a Keating of unusual public warmth made that inspirational speech in which he thanked the faithful and promised a government of inclusion for all Australians, he was as close as he'd ever come to being a prime minister the electorate as a whole could embrace.

From there on, for the next three years, it was mostly downhill.

Keating ignored his reprieve and took his victory as business as usual. He handpicked his ministry, governed by cronyism and the dictates of presidential fiat, ignored his Caucus in the same way he ignored Parliament, forgot all about normal prudent political management in his obsessive pursuit of his 'big picture', and was utterly contemptuous of criticism.

And what did the Labor Party do?

Nothing! It let Keating do as he liked. His party rolled over in the same way his Cabinet and his Caucus rolled over. The only person who didn't roll over was John Dawkins, the Treasurer who hit the faithful with a raft of tax increases in his first Budget after the election. Dawkins quit when Keating ignored him a year later and insisted, unilaterally, on going ahead with tax cuts Dawkins argued the economy couldn't afford.

Then Dawkins quit Parliament too and Keating let him go, just as he let Ros Kelly go after she was driven out of Cabinet, not by principle but by her own incompetence. Dawkins's departure brought to Canberra Carmen Lawrence, a political time bomb nobody recognised when she arrived. Kelly's departure brought the worst by-election defeat any government has suffered since Federation. Did the Government learn anything?

Not a bit. Keating went on looking down his nose at everybody and behaving exactly as before, contemptuous as ever. He plunged into his big picture of Mabo and APEC and ignored all the little ones. In doing so, he was massaged by 14 months of John Hewson's discredited leadership and then eight months of the political adolescence of Alexander Downer.

When John Howard re-arrived a year ago, recycled and rehabilitated, Keating greeted him as just another pushover. He never believed Howard could possibly be a threat.

And his party, conned by the election victory in 1993 that nobody really thought was possible, behaved as if it would all be right on the night. Once they got into the campaign, irrespective of what might or might not have been going on in the three years beforehand, Keating would just steamroll the Opposition as he'd done before.

It's all been such a waste.

Keating is a true leader like this country has not seen for a long time. He has courage, commitment and passion. And yet all this he squandered, along with the vast store of electoral goodwill that came with Labor's reprieve three years ago. He has, in the vernacular, simply pissed it up against the wall. His self-indulgence, his cronyism and his arrogance have undone him more thoroughly than John Howard ever could.

The Liberal leader has simply bided his time, kept his nerve and played the basic politics more cleverly than his opponent ever gave him credit for.

Howard may be dull and uninspirational and lead an Opposition as undistinguished and ordinary as any we've seen in a very long time. But he is not a fool and he is not weak and Paul Keating has underrated him as an opponent as surely as he has misread the anger and forbearance of much of the community.

So it was all rather melancholy when Keating stood at the National Press Club two days ago and told his audience: 'The main issue of the election is whether the real government of Australia—not the pretend one, the real one with the real policies, the real beliefs and the real imagination—goes on to continue driving and guiding this country, and believing in this country; or whether we have a group of people who think the only reason they can get into office is buy their way back with money they don't have. I don't think it's come to this, and I don't think the Australian public will, either.'

I think you're wrong, Prime Minister. I think it's all over and you only have yourself to blame. It could have been so different. Thirteen was the beginning and now the end.

Alan Ramsey

# Payday For Perseverance

**APRIL 27, 1996**

IT'S BEEN a long journey. When the new Parliament first meets in three days' time, and John Howard takes his seat, for the first time as Prime Minister, at the centre table of the House of Representatives, he will do so on his 8,017th day in public life. Tuesday marks 21 years, 11 months and 12 days since Howard was first elected to Parliament on May 18, 1974.

It also marks 10 years, seven months and 25 days since his Liberal colleagues first made him leader on September 5, 1985; and just nine days short of seven years since they turfed him out of the position on May 9, 1989; and much longer—14 years and 22 days—since he became deputy leader to Malcolm Fraser (and then a year later, Andrew Peacock) on April 8, 1982; and exactly 15 months since his despairing party finally made him leader a second time on January 30, 1995.

And, of course, just two months since he led the Coalition to victory.

This has been the central quality of John Howard's political career: he wouldn't stay down. He kept getting sandbagged. He even sandbagged himself. He kept getting up again. In a party bereft of leadership talent and riven by its own poison, he wouldn't go away. He outlasted all his rivals, just as he outlasted Paul Keating and drove him out of politics.

Nobody was ever able to do the same to John Howard.

Ten years ago, Keating stood on the front steps of Old Parliament House and promised to 'crucify' him. Ten years later Howard is Prime Minister and Keating is gone from political life, sliding out the back door seven weeks after Labor's worst defeat since 1931 and just a week before the new Parliament was due to meet.

For all Keating's political courage over the years, for all his impact on the political life of this country since 1983, for all his commitment to his perceptions of Labor's cause, when it came to the end of the road one of the most significant and formidable political figures of postwar years either squibbed it or thumbed his nose at the Parliaments he'd either dominated or debauched for so long.

And for those who think it heresy or bile to say so out loud, consider the fact that no fallen Labor Prime Minister—not one—has ever before declined to confront the Parliament and face his victorious opponents after electoral defeat. Whatever his reasons, whatever excuses are offered by his apologists, Paul Keating is the first.

Hawke slunk away after his party voted him out of the leadership, not the voters. He never came into the Parliament again after that party room vote deposed him for Keating

in December 1991, instead resigning on commercial television for a fee the following February. It was as grubby an exit as Keating's subsequently was to be so disappointing.

Labor has only ever produced 10 prime ministers. Watson stayed on in Parliament six years after his Government, Labor's first, collapsed on the floor of the House in September 1904. Fisher formed three administrations, the third after he came back from defeat at the polls in 1913 to win his second election in 1914.

Hughes ratted to an anti-Labor Coalition in 1917 in the midst of the great conscription battles of the time, and went on to serve in conservative governments for years afterwards before dying in 1952, at the age of 90, while still a member of Parliament. Scullin stayed an MP another 18 years—all of them in Opposition or on the Government back benches—after his Government was slaughtered by voters in 1931.

Curtin died in office. Chifley went on to lead Labor to another election loss after his Government was defeated in 1949, before dying, as Opposition leader, in June 1951. Frank Forde was an interim leader for a week between Curtin and Chifley. And Gough Whitlam endured a second election loss, as well as a subsequent six months on the back bench under Bill Hayden's leadership, after his Government went down the tubes in 1975.

So Fisher, Scullin, Chifley and Whitlam were, until Keating, the only Labor prime ministers defeated in general elections. Not one of them beat an instant retreat from politics. All returned to Parliament, two of them, Scullin and Whitlam, to sit subsequently on an opposition back bench. Fisher even came back to win a third term as Prime Minister.

Paul Keating is the exception, the only Labor Prime Minister to lose office at the ballot box and then to resign before the resumption of

Parliament. He couldn't bring himself to sit even for a day opposite a new Government and a new Prime Minister he'd been pouring contempt and ridicule on for 13 years. Not even for a resignation speech.

Instead he resigned in absentia and left it to his colleagues to defend his actions, just as others wrote his press statement of resignation. It was an exit as ignominious in its own way as was Hawke's. And those True Believers who shriek in his defence ignore the irony that the only recent parallel they can call on to excuse Keating's behaviour is, of all people, the despised Malcolm Fraser.

Even Billy McMahon, the Liberal Prime Minister Keating would lampoon unmercifully at times in recent years, returned to the Parliament to sit on an opposition back bench—not for days or months but for years—after he led the Liberals into Opposition in 1972 from the Coalition's 23 glory years of the 1950s and '60s.

But not Paul Keating. History may well treat his Government and his profound political influence over the years far more generously than did the voters eight weeks ago. But it won't ever have much good to say about the manner of his leaving Parliament. Neither it should.

That brings us back to the man who will look across the centre table in Parliament on Tuesday and see instead Kim Beazley and not the opponent who pledged to crucify him. John Howard came into politics amid as much tumult as Keating left it. Indeed, leadership turmoil has been part and parcel of the Liberal Party ever since Menzies quit 30 years ago.

By May 1974, the month of Howard's arrival, there'd already been four leaders in eight years—three of them prime ministers. Within a year, yet another leader, Fraser, had bulldozed his way to the top over the body of Bill Snedden. Another seven months and Fraser was Prime Minister. In the next 20 years, from 1975 to 1995, the instability and turmoil of another six Liberal leadership changes would come and go.

Two would involve Andrew Peacock and two Howard himself. In between were John Hewson and Alexander Downer, one an inspired amateur and the other a complete misfit. Through it all, plus five election defeats on the trot, at least two of them utter debacles in which the Coalition butchered what should have been victories, Howard survived. Now the debacle belongs to the other side and the prime ministership belongs to him.

Who would have thought it as recently as two years ago?

Yet his is a victory for perseverance and stoicism rather than anything else. Howard has endurance, but then so must almost all leaders who make it all the way into The Lodge.

Harold Holt was in Parliament 30 years and four months before he became Prime Minister. Whitlam and Fraser both had to wait 20 years; McMahon more than 21 years. Gorton got there in 18 years but only under the most bizarre circumstances, the first Prime Minister to travel via the Senate. Hawke is the exception: a mere two years and four months from his election as an opposition MP to his election as Prime Minister.

But the political and electoral circumstances involved were exceptional, too.

Yet while John Howard seems to have been around forever, the perennial pursuer of politics' holy grail, he has waited no longer than Paul Keating was forced to endure. In fact, Howard made it to the prime ministership three months quicker. From the day of Keating's election to Parliament on October 25, 1969, until his party ousted Hawke on December 20, 1991, and Keating was sworn in as PM the following day, was 22 years and two months.

Howard's long journey just pips him.

Both have each won and lost one election as their respective party's leader. Only now Keating's prime ministership, like his career, is over. Howard's is just beginning. What he does with it and how long he lasts we'll see. For the moment, for John Howard, it's enough that he's arrived and Paul Keating is gone.

Alan Ramsey

# The Big Picture a Wasteland

**MARCH 9, 1996**

WHEN PAUL Keating packed the family Mercedes onto a truck this week and moved out of the The Lodge and out of Canberra, he left behind a Labor Party shattered like no Federal Labor Government in 65 years. Labor in office in Canberra never loses small. When they go, defeated Labor prime ministers go on the grand scale. Voters have ousted four Federal Labor governments in the last seven decades, all of them by crushing margins. But not since 1931 has Labor been flogged like the Keating Government was flogged last weekend.

Its national primary vote, at 39.1 per cent, was Labor's most paltry since the Scullin Government disintegrated internally and went on to poll 37.7 per cent at the subsequent election in 1931. It was then 10 years before Labor, under Curtin, made it back to the Treasury benches. The defeats suffered by Chifley in 1949, with a 46 per cent primary vote, and

Whitlam in 1975, with 42.8 per cent, were relatively modest by comparison.

Labor took 23 years to return to power after the Chifley Government lost office and seven years after the Whitlam Government's defeat. How long this time?

Well, if what happened in NSW and Queensland is any guide, it could be anything you like to name. These two States, over the years, have been arguably Labor's two most loyal, irrespective of the degradation of Labor's Queensland vote after the party split in 1955. Yet, this time, Labor's primary vote in Queensland was a soul-destroying 33.4 per cent—its worst ever Federal vote in that State in the 95 years since Federation.

Not even in the debacle of 1975, when Bill Hayden emerged as the sole remaining Labor MP north of the Tweed, did Labor's vote hit such an appalling level. Its Queensland primary vote that year was 38.8 per cent. This time, in the fastest growing State in the Commonwealth, it's left with just two of the State's 26 seats—both of them in Brisbane.

Every seat on the vast Queensland coastline, from the tip of Cape York to the Tweed River, is now held by the Coalition. Indeed, nowhere in mainland Australia does Labor now hold a seat outside any of the capital cities, except for two pockets of loyal Labor resistance in the industrial heartlands of Newcastle and Wollongong.

It could have held Kalgoorlie, the vast West Australian hinterland, except it took the incumbent Graham Campbell's Labor endorsement away from him and he went on to hold his seat as an Independent with an even bigger majority than the 10 per cent margin he'd built up over the 15 years he's been there.

So vicious was the anti-Labor mood in Queensland and NSW that John Howard could have won the election in either State alone without having to win a single seat anywhere else. Howard went into the election needing a net gain of nine seats to form a government. The Coalition swept 13 Labor seats in NSW—with Michael Lee still fighting to the absolute fag-end to retain Dobell, south of Newcastle—and took another 11 Labor seats in Queensland.

Labor was dead and buried an hour into the election count.

And nowhere was the debacle more devastating for the defending Prime Minister than in his home State. NSW has been the rock of Labor's electoral base for all the 13 years it was in power in Canberra and for many more years before. It sustained Bob Hawke when he should have lost in 1990. It gave Paul Keating his highest primary vote (48.3 per cent) recorded by any State in 1993 and Labor's best vote anywhere outside Canberra in nine years.

This time Labor's NSW vote disintegrated.

You have to go all the way back to 1906 to find a Federal election where Labor's primary vote, at 38.5 per cent, is smaller than the NSW vote it got this election. In the 1930s and 1940s, despite the split between official Labor and Lang Labor, the NSW Labor vote held up, never once falling below 40 per cent, just as it held after the Great Split in the mid-1950s and at the time of Gough Whitlam's humiliation in 1975 and 1977.

The closest it ever got to breaching the 40 per cent mark in those 90 years between 1906 and now was the 40.7 per cent Labor gained in NSW in the Vietnam election of 1966.

And now, under Paul Keating, it's happened.

It wasn't just the 13 NSW Labor colleagues who lost their seats, all but two of whom held electorates either well outside or on the fringes of the Sydney metropolitan area; it was the massive desertion of voters, too, from many of Labor's safest city seats in the southern and western suburbs. True Believers turned their backs on him, quite literally, in their tens of thousands, right there in Keating's own State and his own capital city.

For all his commitment and passion over the years, for all his ever-changing big picture, Keating's electoral legacy is utter Labor devastation.

His political legacy to his own party isn't much better.

He and Hawke between them, in the 13 years they ran Australia, ran the Labor Party into the ground. They disillusioned the faithful, alienated the loyal and disenfranchised the activists. Perhaps it was inevitable. Perhaps the changes forced on Australia but implemented by Labor could not be denied, whoever was in power. Whatever the case, Hawke and Keating changed the Labor Party irrevocably and maybe forever.

What remains is unrecognisable from the Labor Party Bill Hayden handed over to Hawke in the last days of January, 1983. Perhaps that is inevitable, too, for Hayden himself is unrecognisable from the Labor leader of 13 years ago. Just last year, in his last months as the Queen's Man, Hayden stood in the citadel of Australian capitalism, the annual dinner of the Sydney Stock Exchange, and all but apologised for having been so wrong-headed about democratic socialism.

No wonder Labor loyalists wonder what's going on.

Well, what's going on is that Labor's now left, as a party, out of power everywhere in the country except NSW, including both Territories, and with just 47 seats in a House of 148, with maybe two still to come from the three remaining doubtfuls. Its numbers are 19 out of 50 seats in NSW, 16 out of 37 seats in Victoria and a miserable two seats in each of Western Australia, South Australia and Queensland.

Those three latter States have a total 52 seats between them. Labor holds just six! Or seven, if Kim Beazley finally makes it in the west, as it seems he will do after a see-sawing week. Only in Canberra, the national seat of government where it rains money every fortnight, does Labor hold all three seats. And only in little Tasmania, where it has three of the State's five seats, does it have a majority in any of the States.

That's the real legacy of 13 years in office.

If all that isn't enough to emphasise Labor's absolute humiliation, then consider this: when John Hewson lost the unlosable election to Keating three years ago, Labor gained 4,751,390 primary votes across the whole of Australia—70,000 more than the Coalition's 4,681,822 votes. In the three years since, another 300,000 voters have come on the roll.

Yet, when counting ended last Saturday night, Labor had lost not only the 70,000 lead of three years earlier but another 743,438 voters as well. By 10 o'clock yesterday morning, after a further five days of progressive counting, even though the outcome of the election was cut and dried, the Coalition's national lead over Labor, in primary votes, had stretched to 810,724. The longer the count lasted, the further ahead went the Coalition.

What that means, simply, is that over the three years, while Paul Keating thought his big picture was dazzling everybody, Labor lost almost 900,000 voters, gaining none, in absolute terms, of the additional 300,000 new voters in this election.

Thank you, Paul. Thank you, Bob.

*Alan Ramsey*

# A Wretched Way to Leave

APRIL 24, 1996

MOST LABOR people felt sure this was Paul Keating's last week in politics. While he kept his own counsel, confiding in very few, his colleagues expected him to resign before the new Parliament met for the first time under new management next Tuesday. So did John Howard. Keating told him the day before he moved out of The Lodge a few weeks ago.

It's a pity he meant what he said.

Keating might argue he owed nobody but his family anything, but that is not the point. To simply walk away from public life, resigning in absentia and leaving the Parliament with only a press statement to explain himself, is a denial of much of his political career.

Over the years, Keating has rarely walked away from anything, sometimes to his cost. It's not the nature of the man. To do so now, particularly after the flogging his Government got seven weeks ago, is a wretched note on which to sign off the greater part of 27 years of his life. Besides, he's wrong if he thinks he owed nobody.

He owed the Labor Party and he owed the Parliament, both of which made him. He owed the voters, too. These he variously seduced, manipulated, delighted and infuriated for more than a quarter of a century. In the end they shredded him, but not before they gave him everything, and more, a professional politician can reasonably expect from public life.

That Keating couldn't have waited a few more days to announce his resignation before his peers, however difficult that might have been in the circumstances he was leaving, is the ultimate rejection of Parliament.

So was the fact he tendered his resignation to Government House yesterday. Only ministers resign to the Governor-General, for it is the Governor-General who gives ministers their commissions. Ordinary members are responsible to Parliament and resign to the Speaker.

Not Paul Keating, though, apparently.

After what's happened in recent years, that could have been expected. Nothing more traduced and diminished Parliament than the standards set, as Prime Minister, by the former Member for Blaxland. It's just that, when it came to the crunch, I thought Keating would behave differently. Gough Whitlam certainly did, and he was flogged twice. I should have known better.

Besides, if Keating really meant to quit after his Government's defeat, why wait seven weeks until just before the resumption of Parliament to do so? Why not get out immediately, rather than go through the humbug of hanging around, using his parliamentary office as an employment recruiting agency for former staff, and picking up seven weeks' parliamentary salary, courtesy of the voters who had just rejected him? It's an uncharacteristically mean and miserable way to go.

Alan Ramsey

# The Election Nobody 'Won'

**JULY 26, 1997**

*THE VICTORY The Inside Story of the Take-over of Australia,* by Pamela Williams, Allen & Unwin, 370pp, $24.95 ISBN 1 86448 405 5

THIS IS less a book about victory than about defeat. It is not about a takeover but a hando-ver. Its core is a wilful Prime Minister who destroyed himself, blaming everyone else, and an unwanted leader who remade himself long enough to win by default. It is about a govern-ment corrupted by 13 years of power and an opposition ravaged by 13 years of irrelevancy. It is about a competent Government gone to seed and an incompetent alternative which, finally, learnt how to win by not losing.

It is about leadership, both fatally flawed and invisible. It is about shrewd foresight and blindingly brilliant hindsight. It is about rationalisation and realisation, home truths and half-truths, self-defeating decisions and self-serving excuses. It is about cynicism, pragmatism, stoicism, ego, paranoia, self-delusion, decay and discipline.

Needless to say, it is a book about profes-sional politics.

Sadly, in defeat, it is as much a book about the disintegration of personal relationships as it is about the disintegration of a govern-ment. Just as sadly, in victory, it is more about shrewd and ruthless manipulation than it is about honest exultation.

There is nothing uplifting in this book, either in the manner of the winning or the losing. While that may disappoint the naive and the romantic, it will make just that bit bleaker the outlook of those who give more than a passing thought to the inexorable 'Americanisation' of the political process in this country. Or it should do.

What this book is mostly is a great piece of journalism. Pamela Williams, a writer with *The Australian Financial Review,* had the luxury of total access to the Liberal Party's campaign headquarters in Melbourne throughout much of the five weeks of the 1996 formal election period. As a fly on the wall, she heard and saw everything that went on at the heart of John Howard's winning campaign. And she reports it superbly, with detail and insights most of her colleagues would kill for.

It is all there, from the army of 60 people under Andrew Robb's direction as national campaign director; to the complete funk Howard's team went into when Pauline Hanson started the racism issue running in the first week of the campaign; to the mil-lions funnelled by big business into Howard's campaign coffers through Ron Walker, the millionaire Melbourne 'bagman' as adept at winkling 2,000 meal vouchers out of McDon-ald's for Robb's campaign team as he was at raising money; to the two hessian doormats stencilled with Paul Keating's face that James Packer sent to Walker and Jeff Kennett (think carefully about that!); to the Howard staffers who 'privately vowed revenge' on the ABC for what they saw as a 'typical ABC hatchet job' on Howard by *Four Corners* during the campaign (which, in retrospect, explains a few other things, too).

The book's real meat, though, is the job Keating did on himself, aided and abetted by the blinkered loyalists he surrounded himself with.

Two days after Labor's defeat, Don Russell, the former staffer Keating had brought back from Washington to hold his hand during the campaign, phoned a journalist colleague of mine he had known for years to ask, quite genuinely: 'Why do you think we lost?'

Remarkably, he still didn't understand. Yet Russell as much as anyone had insulated Keating from reality and kept him wrapped in the delusion that only he knew best and that what was going wrong was everyone else's fault. As Robert Ray, one of Keating's senior ministers, would later tell Williams, the problems were there for everyone to see, but nobody could get to Keating. 'There was an impenetrable barrier around Keating of (his senior staffers) Russell, Watson, Bowan and Bowtell,' said Ray. 'They weren't sycophants. They were just like-minded people.'

Don Watson, Keating's speechwriter, was as embittered as anyone. He mostly blamed the political reporters, telling Williams he 'would not have crossed the road to rescue a member of the press gallery from a rabid dog'. Nor would Keating have done so for Gary Gray, Labor's national secretary and the campaign director he treated with contempt.

The disintegration of Keating's relationship with his party machine is recounted by Williams in all its bilious detail. It is a very destructive story.

It is also self-serving. Williams writes first-hand of Howard's ascension. She was there.

Yet the death of Keating is a grave-robber's tale. Williams has to rely on what Labor's key players told her after the funeral. And most of them talked to her—all except Keating. Understandably, they all look better at his expense. Political history in the third person usually does. Human nature and self-interest say so.

That is the book's other flaw: Williams makes no judgments of her own. She tells a story and leaves it to sit there, the work of a meticulous but detached observer. Readers must draw their own conclusions. In reality, Keating debauched whatever chance his Government had, not in the death throes of a botched election campaign but over the whole of the three years from Labor's reprieve in 1993.

And his colleagues, all of them, from top to bottom, whatever their fears, just sat by, intimidated into silence, and let him do it. They all share the blame. Labor's self-destruction is a great political story. That it should be wrapped up and sold as a 'victory' for the mediocrities—small in mind and mean of spirit but stoic in their discipline—who replaced them is both to misread and distort what occurred.

Alan Ramsey

# Chapter 13

# Mates, Twerps and Deadbeats

## The Mick Mates

APRIL 10, 1996

ALMOST THE last time John Howard made a substantive speech about Mick Young, he insisted his ministerial conduct 'totally disqualified him from membership of the Government of this country'. That was in August 1984, a time when Howard was Andrew Peacock's deputy Opposition leader and Mick Young was Labor's friendly fixer who, as a minister, kept coming unstuck.

Yesterday, almost 12 years later, Howard, now Prime Minister, announced that his new Government, after Young's death from cancer last week, would accord Mick a State funeral in 'recognition' of his 'distinguished contribution to the nation, and as a mark of respect'.

The 'mark of respect' I understand. Young was a formidable political servant of the Labor Party and a considerable figure, in organisational terms, in Labor's electoral and political rehabilitation in the late 1960s and 1970s. But his 'distinguished contribution to the nation'? Nobody would be more embarrassed than Mick himself.

Mateship, the institution of the long lunch, a huge appetite for life, his political instincts, his sense of humour and his organisational and parliamentary skills were Mick Young's long suits. As a minister he was utterly undistinguished, at times an abject pain in the Government's rectum and a highly embarrassing political one to boot.

Three times in five years his careless disregard for prudent ministerial behaviour endangered his career and embarrassed his Prime Minister. The first time, he was forced to resign his portfolio and sit out almost six months on the back bench. The second time, he was made to stand down from Cabinet while an inquiry investigated his next stupidity, finally exonerating him of 'improper' behaviour.

The third time he simply up and quit politics altogether, walking out on the Government in circumstances and at a time when the political fallout could hardly have been worse. How all or any of this can be thought of as a 'distinguished contribution to the nation' I have no idea. Nor, of course, did anyone else think so at the time.

Death always has this ability to make the absurd acceptable. This is particularly so with public figures, not least politicians. So it is that John Howard, in Opposition, can brand Mick Young a ministerial disgrace and then, years later as Prime Minister, honour his memory as a distinguished servant of the people with a State funeral.

Mick, of course, was a character of larrikin charm and personality, and that can excuse a great deal, as well as blur, if not obliterate, the memory. I remember him most for the small network I once wrote about as the Mick Mates, those with enduring personal friendships and deep loyalties to each other who coalesced around Young all that time ago in the late '60s when he was beginning to make his mark in the Labor Party.

The bond that brought them together was Gough Whitlam's drive for The Lodge, and now, 30 years later, the Mick Mates remain as close as ever. Eric Walsh, the lobbyist and former Murdoch journalist who got Mick into so much trouble in the grubby Ivanov/Combe business in 1983 and who was probably his closest friend, was there when he died of cancer last week. John Menadue, whose relationship with Young incestuously helped sustain each of their careers over the years, signed his name to one of the more generous obituaries yesterday.

Brian Johns, another old Mick Mate whom Young first lobbied in the Hawke Cabinet to head up the ABC long before the Keating Government appointed him, was a founding member of the group. So was Stephen Fitz-Gerald, the former Ambassador to China.

The group's patronage of each other and their parallel careers, all sponsored by Labor and owing much to Young's influence, was one of the constants of contemporary politics.

They were known as Labor's Irish Mafia. Some day someone will write a book about them and, if they get it right, it will be as heady a political journey as you could read.

I also remember Young's role in the Hayden years of Labor leadership when Mick went from being one of his closest colleagues to complete alienation after Hayden, in a blazing row over the phone, dumped him as parliamentary manager of Opposition business, a role in which Young was supreme. And then later, with Young now a Hawke ally, Hayden manoeuvred to kill Mick's chances of becoming Labor's national president in 1980.

He succeeded, too. Years later, after they'd become allies if not friends again, Young got the presidency Hayden had denied him years earlier. Now all will be forgotten, like much else, at Friday's State funeral.

Alan Ramsey

# One of Life's Pleasures

**MARCH 30, 1996**

GORDON BILNEY was never your stereotype politician. He was a professional diplomat for 16 years and a Whitlam Government adviser before the Parliament claimed him as a Labor MP in 1983, yet diplomacy was never his strong suit, at least in politics. A free and roly-poly spirit, he moved through 13 years of national political life, six of them as a minister, with considerable style and acerbic wit before the voters of Kingston, in Adelaide, caught up with him four weeks ago and turfed him out.

And in going, as was Bilney's wont in many things he did, he'll not be forgotten for the manner of his leaving, at least in South Australia.

First, some background.

On Australia Day—the day before Paul Keating called the election that ended his Government and Gordon Bilney's political career—the people of Noarlunga in Adelaide took part in local festivities to mark the national occasion. As *The Advertiser*, the city's only daily newspaper, reported two days ago, 'community groups gathered to display their achievements in front of a large and admiring crowd of residents, council staff and local identities'. Among these 'community groups' was Bilney, the local Federal MP, who took advantage of the occasion and the crowd and the coming election to display a stand of Labor Party posters and electioneering material.

That did not sit well with the event's organising committee. And when its chairman, John Seamer, remonstrated with Bilney and asked him to remove his political wares, according to *The Advertiser*, 'a heated argument' ensued— an 'altercation' that so angered Seamer he later wrote to Bilney accusing him of 'discourteous and unco-operative' behaviour.

Seamer's letter, dated February 26, said in part: 'As your application stated your stall was for the purpose of promoting Australian citizenship and you were advised that no political material was to be displayed, the committee was well within its rights to ask you to leave.'

Bilney saw it differently. In a letter dated three days after his election defeat, he said so—in very specific and cogent terms. It was this letter that saw SA's Liberal Premier, Dean Brown, rise in the State Parliament this week and declare portentously: 'I think it is a disgrace that a Federal minister of the Labor Government should send a letter like that to a local government body . . . To have carried on in that manner, to have written that style of letter, whether he has just been defeated or not, shows he is not fit to be in Parliament.'

John Seamer said of Bilney's 'bloody insulting' letter: 'I would have belted him on the nose.' And what did Bilney's letter say?

'Dear Mr Seamer,' he wrote on March 5.

'I saw today your letter of 26 February, 1996. One of the great pleasures of private life is that I need no longer to be polite to nincompoops, bigots, curmudgeons and twerps who infest local government bodies and committees such as yours. In the particular case of your committee that pleasure is acute. Yours sincerely,

'Gordon Bilney.'

Alan Ramsey

# A Matter of Opinion

**MARCH 27, 1996**

WHEN VICTORIA'S Premier, Jeff Kennett, appeared on two interview programs on commercial television at the weekend, he spent much of his time slagging the interviewers, and the media in general, as a convenient means of avoiding answers to questions he didn't like, particularly the wretched issue of the tender process for Melbourne's casino.

The overt or implied you're-an-idiot technique of dealing with the press is, of course, not new among politicians. Joh Bjelke-Petersen and Bob Hawke each made it an art form, Bjelke-Petersen with his patronising don't-you-worry-about-that approach, and Hawke, when aroused, with his more malevolent personal intimidation.

Most times it worked, too.

All politicians know how successful the personal put-down can be as a device to kill off or divert an unwanted line of media questioning. Not all, however, have the force of personality to use it effectively. Kennett does. So did Bjelke-Petersen, Hawke, Neville Wran and, of course, Paul Keating, to name the more obvious.

What they also had in common was an intense dislike of and contempt for the media, or sections of it. Wran and Keating despised the Fairfax papers, in particular the old *National Times* and this newspaper. Keating was also contemptuous of the former Melbourne-headquartered Herald and Weekly Times group as an establishment Tory bastion, and he revelled in its takeover in 1986 by the rapacious Rupert Murdoch.

Kennett's bete noires are the ABC and *The Age*, the Melbourne broadsheet he refers to as 'the Spencer Street Pravda' and which he has publicly wished would go 'bankrupt'.

In 1992, during the election campaign that brought Kennett to power, two incidents poisoned him irrevocably against the national broadcaster. In one, a *7.30 Report* television crew followed him into a lavatory to film him at the urinal. In the other, a reporter from the same program asked him a series of personal questions that so infuriated him he cut the interview short and ordered the reporter and her crew out of his home.

Kennett was still livid when a Liberal colleague arrived an hour later. Although the interview was not broadcast, Kennett never made himself available to the *7.30 Report* again. As Premier, he blackballed the program, an attitude since extended to its current affairs parent, *Four Corners*. He has not relented in the four years since.

And Kennett still rails against the ABC every chance he gets, as viewers of either of his two weekend interviews could hardly have failed to notice.

Kennett's feud with *The Age* is no less bitter. It goes back years and has much to do with his prejudices and perceptions of the newspaper's political coverage, an attitude reinforced after Kennett closed a small advertising business run by his wife, Felicity, following politically uncomfortable disclosures by *The Age* after Kennett became Premier.

So deep is Kennett's animosity that when *The Age* last year offered a discounted price to new readers, he claims to have cancelled all State Government departmental subscriptions and re-ordered at the discount price, supposedly saving taxpayers $56,000. Kennett still tells the story with malicious glee.

Kennett can do little to influence *The Age*'s political reporting or its publishing future, but God help the ABC should he ever be in a position to do it dirt. As he said last Sunday, with obvious feeling: 'The ABC is lucky I don't have any authority whatsoever in determining their outcome . . . If I had my way, I'd like to hang on to my eighteen cents a day and invest it more wisely.'

The real problem, of course, is that most politicians like the media to be uncritical propagandists and want to believe you're a fool or an enemy if what you write or broadcast does not advantage their individual or party political interests.

Six months ago the then Prime Minister suggested in a friendly phone call that what I should be doing each Saturday is 'putting a bazooka right up that little (expletive)'s backside'. Two weeks into the recent election campaign, after I suggested Labor was going to lose, he phoned in less friendly terms to tell me I was a 'deadbeat'.

A matter of opinion.

Alan Ramsey

# $7.5 million for Sour Grapes

**MAY 12, 2004**

REMEMBER THE Hewetts? The last time I wrote about the brothers was on November 27, 2002. The time before was April 13, 2001. Hal and Don Hewett had this idea 19 years ago to export table grapes to Europe. But they lost everything: their grand plan, their Riverina vineyards, their financial backers, their livelihood, their 28-hectare family farm, even their marriages. And in losing everything they blamed the bureaucratic sludge of two government agencies.

The Hewetts' nightmare grew out of the simple premise they wanted to grow and sell overseas 'natural sultana' grapes, but were opposed by the Victorian Department of Agriculture, which didn't want them undermining its own scheme, adopted by most Sunraysia grape growers in Victoria, to export a rival variety, the Thompson seedless.

To thwart them, the Hewetts insisted, the State body had acted in concert with a federal agency, the Australian Quarantine and Inspection Service (AQIS), 'deliberately, unjustly, unethically, vindictively and illegally', by banning the export of natural sultana grapes. And that is what the bizarre fight for the past 19 years has been about.

It has involved, at various times, five governments in Canberra and Melbourne, a raft of senior ministers across the years including Labor's John Button and John Kerin and the Coalition's Tim Fischer and John Anderson, the former ACTU secretary Bill Kelty, Paul Keating's speech writer Don Watson, various Senate committee hearings since 1995, and internal departmental inquiry rejected as a fit-up, and an investigation by the Commonwealth Ombudsman that, in 1999, upheld the core of the Hewetts' claim.

You see, despite everything, the brothers never gave up. Thus on September 11, 1999, after the Ombudsman had found in their favour, the Howard Government wrote to the Hewetts and asked them to submit a compensation claim. This they did under a wondrous bureaucratic creation called the Scheme for Compensation for Detriment Caused by Defective Administration. And yes, I'm serious.

What the Hewetts asked for was $68 million, itemised to the last dollar ($68,074,768). And they went on persisting for the next 4 1/2 years, just as they'd done over the first 14 years. Hal Hewett could be seen in Parliament's corridors from time to time with his shopping trolley of documents, relentless in his lobbying. He was once even banned from the Prime Minister's office.

And for 4 1/2 years, while the Government's lawyers considered the claim, Labor's Kerry O'Brien kept pushing at Senate estimates hearings for 'the latest' on what was happening. As in the following exchange, at a Senate hearing on November 3 last year.

Senator O'Brien: 'We have raised the Hewett matter a number of times.'

Official: 'Yes, Senator.'

O'Brien: 'It is no laughing matter, is it?'

Official: 'No, it isn't, Senator. It is very close to resolution.'

O'Brien: 'Those are very brave words. I might quote them back to you next year.'

And, three months later, on February 16, he did. O'Brien told the same 'brave' official from November: 'Is it true the matter remains unresolved?'

Official: 'That is true. We have been working hard (on the claim) since 1999. It has been a difficult matter because it goes back to the mid-'80s, which makes it nearly 20 years old. It has not been an easy. But I can happily report an offer [has been made to the brothers] . . .'

O'Brien didn't say so, but he might well have cried, 'Hallelujah!' I know the Hewetts did. Nineteen years is a long time. So what happened? Well, I can't tell you. Not in detail. The Howard Government, in making its offer, insisted on a confidentiality agreement. And it refused, to the Hewetts' immense disappointment, to publicly apologise. But this I do know. The Hewetts accepted the offer.

They had no choice. Everyone involved over the years, in their pursuit of bloody-minded bureaucracy, told them, brutally: 'Take the (expletive) money.' And they did. The cheque has been paid and cleared. What the Hewetts got, I understand, was $7.5 million.

Hallelujah!

Alan Ramsey

# Chapter 14

# John Howard's Australia

## Anatomy of a Web of Lies

MAY 30, 1998

TELLING A lie is easier than killing it, even for a prime minister. A lie is a lie, and once it is out on the main street no amount of passing traffic can ever truly skittle it. John Howard told a lie on May 2, 1995. Then he told more lies to reinforce the first lie. He had no choice. To protect himself from what he judged a serious threat to his last chance ever to become Prime Minister, John Howard lied then went on lying.

Now, three years later, he is telling still more lies to hide that first lie.

They are not even clever lies. How can they be when they are so easily exposed by plain English and the public record? That Howard should now pretend he said one thing three years ago when he said something totally different is not only foolish but desperate. It's as if he believes that should he now insist often enough that black is white then maybe he can convince us we're all really colour blind.

See what you think. This column has three times, since May 1995, written about what happened on May Day 1995 and in the subsequent 24 hours. Pulling it all together in an anatomy of The Great GST Lie presents an open and shut case of how 'Honest' John is just as quick as the next political shyster to try to sneak the wool over voters' eyes should the circumstances warrant. And, in May 1995, he certainly did that.

The great irony is that in the beginning Howard told the truth. Absolutely and utterly. But then the truth panicked him and he bolted and he's been running ever since.

May Day 1995 was a Monday. That day Howard, as Opposition leader, was guest speaker at a Bankers' Trust lunch in Sydney. What he had to say was mostly about what he thought the Keating Government should do in the Budget the following week. He spoke from notes. His office later issued a transcript. It excited little news interest. ABC radio carried a brief report that night and *The Australian Financial Review* had a story next morning. Neither report mentioned the GST.

Howard's speech made only a brief, negative reference to the GST, repeating yet again that voters had passed judgment on John Hewson's GST proposal at the 1993 election and 'nothing remotely resembling it' would be included in Coalition policy at the next election. This was hardly news, which was why it was ignored.

However, after his speech Howard took questions, and a businessman asked why, if a GST was so economically sound, Howard would not again support it? That's when Howard told the truth, and the whole truth. He said: 'At the last election, the Opposition put all its eggs in the GST basket. I mean, you

can criticise the marketing. You can say, with the benefit of hindsight, that it was very, very poorly marketed.

'It WAS poorly marketed. But it was the subject of one of the most dishonest fear campaigns I've ever seen in Australian political history, and that was orchestrated by the current Prime Minister (Keating). Of course he knew it was a good reform; and in 1985, when he went to the (Hawke Government's) tax summit and he and I were on talking terms, I went to see him the morning the White Paper (proposing Keating's version of a GST) came out, and he gave me a signed copy and said, "This is a moment in history, John."

'I gave him very strong support in 1985. As shadow Treasurer (to Andrew Peacock as Opposition leader), I was the most vociferous supporter, politically, of the GST anywhere in Australia, apart from him. But, when the roles were reversed (eight years later), he squibbed it. He ran the most ferocious fear campaign against it. Now, to say, in the face of all that, that the Liberal Party has got to do that again, well, you know, we would occasionally like to win, you know.

'The fact is that the last election was a referendum on the GST. There is no way we can have it as part of our policy for the next election. As to what happens some years in the future, I don't want to—I don't know. But the GST cause was lost in the last election because of a highly political, highly success-ful campaign, run by Paul Keating against his better instincts as to what was good for Australia's economic future.

'Hewson campaigned hard for it. I sup-ported him. But the electorate said no, and in a democracy you've got to take note of that. What happens in the future I don't know. But I have to say that it won't be part of our policy in the next election, and you can thank Mr Keating for that, and nobody else.'

Nothing could have been more honest. The remarks reflected Howard's attitude exactly. He was no less in favour of a GST than he'd ever been, but he wasn't prepared to risk another massive rejection by voters given how Labor's adroit campaigning had mangled Hewson the previous election. As Howard said, he wanted to win. For the time being, therefore, a GST was off the Liberals' agenda. As to the future, who could tell?

And that, of course, was the real news.

Here was Howard still keeping open the GST option for some undefined time after the coming election. But the story went beg-ging. Howard's GST answer was not included, for whatever reason, in the transcript released later that day to the Canberra press gallery by Howard's office. And those reporters at the lunch, including some of the best known economic writers in the country, didn't wake up to what he'd said.

All except one.

Robert Garran of *The Australian* taped the whole thing. And that night he wrote a story saying Howard had 'left open the possibility of the Coalition reconsidering a GST some years in the future'. His paper ran it as a single column on its front page next day. And that's when John Howard panicked. It's also when he told his first lie, although we didn't know it was a lie at the time.

On the morning of May 2, in response to Garran's story, Howard's office issued a four-sentence statement headed 'Tax report is wrong'. The statement said: 'Suggestions in today's *Australian* that I have left open the possibility of a GST are completely wrong. A GST or anything resembling it is no longer Coalition policy. Nor will it be policy at any time in the future. It is completely off the political agenda in Australia.'

Having missed the real story the previous day, the press gleefully pursued the denial. The Opposition leader campaigned that day on NSW's Far North Coast, and when he appeared at the Tweed Heads Civic Centre at lunchtime, the rat pack was waiting. And Howard, now committed, went on lying.

Q: 'You've left the door open for a GST, haven't you?'

Howard: 'No. There's no way a GST will ever be part of our policy.'

Q: 'Never ever?'

Howard: 'Never ever. It's dead. It was killed by the voters last election.'

Q: 'Were you misquoted in today's *Austral-ian* then?' Howard: 'Well, any suggestion that I left the door open is absolute nonsense. I didn't. I never will. The last election killed the GST. It's not part of our policy, and it won't be part of our policy at any time in the future.'

Q: 'So Robert Garran got it wrong?' Howard: 'Yes.'

No, he didn't. Garran got it right. He had quoted Howard accurately. And now, three years later, we know he interpreted Howard's attitude with absolute precision, too.

Paul Keating seized on the remarks at the time as evidence Howard 'wants to do by stealth what John Hewson failed to do by fanatical advocacy'. Generally, however, the press ran the sort of headline Howard desperately needed: that he had 'ruled out a GST as Coalition policy at any time in the future'. It was an absolute political imperative that Howard get the GST back into hiding.

And he succeeded.

By lying.

The story was overwhelmed by what would prove the Keating Government's last Budget a few days later. It simply vanished in the face of Howard's unequivocal, unqualified, bald-faced assertions. Vanished, that is, until 27 months later. Then, with the election safely won and Howard as Prime Minister, he announced in August 1997 his 'great adventure' in tax reform that he wanted to 'share with the Australian people'.

Ten months later we are still awaiting any detail. So far nothing. Zilch. All we know is the GST that Howard insisted three years ago would 'never ever' be 'part of Coalition policy' at 'any time in the future' is now to be the core of his 'great adventure' into tax 'reform' should he be re-elected. And how does he explain this stunning reversal?

Two days ago Howard pretended he didn't understand what 'all the fuss' was about, just as he pretended that 'never ever' had only ever meant his Government's first term. He told Radio 2UE: 'When you say your position is X, and you have an election and you stick to that, what is wrong with then saying, "We have changed our position, but before we implement our changed position we are going to give you a chance to vote against us"?'

He told Parliament the same day, with similar breathtaking glibness: 'Apparently there is something wrong with a political leader going to the public and actually telling them what he is going to do if he gets re-elected. I went to the 1996 election saying there would not be a GST in our first term [sic]. I go to the coming election saying we are going to reform the tax system and I will tell them how we are going to reform it.

'The reply of the leader of the Opposition is that, even if the public votes for our reform policy, he will try to stop it. I operate on the principle the Australian public are the political masters of this nation. They will decide. The Australian public are entitled to be told before an election what a government will do after the election. They do not deserve to be misled. They do not deserve to be deceived. They will not be misled and deceived by me . . .'

Pardon, Prime Minister?

Could you repeat that?

Alan Ramsey

# The Never Ever GST

**MAY 29, 1999**

SO ANTS is here, ready or not. You know, A New Tax System, as the Government promotes its new GST regime. It isn't the same beast John Howard first let loose on voters eight months ago, but the Prime Minister is in no state to be picky. He must take what he can get. And the cut-down, revamped GST finally unveiled early last night is all that Meg Lees and her Democrats, with their Senate balance of power, will let him have. For the present, anyhow.

I've been looking at that paragraph for three hours. It is now 5pm the next day (Friday). So far the 3pm unveiling of the detailed agreement promised by the hasty phone call earlier this afternoon has not materialised. The editor of this Saturday page is getting nervous. The editor of this newspaper is even more nervous. There is a vast space to fill and nothing yet to fill it. Time is running out. I understand now how John Howard must have felt as he waited each day, every day, this week for Meg Lees to tell him if he'd won the lottery.

A phone call just after lunch claimed he had. Broad Senate agreement with the Democrats had come, at last, the previous night, said the caller. Now the boffins, that morning, had finally got the figures to tally. The big press conference announcement could only be a matter of time. Would only be a matter of time. Yet as the afternoon wore on and nothing happened I recalled the shrieking headline on *The Australian*'s front page two days ago ('PM, Lees close to deal') and wondered if this was another massive leg-pull by a government with a sense of humour after all.

We learned at 5.50pm it wasn't.

That's when Howard's office called a press conference for 6pm in what is known as the Blue Room, a truly apt venue for all those who think, like Tasmania's Brian Harradine, that a GST may be the economic pits. It is a small room just down from the Cabinet room and almost immediately opposite the Prime Minister's suite; and on the dot of 6pm, there was Howard, flanked by a sombre Peter Costello, announcing for the history books: 'This is a truly historic moment in the economic modernisation of Australia. We will have, after the passage of the legislation, a new tax system for the new century.'

Howard has been wanting to say that ever since the elections.

Now Meg Lees and her Democrats have made it possible. Lees drove this agreement through her party and, in doing so, made politically redundant a Labor Opposition which, for almost two years now, has insisted the only good GST is no GST. Kim Beazley and his troops must now sustain their rage until the next election more than two years

away and hope the GST proves as voter unfriendly as they think. Labor has nowhere else to go.

Yet neither Howard nor Costello looked like politicians who'd got the jackpot. Howard had all his lines ready. It was a 'great breakthrough for Australia', he told us. 'All the major elements' of his original ANTS proposal 'remain intact'. 'The full measure' of the original income tax cuts 'have been preserved'. But they were lines delivered with all the verve of an obituary. You felt, instantly, despite the Prime Minister's rhetoric, that the concessions he'd had to make to Meg Lees must surely have been huge.

And when Howard and Costello left, and Lees took their place before the cameras and the microphones, her effervescent manner suggested the Democrats indeed had got what they wanted, and more than they expected. Lees, carefully, announced 'in principle' agreement with the Government. What the Democrats had wanted, she said, was to negotiate a 'fairer package'. And she added, beaming: 'Well, we've certainly done that.'

We shall see. At 6.30 on a Friday night the first blush tells us nothing, and there was no time to examine the fine print. Newspaper deadlines say so. I kept thinking it was all very deliberate by the Government, just to keep the initial newspaper punditry to a minimum.

But if immediate impressions are anything to go by, John Howard has had to concede far more than he was letting on last night, and certainly much more than his hardline Treasurer on his own would have given. It was, after all, Peter Costello who, during the election campaign last year, gave an interview in the final fortnight in which he asserted, without qualification, that ANTS was 'non-negotiable' and, if rejected by a hostile Senate, would mean a new election.

And everything about the Treasurer's body language during the eight days of negotiations since Meg Lees and her colleague, Senator Andrew Murray, flew to Melbourne to see Howard last week, suggested Costello hated giving an inch to the detested Democrats and he would have done just about anything not to have been there with his Prime Minister. Or so Lees would later indicate to her party room this week.

The breakthrough came on Thursday night.

The last round of negotiations went from 10.30pm until 12.40 yesterday morning. Howard had cut short dinner at The Lodge at 8.30 with Max Walsh, the new editor-in-chief of *The Bulletin*, and Paul Bailey, *The Bulletin*'s editor, to return to his office in Parliament House to await the outcome of the Democrats' latest party room meeting—their seventh in four days.

That meeting went for three hours. And when Lees and Murray finally arrived at Howard's office after the Prime Minister had waited almost two hours, the talks that followed in the Cabinet room went on until well after midnight. After Lees and Murray left, Howard and Costello stayed on another hour with their advisers. Howard did not get back to The Lodge until 2am. It had been a long night.

But a win is a win. And Howard's political need for an agreement with the Democrats was absolute. Whatever the cost in concessions, the political cost to his leadership could have been graver had the Government not given ground. Now Howard must sell his revised package, with its part food mix and other Democrat giveaways, to the electorate at large all over again.

Alan Ramsey

# Obscene and Vulgar Behaviour

**FEBRUARY 12, 2000**

NOBODY COULD be sure exactly where obscene and vulgar behaviour, corporate and political, began and ended this week. Not just with George Trumbull's $13.2 million pay-off for having been tipped out of AMP, you can bet. And if Stan Howard, from his comfortable address in Sydney's eastern suburbs, wasn't looking too flash as corporate chairman of a failed regional textile company in the Hunter Valley, how much worse do you think brother John was looking as political chairman of the board in Canberra?

That wasn't all, of course. The day the NSW Premier, Bob Carr, sounded off in Sydney about the 'obscene and vulgar largesse' handed out by the AMP board to see off Trumbull was the very same day in Senate estimates we learnt that John Moore, our extraordinary Defence Minister, last October hired another fallen corporate giant, John Prescott, former head of BHP, as a part-time adviser to the minister at a fee of $3,000 a day.

This is the same John Prescott who walked away with $11 million when he stepped down as chief executive of BHP in 1998 and BHP shares instantly jumped in value. Coincidentally, Carr on Wednesday lumped the financial largesse accorded Prescott when he left BHP in 1998 in exactly the same 'obscene and vulgar' category he put the Trumbull payout. In Canberra, though, Moore seemed either to be unaware or not to care.

What, you wonder, has happened to everyone's political judgment in the Government? Here we have the Prime Minister being accused by Rupert Murdoch's national newspaper of 'favouritism if not corruption' because of his foolish involvement in the

Government's 'special' rescue bailout of $6 million from taxpayers to the workers of brother Stan's busted textile company, at the same time as a senior member of his Cabinet is hiring a millionaire corporate heavy as a part-time adviser at a cost to taxpayers of $3,000 a day.

Obscene and vulgar behaviour, indeed. Certainly politically.

And what will Prescott do? In a letter stamped commercial-in-confidence, Moore wrote to Prescott on October 29: 'Following Cabinet's acceptance of the report you prepared with Sir Malcolm McIntosh (head of the CSIRO who died this week) on the Collins Class submarines, I have decided it would assist me to receive independent advice on the industry arrangements to support a sustainable Australian submarine capability. I am most grateful you have indicated you would be prepared to assist me in this matter, and accordingly I am writing to appoint you as the Australian Government industry representative, submarine industry arrangements . . .'

The multibillion-dollar Collins Class submarine program is a supposed development nightmare that remains one of the most underreported stories in Canberra. Prescott is welcome to it, even at $3,000 a day part-time, though taxpayers are unlikely to thank him for it. Sooner or later, though, the bedevilled submarine program is likely to make the same sort of headlines as the Government's rescue of National Textiles' 340 workers is now doing. Maybe then $3,000 a day to help fix it won't look so great.

However, this is not what Howard was thinking after he read *The Australian*'s front page on Thursday morning and its editorial inside. It was a good old-fashioned bake, the like of which we have not seen for a very long time, and the Government's inherited submarine program and its multiple problems would not have been further from the Prime Minister's

mind. At 10.50 that morning, after much discussion in Howard's office, his press secretary walked upstairs in Parliament House to alert the press gallery to an 11.30 press conference.

Paul Kelly wrote during the 1990 election campaign that Andrew Peacock, then Opposition leader, was unfit to be Prime Minister because of the Liberals' attempt to exploit what Kelly saw as a racial issue. But not, in my memory, has anybody outside the heated daily exchanges by the politicians themselves actually suggested a serving Prime Minister could be guilty of corruption. Not until this week, for that is what *The Australian* did.

Later, much of the reporting would talk of an 'angry' Howard 'lashing out' at the attack against him. Fiddle. What was remarkable about his press conference in the concrete courtyard outside his office on Thursday morning was just how controlled Howard seemed, given the gravity of *The Australian*'s accusations. There was very little outward evidence of real anger at all, despite occasional language such as 'this rotten attempt' and 'despicable slur'. Howard's language was quite temperate in the circumstances, and so was his demeanour. Cold maybe, but not cold anger.

What betrayed Howard's nervousness was his stumbles over words. His opening statement, clearly rehearsed, was as strong and forceful as you would expect. But when, 'for the record', he reeled off a series of denials in support of his handling of the issue of his brother's company: 'I deny absolutely the decision undermined my probity, I deny the decision was improper, I deny the decision amounted to "favouritism, if not corruption" in the words of *The Australian* editorial' he blurted out the word 'desire' the third time before quickly correcting it to 'deny'.

Later, to questions about what was different between the National Textiles workers in the Hunter Valley, to whom the Government is giving $6 million, and the Pelaco workers at

Braybrook, on the outskirts of Melbourne, who've also seen their factory go bust and their jobs and their entitlements with it but to whom the Government is giving nothing, Howard referred to the 'Braidwood matter' instead of 'Braybrook'.

Small points, but slips like this say much about how a politician is feeling the pressure. Howard is an old hand at handling pressure, yet he was showing it on Thursday. And not, I don't think, because of *The Australian*'s accusations. These, in context, were proper concerns, given the Prime Minister's direct involvement.

No, what Howard has been exposed doing is not so much playing favourites with his brother but open and direct favouritism to the political issue so baldly exposed: the plight of a group of workers in a threatened industry in a country area. To ignore them was to feed even more the political monster alive and thriving outside the cities that government, all governments, are letting rural and provincial Australia simply die bit by bit.

It was the bush vote, the country vote, that galvanised Howard and his Cabinet, not Stan Howard's difficulties as chairman of the company concerned. The Government has been under immense pressure from its own rural backbench members and the reality of what happened to a complacent Kennett Government in Victoria [swept from office just months earlier]. In responding to this electoral imperative, it downplayed or misunderstood the equally dangerous political problem of the Prime Minister's brother's involvement.

So did Howard.

He told us at his press conference how he had fully briefed Cabinet this week on Stan Howard's involvement in the issue and his own limited, as he saw it, discussions with his brother. He had intended to leave the ensuing Cabinet discussion and decision. Instead, his colleagues had encouraged him to stay. So he did. 'I commenced to give affect to an intention to leave the Cabinet room while the final decision was taken,' Howard would explain later. 'But I was encouraged by my colleagues to remain because they could not see any point (in his leaving), having made a full disclosure of the association.'

It was clumsy language, but an even clumsier decision. Clearly, everybody's political antennas had shut down. Either that, or the smarter ones kept their mouths shut and said nothing. Worse, despite the Prime Minister's insistence he remained at arm's length from his brother and his company, the reality is he did not.

When two of its directors came seeking the Prime Minister's ear a year ago, Howard's door was open. He saw them. They got nothing in the end, because Howard told the relevant industry ministry, Nick Minchin, to handle the request on its merits and Minchin ruled their request did not qualify for government assistance.

But they got to the Prime Minister's office. And they got in the door because of brother Stan and the identity of one of the directors, whom Howard described on Thursday as 'one of the most prominent people not only in the Sydney business community, the Sydney Jewish community, but also the textile industry in Australia'. They got a hearing. They got access. And several times later, by phone, Stan Howard got access, too.

John Howard can't see this as involvement. Maybe he does now that it's blown up in his face, but he won't admit it. And because none of the journalists travelling with him, when he saw the delegation of Hunter Valley textile workers nine days ago, said anything at the time or raised any queries about the propriety of the meeting, Howard came to Canberra this week perhaps under the false illusion it didn't matter. That, at least, is what some in the Government were arguing yesterday.

It is a silly argument.

And when the Prime Minister openly admits he gave a hearing to prominent corporate businessmen involved with his brother's company, even if they got nothing, but also concedes he wouldn't see a group of the dispossessed Melbourne textile workers when they came to Canberra before Christmas to plead their case, you have to say the Government deserves all it gets.

It was Howard in the 1996 election campaign who pledged: 'The most important thing any government can do is build a sense of trust, a sense of integrity, a sense of honesty (with) the Australian people.' In a climate of obscene and vulgar political behaviour, it is a pledge looking pretty ratty four years later.

Alan Ramsey

# The Stolen Generation

AUGUST 4, 2000

'I WAS at the post office with my mum and auntie and cousin. They put us in the police ute and said they were taking us to Broome. They put the mums in there as well. But when we'd gone about 10 miles [16 kilometres] they stopped and threw the mothers out. We jumped on our mothers' back, crying, trying not to be left behind. But the policemen pulled us off and threw us back in the ute. Our mothers were chasing the car, running and crying. We were screaming in the back. When we got to Broome they put me and my cousin in the lock-up for two days waiting for the boat to Perth.'—**Confidential evidence 821, WA. The incident occurred in 1935, shortly after Sister Kate's Orphanage opened in Perth to receive 'lighter skinned' children.**

'By the late 19th century, it had become apparent that although the [fullblood] indigenous population was declining, the mixed descent population was increasing. The fact they had some European 'blood' meant there was a place for them in [white] society, albeit a very lowly one. Furthermore, the prospect this mixed descent population was growing made it imperative to governments [these]

people be forced to join the workforce instead of relying on government rations. In that way the mixed descent population would be both self-supporting and satisfy the needs of the developing Australian economy for cheap labour.'—**From _Bringing them Home_, 597-page report in 1997 by Sir Ronald Wilson, former High Court judge and president of the Human Rights and Equal Opportunity Commission (HREOC).**

'Mr Neville, the Chief Protector of WA, holds the view that within 100 years the pure black will be extinct. But the half-caste problem was increasing every year. Therefore, their idea was to keep the pure blacks segregated and absorb the half-castes into the white population. Sixty years ago, he said, there were over 60,000 fullblood natives in WA. Today there are only 20,000. In time there would be none. The pure blooded Aboriginal was not a quick breeder. On the other hand the half-caste was.'—**Brisbane's _Telegraph_ newspaper, May 1937.**

'In Neville's view, skin colour was the key to 'absorption'. Children with lighter skin

colour would automatically be accepted into [white] society and lose their Aboriginal identity. Assuming the theory to be correct, argument in government circles centred around the optimum age for forced removal. At a Royal Commission in South Australia in 1913, 'experts' disagreed whether children should be removed at birth or about two years old.'—From ***Bringing Them Home***, HREOC report, 1997.

'Every morning our people would crush charcoal and mix that with animal fat and smother that all over us, so that when the police came they could only see black children in the distance.' —**Confidential evidence 681, WA, of events in the 1930s.**

'I remember all we children being herded up, like a mob of cattle, and feeling the humiliation of being graded by the colour of our skins for the government records.'—**Confidential submission 332, Queensland. Woman removed in the 1950s to Cootamundra Girls' Home.**

'Another method of forcing people of mixed descent away from their families and communities was to change the definition of 'Aboriginality' in the protection legislation. People with more than a stipulated proportion of European 'blood' were disqualified from living on reserves or receiving rations. This tactic of dispersing Aboriginal camps was used in Victoria and NSW. An analysis of the definition of 'Aboriginality' has found more than 67 definitions in over 700 pieces of legislation.' —**From HREOC report, 1997.**

'As the ultimate purpose of removal was to control the reproduction of [mixed blood] people with a view to 'merging' or 'absorbing' them into the [white] population, girls were targeted for removal and sent to work as domestics. Apart from satisfying a demand for cheap servants, it was thought the long hours and exhausting work would curb the sexual promiscuity attributed to them by non-indigenous people.'—**HREOC report, 1997.**

'The policeman patted his handcuffs, which were in a leather case on his belt, and which my sister, May, and I thought was a revolver. "I'll have to use this if you do not let us take these children now." Thinking the policemen would shoot mother because she was trying to stop him, we screamed, 'we'll go with him, Mum, we'll go.' Then the policeman sprang another shock. He said he had to go to the hospital to pick up Geraldine, my baby sister, who was also to be taken. The horror on my mother's face!'—**Tucker, 1984, quoted in HREOC report.**

'In 1883 the NSW Aborigines' Protection Board was established to manage the reserves and control the lives of the estimated 9,000 Aboriginal people in NSW. By about 1890 the board had developed a policy to "remove children of mixed descent" from their families to be "merged" into the White population. The board reasoned that if the Aboriginal population, described by some as a "wild race of half-castes" was growing, then it would

somehow have to be diminished. If the children were to be de-socialised as Aborigines and re-socialised as Whites, they would have to be removed from their parents.'—**Dr Peter Read, submission 49 to HREOC.**

'According to the then Acting NSW Premier [in 1909], ". . . quadroons and octoroons will be merged in the white population, and the camps will merely contain the fullblooded Aborigines and their descendants . . . By this means, considerable savings will be effected in the expenditure of the Aborigines' Protection Board. There is hope in years to come the expenditure in respect of Aborigines will reach vanishing point."'—**Quoted by NSW Government submission, HREOC report.**

'The NSW Aborigines' Protection Amending Act 1915 gave total power to separate children from their families without having to establish neglect. No court hearings were necessary. The manager of an Aboriginal station or a policeman in a town might simply have them removed. The racial intention was obvious enough. Some cut a long story short when they came to that part of the committal notice, "Reason for board taking control of the child". They simply wrote, "For being Aboriginal".'— **Dr Peter Read, 1981, quoted by HREOC report.**

'Some parliamentarians of the day, such as the Hon P. McGarry, strongly opposed the 1915 amending Act. According to McGarry, it allowed the board "to steal the child away from its parents". This "act of cruelty" was a scheme to take the children "prisoners" and "to gain absolute control of the child and use him/her as a slave without paying wages". Another MP assessed the amending Act as tantamount to the "reintroduction of slavery in NSW".'—**NSW Parliamentary debates, 1914/1915, quoted by HREOC report.**

'By 1921, 81 per cent of the children removed in NSW were female. That proportion had decreased only slightly by 1936. Girls were sent to Cootamundra Girls' Home, established in 1911, until the age of 14, then sent out to work. In any one year in the 1920s there would have been between 300 and 400 Aboriginal girls apprenticed to white homes. Many girls became pregnant, only to have their children in turn removed and institutionalised. Generations of Aboriginal women passed through Cootamundra Girls' Home until it closed in 1969.' —**Quoted by HREOC report.**

'When the girls left the home, they were sent out to work in the homes and outlying farms of middle-class white people as domestics. On top of that you were lucky not to be sexually, physically and mentally abused, and all for a lousy sixpence [a week] that you didn't get to see anyway. Also, when the girls fell pregnant, their babies were taken from them and adopted out to white families. They never saw them again.'—**Confidential submission 617. NSW woman removed at eight years with her three sisters in the 1940s, and sent to Cootamundra Girls' Home.**

'In 1937, the first Commonwealth/State Native Welfare Conference was held, attended by all States (except Tasmania) and the NT. Although the States had been influenced by each other's practices to that time about the "Aboriginal problem", this was the first time [the issue] had been discussed at national level. Conference was sufficiently impressed by the idea of "absorption" to agree that, "This conference believes the destiny of the natives of Aboriginal origin, but not of the fullblood, lies in their ultimate absorption by the people of the Commonwealth, and it therefore recommends all efforts be directed to that end". In relation to children, the conference resolved that ". . . efforts of all State authorities should be directed towards the education of children of mixed race blood at white standards, with a view to their taking their place in the white community on an equal footing with the whites".—**From HREOC report, 1997.**

'The children were screaming, and the little brothers and sisters were just babies, of course, and I couldn't move. They were all around me, around my neck and legs, yelling and screaming. I was all upset and didn't know what to do and didn't know where we were going. I just thought, "well, they're police, they must know what they're doing. I suppose I've got to go with them, they're taking me to see Mum." That is what I honestly thought.' —**Confidential submission 318, Tasmania. Removal from Cape Barren Island, Tasmania, of eight siblings in the 1960s.**

'There was never a "generation" of stolen children.' —**From executive summary of Howard Government's 55-page submission to Senate inquiry, April 2000.**

Alan Ramsey

# Reality Overboard

**FEBRUARY 16, 2002**

OCTOBER 5, 2001 was a Friday. That was the day John Howard drove to Government House and secured his November 10 election. He announced the date early that same afternoon. Next morning, several thousand kilometres distant, a patrolling naval aircraft spotted an Indonesian fishing boat near Christmas Island in the Indian Ocean. The frigate HMAS *Adelaide* was directed to intercept the fishing boat with its 223 SUNCs ('Suspected Unauthorised Non-Citizens') and five crew. The local time was 4.14 in the afternoon of Saturday, October 6.

Four months later and what followed between the fishing boat and the Australian ship of war still infests and infects national political debate in this country. Consider the sequence of events.

This account comes from the military, not the politicians or the bureaucrats. It was put together by Major-General Roger Powell, a 30-year army career officer, at the direction of Admiral Christopher Barrie, chief of Australia's defence forces, who in turn had been directed by the Prime Minister.

Howard wrote to Barrie on November 13, three days after his winning election. Barrie wrote to Powell on November 20. Powell completed his 30-page report on December 14. Howard tabled that report in Parliament three days ago. With it he tabled a second report, this one of 60 pages, drawn up by a middle-ranking bureaucrat, Jennifer Bryant, in Howard's own department.

But it is the military account here, dealing as it does with the actual events off Christmas Island on the three days in question Saturday to Monday, October 6 to October 8 inclusive. It puts what happened into perspective, irrespective of what politicians might or might not

have done in using or abusing the detail to suit their own ends. Which, unsurprisingly, they did. That is, politicians of both sides, along with a frenzied media.

In his directive, Barrie instructed Powell to 'conduct by way of routine inquiry' a factual survey 'of the proximate cause, events, circumstances and imperatives' surrounding 'the rescue at sea' by HMAS *Adelaide* of 'the children and other passengers and crew' of the Indonesian fishing boat designated SIEV 4, a navy acronym for the 'fourth Suspected Illegal Entry Vessel'. Powell was also to develop a chronological 'key events narrative' of 'the making, custody, handling, transmission and receipt of all records and policy advice' about the rescue, 'including written notes, recorded telephone conversations, photographs and film, reports of proceedings, situation reports, electronic message traffic, and ministerial submissions and correspondence'.

Powell did so. His 13-page chronological narrative begins with the frigate *Adelaide* shadowing the fishing boat from 10 nautical miles away late on the afternoon of Saturday, October 6, and continues: '7.55pm Long-range rigid hull inflatable boat (RHIB) departs *Adelaide*. 8.41pm RHIB alongside SIEV. 9.13pm Warning one given to master of vessel. Ignored. RHIB returns to *Adelaide*.'

Sunday, October 7: '4.30am RHIB continuous attempts to issue [verbal] second warning (imprisonment penalties). Ignored. 4.53am Second warning issued. (Tied to bottle and thrown onto boat. Examined by SUNCs and thrown overboard.) 5.16am Boarding party ordered to be prepared to board SIEV if it enters Christmas Island contiguous zone. 6.35am *Adelaide* directed to conduct a positive and assertive boarding. 6.59am Four aimed 5.56mm

warning shots fired 50 feet in front of vessel. No response. Department of Immigration warning passed again. 7.01am SIEV 7 nautical miles inside Australian contiguous zone.

'7.02am Aimed burst 5.56mm fired 50 feet in front of vessel. No response. 7.14am Boarding party advised that if 50-calibre warning shots do not cause vessel to stop it is to aggressively board vessel. 7.18am *Adelaide* fires 23 rounds 50cal into water ahead of SIEV. No response. 7.37am Boarding party ordered aboard. 7.45am Boarding party in control of SIEV. 7.50am CJTF 639 [commander of joint military task force, based in Darwin, Brigadier M.J. Silverstone] has a clear and well-documented phone call with commanding officer, *Adelaide* [Commander N.S. Banks] and determines that the vessel has disabled steering, is dead in the water, 7/8 nautical miles south of contiguous zone. SUNCs threaten mass exodus. Man in water, child thrown over the side.

'8.02am Number of SUNCs threatened to commit suicide and throw children overboard unless taken to Australia. Disturbance on SIEV. [Radio] aerial ripped from mounting and thrown over side. 8.40am Boarding party prevented a number of SUNCs from jumping over the side. 8.43am Man overboard declared. Five SUNCs in water. 8.45am All SUNCs retrieved by RHIB. 8.49am Six more SUNCs overboard. 8.56am SUNCs appear to be destroying the SIEV upper-deck fittings. Additional SUNC overboard (12 total by this time).

'8.57am SUNC on top of coach house dressing small child in life jacket and preparing to throw small child overboard. Child not thrown overboard. Child and father returned to wheelhouse. Boarding party officer advised child and father under observation. Some SUNCs being returned to SIEV from overboard. 9am IDC meeting [of bureaucrats in Canberra] chaired by Ms Jane Halton from [Prime Minister's Department] attended by Mr Bill Farmer [head of Immigration Department] and Group Captain Walker, Strategic Command. At this meeting Ms Halton stated that 14 SUNCs were in the water and that they were throwing children in. During this meeting, Mr Farmer takes a call from Minister Ruddock and reports that a child has been thrown over the side of SIEV 4.

'9.01am Boarding party Bravo inserted in SIEV. 9.08am Steering capability lost on SIEV. Appears steering sabotaged by SUNCs. 9.26am Male SUNCs in view of wheelhouse threaten to throw women and children overboard. This did not occur. 10.28am Main engine disabled by SUNCs. Cooling lines slashed and fused to engine head. Rags and plastic thrown on casing to produce thick toxic smoke. 10.42am Final SUNC overboard. Returned to SIEV (13 total).

'10.49am *Adelaide*'s damage control team embarked on SIEV to repair main engine. Repairs complete. SIEV under way. 12.57pm SUNCs light small fire on deck. Fire extinguished. 1.31pm Boarding party extracted. 1.38pm Four photographs of man overboard incidents sent to CJTF 639 by Adelaide's secret email system. 5pm Group Captain Walker reports to IDC he had no documentary evidence to indicate any children had been thrown from SIEV 4. There is some discussion as to who originally had stated [children overboard] at the morning IDC meeting. Farmer claimed it was Group Captain Walker. Walker claimed it was Ms Halton. Halton made no comment.

'5.11pm SIEV displays distress signals. Sabotages steering [again]. Engine damaged [again]. Water in fuel. Starter motor engine damaged. PM [time uncertain] During a reception aboard HMAS Kanimbla, Rear-Admiral G.F. Smith [head of the Australian Navy] remarks to Brendan Nelson, parliamentary secretary for Defence, that "the [navy's] task was very difficult, made even more so by the most recent boatload jumping/pushing people into the water, including children".'

'8.31pm [Defence Minister] Reith receives a paper on his home fax from [the Prime Minister's department] entitled, "Options for handling unauthorised arrivals, Christmas Island boat". The report stated that the efforts of *Adelaide* to return SIEV 4 to international waters were "met with attempts to disable the vessel, passengers jumping into the sea and passengers throwing their children into the sea".'

Monday, October 8: '8am SIEV lost power. Water ingress increases. Pumps provided by *Adelaide*. 3pm SIEV under tow. 7.26pm Water coming into SIEV over freeboard. 8.08pm SUNCs start entering water as bow dips under. *Adelaide* orders first life raft released. Tow cut. 8.12pm *Adelaide*'s ship's company enter water to assist SUNCs into life rafts. 9.06pm SIEV three-quarters submerged. Children into RHIBs. Adelaide launches three life rafts. 9.12pm All children in life rafts. 10.08pm All 223 SUNCs on board Adelaide.'

And then SIEV 4 sank with all its SUNCs safe.

No thanks to the SUNCs, of course. Their purpose was obvious. They intended doing whatever it took to reach Australia. They sabotaged their own vessel, issued various threats of self-destruction, carried out none, and ignored the navy's every attempt to turn them back to Indonesia. They were as determined to get here as the Government was to stop them.

And in the end it got them nowhere.

They never got to Australia but they did get taken aboard the Adelaide. In turn, they were offloaded in Papua New Guinea and/or Nauru. There they stagnate, still, in detention camps. No 'suspected unauthorised non-citizen' coming down the people-smuggling route has made it to the Australian mainland since the *Tampa* defied Howard and the Government saw its chance. And if anyone thinks that what has been going on in the new Parliament this week, four months later, with a Labor Opposition still desperate for an excuse to explain its own political ineptness and lack of policy courage, is anything more than the emptiest of political farces, then they should think again.

Boat people and their attempts to manipulate their way into this country by whatever means possible, including ramping up the media, was always the Government's issue, however it played—honestly, dishonestly, opportunistically, ineptly, over-enthusiastically, whatever. The Australian community at large was never going to cop them. They still won't, whatever the new Labor leader's sterile effort to refight the election.

There is no cover-up. Confusion and stupidity and some panic among some players who should have known better. But Howard himself has released the two reports Labor is trying to hang him with, just as he released the supposedly damning navy video two days before polling day. All the supposed furore is political smoke, no more.

*Alan Ramsey*

# Whites Only on the Gravy Train

JULY 19, 2003

GEOFF CLARK is a blackfella who looks like a whitefella. Even worse, he thinks he can behave like one. When Clark went to Ireland last year on a trip as the most senior elected official of Australia's peak Aboriginal organisation, ATSIC, he took his wife. Clark's board had approved the trip. Clark's minister, Philip Ruddock, approved Clark's wife going with him on the basis she had 'significant duties'. Taxpayers weren't asked but they paid the bill. Taxpayers always pay the bill. The Clarks were away for 10 days. Their trip cost $31,000. Last year, just before the Clarks went to Ireland, Philip Ruddock spent 15 days in Switzerland, Canada, Malaysia, the Philippines and Korea. The cost was $113,404 and 67 cents. Taxpayers paid that, too.

Ruddock's trip in October followed an earlier overseas visit in August. This first trip lasted 18 days. It took him to South Africa, 'Yugoslavia', Greece, the Czech Republic, Austria and Britain. He also took his wife, Heather, with him. This time it cost taxpayers $122,165 and 58 cents. Indeed, Heather Ruddock went on both her husband's trips last year (total cost: $235,570.25). I do not know if she had any 'significant duties' or if she just went shopping and sightseeing and enjoyed herself. Nobody asked the Ruddocks before they left, least of all the Prime Minister.

John Howard, too, was busy overseas last year, you'll remember. Very busy. And, like Trudy Clark and Heather Ruddock, Janette Howard went along as well, also at public cost. You'll likely be a bit stunned to learn what that cost was. That is, the cost during the calendar year 2002 of the overseas travels of the Prime Minister, wife and entourage. Total: $3,551,035. Yes, I blinked, too. For this the Howards went to the United States twice for 10 days in January–February ($1.15 million) that included Singapore and Indonesia, and a week in June ($467,480). They also went to Britain twice, in March and April (total cost: $323,730), which included the Queen Mother's funeral.

Then there was the trek through Europe—Germany, Greece, Italy, Belgium and France in the first fortnight of July. That was the trip that got all the publicity a few months back after we learnt, at Senate estimates, that our own Kirribilli royal couple had paid $171,000 including a $10,000 late checkout fee to spend four nights in the so-called royal suite of a swank Rome hotel. Those two weeks in Europe ended up costing Australian taxpayers a tick over a million dollars ($1,025,638). We got the final cost a few weeks ago on Parliament's last day before the winter recess.

Only you had to look hard to find it.

The Government tables parliamentary travel costs every six months. In doing so it buries the ministerial travel in with the travel of all the parliamentary other ranks. Often the figures can be misleading. For example, the 561-page phone book of figures on overseas travel for the first six months of 2002, which was made public in December, put the cost of the Europe tour at $268,907 (and 75 cents). The most recent 524-page release three weeks ago, covering travel for the second six months of last year, simply added another $756,731 (and 1 cent ) to the cost of that particular trip, without any reference to the earlier figure.

The same thing happened in relation to the Howards' trip to the United States in June last year. This time $54,697 of the cost showed up in the parliamentary release last December, and then another $412,783 three weeks ago. It's a neat way of hiding some of the costs, if you think politicians would resort to such weak and sneaky behaviour.

That brings us back to Clark and his $31,000 trip to Ireland with his wife. A couple of weeks ago, the Murdoch daily *The Australian*, got very shrill over its disclosure that Clark had, it claimed, spent only two days at a week-long conference in Ireland last November, and it fumed and fulminated about the dastardly waste of money and presumed fraud. This week, as the Ruddocks once more left Australia on yet another trip to Britain and elsewhere, a letter went out under the minister's name calling on Clark to 'show cause' why Ruddock should not dismiss Clark as ATSIC chairman for supposed misbehaviour.

I mean, $31,000 of taxpayers' money is, after all, $31,000, even when your own international travel bill (fully met by taxpayers) is, as Ruddock's was for calendar 2002, $280,276 (and 41 cents). But if Ruddock, urged on by the urgers, is out there watching Clark's overseas spending, who is watching Ruddock's?

Not John Howard, surely, with his $3.55 million travel bill for the year carefully tucked away in 1100 pages of eye-glazing arithmetic? Perhaps *The Australian* might get off its sanctimonious bum and have a look at the Prime Minister's costings for a change, because the Parliament surely is not. It is, though, much easier to plant a good front-page kick up the backside of the reviled blackfella who not only looks like a whitefella but thinks he can behave like one, too.

The parable does not end there.

John Anderson, the nice National Party family man from north-west NSW who has proved himself one of the country's most ineffective and least knowing politicians, not to mention, God help us, senior ministers, decided that, with Ruddock and Howard absent overseas, he would have a few words to say on ABC radio about the naughty Clark and his $31,000 overseas trip. What was needed, said the nice

Mr Anderson, were some 'sound explanations' and ' I think it is appropriate he be given a proper opportunity to explain himself'.

Really? This is the same Anderson who shows up in the parliamentary travel records as one of the Government's most dedicated users of the RAAF's domestic VIP jet fleet in recent years, more particularly since he became deputy PM , on the departure of Tim Fischer, another who was a ferocious user of VIP jets as well as a dedicated international traveller (as Trade Minister) at public expense.

Over the last six months of 2001 at the very time, coincidentally, that a difficult federal election campaign was being waged, Anderson, the farmer who lists his home base at Gunnedah, got into taxpayers' pockets to the tune of half a million dollars in VIP flights and charter aircraft ($297,885 for VIPs, and $204,654 for charters). In the first six months of the following year, Anderson's use of the VIP fleet was also formidable ($149,657 for VIP flights, $182,297 for charters) and still exceeded $200,000 in the last six months of last year ($196,180 for charters, $30,446 for VIP flights). Maybe Anderson, too, could 'be given a proper opportunity to explain himself'.

I mean, why do some ministers use VIP flights and charters like a local taxi service? The Prime Minister, of course, never travels on scheduled domestic services these days, racking up VIP flight bills like I don't think we've ever seen, even though there have been some pretty heroic Labor users of the VIP fleet, among them Kim Beazley. John Howard's VIP flight bills for air travel within Australia: $1,072,315 last year; $715,724 in 2001; $569,790 in 2000; $480,387 in 1999; $840,000 in 1998 (an election year!); $321,120 in his first 18 months of office.

In all, the better part of $4 million in seven years.

And this by a prime minister who came to office promising an end to waste and extravagance, and who sees nothing wrong in blowing $4 million on his RAAF domestic taxi service. Terrific. A bit more Howard free spending, now that you've got the taste. His personal staff of 42 (annual collective salary: minimum $2.75 million) consumed just on half a million ($498,201) in tax-free accommodation allowances in election year 2001.

Last year these allowances collected by the prime ministerial staff totalled $226,964; plus $258,696 in the Government's first 18 months (1996/97) and $175,255 in 1998. A total $1.1 million, tax free, for 42 staff in a bit more than four years.

There are many more horror figures from the official lifestyle of this Government that promised so much in ridding us of 'waste and extravagance' in public life, yet seems to have forgotten about abiding by its own harsh, uncompromising attitude to the unemployed and myriad other unfortunates in the community whom this Government always seems to be lecturing about good work habits and poor behaviour.

We can drown in figures, and that is easy to do when you try to wade through seven years of parliamentary dossiers that each look like phone books. But if we take just one year, the most recent calendar 2002 then our Prime Minister cost the nation, over that 12 months, just under $8 million in VIP flights, personal car usage ($167,000), domestic travel allowance, staff allowances and car usage, overseas travel, and staff salaries.

To that you can add Howard's own salary and allowance package ($294,476 a year) plus the cost of full board and lodging and security at two official residences The Lodge in Canberra and magnificent Kirribilli House in Sydney. These latter figures are ferociously hidden but they would not be less than $2 million a year.

So there you have it. John Howard, the Prime Minister who promised to make us all relaxed and comfortable, mucks along, in the eighth year of his prime ministership, at a cost to Australian taxpayers of nothing less than $10 million a year.

Alan Ramsey

# Anniversary Sludge

MARCH 8, 2003

JOHN HOWARD wants to fudge the present and Bob Hawke wants to rewrite the past. Listening to Howard you wonder at the audacity of his Government's charade these past six months in its quite shameless pretence over the impending war on Iraq. Listening to Hawke and his acolytes reminisce over the Second Coming 20 years ago you wonder how it was his 26 ministers in that first Hawke Government in 1983 had anything more to do than sit about and marvel at the wondrous feats of their new messiah.

Some reality, please.

Labor's vote under Hawke diminished every election after 1983. His Government in those first four years from 1983 until its third election win in June 1987 was likely as good as anything this country has seen and much better than we're used to. But the reason why this was so is that the Government was, essentially, run by five people, not one.

Four of those people were Paul Keating, Peter Walsh, Ralph Willis and John Dawkins. The fifth was Hawke, and his economic surrogate, Ross Garnaut. These five (plus Garnaut) were the members of the Labor Government's initial expenditure review committee, its cabinet within a cabinet. They were the very heart and soul (plus Coalition dills) of the longevity of Labor's 13 years in office.

Three nights ago, when Labor gathered in Canberra to remember that first winning election 20 years earlier, four of the key five people were absent. Only Bob was there, drinking in the adulation, feasting off much of the bullshit backslapping in the media, particularly the Murdoch papers, reliving where he always liked to be and wanted to remain, at the very centre of the political universe.

But from 1983 it was downhill all the way, through three more election victories, each one finagled on a smaller aggregate vote than the one previously, until in 1990, his last election victory as leader, the Coalition under the despised Andrew Peacock clearly outpolled the now-silver-maned messiah.

And a year later, when Keating exiled himself for six months on Labor's backbench after Hawke broke his word and his bond to his deputy and Treasurer, the Hawke Government fell apart. Excuse me, but remember, Bob? John Hewson was doing you like a dinner. You and those who'd saved you from Keating in June 1991—Beazley, Gareth Evans, Robert Ray, Michael Duffy, Nick Bolkus and Gerry Hand—in the main had no idea how to deal with Hewson's consumption tax agenda. None.

Labor's support plunged. So did Hawke's. People forget by just how much, and the resulting Labor panic. By Christmas Hawke was gone, the first Labor Prime Minister turfed out by his party while still in office. Keating was the new messiah, and deservedly. And he managed yet another election victory when Labor had no business doing so. And he did it by exactly the same means John Howard has skewered Labor under Kim Beazley and now Simon Crean for the last seven years—by sheer political mastery.

So please, while Wednesday night's anniversary dinner might have been old Labor folks night, run by Beazley and Ray and their new partner in Labor cabaret, John Faulkner, don't anybody kid themselves the Hawke years were anything more, politically, than the journey of a skilled and relentless narcissist whose high water mark was that very first election victory 20 years ago and who then remained Prime Minister for the next eight years largely by the ability and energy of those band of colleagues who first made him and then unmade him and the idiocy of his Coalition opponents.

Anyone who thinks differently has been eating the same mushrooms too many of the Hawke toadies have been feeding off all these years.

Alan Ramsey

# At Home in a Mugs' Lair

SEPTEMBER 9, 2006

JUDITH WRIGHT died six years ago. Yet when the Federal Parliament next met four weeks later there were not condolences, no eulogies. The death of one of Australia's most eminent daughters and literary figures was ignored by John Howard and Kim Beazley and pretty much every other politician. Only two MPs, both backbenchers, acknowledged Wright's death for the parliamentary record. A.D. Hope's death 18 days later went unremarked altogether.

I thought Colin Thiele's death on Monday this week was going to be similarly passed by, until the Democrats' Natasha Stott Despoja, of Adelaide, got to her feet in the Senate on Wednesda afternoon and intoned: 'I move that the Senate notes the death of Colin Thiele, a children's writer from South Australia; recognises that Mr Thiele helped form children's respect and love for the Australian landscape as well as telling good stories; and notes that Mr Thiele loved writing for children.'

The author of the much-loved *Storm Boy* and 80 other children's books of the past 60 years would surely have agreed. The Senate did as it was asked, formally and without ceremony. Nobody else said a word.

To make your mark by the power and eloquence of the written word, unless you are a Nobel laureate, is nowhere near enough in this country. It seems you have to wrestle crocodiles and poke snakes and generally act like a mug lair, if not an idiot, for the amusement and wonder of the television masses, if your passing is to attract the attention and rhetoric of our political leaders.

Said a suitably sombre Howard the instant the Parliament met on Tuesday: 'I seek the indulgence of the House to say a few words. Steve Irwin's death yesterday in bizarre, tragic and in some respects quintessentially Australian circumstances has not only shocked and horrified the people of Australia, it has brought forth around the world an outpouring of grief and emotional expression of regard for this remarkable man. As the Cinderella Man, Russell Crowe, put it so well: "The crocodile man was the Australian many of us aspire to be . . ."'

A fawning Beazley was no less inspired.

'I echo the remarks of the Prime Minister,' Beazley intoned. 'I know they are heartfelt. We are all aware of the strong relationship the Prime Minister had with Steve and his family. The Prime Minister in particular would have been hurt by the events of yesterday as he contemplated the words to say in this chamer today. The nation went to bed in shock last night and this morning it arose in sorrow . . .'

Germaine Greer [who dismissed Irwin as a 'self-deluded animal tormentor'] was, if anything, gentle. However, the Liberals' Michael Keenan (WA) reflected the quality of the Government's gene pool when he fulminated in the House on Thursday night: 'I am sure almost all Australians have taken offence at the latest outrage from one of Australia's least favourite exports. Germaine Greer's tasteless diatribe attacking Steve Irwin is exactly what Australians have come to expect. However, this is unforgiveable, even for her . . .

'I normally would not consider it particularly good practice to single out a particular individual for criticism [under parliamentary privilege], and it is not something I would normally do. But I think her comments deserved to be repudiated for the rubbish they are. Germaine Greer once said Australians are 'too relaxed to give a damn'. But I can say, from the correspondence I have received today, this is definitely not the case. They do care when the feelings of a grieving family are so wilfully disrespected so a second-rate expatriate can insert herself, yet again, into the media spotlight.'

And political second-rates do, what?

Alan Ramsey

# A Decade of Indulgence

**FEBRUARY 25, 2006**

SO THE Howard Government is a decade old. Ten years ago this Thursday voters replaced Paul Keating's mob with John Howard's mob. Already our newspapers have published near as much gush as they gave a dead Kerry Packer a month ago. Robert Hill celebrates in his own way. Four weeks ago, on January 20, he quit as Defence Minister and Senate leader. On the Government's birthday he quits the Parliament. Both Houses then close for three weeks for the Commonwealth Games, would you believe. Hill won't be back when Parliament resumes on March 27. After a quarter of a century in political life he says goodbye to the Senate on Thursday. His decision sets two bars.

Hill is the 32nd minister in the Government's 10 years to resign, either by choice or by force—an average of a bit over three a year. And he'll be Howard's 15th appointment of a Liberal Party politician to a lucrative (mostly), prestigious overseas post. All but three— former leader and rival, Andrew Peacock; his former Sydney colleague and defeated MP, John Spender; and the disgraced former South Australian Premier, John Olsen—were members of Howard's Government.

The Prime Minister's patronage of his own side of politics is not modest. The major capitals to which Howard has sent his party mates have been London (3), New York (2), Los Angeles (2), Washington, Paris, Chicago, Pretoria, and Dublin/the Holy See (2). Minor appointments have sent other Liberal politicians to Cyprus, Norfolk Island (2) and Christmas Island. Now Robert and Diana Hill are going to the United Nations.

There is a lovely story about the UN post.

Our ambassador there lives in one of two Manhattan apartments the Menzies Coalition Government bought in the early 1950s. The multimillion-dollar address is a very upmarket 1 Beekman Place, overlooking the East River. Both apartments are on the fifth floor. Apartment 5A is the New York residence of our UN ambassador. Apartment 5C is the residence of our consul-general to New York. Apartment 5A is the bigger of the two, though 5C is anything but a slum.

In 1978, when Malcolm Fraser had one of his ministers, Bob Cotton, knighted, and sent him to New York as consul-general for three years, Cotton insisted on having the bigger apartment, 5A. The Government acquiesced and our UN ambassador, a career diplomat, was moved into the smaller 5C.

Much later, after the Fraser Government brought Cotton home and made him, briefly, a director of the Reserve Bank before posting him as ambassador to Washington in 1982, Labor came to office and the Hawke Government felt apartment 5A had to be taken away from the Liberal appointees who'd infested it in the lesser guise of consul-general and returned to the professional diplomats forced to make do as our ambassador to the United Nations.

This Labor achieved in the mid-'80s, despite determined efforts by various consuls-general to wrest 5A back. They never succeeded.

The bigger apartment has remained the residence of our UN representative for the past 20 years. Now Adelaide's Robert Hill is to become the first politician, Liberal or otherwise, ever to fill the post, while his neighbour, in 5C—appointed consul-general on Pearl Harbor Day (December 7) last year—is his hated factional Liberal opponent from his home city, John Olsen, who has just completed three years as Australia's consul in Los Angeles. Howard appointed Olsen both times.

And if you want to know why, understand that Olsen resigned as Premier of South Australia on October 18, 2001—which just happened to be slap-bang on the eve of the Howard Government's second re-election campaign, the vicious battle now remembered as the children-overboard campaign that saw the Coalition sweep to its third successive victory and Kim Beazley suffer his second leadership defeat.

Olsen had got caught up in an inquiry into a deal between his Government and the US Motorola corporation involving $240 million of public money. An Adelaide QC who headed the inquiry eventually brought down a 200-page report scathing of Olsen's 'misleading, inaccurate and dishonest evidence' to the inquiry about documents which had gone missing. Olsen strenuously denied the accusations and shed tears at his resignation announcement. But in Melbourne, with three weeks to polling day, federal Liberal campaign headquarters was delighted. Adelaide's Liberal marginal seats could now concentrate on the big canvas.

A year later, in November 2002, with victory behind him, Howard honoured a political debt and sent Olsen to Los Angeles. Three years later he sent him to New York. Now the Prime Minister is to send Hill to New York, too. And when the neighbours of apartments 5A and 5C, 1 Beekman Place, enter their common ground floor entrance, Hill—'the wet'—will turn right to reach the lift that takes him up to apartment 5A while Olsen—the arch-conservative—turns left for the lift that goes to apartment 5C.

Hill and Olsen have been factional enemies in South Australia for all the years Hill has been in politics. The exquisite irony of where both are now to end up delights their

colleagues in Canberra. Me, too. Absolutely wonderful.

Hill could have gone to Washington a year ago. He declined. He did not decline the UN appointment. His wife Diana is the president of UNICEF Australia, a post she's held for five years. The Hills have been going once a year to New York for many years now. They love the city and the many friends they've made there. The couple first went to New York in the mid-1980s. Hill, then in Opposition, 'paired' the Labor Government's Nick Bolkus for the annual three months two Australian MPs are sent each year for the meeting of the UN General Assembly.

They are still remembered in foreign affairs for their enthusiasm as working members that year of Australia's UN delegation.

The UN post has another huge plus for Hill. As our UN ambassador he is not obliged—as the Washington post is—to be at the beck and call of the visiting Foreign Minister, Alexander Downer. Having to rise in the 'middle of the night' to 'welcome' Downer at the airport on his many visits to New York over the 10 years the Coalition has been in office is the burden, in New York, of our consul-general, not our UN ambassador. It never has been, unlike Washington. Richard Alston, now our High Commissioner in London, fills a similar chore.

This, too, delights their old Canberra colleagues.

For the record, Howard's other political appointments over the years have been: Michael Baume, ex-Sydney MP and senator, to New York in 1996 for five years; Peacock to Washington and Spender to Paris in 1996; Victoria's Jim Short, who resigned as Howard's assistant Treasurer—just seven months after they won office in 1996—after breaching Howard's much trumpeted (and soon forgotten) code of conduct. Short used to share a rented Canberra house with Howard in Opposition. After his fall from grace in 1996, Howard sent him to London, with the European Bank, in 1997, then to Cyprus in 2000.

In 1998 David Connolly, who lost Liberal preselection (after 22 years an MP) to Brendan Nelson for the plum Sydney seat of Bradfield on the eve of the 1996 election, was appointed by Howard for three years as ambassador to South Africa. Melbourne's Bob Halverson, a failure as Speaker, was sent to Dublin the same year, and WA's Alan Roche, a Howard loyalist, got three years as consul in Los Angeles, to be replaced by Olsen.

Melbourne's Peter Reith got Short's old job at the European Bank after the 2001 election, Queensland's John Herron was sent to Dublin after Halverson completed his three years, Alston got the London plum as high commissioner two years ago, and Melbourne's Bob Charles was sent to Chicago the same year.

The roll call of the 32 ministers who came and went from political life over the decade should not be forgotten, either. Only one of them—the Nationals' Peter McGauran, from Victoria—made it back into the ministry after a year in the sin bin of backbench exile for funny buggers with his travel allowance claims. The other 31: John Herron (Qld), Jim Short (Vic), Andrew Thomson (NSW), Warwick Smith (Tas), David Kemp (NSW), Peter Reith (Vic), Jocelyn Newman (Tas), Tim Fischer (NSW), John Anderson (NSW), Warwick Parer (Qld), Robert Hill (SA), Richard Alston (Vic), Ian Macdonald (Qld), John Moore (Qld), Geoff Prosser (WA), Ian McLachlan (SA), Bronwyn Bishop (NSW), Bruce Scott (Qld), John Sharp (NSW), Alex Somlyay (Qld), Michael Wooldridge (Vic), John Fahey (NSW), Judi Moylan (WA), David Jull (Qld), Daryl Williams (WA), Wilson Tuckey (WA), Jackie Kelly (NSW), Larry Anthony (NSW), Danna Vale (NSW), Kay Patterson (Vic) and De-Anne Kelly (Qld). They include some very bitter people.

Happy birthday, John Howard.

Alan Ramsey

# Police State Business

**JUNE 21, 2003**

SIX MONTHS ago John Howard pulled on his balaclava and strode into the Parliament with his sledgehammer. It was 11.59am, Thursday, December 12. Our Prime Minister was in full ASIO raid mode. His target was the Labor Opposition. His motive was political. His intent was resolute. And, thus fortified, morally and spiritually, he stood at the dispatch box and told a 'monstrous lie'.

During a 12-minute speech what Howard said, in part, was: 'Labor's amendments will wreck the bill and render it inoperable. From the very beginning Labor has not been serious about serious and necessary amendments to the ASIO legislation. Labor is not fair dinkum . . . The Labor Party realise they are going to be judged as soft on this issue. The Opposition leader knows his amendments will destroy the [Australian Security Intelligence Organisation Legislation Amendment (Terrorism)] bill. We have no intention of parading a pretence, a fabrication, a fraud to the Australian public.

'We have no intention of going out and saying, "We have passed a bill which will guarantee ASIO has the necessary additional

powers," when we know in our hearts that would be a monstrous lie . . . We do not accept the Senate's amendments. Labor are weak on this issue. Labor are very weak, just as they were weak on border protection. They remain weak . . .'

On that note Howard sat down, took off his balaclava and put away his sledgehammer. Thirty-five minutes later he closed the Parliament for the year and went home to Sydney for Christmas.

If the Prime Minister couldn't have the bill he wanted, there'd be no bill at all. If ASIO couldn't have the unfettered and unchallengeable right to pick up, on special warrant, people as young as 14, anywhere, any time, detain them in secret, tell nobody, question them for as long as a week, charged with nothing, suspected of nothing except maybe—*maybe*—having information they may not even realise they possessed, then ASIO would get no new powers of any Kind.

So what had Labor done?

Or, more correctly, what had Labor's Senate leader, John Faulkner, in alliance with the Greens' Bob Brown and the Democrats done? How had their Senate majority 'wrecked' the Government's ASIO bill, made it 'inoperable' and 'unworkable', a 'pretence, a fraud and a fabrication', and 'vandalised' it to the point that 'it failed the national interest'?

What the Senate did was make 35 amendments, 34 of them Labor's. In doing so, the key changes that so 'vandalised' the 'national interest', all of them voted against by the Government in the Senate and, ultimately, rejected by the Prime Minister's majority in the House were, what?

In summary: 1) the proposed new ASIO 'investigative' powers automatically would lapse after three years unless Parliament re-endorsed the legislation; 2) the legislation would apply to nobody under the age of 18; 3) the bill's denial of the right to silence was circumscribed by specific civil rights protections, including against self-incrimination in any future charge; 4) a person could only be detained for questioning and not simply for the purpose of detention without charge; 5) detention under a single warrant could last no longer than a total of 20 hours of questioning, broken into three periods of four hours, eight hours and eight hours; 6) a judge or retired judge would have to be present during any and all questioning; 7) the right of immediate legal representation of choice; and 8) no person would be subjected to more than one broken session of 20 hours of questioning in a seven-day period, while no person already questioned for a total of 20 hours could be held in detention.

These were the Senate changes to ASIO's proposed new secret police state powers. They were, as the Government proposed them, no less than this that the Prime Minister insisted, in the strongest language, would mean the end of civilisation. Six months later and his own words are proved meaningless. Why? Because most of the changes Howard fumed against last December his Government now accepts. The ASIO powers bill Howard 'killed' six months ago has been resurrected and redrafted. In it are most of the changes Howard insisted six months ago were 'inoperable, unworkable, a fraud and a fabrication'.

And that is Howard's great lie.

His change of heart exposes him, again, as a crafty humbug more intent on milking the threat of terrorism for political advantage rather than legislative action in 'the national interest'. If you think 'monstrous lie/great lie' too harsh, consider this.

The Government's original stance on ASIO's proposed new powers included: indefinite secret detention, no legal representation, no judicial supervision, no age limit, no protocols, no right to silence, no sunset clause to limit the duration of the bill, no reporting mechanism to Parliament of any kind, no parliamentary review. The revised bill the Senate debated for most of this week and will go on debating most of next week excludes or qualifies most of these powers. The new bill, however contentious it might remain, is light years in advance of what it was.

The only age limit in the original bill announced in March last year, was a lower age limit of 10 for detainees who could be strip-searched. How draconian can a government be and still pretend it's democratic? (Sub-10-year-olds, I remind you, were to be, or could have been, legally detained by ASIO indefinitely, with not even their parents told. The whole purpose of this police state power was to pick up kids to get them to inform on family members, and to go on holding them, in secret, so they couldn't alert anyone to what was going on.)

By last December, the Government had shifted ground to adopt a lower age limit on 'investigative' detention of 14. The Labor/ Greens/Democrats lower age limit was 18. Labor and the Government have now compromised on 16. And only 16- to 18-year-olds that is, juveniles suspected of actual terrorist activity, can be detained. The Government has dropped its earlier insistence of ASIO's right to detain juveniles, as they will be able to detain adults for questioning only about information they 'may' have, knowingly or otherwise.

The Government also has adopted the Senate's insistence the legislation lapse after three years if not re-endorsed by Parliament. So, too, has it agreed to: 1) supervision by a judge of all ASIO questioning of detainees; 2) a detainee's right to immediate legal representation of choice; 3) protocols governing the actual operation of the powers to be tabled in Parliament; 4) parliamentary supervision of the numbers of warrants issued to ASIO for detention and the numbers of hours of ASIO questioning.

The hardline sticking points concern three key issues: 1) the length of time a detainee can be held under a single warrant; 2) the issue of onus of proof in removing a detainee's right to silence; and 3) the crunch issue of continuous periods of detention. This last matter could see the whole of the Government's grudging co-operation shattered. Debate adjourned two days ago. Labor will not support a regime of rolling warrants to detain a person indefinitely. Neither will the Greens nor the Democrats.

If the Government insists ASIO must have such a right, then, for the third time in the 15 months Howard has been trying to get his ASIO powers bill into law, the legislative process will founder in Parliament.

Understand two things. The Government and Labor now agree on a maximum questioning period for a single detainee of 24 hours, broken into three blocks of eight hours with no one session being longer than four hours without a break. But the Government wants the 24 hours to have a time frame across a maximum of seven days' detention. Labor says no, it must be 24 hours across three days only, then the detainee must be released, permanently.

Also, the Government is arguing the right to seven days' detention under a single warrant, and then a further warrant for another seven days, and so on indefinitely, if necessary. In other words, indefinite detention without charge, plus continuous rolling periods of questioning.

This is exactly what the United States imposes on the several hundred terrorist 'suspects', including two Australian citizens, it still holds and has been holding in isolated military detention in Cuba's Guantanamo Bay for more than 18 months, all without charge, all without recourse to any legal assistance. You see where our Government gets its creative impetus from for 'combating terrorism'?

Good ol' George and the boys.

Alan Ramsey

**Postscript:** *The Howard Government's ASIO legislation was still intact six years later and 18 months after voters had buried its enthusiastic parent. The same was true for the former government's 30 or so pieces of associated 'anti-terrorism' and 'security' legislation, much of it hugely intrusive of individual rights, more particularly the increased powers given the Australian Federal Police and State police forces to 'monitor' the Australian community.*

# Chapter 15

# Rats in the Ranks

## Slithering Around Pauline

**NOVEMBER 16, 1996**

*'An obsessive and disproportionate preoc-cupation with the speech of one person can produce consequences that are not in Australia's interests, and I do think there has been an obses-sive reaction by some sections of (the ABC) in particular and by* The Sydney Morning Herald. *I single those two out as having really sort of gone overboard on this issue.'* —John Howard, November 8, 1996.

JOHN HOWARD'S Government is eight months old. Pauline Hanson's speech is nine weeks old. Probably no new Prime Minister ever got a more sympathetic media in his first months in office. Probably no single backbench politician ever created more continuing controversy—or struck a more responsive public chord—with his or her first parliamentary speech. Now the latter is interfering with the former, who do you suppose is getting the blame?

If only we would all ignore her, the Prime Minister says, 'this lady' as he calls her—Howard never refers to Hanson by name—would simply go away, taking with her the political difficulties she creates, mainly for him.

This is the great inconsistency of Howard's rhetoric. While he persistently applauds 'robust' debate on immigration and Aboriginal policy in what he insists is a new, enhanced climate of freedom of speech, he wants nobody to debate Queensland's Pauline Hanson and what she stands for, least of all him. We're all to pretend she's not there.

When Paul Keating told the University of NSW on Monday night he thought it the responsibility of government to turn back the tide of prejudice, and that Hanson's views were 'shamelessly regressive', Howard responded on radio next day: 'Well, I guess he would say that, wouldn't he? I mean, he's hardly been my number one fan over the years . . .

'I've made my position clear on her (Hanson). And I think one of the positions I've made clearest of all is that I think it is ridiculous—and he (Keating) repeated the ridiculous situation in his speech—to imagine that a speech of one Independent member of Parliament is going to do irreparable damage to this country and our region. I mean, I reject that 100 per cent. I think it's an absolute absurd proposition.'

Paul Keating, therefore, like everyone else who disagrees with John Howard's ambiguous behaviour towards Hanson over the past two months, is apparently disqualified from the debate.

And Keating, too, is to blame, it seems, just like the media, for prolonging it, along with others such as the Governor-General, Malcolm Fraser, Jeff Kennett, Tim Fischer,

and various church leaders, all of whom have been disquieted by Hanson's ignorant views and have publicly repudiated them, either explicitly or implicitly.

But not the Prime Minister.

As Howard said the day after Keating's speech, this time on Kerry Packer's national television network: 'I think people reacted, many of them, very foolishly (to Hanson's speech). I mean, my reaction was one of not overreacting to the speech of an individual. And every week that has gone by has confirmed my view that that was the right reaction. I think those people who chased it were wrong and I don't think they did Australia a great service.'

What John Howard refuses to accept is that it is his behaviour that now does Australia no service, not Pauline Hanson's or the media's or anyone else who challenges what she has to say. If the Member for Oxley lit the fire, the Prime Minister's stubborn and persistent refusal to denounce her bigotry keeps it alight, for the unassailable truth is that at no stage since Hanson's speech on September 10 has he made his 'position clear on her' at all.

This is why the debate continues. For Howard to claim otherwise is to ignore the public record or to try to rewrite it.

The great irony of the circumstances of Hanson's speech is that it was only modestly reported at the time she actually made it. The first person to react was one of John Howard's own Liberal backbenchers, Victoria's Peter Nugent, who replied in the Parliament two days later by factually countering each of Hanson's simplistic assertions, and concluding: 'It seems to me she does neither the House, her electorate nor this country any service by making those comments. I will challenge them and I will rebut them at every opportunity.'

Nugent's speech went unreported.

Neither John Howard nor Kim Beazley made any public comment. Three days later

Howard went overseas to Jakarta and Tokyo. The day he left, his Immigration Minister, Philip Ruddock, appearing on the Nine Network's *Sunday* program, gave the first response by any member of the Howard Government. Ruddock thought Hanson's speech 'unfortunate' and 'very unhelpful'.

Asked why the Prime Minister hadn't condemned it, Ruddock replied: 'It's a matter of judgment that you make at a particular time as to the extent to which you draw attention to particular comments. I was hoping, in the way in which the particular speech was given, that there would not be a great deal of public interest . . .'

Ruddock's naive judgment mirrored the Government's silence. But on September 22, 12 days after Hanson's speech, Howard flew back to Australia and, speaking in Brisbane to the Queensland State Liberal Party Council, gave the speech that lifted the Hanson Factor onto the front page of just about every newspaper in the country.

That was the speech where we learned 'the pall of censorship on certain issues' had been lifted since his Government's election, where 'one of the great changes' that had come over Australia since March 2 'is that people do feel able to speak more freely and a little more openly about what they feel'.

If the Government's strategy was, as the Prime Minister has since exhorted everyone else, to ignore Hanson and somehow isolate her speech in a no-speak vacuum, Howard's Brisbane speech demolished it. Neither he nor Hanson nor Asian immigration has been out of the news since.

Hanson's appearance on Nine's *Midday* program at the time, cemented her celebrity status. Howard's Brisbane speech, with no censure either of Hanson or the ignorance of her views, was instantly interpreted as encouragement if not endorsement. Three days later, on September 25, he reinforced this assessment when he appeared on *A Current Affair*.

That was the first occasion Howard was quizzed about Hanson's speech. And when the opening question was, 'Should Australians, other Australians—Aborigines and Asians—be protected from people like Pauline Hanson?' he immediately dropped into the ambiguous format of reply that has fuelled the debate ever since.

'Well, are you saying that somebody shouldn't be allowed to say what she said?' he asked Ray Martin. 'I would say, in a country like Australia, people should be allowed to say that. I'm not going to respond specifically to what she said because I don't announce the policies of my Government by reference to the speech of another. If you want to ask me questions about my Government's policy on immigration or anything like that, I'm happy to answer them.'

And he did. But he wouldn't talk about Pauline Hanson, just as he didn't offer a single word of censure of her views. Five days later, with Asian immigration steadily building as a major political story, Howard only added more petrol when he was asked by 2UE's Alan Jones: 'Do you believe in anything that Pauline Hanson said?'

He replied, in part: 'I certainly believe in her right to say what she said. I thought some of the things she said were an accurate reflection of what people feel. I think she said, as I have said, that there were many times under the previous Government where people felt intimidated out of saying what they really believed. I don't agree with her when she implied that Aborigines as a group are not disadvantaged . . .'

Implied? Pauline Hanson never 'implies' anything when she articulates her prejudices. She asserts them, aggressively. But this is the sort of soft language Howard uses most times to slip and slide around anything to do with the Member for Oxley.

And yet, almost two months further on, with the Hanson Factor showing no sign of diminishing in the public consciousness, despite increasing wariness in the Government of where it could be leading the whole political debate in this country, who does the Prime Minister blame? Who else, but the media, like every political leader before him when things get out of hand.

Alan Ramsey

# The One Nation Aberration

**JUNE 13, 1998**

PETER BEATTIE often goes for an early morning walk. The man who would be Labor's second Queensland Premier in 41 years mostly takes his dog, Rusty, with him. Like a good citizen Beattie always has a plastic bag to take home what Rusty leaves behind. It is the ultimate metaphor for Beattie's political career. He was made State leader 28 months ago to do for Queensland Labor, after the electoral debacle of the Goss years, exactly what he does for his dog each morning: clean up after them.

Three years ago, during an election campaign Labor's own polling had been telling them for two months could be a disaster, Peter Beattie sat in his North Brisbane electoral office utterly unwanted by the State ALP machine that had gone so sour. He was a factional outcast, a political leper in a government rigidly controlled by Wayne Goss and his AWU-sponsored allies, chief among them Wayne Swan, the former State ALP secretary by then a backbencher in the Keating Government in Canberra.

But when State Labor lost nine seats in that election and barely retained office with a majority of just one, Goss reluctantly brought Beattie into his ministry in a junior portfolio. And then, six months later, when the Mundingburra by-election brought Goss and his machine crashing down, Beattie, as the only Labor cleanskin of any public standing, became Opposition leader to Rob Borbidge's minority Coalition Government.

The irony remains that a number of the key players in Beattie's party hate the thought they needed him to remake Labor's image. After six years of the cold, clinical Goss, Beattie's smiling 'nice bloke' manner and high public regard have been the key to whatever Labor's chances of election today might be. Yet nothing, in machine terms, has changed: the Beattie campaign has been every bit as tightly controlled and presidential as each of the three Goss campaigns always were. Nobody else in Labor got a look in.

And now Pauline Hanson's One Nation has come thundering onto the scene with a force more destructive of established political mores than anything in Australian politics since the Labor split of the mid-1950s.

Peter Beattie's Labor Party may well be the only party that can win today's election in its own right. Beattie himself may well have done all Labor could have asked of him in cleaning up the political crap left behind by the discredited Goss administration. His party may well have successfully disguised itself throughout the campaign as 'today's Labor', an obvious parody of Tony Blair's New Labour. But there was not a thing more it could have done to stem the onrush of Hansonism.

By the time of the Queensland campaign it was much too late. And now all Beattie can do, like Rob Borbidge and John Howard and Tim Fischer and Peter Costello and even NSW's Bob Carr, is see what tonight's count visits upon them all. The opinion polls are

still rolling out, as they have done for the past fortnight, heightening the fear and loathing of what could be happening 'out there' in the real world of fed-up voter attitudes.

Look at it this way: Queensland is two countries, one of which sees Pauline Hanson with all the religious fervour of Joan of Arc and which is utterly determined to make political war on the rest of the State. The voters of this 'country' have had enough of 'bullshit politicians' they perceive as incapable of either listening to them or acting in their interests. They hear Pauline's populism in language they understand and they react almost instinctively.

And if any politician anywhere thinks this stark division in Queensland is some sort of electoral aberration quarantined north of the Tweed, then they misread entirely what is going on, in varying degrees, right across the Australian community.

Hansonism will surely implode sometime. But not yet and not while the established parties refuse to take seriously the scapegoating issues she highlights, however uncomfortably—among them alienation, insecurity and, dare it be said, Asian immigration. They will not go away simply by abusing Hanson as an ignorant bigot, or wishing them away by politicians who don't want to face up to the electoral forces she has set loose.

Just how serious this all is we learn today. The opinion polls have been increasingly blunt. Election-eve research is stark. Yet even three nights ago the best amalgam of hardheaded analysis I could find from across all three of the major parties saw One Nation maybe winning up to nine seats in provincial Queensland: five from the Labor Party and four from the National Party.

Labor in turn would win four seats from the Liberals, including a minimum of two in Brisbane, where the Liberal vote is seen to have shattered. Another two seats, both Liberal, in outer suburban Brisbane, were regarded as highly doubtful, while a further three Liberal seats were seen as 'somewhat' doubtful.

The possible One Nation gains were seen as coming from: Maryborough, Hervey Bay, Whitsunday, Thuringowah and Fitzroy—all Labor-held provincial seats; and the National Party seats of Gympie, Barambah, Mulgrave and Burdekin. Liberal losses to Labor were counted as Mundingburra (ironically, the seat that brought down the Goss Government in February 1996), Barron River, Greenslopes and Redlands, with Mount Ommaney and Springwood regarded as 'highly doubtful'.

On this basis, the best result Labor could hope for is an absolute majority of one, perhaps three, but more likely a hung Parliament with One Nation holding the balance of power. In that case Rob Borbidge would certainly remain Premier of a minority government. Whatever, One Nation was seen as certainly winning seats. It's more a question of whether Labor can hold enough of its electoral ground outside Brisbane to benefit from gains at the Liberals' expense in the greater metropolitan area.

We're guessing of course, but this is a best guess from inside the major parties, not from the public opinion polls. The public polls keep insisting Labor's State-wide vote on a two-party preferred basis has it well ahead. Well, that may be so. But as all the political parties know, the result isn't that simple. Who wins will be determined by where the votes actually fall, not on an aggregate basis across the State.

Three years ago the Coalition's primary vote went up 4.8 per cent State-wide, and its final two-party preferred vote was 53.3 per cent. Yet it still lost the 1995 election by a single seat. Labor's aggregate vote slid 5.8 per cent and its two-party preferred vote was a miserable 46.7 per cent, the lowest winning vote anywhere in Australia since the gerrymandered Playford era in South Australia in the 1960s. Yet the Goss Government still hung onto power, at least for a further six months.

So overall aggregate votes are meaningless, a reality complicated quite massively by One Nation bleeding votes from everybody, in Brisbane as well as out in the provincial cities and, most strongly, in deeply conservative rural areas. A panicking Labor Party trumpeted this message all week in its efforts to offset any voter backlash against public polls suggesting a sweeping Labor win.

So great was Labor's concern with these public polls, even though they showed One Nation surging, that ALP head office itself 'leaked' an internal memo from its party pollster which warned Labor had only an even chance of victory and that Peter Beattie should prepare himself for defeat. Whether a set-up or not, copies of the memo went to local Brisbane commercial television and to *The Courier-Mail*, and the resultant publicity was everything the Labor Party wanted. Labor has been hosing down its prospects ever since.

By Thursday Beattie was publicly conceding One Nation had hijacked the campaign and 'certainly would win seats'. He told a Brisbane television interviewer: 'Of course One Nation will win seats. But the choice is between the stable government I offer and the risky three-way arrangement of a Coalition minority government in which Pauline Hanson is judge and jury on every decision it makes.'

The Nationals' Borbidge conceded nothing. The day his security man bowled over a Wilderness Society protester in a koala suit who gatecrashed a lunch speech the Premier was making at a Brisbane hotel, Borbidge later said on television: 'I still don't believe One Nation will win a single seat. But I think they'll poll well, and they could most likely determine the outcome. But come Sunday only two people can be Premier: either Peter Beattie or Rob Borbidge. It won't be a One Nation government. That is the reality.'

Borbidge is right, of course. Only he or Beattie can be Premier. But he's wrong about the timing. Nobody thinks, whatever their guess about the outcome, that we'll know on Sunday. It's going to be a long count. What we will know is that Hansonism isn't a one-election wonder.

Alan Ramsey

**Postscript:** *Borbidge was wrong. Hanson's One Nation Party, with almost a quarter (22.7 per cent) of the Queensland popular vote, swept up 11 seats from Labor and the Nationals, mostly in provincial centres, shocking the socks off the established parties. But Labor in turn matched its losses to One Nation by winning an equivalent number of seats from the Coalition in and around Brisbane and in coastal centres. Thus Peter Beattie, with 44 seats, was able to form a minority government in the 89-seat State Parliament with the support of a non-aligned country Independent. Beattie would go on to win another three State elections in the following nine years, all by big margins, before he resigned in September 2007 as Queensland's longest serving Labor Premier and took himself off to a wondrous taxpayer-funded sinecure as his state's trade representative in Los Angeles. One Nation's meaningful political life was mercifully short, even though it maintained a withered parliamentary presence for 11 years. Its 11 Queensland State MPs elected in 1998 wrangled constantly. Within 18 months, all had resigned, either from the Parliament or from One Nation. In the 2001 election, their parliamentary numbers were reduced to three, then to just one in the subsequent two elections, 2004 and 2006. The Queensland Parliament that returned Labor's Anna Bligh in her own right as Premier in 2009 did not have a single One Nation MP. The party was over. Hanson herself was swept out of the Federal Parliament in John Howard's second election in October 1998, just two months after her One Nation Party's stunning Queensland debut. Multiple attempts by Hanson at re-election in the years since failed, although her personal vote in the 2004 and 2007 Senate elections was strong enough to qualify her for public funding—to Hanson personally—in excess of an aggregate $400,000.*

# Another Queensland Quisling

AUGUST 21, 1996

FOR 21 years Queensland's Mal Colston took everything the Labor Party had to offer. Finally, when the well had run dry, he walked out, without so much as the courtesy of telling his leader, Kim Beazley, he was going. The repercussions of what Colston has done are as profound as they are a sickening blow to the political party he has quit.

Colston resigned by letter faxed to the Brisbane office of the Queensland State ALP at 11.30 yesterday morning. When the Senate met at 2pm he took his seat as an Independent for the remaining three years of his six-year term. And at 6.03pm, as the nominee of John Howard's Coalition Government, he was elected, amid bitter scenes, the Senate's new deputy President.

Six years ago the Labor Party gave Colston the deputy presidency after the 1990 election, but he lost it when the Senate numbers changed after the 1993 election. The Liberals' Margaret Reid, now the new Senate President, instead became deputy, with Democrat support, to Labor's Michael Behan as Senate president.

But now that Behan has gone, along with the Keating Government, the Coalition parties are in power, and Colston, 58, and with only three years to go before retiring from politics, wanted his old job as deputy president to end his career. It wasn't available.

A year ago he sought possible appointment as Administrator of Norfolk Island, but that was denied him, too. And when he sought Labor's nomination in recent weeks to regain the deputy presidency of the new Senate, he was told 'no' again . . . The Labor factions instead agreed to nominate NSW's Sue West. Colston's appeals fell on deaf ears, at least among his Labor colleagues.

John Howard was far more receptive.

And when Parliament resumed yesterday for the Budget session, Mal Colston—without telling his leader, his Caucus, or Labor's national head office—issued two statements severing 35 years of Labor membership and 21 years as a Labor senator. The first was his letter of resignation faxed to the Queensland ALP State secretary, Mike Kaiser, in Brisbane.

That said, enigmatically: 'Dear Michael,

'Since the Federal election in March, significant differences have developed between me and some other members of the Federal Parliamentary Labor Party (FPLP). As a result, I am no longer prepared to be a member of that body. It would be untenable for me to remain a member of the ALP if I am not a member of the FPLP. I therefore tender my resignation . . . to take effect immediately.'

An hour later, with his party in turmoil, Colston announced his decision in a public statement just as coy about his reasons for leaving. Significantly, however, he announced his 'voting pattern' as an Independent for the next three years would be 'influenced by my long-held Labor beliefs, by an acceptance that the present Government has an electoral mandate to pursue a number of issues, and by what I judge the most appropriate course of action for the people of Queensland.'

It is the second of these that now has so much significance for John Howard, for his Government, for the Coalition's policy agenda, and for the Senate. Of a sudden, one of the two elusive Senate votes the Government needs to control the Upper House for the next three years is, at the very least, within negotiable reach.

That it should come from within Labor's ranks is as much an irony as Colston's history of how he came to politics 21 years earlier.

In September 1975 Colston was the Queensland Labor nominee that the Bjelke-Petersen Government refused to accept to fill a Senate casual vacancy after Labor's Bert Milliner died. Instead, the infamous Albert Field was sent to Canberra in Colston's place, thus making possible everything that followed in the constitutional upheaval of the Whitlam Government's dismissal two months later.

Colston was elected in the subsequent double-dissolution election of December 1975 and has been a Labor senator ever since. That is, until yesterday. He will no more be forgotten by the Labor Party than is Albert Field.

*Alan Ramsey*

# Impeccable Judgment

DECEMBER 7, 1996

FEDERAL LABOR has had better years. It lost government, it lost 30 Labor seats in an election in which it suffered its worst primary vote in 60 years, it lost its former Prime Minister, it was humiliated in losing Sydney's Lindsay by-election, and it lost the fight on behalf of its union base against the new industrial relations laws. Now, in losing the Telstra battle in Parliament, the ultimate indignity: Labor loses it on the votes of two ex-Labor members—one it expelled two decades ago and one who, after 21 years of Labor patronage, 'ratted' for a better offer from Labor's opponents.

Kim Beazley and Labor won't easily forget 1996.

Nor should anyone ignore the irony of it all. Tasmania's Brian Harradine was once a senior figure in both the political and industrial wings of the labour movement. In 1968, in one of those ugly Left/Right confrontations that always seems to be tearing at Labor, Harradine, although backed by Gough Whitlam and the party's Right, lost his seat on the ALP Federal Executive, even though he remained, as secretary of the Tasmanian Trades and Labour Council, for another eight years a member of the ACTU executive.

Now, all these years later, here he is doing his old party in the eye with the same adroit political quick-stepping that has enabled Harradine to survive as a Senate Independent ever since his election in December 1975 in the same upheaval that confirmed the end of another Labor Government and another Labor leader—the very same leader who'd put his leadership on the line for him seven years earlier!

Yet John Howard couldn't have won the Telstra battle on the vote of Brian Harradine alone. Had Labor somehow kept Queensland's Mal Colston content within the party that had been his political meal ticket for so long, the Telstra legislation could not have succeeded. At best, with Harradine's support, it would have been defeated on a tied vote. That's how significant was Colston's defection. Just to complete the symmetry, Colston, too, came into Parliament in the same election that sent Harradine to Canberra.

So how do you think Labor's Senate leader, John Faulkner, must feel?

Last year, with Labor in office, Colston made known his wishes to end his career with his appointment to the coming vacancy of Administrator of Norfolk Island. Faulkner, the relevant minister, flatly rejected the overtures. From that point on, Colston's loyalty to Labor was under strain, finally to give way when the Coalition was more than delighted to accommodate his nomination as the Senate's deputy president last August.

Colston resigned from the Labor Party a matter of hours before the Howard Government voted him into the job, as its nominee, on Budget day. He has, with one exception, been a reliable Coalition ally in every Senate vote since.

Imagine the 'what ifs?' What if Labor's Left hadn't persecuted Harradine all those years ago? What if Harradine had come to Canberra as a Labor Senator and not an Independent? And what if John Faulkner had appointed Mal Colston to Norfolk Island when Labor had the chance?

Alan Ramsey

# The Ugly Colston Cover-Up

**APRIL 19, 1997**

TUESDAY, AUGUST 23, 1983, reflected change. That night, Paul Keating would bring down his first Budget as Labor Treasurer. When Parliament met that afternoon, a new Liberal MP was sworn in to replace Bill Snedden, the sometime Liberal leader who'd quit politics after the defeat of the Fraser Government in March. It was the same day Parliament acknowledged the resignation of Jim Killen, another former Coalition veteran. It was the day, too, that Bob Hawke formally advised the House of his revamped ministry following Labor's first political casualty after just four months in office.

Mick Young had resigned as Special Minister of State (SMOS) on July 14 for 'certain improper and unauthorised actions' in the Combe/Ivanov spy melodrama then convulsing Canberra. Hawke replaced him with Kim Beazley, his protege and junior Minister for Civil Aviation. By August 23, Beazley had been in the new job a bare five weeks. And when he got there he found Mick had left behind a dead cat.

That day, amidst the heightened mood of Parliament, Roger Holdich wrote a minute for his departmental files. Five years later Holdich would become Director-General of Security and Intelligence. In August 1983, he was deputy secretary of Kim Beazley's new department. The subject of his file note that day: Malcolm Arthur Colston.

It read: 'Mr Brazil (head of the Attorney-General's Department) telephoned this afternoon. He said he had been able today to speak to the Attorney-General about the problem . . . The Attorney had made the point he wondered whether there was not an option (other than) to investigate at this stage, such as counselling. (I said that the senator had already been counselled in respect of earlier apparent misuse of air tickets.) The Attorney felt that any action that might be taken should stop short of investigation. The Attorney said he would be happy to talk to the minister about it if Mr Beazley wished.'

The Attorney-General was Gareth Evans. The 'problem' was Colston's creative attitude to his parliamentary 'entitlements'.

Fourteen years later, when Labor's cover-up of the Colston 'problem' in 1983 would become an even graver political embarrassment for Beazley and Evans than Colston's recidivist behaviour posed for John Howard, Evans would lamely excuse the early Mal Colston as having been a 'young mistake-maker' who deserved 'tolerance'.

The paper trail suggests the only 'young mistake-maker' was Evans himself, almost three years Colston's Senate junior. Worse, Evans' misjudgment was compounded by Beazley's leniency. Both ministers not only rejected departmental advice to call in the police, but Evans stepped in to stop such an investigation as 'premature'.

Five days before Holdich wrote his August 23 file note, he and Pat Lance, head of the branch that dealt with parliamentary allowances, sought 'informal advice' from Pat Brazil. They gave Brazil a number of documents. Brazil later reviewed these documents with Tom Sherman, Acting Crown Solicitor and later to become chairman of the National Crime Authority.

Their findings, as recorded by Holdich on August 22: 'The informal conclusion of this study (by Brazil and Sherman) has been that if a further step is to be taken it should be (police) investigation.' And what had they reviewed? The circumstances of payments to Colston, through a family company, totalling $6,444 over two years, plus a new, seemingly 'artificial' claim Colston had lodged on June 29 that year for $1,452, but which he then withdrew on August 5 after Pat Lance challenged it.

Ten days later Holdich wrote to Beazley.

His letter, stamped 'in confidence' and dated September 2, said: 'The Secretary (of SMOS, John Menadue) and Miss Lance recently discussed with you concerns the department had about claims for payment . . . (to Colston). You had asked that we seek informal advice from the Attorney-General's Department. Mr Brazil and the Acting Crown Solicitor are of the view that if a further step is to be taken, it should be investigation and this would be a matter for the Australian Federal Police (AFP) . . .

'Mr Brazil said that, in his view, any charges that might be laid would be charges under the Crimes Act. A decision on prosecution in such a case would be a matter for the Attorney. Mr Brazil has informed the Attorney of our inquiry. The Attorney expressed the view that any proposed action should stop short of an

investigation. We do not know however, whether he is aware the senator was earlier counselled in relation to his use of airline tickets.

'We believe we have no option but to ask the AFP to initiate an inquiry into the payments by the Commonwealth amounting to $6,444 . . . In reaching this view, we have had regard to the pattern of Senator Colston's previous claims against the Commonwealth, viz. irregularities in his use of airline tickets (involving repayment of $4,200). You may wish to inform Senator Colston of the inquiry which the department proposes to initiate. Alternatively, you may prefer the secretary or me to do this. You may also wish to inform the Prime Minister.'

Beazley was in New Zealand at the time. His departmental head, John Menadue, would later note to Pat Lance: 'Spoke to minister during 3/4 September in NZ. He agreed the course of action proposed—investigation by AFP—was the appropriate course. It was decided in the meantime he would speak with PM and ministers and also ask Colston for further explanations . . .'

And then Gareth Evans intervened.

On September 7, five days after Holdich's letter, Evans wrote to Beazley: 'This is to confirm my oral advice to you as to the most appropriate course of action to be followed in respect of the possible irregularities which have appeared in Senator Colston's chartered transport claims over the last two years. My view is that before entering on a police investigation, which might have quite profoundly disturbing implications for Senator Colston's apparently delicately balanced family situation, quite apart from causing grave damage, whether unfairly or not, to his reputation in the event that the fact of the investigation became public knowledge, Senator Colston should be asked to provide a full and detailed explanation of the circumstances of his claims and be given time to pursue any documentation required . . .

'In all the circumstances, and given in particular that any such possible irregularities are routinely handled in private commercial organisations and other institutional settings, I believe it would be premature to set in train a police investigation. In the event, however, that Senator Colston's explanation were unsatisfactory, I agree there would be no alternative but to involve the police . . .

'I mention my conversation with Mr Brazil in order to clarify a somewhat inaccurate report of that conversation which appears in a minute to you signed by your deputy secretary, Roger Holdich, dated 2 September. The view which I expressed to Mr Brazil was not that 'any proposed action should stop short of an investigation', but rather that 'it should stop short of an investigation at this stage . . .'

Beazley spoke to Colston that same day. Five days later, on September 12, Colston wrote to Beazley: 'I refer to conversations I had with you on September 7 and 8 . . . I mentioned to you that I regarded the claims to be valid. I still contend they were . . . However, it has been mentioned by you that the claims involved a conflict of interest. Because of this reason, and this reason alone, I have decided it would be proper for me to repay the total amount which was claimed. A cheque for $6,444 is thus enclosed.'

And that was that.

Although Beazley would later write three times to Colston, insisting he 'regularise' the dubious way he made claims on his 'entitlements'—appeals that, according to the files, Colston would ignore—any further talk of police investigation was shelved.

In a departmental aide-memoire dated September 18, six days after Colston sent his cheque for $6,444 to Beazley, Pat Brazil wrote, following a meeting with Evans and Sherman on September 14: 'The Attorney indicated that, in these circumstances, no further action was being contemplated at this stage. Both Mr Sherman and I indicated we thought that this was an appropriate course to follow . . .'

And 'these circumstances' were? As Brazil noted them: 'In one case the claim (for $1,452) was withdrawn. In the other case, repayment (of $6,444) was made. The public interest, in ensuring properly-based claims in the future, had not been prejudiced . . .'

In hindsight, what a joke.

From the moment the word 'police' was mentioned, the matter was settled in three weeks. It was the bureaucrats who wanted the police called in. It was the politicians who kept them out. Beazley and Evans, with the Government's apparent support, were responsible. Their departments acquiesced only after the two ministers resolved the 'problem' behind closed doors.

It remains the most exquisite irony that, with Beazley and Evans now Labor's national leaders, the very investigation Labor stymied 14 years ago should now involve not only Colston's inventive behaviour over the years but their own roles in shielding him from exposure in 1983.

Alan Ramsey

# Judas Declines to Mort

APRIL 24, 1999

ACCORDING TO his lawyers, Malcolm Arthur Colston should be well and truly dead by now. They told the legal system in November 1997, in arguing for the withdrawal of 28 fraud charges against the ample Queensland senator, that he 'likely' had only 'six to 12 months' to live. Colston, his lawyers said, was a 'very sick man' whose 'long-term outlook is bleak'.

They went on: 'His health is such that proceeding with the prosecution can, on any reasonable view, only have the effect of accelerating his death.' The Commonwealth Director of Public Prosecutions (DPP) was unmoved. Six months later, on May 18 last year, so was the ACT Magistrates Court. It committed Colston for trial, at a date to be fixed, in the ACT Supreme Court.

Eleven months further on and, despite his lawyers' dire warnings, Mal is still with us. Mal de mal maybe, but not Mal de mort.

Nothing has accelerated, least of all the start of his trial.

Twenty-one months after Colston was first charged, by summons, on 28 counts of rorting his travel 'entitlements' as an MP, and 17 months after his lawyers pleaded, in writing, that 'the interests of justice will not be served by continuing the prosecution', Colston has defied the setting of a court trial as thoroughly as he has defied the undertaker.

There are constant alarums concerning his pending death, but nothing concerning his pending trial. Neither one nor the other is ever incited by the passage of time. I asked the DPP's office this week why it was that Colston's trial seemed so slow in materialising, given it was nearing two years since he'd been charged. When I sought to learn if Colston's lawyers, or anyone else, had made representations for his trial's delay, on whatever grounds, I was told, after several phone calls, to essentially mind my own business. Any such discussions between the DPP and Colston's lawyers were their respective concern and 'not a matter this office would disclose'.

As for a trial date, well, Colston's matter was in the Supreme Court list. A date would be decided by the court itself, as was always the case. The next call-over was in early May. In the meantime, please go away and annoy the politicians, not the DPP's office. Nobody actually said so, but they might as well have. The DPP's media spokesperson is a courteous young woman as informative as a recorded message. She does as she is told, which is very little indeed.

Colston doesn't do a great deal these days either, apart from rail and fume at the Labor Party through press releases drafted by his two sons, Douglas and David, and inspire stories about his fight with cancer, a well-publicised trauma from since somewhere between the time his office secretary blew the whistle in April 1997 on Colston's abortive attempt to get her to lie an alibi for him and the announcement of the DPP's 28 fraud charges in July the same year.

In April 1998, the month before he was committed to stand trial, Colston told the DPP, in writing: 'I consider it better to be in Parliament House, even though I am not functioning at an optimal level, rather than remaining at home waiting to die.' John Howard, now the election is over, would prefer him in Parliament, too, even though the Prime Minister prudently abandoned Colston (and his vote) to the police the same time two years ago that Colston's secretary said she couldn't lie for him any longer.

On Monday, with the GST debate nearing its ultimate Senate orgasm, Colston reappeared, after an absence of several months, to announce his readiness to cast his vote, even if in the first four days of debate he declined a single word in explanation of his reasons. By Thursday night, Colston had voted 26 times this week, including 24 in support of the Government and twice (in tandem with Brian Harradine) with Labor and the Democrats.

And did the Government accept his vote? You bet. Like a big, hungry dog. The Prime Minister's conversion from denial to full embrace is as wondrous as Colston's stoic defiance of his lawyer's grim prediction of his impending death 17 months ago.

Consider the following:

John Howard, April 16, 1997, in an interview with ABC radio 4QR in Brisbane: 'We discussed this matter yesterday at our Cabinet meeting at very great length, and I'm making it clear this morning that, in all the circumstances, if Senator Colston remains a member of the Senate, we will not, in future, accept his vote.'

Q: 'Is that right?'

Howard: 'We won't. We have decided that if he remains a member, if he purports to vote with us, we will arrange for one of our senators to absent himself or herself. And we've taken that decision because we think that is the right response in all the circumstances ... The question of whether he stays in the Senate or not is ultimately a matter for him and the operation of the law, but for so long as he stays, and until this matter is resolved, we won't accept his vote ... What I am announcing is a very, very clear message to the people of Australia that, until this matter is cleared up, we are not going to accept his vote.'

Howard, same day (April 16, 1997), to a Brisbane Liberal Party lunch audience: '(Senator Colston) is entitled to a fair trial. Equally, we are entitled to make a value judgment about the damage the issue (of the travel rort allegations against him) may be doing to people's perception of the institution (of Parliament). And what I've said on behalf of the Government is that when Parliament resumes, if he votes for us on a particular measure, then a Liberal or National Party senator will be absented so that we don't benefit from his vote.

'We believe that is the right thing to do. It may not, in the short term, be the most comfortable thing to do. But in the long term, I think it is the right thing to do for the institution of Parliament. This is a unilateral decision on our part. I would expect the Labor Party to match it, but if it doesn't, well, that's for the Labor Party to explain ...'

Senator Robert Hill, July 12, 1997, in an interview with Glen Milne on the Seven network's *Face to Face*: 'The Prime Minister made a decision some time ago, and the Cabinet supported him, that in circumstances where

(Colston) was facing trial for serious offences, we didn't think the Australian people would believe that we should accept his vote where that vote would determine the passage of major pieces of legislation. We have stood by that as a matter of principle, and I don't expect the Prime Minister to change his mind.'

Oh, really?

Come forward to October 14, 1998.

The election has been run and won, albeit with a minority Coalition vote and the loss of 19 Government seats. John Howard is claiming a mandate for his GST package, which he insists must be passed through Parliament before the Democrats regain the Senate balance of power on July 1, 1999. At his first post-election press conference with the Canberra press gallery, he is asked: 'Will you be accepting the vote of Senator Colston?'

Prime Minister: 'Well, it's something that needs to be looked at again, because at the moment (Colston) has been treated worse than anybody else who's charged with a crime. I mean, nobody else has been treated like that. He is, at the moment, being denied the presumption of innocence. But, as I say, it's something to be looked at.'

Q: 'But you refused his vote?'

Howard: 'That's right, we did. So I don't think anybody can accuse us of being particularly venal on the subject. I think now that you've had an election (in which all the policy points of view were debated), I was asked a question. I think it's something that should be re-examined.'

Three weeks later, on November 6, 1998, Howard's view had come full circle from 'the matter of principle' he'd announced so forthrightly in Brisbane 19 months earlier when Colston's name had become mud across the community. In an interview on radio 2UE, the sycophantic Alan Jones smarmed: 'We have developed this rather strange notion

that someone democratically elected to the Senate is either not entitled to vote, or his vote is somehow inferior to that of others. Is that argument used in relation to Carmen Lawrence?'

Howard: 'Oh, no, no, no. The argument about presumption of innocence has always been that if somebody being a Member of Parliament is charged with an offence, until that person is convicted, that person is entitled to exercise the full rights of a Member of Parliament. Now, I acknowledge that we adopted a harsher stance in the last Parliament in relation to Senator Colston than that conventional approach. I acknowledge that.

'And, in going back to the conventional approach, we are not adopting as harsh an approach as we did in the last Parliament, but we are adopting the same approach as the Labor Party has always taken.'

Melbourne radio 3AW's Neil Mitchell was less accommodating of the Prime Minister's post-election change of mind. 'But what's changed, Mr Howard, from the days when (Colston's) vote was unacceptable?'

Howard: 'I've looked, and the Government has looked again, and we have come to the conclusion that the stance we then took was inconsistent with the presumption of innocence.'

Q: 'It sounds like a pragmatic decision based around the GST.'

Howard: 'People will say that.'

Q: 'And it's not?'

Howard: 'Well, I said to you, in fact, earlier, that we would use whatever legitimate means were available to us to get through something the Australian public supported. And I say this very directly, I think there is a strong argument that the stance we took (against Colston's vote) in the last Parliament was unreasonable, was a more severe reaction than has normally been the reaction of governments in similar situations. So, they are the facts. People will make their own assessment.'

Indeed, they will. Malcolm Arthur Colston, 61 years old and 24 years a political parasite, is just being Mal Colston. And John Howard, desperate for his vote, is just being an utter political humbug.

Alan Ramsey

**Postscript:** *Mal did not mort until August 23, 2003, almost six years after his lawyers first asserted, in court, he would 'likely' die within 'six to 12 months', and more than four years after he retired from the Senate on July 1, 1999. He never went to trial. Thus Colston was able to leave public life with his taxpayer-funded superannuation fully intact after 24 years an MP, an 'entitlement' he'd have lost had he been convicted of the 28 fraud charges he'd been 'too ill' to defend in November 1997. Yet both sides of politics were culpable for the sleaze that protected his charmed life as a public parasite.*

# The Golden One Walks Out

**OCTOBER 18, 1997**

CHERYL KERNOT was 17 years a member of the Democrats. It took her 10 years to get into Parliament, less than three years to become their leader, another four years to decide she wanted to be one of the bastards rather than simply keep them honest, and a mere 15 minutes to leave. And, in the leaving, with a fortnight's advance booking, first-class, on the train she was catching, with only a cursory phone call to the stunned loyalists she was abandoning on the station, Cheryl Kernot identified herself as just another hustling politician in pursuit of the main chance.

A good one, even a golden one. But just another one, nevertheless. The Democrats were supposed to be different.

It is 80 years since a Federal leader of any party last ratted, and 66 years since a politician did so as successfully as did Joe Lyons in 1931. Lyons, like Billy Hughes, ratted on the Labor Party. He became Prime Minister a year later. Hughes, in 1917, never stopped being Prime Minister. They, too, ratted in the name of principle. Labor, understandably, never forgave either of them. It never does, not with its own rats.

Look at Mal Colston. Remember Robert Ray's venomous outburst of pure hatred that day in Parliament little more than 18 months ago? Ray is one of the modern hard men of Labor who professes little time for his opponents' description of 'the traditional Labor member'. In the Senate a few years back, when the Liberals' Rod Kemp was baiting him one day, Ray, a minister at the time, responded: 'The traditional Labor MP those opposite used to love was a person who couldn't read opinion polls, who didn't know how to raise money, and who couldn't match them in this chamber or outside. I can tell Senator Kemp that times change . . .'

Well, not when it comes to Labor rats, they don't.

In March this year, just six months after Colston sold out the Labor Party to become Senate deputy president as the Howard Government's nominee, Ray let his feelings on the issue get away from him. His voice shaking as it rose in a crescendo, he thundered: 'You resign from this chamber and you go. You do not stay here for grubby venal reasons. You

do not sell your services to the other side. That is a tradition of the Labor Party. And anyone who rats on the Labor Party will get exactly what this quisling Quasimodo from Queensland got.'

Now, 19 months later, Labor embraces its own Queensland quisling, however blonde and green-eyed and politically golden the package.

Harsh maybe, but Cheryl Kernot has to wear it. She did to the Democrats exactly what the detested Colston did to Labor. However different their motives, each was looking after number one at the expense of parties and colleagues that had sustained them for years. And Labor, for all its hatred of rats, was delighted to sweep her up. It had only ever previously happened in reverse.

Colston negotiated in secret with the Government. Kernot negotiated in secret with Labor, supposedly for 'two to three months'. Colston, confiding in none of his Federal Labor colleagues, faxed his resignation to the Queensland ALP the morning he defected. His party got four hours' notice. Kernot, confiding in nobody from the Democrats, phoned her deputy, Meg Lees, 15 minutes before her public announcement to the nation's TV cameras on Wednesday.

She didn't tell even her staff, leaving that to Meg Lees, who walked next door and told them 10 minutes before Kernot appeared on the television screens. Nor did Kernot walk around to her office afterwards to speak to them, preferring instead to remain ensconced for the rest of the day in the Parliament House office suite of Gareth Evans, one of her new Labor patrons.

Only the following day did Kernot start phoning her old staff. Some simply got a faxed letter, as did her former Democrat colleagues. It was a miserable way to leave after 17 years. It was pretty cowardly, too. The party and personal staff who'd been the vehicles of her political success deserved better, even if she was the Golden One.

Robert Ray and Gareth Evans were part of the small Labor coterie who knew all about Kernot's defection long before anybody else did. So was Kim Beazley, of course, and John Faulkner, Labor's Senate leader, and Gary Gray, Labor's national secretary and the bloke who has to find the money to meet Kernot's bills, political and personal, until she comes back to Parliament as a Labor MP, which she will surely do.

Evans and Faulkner, both Kernot mates for years, had a different role. They wooed her in her defection. They were Kernot's conduit into the Labor Party. And they wooed her not for 'two to three months', but for most of this year. It all began a long time ago. Beazley, as leader, was simply there at the end to seal the arrangements the very night before the unhappy Nick Sherry tried so ham-fistedly to top himself.

The press never got a sniff. Everybody at the end was caught up in the uproar over politicians rorting the taxpayers. None of us had the faintest idea Cheryl Kernot was doing the same thing in secret to the Democrats.

Yet Faulkner, too, has no time for rats, not when they're moving in the other direction. A politician who got his grounding in the NSW party machine as the Left's assistant secretary for nine years, he does his best work behind the scenes and has one of the tightest mouths in the business. If Evans was dazzled by Kernot's political skills and personality,

Faulkner would have looked behind both at the political premium her defection to Labor's ranks represented.

But, like Ray, when it comes to Labor rats, his loathing is immense.

The day that Colston did the dirty on his party, the same day Peter Costello brought down his first Budget, a coldly furious Faulkner told the Senate just before the vote that made Colston deputy president: 'We have seen a very sneaky, low-life performance from the Government today. Every possible convention broken, every possible trick in the book, perpetuated by this crew on the other side . . . We can never take your word for anything. Procedures and processes have broken down and the only way through is to get all 76 senators to cast their ballot, and then we will know, without tricks, without sleaze, without slime, without deceit, what the will of the Senate is.'

What Faulkner's real fury was about, of course, was Colston, not the Government. Yet he and Ray kept a rein on their revenge until after the crucial Telstra vote four months later. Then with the Telstra sale bill ensured by Colston's vote—in reality, a Labor vote—they went for him with a ruthlessness that, eventually, destroyed him.

Now the irony is, all these months later, that Faulkner is central to events that do to the Democrats—and, Labor hopes, eventually to John Howard—what Colston and the Government did to Labor and to Telstra.

All Kim Beazley must do now is pretend a rat isn't a rat but is instead a rose. The political marketing of the Golden One began the instant of Wednesday's press conference. It has been going full-tilt ever since, with Beazley and Evans on national radio and TV and Kernot's strategic interviews across the media, some 14 at last count, orchestrated out of Beazley's and Evans's offices. Expect more large dollops this weekend.

And why not? When you snare a prize like Labor is sure it has with Cheryl Kernot you capitalise on the momentum. Yet there is a problem.

Kernot's great asset is her credibility. She made a soaring political career out of being the most honest of the honest brokers. She was the dazzling saleswoman for integrity and incorruptibility in a self-obsessed business where she promised she would keep all the shonks to their word. Last election almost 1.2 million Senate voters believed her. So did almost 750,000 people who gave Democrat candidates their House vote, too.

What happens to that credibility now? How does Kernot expect to remain unsoiled goods after making a career for seven years out of a slogan she renders, by her defection, as worthless as she now says she has come to realise John Howard's Government is? Were all the bastards really only ever in one party after all?

The truth more likely is Kernot began losing interest in the Democrats only when they lost their share of the Senate's balance of power after Colston sold out Labor for 30 pieces of silver. That single act 14 months ago, transferring the balance solely to Colston and Tasmania's Brian Harradine, severely diminished the Democrats' political authority. And with their downgrading went their leader's previously key role in national affairs.

It was a role Kernot enjoyed hugely. In December 1993, with Labor still in office, the ABC's Kerry O'Brien asked her: 'You'd know that politics can be a very seductive process. You are becoming more and more engaged inside the process. You're rubbing shoulders with ministers and the government process. There is a fine line, isn't there?'

She replied: 'Yes, but I know what they're like. I don't believe that, ultimately, the process will seduce us. It's much more important we have the opportunity to be in the mainstream of the debate than to be marginalised, and I guess that's a balance I'll have to find and a tightrope I'll have to walk.'

Cheryl Kernot was seduced by the tightrope but Mal Colston toppled her from it. She has now opted for the Labor Party to put her back where the real power is.

Alan Ramsey

# . . . And for What?

OCTOBER 20, 2001

CHERYL KERNOT would do herself, her family and the Labor Party a good turn by losing on polling day. Herself, in particular. In reality, that won't be hard. The way Labor's Federal standing has soured in Queensland means Kernot's Brisbane seat of Dickson will be among the first to go. Kernot's absurd behaviour in the past week ensures there can be no escape.

Defeat is all the future Kernot has left in politics, no matter what Kim Beazley says.

Politics has destroyed her. Defeat is her escape. Defeat would mean she wouldn't have to be forever publicly agonising over who'd done what to her and how horrid everyone was being, sniff. Defeat gets her out of public life and out of the public eye. It also gets her out of the Labor Party.

When Kernot defected to Labor from the Democrats four years ago almost to the day (October 15, 1997), a *Herald* headline asked:

Could this be her worst decision? It was. Labor is a hard, demanding party. It has 110 years of struggle. It has no time for self-absorbed sooks. Kernot proved too brittle, too precious. And, in the end, too much a victim.

Defeat would give her the chance to get her life back in order. Her relationships, too. She has a husband and a daughter. She could well have neither if she doesn't remake herself. It would be a terrible price. In the meantime, the snapping, yapping bullies of the Government, from the Prime Minister down, see Kernot as fair game. Why they think it so necessary to go on pursuing her is beyond me. It is just mindless blood sport.

If ever a public figure went about remorselessly doing him or herself in, with a political death wish so obvious you cringe, it is the golden-haired one with the green eyes who ratted on one party after four years its leader and is ratting on herself after four years a turncoat.

Now, well into middle age, Kernot must realise she has no political career left, despite Beazley's protective pretence. You sense that only stubbornness has kept her from resigning for at least the past year. Well, now the voters of Dickson will make the decision for her.

She has three weeks left. Her stupidity in lashing out, wildly, at her Liberal opponent nine days ago ('Ask him why he left the police force') was a slur, with no basis whatever, she later insisted was unintended but for which her grudging apology only further diminished her. That grievous misjudgment was compounded by a lot of backing and filling, by her and by the Queensland Labor Government, over a relatively piddling $5,000 concessionary rebate in stamp duty for a $585,000 Gold Coast unit she and her husband bought last year.

No less than six Howard Government Cabinet ministers—the Prime Minister, the garrulous Peter Costello, the relentless Tony Abbott, the departing Peter Reith, the sneaky Richard Alston, even Amanda Vanstone, usually one of the Liberals' less slavering pursuers—have been variously braying after Kernot all week. In Brisbane it has been a big story, with the city's only local daily, *The Courier-Mail*, running a lot of copy, including an editorial that could find no excuse for her.

What did Labor do? The local State machine, quietly furious, went to ground. The party's federal organisation flew a senior minder to Brisbane to put a guard on Kernot's tongue and to shield her from the media and from herself. Beazley and Simon Crean copped questions every day for five days.

By Tuesday, in Adelaide, Beazley's patience was as threadbare as his windy rationalisation on Kernot's behalf. 'I see there are four Cabinet ministers now devoted to attacking Cheryl,' Beazley replied to questions, 'which is an indication of the extent to which this Government has an agenda for the long term, in terms of the capacity of its ministers to focus on matters related to their portfolios and the development of long-term policy. I have confidence in Cheryl. She is defending herself and I'm getting on with the election campaign.'

It is a sad and sorry ending.

Alan Ramsey

**Postscript:** *Three years earlier, when Kernot wrested the marginal Brisbane seat of Dickson off the Liberals, she squeaked in by 176 votes after preferences and a recount. On November 10, 2001 her Liberal Party opponent, Peter Dutton, a former policeman, won Dickson by a landslide margin of 10,000 votes in a ballot of 85,000. Kernot's exit from national political life, after 11 years, including eight soaring years with the Democrats in the Senate, could not have been more humiliating.*

# A Sly Route to the Truth

JULY 6, 2002

LAURIE OAKES galloped out of the press gallery three days ago to rescue 'the truth' and save Kim Beazley. Galloped? As someone named 'Jack' said on talkback radio next day: 'Laurie said he broke the story because he couldn't conceal it by sitting on it. I'm sure Laurie could conceal anything by sitting on it.' A cheap shot, yes. But politics this week seems to have been little else but cheap shots. And Oakes's 'agonising' decision to tell the world that Cheryl and Gareth used to 'do it' for what he asserts was five years had to be the cheapest, grubbiest cheap shot of all.

A political friend of many years standing and not a little wisdom reflected yesterday: 'If ever you wanted to see what a political issue looks like when it's in free fall, this is it. Yet the real human tragedy is that what is in free fall is Cheryl Kernot herself. There is nothing around her any more; no safety blanket, no supportive network, no close political friends, not much family even. She's no longer a political player, nor a political combatant. Her expulsion from politics at the elections eight months ago was about as humiliating as it gets.

'Now she's just part of the debris. And she's alone. Put aside how this happened and why, and how significant was her own often self-obsessed, self-destructive behaviour, and just remember what it's done to her and to others close to her. That's what I mean by the real human tragedy. If ever one of your children, son or daughter, were to say to you, 'I'm thinking about a career in politics', tell them to think about what has happened to this woman.'

Ah yes, but what about 'the truth'.

Oakes's first version of 'the truth' came when he sat down at his computer in Parliament House on Monday morning and banged out his usual column for *The Bulletin* before going off to lunch at their favourite Canberra bistro with his friend of 20 years, Michael Costello, Kim Beazley's former chief of staff. Only there was nothing usual at all about this week's column. Oakes flayed Kernot's book, *Speaking for Myself Again*, which he felt should have been called Making Excuses for Myself Again because 'everything is the fault of the media, the Labor Party, and mostly poor old Beazley'.

Poor old Beazley, indeed.

You see, 'poor old Beazley' apparently is incapable of speaking in his own defence, certainly unwilling, for when Kernot's book was formally released the very day Oakes wrote his column, the former Labor leader took the high road and declined all approaches for comment. Thus Oakes, in the interests of fairness, obviously felt someone should defend 'poor old Beazley', and who better than himself. In the process Oakes took *Bulletin* readers, tantalisingly, to the bedroom door without telling them who was behind it or, even, that the bedroom beckoned when really it was the lavatory.

What, supposedly, most upset Oakes was that Kernot's book did not confess to what he called 'the biggest secret in Kernot's life' which, 'if made public, would cause a lot of people to view her defection from the Democrats to Labor (in October 1997) in a different light'.

Really? And that secret was?

Well, for another 48 hours, it was still too secret for Oakes to say. But he thundered in his column: 'While it is one thing for journalists to stay away from such a (secret) matter, it is quite another for Kernot herself to pretend it does not exist when she pens what purports to be her ill-fated change of party allegiance. An honest book would have included it . . .'

An honest column, even if a grubby, sanctimonious one, would have included it, too. It did not. Twenty-four hours later, early Tuesday evening, *The Bulletin* in Sydney faxed the major newspaper bureaus in the Canberra gallery with a press release and a copy of Oakes's article. Nobody I'm aware of took it up, though they all knew instantly what cat Oakes was belling.

Next day, with the column's publication, Oakes sought to defend: 1) his 'revelation' of a secret secret; and 2) his coyness in not disclosing the secret, given he had argued it was such a significant omission from Kernot's book. Yet, apart from the grubbiness of what he was doing, the rank hypocrisy of a press gallery journalist throwing such dangerous stones, albeit one as venerable as Oakes, seemed not to dawn on him.

So Oakes that night, as political editor of the Nine Network, sister media arm of the Packer company that publishes *The Bulletin*, went to air on the network's 6 o'clock bulletin with his new version of 'the truth': a story bluntly asserting a five-year 'affair' between Kernot and Gareth Evans, the memorable and much-quoted former Labor Foreign Minister and deputy leader now almost three years gone from Parliament. For his evidence Oakes cited an email he claimed Evans had sent Kernot, and, sprinkled throughout his sordid little tale, were, of course, the ubiquitous 'Labor sources', fount of all truth, light and understanding.

Have you ever thought what political writers would do if: 1) they were compelled, in such instances as Oakes's 'revelation', to identify sources of information or quotes; or 2) if they always had to take direct responsibility for what they wrote or said rather than hiding behind the wondrous catch-all of 'Labor sources', 'Liberal sources', 'backbench sources', 'government sources', 'cabinet sources', 'senior ministers said' (never 'junior' ministers, you'll note) etcetera? Or even 'a political friend of many years standing'? They're always so wonderfully anonymous.

You might remember the pundit who Janette Howard recently bollocked publicly for something she insisted was wrong. If so, you'll remember, with delight, the pundit responded that no, it had not been him at all who'd made the written claim the Prime Minister's wife was challenging, it had been the anonymous 'senior ministers' he'd simply been quoting. Such sophistry warms us all on a cold Canberra night. I wait, joylessly, for the day a journalist, myself included, attributes a story to some 'self-serving politician or staffer or party official whose back (he or she) scratches in return for information, preferably in document form'. Nobody can deny a document.

Or an email, these days.

Yet even Channel Nine had difficulty taking responsibility for Oakes's assertions of the old, clandestine Evans/Kernot poking, though it had no difficulty reporting them. In late night and early morning bulletins on Wednesday and Thursday, its political editor's 'revelations' of two former MPs, both adults, doing what many adults, married or single, even journalists, believe it or not, often do (shocking!), one of whom, given the chance four years ago, decided to fib rather than publicly confess his infidelity (even more shocking!), were reported by the Nine Network as 'claims of an alleged affair', a claim made only by Oakes but parroted, in turn, by all the next morning's newspapers, none of which could possibly have verified the claim, though all had been aware of the gossip for years.

But then Evans, an honourable man, whatever you think, did the honourable thing, when, as a private citizen, he could have told everybody, Oakes and Simon Crean included, to go take a running jump, it was none of their bloody business. With much of the media in a sanctimonious frenzy and a silly Crean adding his silly two cents' worth from as far away as London, ex-politician Evans, three years a private citizen, admitted 'his actions' with the blonde, green-eyed Cheryl, 'deeply' regretted 'the hurt' he'd caused all concerned, 'above all my own family', and confessed the four-year-old lie he'd committed 'to protect my marriage'.

And you can bet that when Oakes went on TV on Wednesday night to reveal 'the truth' he felt the whole country had to know in fairness to 'poor old Beazley', there would have been politicians by the truckload, past and present, right across Australia, who would have felt an instant icy chill, each shuddering at the reality, 'There but for the grace of God . . .'

My political friend of many years standing believes, only half jokingly, the moral of the Oakes dictum on truth above all: 'All new MPs should be told, don't go rooting people you shouldn't be rooting. You don't have to stop rooting; just root the right people. Basic and all as it is, that's a lesson, as you well know, that so many in politics, from prime ministers down, including the press gallery and other parasites and excluding no-one, have never learnt. And don't ever think, just because people with whom you associate would root a running doughnut, that they won't be holier than thou if they get half a chance.'

No, indeed.

As for Crean, you have to wonder. His London press conference on Wednesday was meant to justify what he was doing in Europe by detailing 'wide-ranging discussions' on refugees. It was a disaster. All Crean got was a rush of questions about 'Laurie Oakes's allegations'. Unbelievably, given they had nothing to do with Crean's responsibilities whatever, and both Evans and Kernot were long gone from Parliament and the Labor Caucus, Crean stumbled on and on about a supposed 'requirement' they each make 'a full explanation'.

Why? And says who? Of course, for 'poor old Beazley'. Oakes told ABC radio on Thursday: 'I hope I made the right decision. As I say, I agonised, I worried, and it's a very hard thing to make a decision about.' Be assured, I didn't agonise at all.

Alan Ramsey

# Chapter 16

# A Brief Interregnum

## A Bloke and his Cow

MAY 10, 2003

PAUL BONGIORNO used to be a priest in country Victoria, until one day, in the confessional, a troubled man told him he'd been having sexual relations with a cow. If the late Spike Milligan were telling the story he might have said Bongiorno had replied, gravely, in modulated tones now known to many Australians: 'Have you ever thought of trying it with a woman?'

Instead, what the young Father Bongiorno supposedly mumbled was, 'There's not much I can do for you.' But that, apparently, is not true either. What the incident did, though, was start the young priest thinking that maybe the cloth, after all, was for him the wrong calling.

Bongiorno would quit the church in 1974 to become, along the way, a television weather man (what else?) before, in 1987, arriving in the Canberra press gallery, via nine years in Brisbane, to report for Network Ten on national politics (what else, indeed?). TV journalism has much for which to thank that much put-upon cow.

(Just for interest's sake, the head of Ten's Canberra bureau at the time Bongiorno arrived was Kerry O'Brien, later to return to the ABC, while one of his producers was Tony O'Leary, now and for the past eight years John Howard's press secretary. That, too, was the same year I began filling this space in the *Herald* each Saturday.)

And the point of any of this?

No reason other than, in a bad week for sane news and decent standards, I thought it more satisfying to write: a) that the national press gallery has some genuinely interesting people you'd never suspect; and b) how we all need a sense of humour to cope with the slugs, the spivs, the mendacity and, above all, the mediocrity in this country's public life.

'Bonge', as we know him, and that sad bloke and his cow, helped rescue the week. It is 32 years since Bongiorno officiated at a wedding. But at Sydney's Botanic Gardens last weekend, before 120 invited guests—an eclectic mix of egos (Liberal and Labor politicians, staffers, party officials, journalists, friends and family) you'd never have thought could enjoy themselves together, but did, and with style—Bonge married, jointly with a licensed celebrant, the Seven Network's Glen Milne and Canberra lobbyist Jannette Cotterell. It was during the speeches afterwards that we heard about the cow and its penitent abuser.

We learnt, too, a wonderful story Milne told against himself. He had a cancer scare last year, and after he returned to work following surgery, Howard had him round to his office to welcome him back. The thrice-married Milne took Georgia, one of his teenage daughters, with him. Afterwards, as they were leaving, Milne remarked how impressed his daughter must have been at meeting the Prime Minister. To which she replied, matter-of-factly: 'Not really. Two short men in big chairs trying to look important.'

Peter Costello laughed like a drain.

The self-deprecating anecdote says something, which too many politicians these days ignore, about what we like to think is fundamental to the Australian character: not taking ourselves too seriously. The perception of being 'up yourself' can be hugely self-destructive, a truism Peter Hollingworth seems never to have understood.

A great story defining Australian character comes from the marvellous book *Australian Accent*, written in 1958 by John Douglas Pringle, a distinguished *Herald* editor and a Pom who settled and died here. Writing of Australians' resentment of authority, Pringle told how a young Yugoslav migrant in the early 1950s had rescued a policeman from 'the death grip of a certified lunatic while a crowd of Australians stood by cheering the lunatic'.

The migrant, for his trouble, was 'rewarded' by the then Victorian Premier who, at an official ceremony, 'presented him with a copy of *100 Years of Responsible Government in Victoria*, left over from the previous year's jubilee celebrations, and clapped him on the back, saying, "Well, son, you're a dinkum Aussie now."'

Ava good weegend.

Alan Ramsey

# Up There, Cazaly

**MARCH 16, 2002**

DID YOU see Simon Crean on ABC television's *7.30 Report* two nights ago? National political life has been in turmoil all week over political accusations against a High Court judge supposedly having his way with a 17-year-old 'rent boy', and there was the latest alternative Prime Minister on national TV pontificating about the 'tragedy' of the Melbourne AFL footballer caught having his way with his vice-captain's wife!

It could only happen in Australia.

Fran Kelly, the program's political editor: 'Simon Crean, how do you feel about Wayne Carey leaving (the North Melbourne Kangaroos AFL club)?'

Crean, the Kangaroos' No. 1 ticketholder: 'Well, I feel shocked and I feel saddened. I think it is a terrible blow for him, for the families involved, for the club and for footballers generally [not to mention the vice-captain]. He is the best player I have ever seen, and he will be a great loss to the game.'

Kelly: 'Can you understand the Kangaroos, the players, wanting him to go? I think they went on strike, didn't they (in support of their vice-captain)? I mean, is that fair enough, given the standing of their response [sic]?'

The 'standing of their response?'

Crean rose above Kelly's non-sequitur with ease and took the question with sure hands. 'I've had a few other things on my plate,' he said, 'even though this has been a major distraction for me. I don't know the full circumstances, Fran, but clearly when you have got those divisions within a club it would appear the resolution could only have been this outcome. It is a tragedy that the circumstances that led to it happened, and the outcome itself is a tragedy.'

Gallantly if clumsily phrased.

Kelly battled on gamely. 'Some say it is not a very manly response from the club itself; that they should just have had it out in the back room, with their sleeve shirt [sic] rolled up and be done with it.'

Crean, clearly shaken by the suggestion of a good old-fashioned thumping: 'No, no. I think the club has faced up to this. This must have been the hardest decision they have had to take. I have got great admiration for the club, and whilst it will be a blow to them, the club won't be the same without Carey. But the club will go on, and go on in strength. They have done it in the past and they will do it again, I'm confident of that . . . It's sad all round. The club has got to put this behind it. It will be hard, but they will do it.'

Kelly, seriously: 'Could Wayne Carey be

rehabilitated from this position? Could he come back in the future?'

Crean, just as seriously: 'Well, I think all of these things can have some healing associated with it. It requires a real commitment. I hope there can be that healing out of this, but it's going to take a lot of work.'

Kelly, finally: 'What's your view of Carey's behaviour? He is a role model for young Kangaroo fans in particular.'

Crean: 'Well, obviously the behaviour is inexcusable. And by his own standards, he's accepted that. So I think that's an example, in itself, that even with players at their peak, even with indispensables, they can't bend the rules. I think that's an important rule in itself. But Carey will always be remembered for the player. He is a great player, the best I have seen. I think it's going to be a long time before we see another one like him.'

The vice-captain's wife probably thinks so, too. That's what it's like with 'indispensables'. Can you believe it? *Up There Cazaly* won't have quite the same meaning ever again.

Alan Ramsey

# So Who's the Bunny?

AUGUST 24, 2002

THE ONE we used to call the people's bank made a record annual profit of $2.65 billion and immediately announced it would shed another 1000 jobs to make more. The one that used to be the people's airline made an increased $428 million profit as its workforce continued strike action for a decent wage rise. All Australians once owned both, until a Labor Government, after promising not to, sold both. Now, in a single year, the Commonwealth Bank and

Qantas jointly return $3 billion-plus for private shareholders.

A depressing week. Still, there was Geoffrey Barker's email.

Barker is a friend and colleague who plays the trumpet as elegantly as he writes about the curious world of foreign affairs and defence for the *Herald's* sister paper, *The Australian Financial Review*. His office is just down the hall. On a bad day he often lifts my spirits with wonderfully disgusting jokes. An inventive friend emailed him some days ago. Barker shared the email with me. I share it with you.

The CIA, the FBI and the LAPD are each asked to prove their capability of apprehending terrorists. President Bush releases a white rabbit into a forest and tells each agency to catch it.

The CIA goes first. It sends animal informants into the forest. They question all plant and material witnesses. After three months of intensive investigations the CIA concludes rabbits do not exist.

The FBI goes in. After two weeks with no leads it bombs the forest, killing everything, including the rabbit. It makes no apologies; the rabbit had it coming, it insists.

The LAPD go in. They come out after just two hours with a badly beaten bear. The bear is sobbing, 'OK, OK, I'm a rabbit, I'm a rabbit.'

John Howard hears about George jnr's idea and decides to test Australian law enforcement agencies. He releases a white rabbit into Stromlo Forest, near Canberra. The National Crime Authority can't catch it but promises that if it gets a budget increase it can recover $90 million in unpaid rabbit taxes and proceeds of crime.

The Victorian police go in. They're gone only 15 minutes, returning with a koala, a kangaroo and a tree fern, all three shot to pieces. 'They looked like dangerous rabbits and we acted in self-defence,' they explain. The NSW police go in. Surveillance tapes later reveal top-ranking officers and rabbits dancing around a gum tree stoned out of their minds.

The Queensland police go in. They reappear driving a brand new Mercedes, scantily clad rabbits draped all over them. The WA police actually catch the white rabbit, but it inexplicably hangs itself when the attending officer 'slipped out momentarily' for a cup of tea.

The SA and NT police join forces and beat the crap out of every rabbit in the forest, except the white one. They know it is the black ones who cause all the trouble.

The Australian Federal Police refuse to go in. It examines the issues, particularly cost, and decides that because of low priority, high overtime and the projected expense to the AFP as a whole, the matter should be returned to the referring authority for further analysis.

ASIO goes into the wrong forest.

Alan Ramsey

# Well, Baise-Moi!

**MAY 18, 2002**

NOT ALL French farce is on stage and screen. Labor's Chris Schacht confronted the Senate three days ago with a rousing speech on the banning throughout Australia, on the instigation of John Howard's Attorney-General, Daryl Williams, of the French film *Baise-Moi*. Berating 'this ludicrous situation', Schacht said:

'I trust my French pronunciation is right, *Baise-Moi*. As I understand it, that translates into English as 'fuck me'. I don't know whether the French designed the title to attract notoriety, but that is not the issue.'

Neither was Schacht's English translation, which seemed just as deliberately designed to do the same. It succeeded. Julian McGauran, the National Party's enthusiastic Senate Whip (no, I'm not kidding), leapt to his feet 'on a point of order' and insisted on 'a bit of censorship' of Schacht's language. Acting deputy president, Michael Forshaw (ALP, NSW), was busy reading and didn't hear what Schacht had said, but a Senate clerk whispered the dread word and Forshaw responded: 'Senator Schacht, I understand you did use a word regarded as disorderly. I would ask you to withdraw it.'

Schacht: 'If it is out of order to say it in English, isn't it out of order to say it in French?'

Rosemary Crowley (ALP, SA): 'Touche!'

Forshaw: 'As I understand it, the French word you used may be translated in other ways, as well as in the way you put it. But I still ask you to withdraw the word you used.'

Schacht: 'If I now said the translation is 'Effdotdotdot Me', is that in order?'

No, it wasn't. Forshaw insisted Schacht withdraw 'the word'. Schacht argued how could he argue against film censorship when the Senate was censoring a word that was part of the debate? Chris Ellison (Lib., WA) challenged Schacht's translation. He'd read, Ellison said, that another interpretation was 'kiss me', while there were other versions 'which I will not repeat here'. And then McGauran ('I am no prude, but I do not excuse Senator Schacht's French') insisted not only did Schacht have to withdraw 'the word', but he wanted it 'expunged from Hansard'.

At this point acting deputy president Forshaw announced he'd seek a formal ruling from the Senate president, Margaret Reid (Lib., ACT). In the meantime, said Forshaw: 'I ask you now to withdraw the word.' Schacht acceded. And six hours later, Reid went into the Senate and gravely told senators she endorsed the withdrawal of Schacht's 'inappropriate language' and urged all senators to 'respect the dignity of debate'. But she did not expunge 'the word' from the official Hansard record ('As Senate proceedings are immediately public, expungement is not appropriate.')

Wonderful, don't you think?

Well, 24 hours later, on Thursday, 'the word' got another equally forthright outing, this time in quite different circumstances at a closed meeting of the House of Representatives legal and constitutional committee. Kevin Andrews (Lib., Vic.) used to be its chairman. But Andrews is now a minister and Howard has appointed Bronwyn Bishop in his stead. This week's meeting was the first since she took over. Alas, things did not go smoothly.

They were not helped by Bishop's insistence that she would sit on one side of the table and all other members would sit opposite. Proceedings disintegrated into some undignified exchanges over what should be the new committee's first terms of reference, which Bishop had drafted and was insisting would not be changed. Considerable bickering ensued. Finally, Labor's Duncan Kerr (Tas.), used 'the word' with considerable feeling, and left. He was followed by a chortling Daryl Melham (ALP, NSW). The meeting reconvened later in more civil circumstances.

Wondrous indeed.

Alan Ramsey

# Chapter 17

# Other People's Wars

## The First Casualty

**MARCH 20, 2004**

ARTHUR AUGUSTUS William Harry Ponsonby, the first Baron Ponsonby of Shulbreds, son of Sir Henry Ponsonby, private secretary to Queen Victoria, was born in 1871 and died in 1946. In 1928 Ponsonby, most obviously a Pom, famously used the phrase: 'When war is declared, the first casualty is truth.' Yet this was but a slight reworking of the quote, 'The first casualty when war comes is truth,' by an American, California's isolationist Senator Hiram W. Johnson, during a speech in 1917, the year the United States entered World War I.

It was to Johnson that Australia's Phillip Knightley dedicated his acclaimed 1975 book, *The First Casualty*, on the role of the war correspondent as 'propagandist and myth-maker'.

However, if Ponsonby plagiarised Johnson's quote, the book in which the quote appears in the frontispiece was all Ponsonby's own work. This is the anti-war classic, *Falsehood in Wartime: Propaganda Lies of the First World War*, which, as simply Arthur Ponsonby, British Labor MP, he wrote in 1928, two years before Ramsay MacDonald's Government made him leader of the House of Lords.

In his compelling introduction to a piece of research years later described as 'one of the most important archive documents in any library', Ponsonby wrote, in part: 'Falsehood is a recognised and extremely useful weapon in warfare. Every country uses it quite deliberately to deceive its own people, to attract neutrals and to mislead the enemy . . . Lying, as we all know, does not take place only in wartime. But the habit of lying is not nearly so extraordinary as [people's] readiness to believe. It is, indeed, because of human credulity that lies flourish. In wartime the authoritative organisation of lying is not sufficiently recognised . . .

'Authorities do, and indeed must, resort to this practice in order, first, to justify themselves by depicting the enemy as an undiluted criminal and, second, to inflame popular passion to secure recruits. They cannot afford to tell the truth . . . Victories must be exaggerated and defeats minimised, and the stimulus of indignation, horror and hatred must be assiduously and continuously pumped into the public mind . . .

'People should realise that a government which has decided on [making war] must, at the outset, present a one-sided case in justification for action. Facts must be distorted, relevant circumstances concealed and a picture presented which, by its crude colouring, will persuade people that their government is blameless, their cause is righteous and that the indisputable wickedness of the enemy has been proved beyond question. Lies are circulated with great rapidity. The amount of rubbish and humbug that pass under the name of patriotism in wartime in all countries is sufficient to make decent people blush . . .

'Between nations, where the consequences are vital, the most upright men honestly believe there is no depth of duplicity to which they may not legitimately stoop. They have got to do it. The thing cannot go on without the help of lies. This is no plea that lies should not be used in wartime, but a demonstration of how lies must be used. If the truth were told, there would be no reason and no will for war. In wartime, failure to lie is negligence, the doubting of a lie a misdemeanour, the declaration of the truth a crime . . .

'But there is not a living soul in any country who does not deeply resent having his/her passions roused, his indignation inflamed, his patriotism exploited and his ideals desecrated by concealment, subterfuge, fraud, falsehood, trickery and deliberate lying [by] those in whom he/she is taught to repose confidence and to pay respect. None of the heroes prepared for sacrifice, none of the common herd ready for service and obedience, will be inclined to listen to the call of their country once they discover the polluted source of that call and recognise the monstrous finger of falsehood which beckons . . .'

John Howard can hear them coming.

Alan Ramsey

# The Stampede to Battle

SEPTEMBER 26, 2001

ANDERSON DAWSON died, alone, a penniless alcoholic, at the age of 47 on July 20, 1910. Even his wife and children did not attend his funeral. For 90 years his gravestone in Brisbane's Toowong cemetery simply recorded his name and year of death. There was nothing to identify him. Yet Dawson headed the world's first Labor government, in December 1899, and, in April 1904, he became Defence Minister in Australia's first Federal Labor government.

There is a nice irony about Dawson's background, given the domestic political circumstances of the international war hysteria more than a century later.

Australia's first involvement in someone else's war was the conflict between Britain and the South African republics of the Transvaal and the Orange Free State, officially declared on October 11, 1899. At the time, Dawson, a former mining union leader and newspaper editor, was a Labor MP for the seat of Charters Towers in outback Queensland.

A fervent republican and supporter of Federation, Dawson strongly opposed Australian involvement in the Boer War without the approval of Parliament. Yet Queensland had been the first colony in the Empire to offer to send troops to support British forces.

When it did so, three months before Britain declared war, Dawson, as State Labor leader, berated the Queensland Premier, James ('Oily Jimmy') Dickson, and unsuccessfully moved that 'this House disapproves of the action of the Government in making an offer of troops to Britain, thus committing the Colony to an indefinite and practically unlimited expenditure without the sanction of Parliament'.

Despite the 'wave of jingoism passing all over the country', Dawson thundered, the money used in 'sending a mob of swashbucklers to South Africa to show off their uniforms' would be better spent on Queensland 'libraries and hospitals'. His motion was voted down 38 to 28. Britain duly accepted the offer of 250 mounted infantry, who sailed for South Africa on November 1, 1899, farewelled at the docks by 20,000 loyal Queenslanders.

In his wonderful monograph, *Seven Days to Remember: The World's first Labor Government, Queensland, 1–7 December, 1899*, Ross Fitzgerald, professor in history and politics at Queensland's Griffith University, writes of the occasion: 'From Britain's formal acceptance of Queensland's offer, it took the colony less than a month to organise a contingent of 264 troops, including 14 officers and two machine-guns. On 28 October, the Mounted Infantry paraded through the streets of Brisbane, past a large and enthusiastic crowd at Post Office Square.

'There, private W.J. Evans' horse, frightened by the noise, fluttering flags and bunting,

bucked him off, fell on him and crushed him to death. Despite this unfortunate occurrence, the troops continued to the Domain [and], as the band played Soldiers of the Queen, the Lieutenant-Governor, Sir Samuel Walker Griffith [standing in for the absent Governor, Lord Lamington, after whom the iconic cake came to be patriotically named], took the salute.'

On this sombre note, Australia, not yet federated, departed for its first war. And a month after the troops left, the Dickson Government, riven by internal brawling, resigned and Andy Dawson was sworn in on December 1, 1899, at the head of a minority Labor administration, the first anywhere. It lasted just a week, being voted out as soon as Parliament met on December 7.

Yet that first Labor ministry included Andrew Fisher, who in 1908 would become Australia's second Labor Prime Minister after John Watson became the nation's first (for four months) in April, 1904. That short-lived Watson Labor ministry would include Anderson Dawson, by then a Queensland senator, as Defence Minister.

Alan Ramsey

**Postscript:** *On March 3, 1885, 734 volunteers of the colonial NSW Infantry Contingent sailed from Sydney to join British forces putting down a rebellion in the Sudan by followers of the Mahdi after the death in Khartoum in January that year of one of the Empire's most heroic military figures, General Charles Gordon. The unit was in Sudan little more than six weeks before sailing for home on May 17, having suffered just three wounded in minor skirmishing and spending most of its time on guard duty. They arrived back in Sydney on June 19, 1885 and five days later marched through city streets to a heroes' reception, in pouring rain, at Victoria Barracks.*

# A Legacy of Denial

MAY 27, 2000

TODAY IS the 35th anniversary of the Vung Tau ferry. The troop-carrier HMAS *Sydney* made 25 operational voyages from Australia to the open harbour port of Vung Tau in Vietnam's Mekong Delta between May 1965 and November 1972, ferrying 15,600 Australian troops to and from the war and, with its warship escorts, 350,000 tonnes of weapons, vehicles and equipment. Yet no voyage was ever so bleakly instructive as that first one 35 years ago.

It began in the middle of the night. There was no glory, no crowds, no speeches, no television cameras. No bands played. No prime minister or any other politician was there to farewell Australia's latest commitment of combat forces to someone else's war. It was 1.29am on May 27, 1965, when the *Sydney* drew away from Garden Island and slipped out through Sydney heads to join the escort destroyer HMAS *Duchess*.

Aboard were 460 troops of One Battalion, Royal Australian Regiment (1RAR), their heavy equipment and vehicles and a troop of armoured personnel carriers. Three rifle companies would follow by Qantas charter. Eight hundred men in all. Also leaving on the Sydney that night were five pressmen: a TV cameraman, two photographers and two reporters. I was one of the reporters. Perhaps that is why I remember, 35 years later, what the politicians, then and now, like to forget.

That is their Vietnam legacy. No glorious victories to immortalise, no heroic defeats to mythologise. Just the abiding guilt that, first, Australia ever got involved in such a shameful conflict, and, second, the appalling way we treated our troops when they came home. Have you noticed government in this country never commemorates anything to do with the Vietnam War as such? Its beginning, its end or anything in between?

Nothing. We roll it into Anzac Day and forget it. Authority, political and military, doesn't want to know. Like the Americans, we lost in Vietnam, humiliatingly. The politicians committed the troops, solely for political reasons, then scarpered, also solely for political reasons, three years before the Americans did.

It took all of another 20 years, from the time of the last Australian troops to leave, to honour the 50,000 Australians (and 504 dead) who served there, with a memorial and their own parade. Twenty years!

A newspaper account that May morning 35 years ago reported the stark detail of the *Sydney*'s departure: 'The loading of troops took less than an hour. Soldiers with fixed bayonets stood guard as the men filed aboard.

Police launches patrolled around the ship. No wives or families were allowed near, although three carloads of relatives were at the dockyard as the *Sydney* sailed. Troops had to say their farewells before a convoy of trucks drove them through the city at night to the dockyard.'

The *Herald*'s front-page headline that day reflected the cheerless mood. 'Rendezvous in the dark', it said, in part. That accurately, if unintentionally, described exactly how Australia went to war in Vietnam. In the dark. The contrast with Australia's next two military adventures, the Gulf War in 1991 and East Timor last year, could not have been greater.

Bob Hawke, as Prime Minister, and Robert Ray, as Defence Minister, flew to Darwin to farewell, with great ceremony, our commitment of two warships to George Bush's war with Saddam Hussein in late 1990. They went back to Darwin months later to welcome them home with even more ceremony. A popular war never hurt any political leader. And no war is more popular than a winning one against an international bogeyman.

The East Timor commitment was massaged and manipulated even more ferociously. Remember John Howard's Darwin farewell to General Peter Cosgrove and his troops in 1999? There were enough television crews and newspaper cameras to cover the Olympics. Or so it seemed. By my count, Howard farewelled and/or welcomed Australia's troops seven times in a year, including his visit to East Timor, the Parliament House lunch for Cosgrove, the Darwin Christmas party for troops' families, and the Townsville arrival a fortnight ago.

A month ago the Prime Minister was in Gallipoli for the 85th anniversary of the Anzac Cove landings. A week later he visited the WWI battlefields of the Somme, glorifying the memory of his father and grandfather, both of whom fought in France. Howard's press people even handed out photos and diary extracts from the Howard family memorabilia. Two weeks after that, the Prime Minister was in South Korea for the 50th anniversary of the beginning of the Korean War, another Australian military landmark.

And Vietnam? Here we don't mention the war. It wasn't just that our politicians committed Australia to a tragic, losing cause by lying outrageously to justify their actions. Nor was it the dreadful carnage wrought on the Vietnamese people. It was the way the war unfolded in people's living rooms. Vietnam was the war the military and the politicians couldn't censor. It was there, in all its appalling detail, on the TV every night.

Vietnam was never sanitised.

Families at home saw war like it is before the censors make it respectable, if only for morale. The influence of television was never more dramatically realised than its effect on US public opinion in shaping the conduct and ultimate outcome of the Vietnam conflict. And it neither demeans nor challenges the valour of Australian troops to understand the errors and military accidents that occurred in Vietnam.

On August 18, 1971, Prime Minister Bill McMahon, announced: 'The combat role which Australia took up over six years ago in Vietnam is soon to be completed . . . I am now able to announce the Government has decided to withdraw all remaining combat forces . . . Most will be home in Australia by Christmas, 1971 . . . I express the Government's conviction the decision is a mark of the success which has attended our policies and actions in Vietnam over the years . . .'

Three months later, on November 24, 1971, the Parliament, in a 75-minute debate restricted to six speakers, voted its 'appreciation and gratitude' to all Australian forces who had served in Vietnam 'for their courage, dedication and sense of duty'. Not all the troops got home by Christmas.

In February 1972, HMAS *Sydney* sailed from Vung Tau with 457 troops, its last troop withdrawal. Its final trip to Vietnam in November that year, just weeks before the election that defeated the McMahon Government and brought the Whitlam Labor alternative to power, hoisted the last of the Australian forces' equipment aboard and left Vung Tau for the last time. HMAS *Sydney* was sold for scrap and towed out of Sydney Harbour to the breakers in Hong Kong in October, 1975.

Alan Ramsey

**Postscript:** *In more recent years, Australia's 10-year military involvement in the Vietnam War—its longest in duration in any overseas conflict—has seen its pariah status begin to diminish, both officially and within the community, following a very deliberate attempt by the Howard Government and veterans' organisations to make this involvement more sympathetically known and understood.*

# The Horror and Humbug of Vietnam

**APRIL 16, 1994**

IN HIS book, *A Military History of Australia*, Jeffrey Grey, of the Department of History at the Australian Defence Force Academy in Canberra, says, on page 238, that 501 Australians died in the Vietnam War, not 504. He sources his figures to Central Army Records and the Australian Archives.

Grey's breakdown of Australia's involvement is precise. A series of Coalition governments, beginning with the Menzies Government in 1962, sent 'approximately 50,000' Australians to the killing fields of Vietnam during the 10 years 1962 to 1972. Some 17,424 were 20-year-old conscripts, 200 of whom died there, including 184 killed in action.

Of the total 501 Australian dead over the 10-year period, 423 were listed as battle deaths, 74 as 'non-battle' deaths, presumably accidents, and four are still missing, presumed dead. Another 3,131 Australians were either wounded in action or injured in some way, a full third of them (1,062) in accidents of one sort or another. Australia's 10-year casualty toll, both on and off the battlefield, totalled 3,632, or about 7 per cent.

Actual battle casualties, dead and wounded, were about 5 per cent of the total number of Australians who served in Vietnam. As for the conscripts, more than 804,000 20-year-olds registered in the eight years national service operated in Australia between its reintroduction by the Menzies Government in late 1964 and its abolition by the Whitlam Government after Labor came to power in December, 1972. Of these 804,000 registrants, 63,000 were called up for military service under the infamous lottery system and 17,424 were sent to Vietnam.

Grey records: 'In financial terms the war was said to have cost Australia $218.4 million, although the basis on which this was calculated is not clear. Less than 10 per cent of Australia's armed forces were in Vietnam at any one time, compared with one sixth of American servicemen.'

The loss of US blood and treasure was infinitely greater.

In his book, *The Vietnam War: An Almanac,* John Bowman records: 'The US military lost 47,253 in combat and another 10,499 died in Vietnam. There were 313,616 wounded, of whom 153,300 were classified serious . . . Some 10,000 US wounded lost at least one limb, more than all those in World War II and Korea combined . . . The average age of US combat personnel was only 19—compared to 26 in World War II.

'Black Americans constituted about 13 per cent of the total troop force in Vietnam, about the same as their proportion of the total US population, but 28 per cent had combat assignments and only 2 per cent of officers were black.'

Of the cost Bowman records (figures in US dollars): 'It is roughly but reasonably estimated that the war cost the United States $150 billion in direct expense. Indirect expense would probably total at least that. On an average day (for 10 years) US artillery expended 10,000 rounds at about $100 a shell, a cost for this item alone of $1 million a day. One sortie by one B52 bomber cost $30,000 in bombs alone.

'Some 4,865 US helicopters were lost in the war, each costing about $250,000, and 3,720 other aircraft were destroyed. The total tonnage of bombs dropped in Vietnam, Laos and Cambodia came to 8 million, about four times the tonnage dropped in all of World War II. Some 2.2 million tons of bombs were dropped on the infiltration routes in Laos alone between 1965–71.'

All this for humiliating defeat.

Then there was Vietnam itself. The US-authored *Anatomy of a War* reports: 'The United States in Vietnam unleashed the greatest flood of firepower against a nation known to history. The human suffering was monumental. The figures in all aspects of this enormous trauma are inadequate. The Pentagon's final estimate of killed and wounded civilians in South Vietnam between 1965 and 1972 ran from 700,000 to 1,225,000. Senate numbers for the same period were 1,350,000. In a nation of 18 million, the war exacted an immensely high toll.'

Bowman writes: 'South Vietnam reported 185,528 of its military personnel killed in the war, with 499,026 wounded. North Vietnam and the Vietcong reportedly lost 924,048 dead in combat. Vietnam as a whole is estimated to have lost 415,000 civilians in the war, with at least 935,000 wounded.'

In his *Encyclopedia of 20th Century Warfare,* Dr Noble Frankland writes of the Vietnam War: 'The number of North Vietnamese and Vietcong combatants killed in action from 1965 to 1974 was estimated by the American military at 950,765, a figure admittedly inflated by about 30 per cent. South Vietnamese forces killed-in-action during the same period were 220,357, perhaps 243,000 by the war's end (in April, 1975).

'South Vietnamese civilians suffered anywhere from 247,600 to 430,000 dead and 1,000,000 wounded, while an estimated 52,000 North Vietnamese civilians died in the US bombing before 1972.'

In total, on the best estimates available, somewhere between a minimum 1.1 million and 1.6 million Vietnamese, North and South, died after the Americans decided, from 1961 onwards, to 'save' Vietnam from itself. Nor do these estimates include the carnage wrought after Richard Nixon, pursuing 'peace with honour', took the war into Cambodia in 1970, thus creating the circumstances that later brought the genocidal Pol Pot regime to power.

The United States and its allies all but destroyed two countries and ravaged a third.

In the process Lyndon Johnson destroyed his presidency and established the legacy of an entire generation of the most divisive and corrosive forces from which American society still has not recovered.

Australia's role was no less shabby.

It is 29 years, almost to the day, since Sir Robert Menzies stood in the Parliament on the night of April 29, 1965, and announced his Government was committing frontline troops to Vietnam. Three years earlier Australia had sent 30 military training instructors. This had become 100 by the end of 1964. Now we were joining the war itself.

'The Australian Government is now in receipt of a request from the Government of Vietnam for further military assistance,' Menzies announced. 'We have decided, after close consultation with the Government of the United States, to provide an infantry battalion . . .'

By the end of 1967 this initial one battalion of 1,000 troops had been twice increased to a self-contained battle group of more than 8,000. By then Harold Holt, in March 1966, had already committed 20-year-old conscripts to the war—the first time in all the wars Australia has fought that it has sent conscripted forces beyond New Guinea.

Ten years after Menzies' announcement, the Whitlam Government tabled in Parliament, in May 1975, a 35-page document which made a mockery of the professed reasons Australia had gone to war. Menzies' statement had been a hoax, if not a bare-faced lie. We hadn't gone to war at South Vietnam's request at all. Canberra and Washington had manipulated Australia's entry.

The document Whitlam tabled was prepared by the Department of Foreign Affairs. It was based on official cables and memoranda of the day. It said in part: 'Despite the fact the Government of South Vietnam, on 29 April, 1965, announced that the Australian battalion was sent in response to a request from South Vietnam, this is not borne out by the evidence of the documents.

'The requests for military aid were largely generated by initiatives from the US. These initiatives were political and not military in motive. The United States did not need the military aid, but it did desire the military presence of its friends and allies in order to show the world that the United States was not alone in its efforts against communism in South-East Asia . . .'

Bill Morrison, a Whitlam Government Minister, told the Parliament in a debate on the issue at the time: 'The [Coalition] Opposition belong to the very political parties that lied and lied and lied to the Australian people about Australia's involvement in Vietnam.'

All the evidence agreed.

Alan Ramsey

**Postscript:** *Remarkably, the official number of Australian casualties in the Vietnam War have in recent years begun to increase, even though it is almost four decades since the last Australian combat forces were withdrawn from Vietnam in 1971. The reason for this is that although Australian battle and non-battle deaths in Vietnam are fixed at 501, the 'official' overall casualty figures are counted by the names on the Roll of Honour at the Australian War Memorial in Canberra. These figures are subject to change as the surviving generation of young men who served in Vietnam begin dwindling and their eligibility for Roll of Honour status is determined, on application, by a Government-appointed Council for the War Memorial. Thus, by June 1, 2009, the number of Australia's 'official' Vietnam War dead exceeded 520 and was climbing.*

# 'Yes, Mr President'

AUGUST 11, 1990

BOB HAWKE yesterday took Australia into Iraq's war in the Middle East. He did so at the request of an old and powerful friend. He did so in formal response to a phone call from Washington at 7 o'clock in the morning. He did so without the approval of his Cabinet, his ministry, or his parliamentary party.

And he did so in playing some of the same sort of silly buggers that went on between Canberra and Washington 25 years ago to get Australia loyally marching into Vietnam to the sound of American trumpets. The parallel is there even if the politicians and the circumstances are different.

George Bush [the father] asked and Bob Hawke willingly gave. By his own count, only five of Hawke's ministers were party to Australia's decision to join the US naval blockade in the Persian Gulf. None of the five ministers opposed what he was doing. None opposed what the United States wanted him to do. Nobody else in the Government got a chance to say anything.

Nobody else was asked for an opinion. The Americans whistled and the Australian cab, as usual, was among the first off the rank, our Prime Minister at the wheel.

And even this, in the end, involved a bit of play-acting. President Bush knew before he phoned his loyal Canberra mate yesterday morning that President Hawke already had rounded up all the numbers he felt it necessary to consult in agreeing to the US request. Washington had been sounding out Canberra all week through the usual diplomatic links. The decision that mattered was reached in Hawke's office at lunchtime on Thursday.

Present at that meeting were Hawke's deputy and Treasurer, Paul Keating, his Senate leader and Industry and Commerce Minister, John Button, and the Attorney-General and acting Foreign Minister, Michael Duffy. They talked Washington's request through with Hawke for an hour. Two others ministers were drawn into the discussions during the meeting.

Robert Ray, the Defence Minister, was in Cairns. Gareth Evans, the rarely-at-home Foreign Minister, was in Dacca in Bangladesh. Hawke rang them both during the meeting to get their views. He rang no-one else. When the meeting ended, the five ministers were in full agreement with Hawke's proposal to commit Australian warships to the US naval blockade.

All Hawke now needed was for the Americans formally to ask what they had been informally canvassing since the weekend. A cable was sent to Australia's ambassador in Washington advising him to inform the Americans they could have what they wanted. Bob, meantime, sat back and waited for George's call. It came some 16 hours later.

Hawke took the President's call during breakfast at The Lodge. They spoke for half an hour. The only person with the Prime Minister was his office chief-of-staff,, Sandy Hollway. When the call ended, Australia was part of the blockade. It was as simple as that.

As Hawke announced, in suitably grave tones, to a press conference three-and-a-half hours later: 'The decisions I'm about to announce are against the background of Australia's total, unequivocal condemnation of the invasion by Iraq of Kuwait and its subsequent reported annexation. We join with the rest of the world in saying that we will not tolerate, will not stand idly by, while any member of the international community purports to break the rules of civilised conduct in that way.

'We've been considering what more should be done in addition to our joining with the rest of the world in imposing sanctions, to give an additional response to what is happening in the Gulf. We have been in contact with Washington on this issue.

'Let me make it clear that the primary purpose of the multinational naval task force will be to enforce the blockade on Iraq and Kuwait and, of course, to protect the exports from other oil-producing gulf countries and to protect other trade in the Gulf. But by its very nature it's worth saying that the force will contribute to the deterrence, we believe, of further aggression by Iraq . . .'

Unlike the decision three days earlier, supporting UN-imposed sanctions against Iraq, Hawke did not call his Cabinet together. A meeting on Monday of the full Cabinet—17 ministers minus Evans—approved Australia imposing trade sanctions. That meeting had lasted some 40 to 50 minutes. Again, nobody dissented. Neither did the Opposition.

And neither, it would seem, do the Australian people. But that is not really the point. What is the point is that Bob Hawke, as much as any prime minister before him, seems only too anxious to please whenever the phone rings from Washington. When this happens, Prime Minister Hawke and the Westminster system of government become President Bob and the Hawke system of doing what he wants.

Yesterday, at his press conference, Hawke revelled in the personal pronoun of sounding the call to arms. It was all 'I' this and 'I' that as he explained why Australia was rushing to the other side of the world as a good and responsible friend to our large and powerful ally.

Question: 'Wouldn't it have been better to wait for the United Nations, or seek a (UN) response before committing ships?'

Hawke: 'We can always find a reason and an excuse for not playing a responsible role in a threatening situation, and if we had wanted to do that, yes, we could have easily done that. But

I believe the gravity of the situation is such that it warranted this action at this time by Australia. Obviously I believe it would be the preference of the US, as well as of Australia, that there could be a United Nations-flag operation, and that is not out of the question. But, in circumstances of this kind, I think it's not appropriate to wait until the ideal actually emerges . . .'

Nobody asked why it wasn't appropriate, given that large numbers of US warships already are in the Gulf, and the two little frigates we're sending, however worthy, aren't going to make that much difference, not now and not if anyone actually starts shooting. Besides, the admiral, in all his braid, who

was sitting behind the Prime Minister with Defence Minister Robert Ray, the two like a couple of well behaved props, admitted it will be a full three weeks before our ships—Hawke insisted on using the defence jargon of calling them 'assets'—arrive 'on station' in the Gulf.

It all seemed a bit precipitate, like World War I, when young Australians rushed to join up and 'get over there' before it ended. Yet behind all the haste yesterday in getting to the front was the overwhelming feeling we're going for one reason only. And that's because Bob Hawke can't say no to Washington.

We never do.

Alan Ramsey

# Australia Never Says No

**FEBRUARY 14, 1998**

JOHN HOWARD calls it 'the hardest decision I have taken as Prime Minister'. It wasn't. There is nothing hard about getting into a war you can't lose. The hardest decision would have been to say no to Washington. Instead, when Bill Clinton phoned last Saturday to ask for Howard's help to make war against Iraq, the Prime Minister did what every other Australian leader has always done.

He said yes. Australia for more than a century has been going to other people's wars. This time is no different. Neither is the rhetoric. Once it used to be Britain's Prime Minister that phoned. Now it is the American President. Britain took us into the Boer War, two world wars, the Malaysian insurgency and confrontation with Indonesia.

The United Nations took us into the Korean War. The United States asked for, and got, our involvement in Vietnam and the Gulf War. Now we're ready, at Washington's request, to

make war against Saddam Hussein for the second time in eight years. Nothing changes.

Lyndon Johnson phoned Bob Menzies in 1965. George Bush phoned Bob Hawke in 1990. Bill Clinton phoned John Howard last weekend. Clinton phoned a second time three days later, on Tuesday, to say thank you. Howard was waiting in his office. So were the cameras that would record the moment for posterity and for the voters. Photos of John Howard standing at attention behind his desk, talking to the most powerful man in the world, were all over newspaper front pages next day.

That's another thing about getting into wars you can't lose. They usually make political leaders look good. Ask Margaret Thatcher and Ronald Reagan. Thatcher went to war in the Falklands in 1982 and Ronald Reagan indulged his military establishment in tiny Grenada in 1983 and with a bombing strike on Libya in 1986. Thatcher later won another

election and Reagan retired the most popular president in American history.

It's only when wars go bad, such as Vietnam, that politicians have regrets. Short, sharp wars far away in somebody else's country are always the best. The Falklands, Grenada, Libya, the American invasion of Panama in 1989 and the Gulf War in January/February 1991 are the best sort. And so, if Iraq remains intransigent about letting UN inspectors in to see whatever it might be doing that US spy satellites can't detect, is the latest proposed American military adventure.

For the moment, all we have is the rhetoric of justification . . .

Eight years ago, when Bob Hawke said yes to George Bush Snr, it took months for hostilities to begin. Thinking it had the Americans' tacit support, Iraq only discovered its mistake after it had invaded Kuwait. Five months went by, from August 1990 to January 1991, before Saddam Hussein learnt the folly of his misjudgment. This time we're told the waiting won't be so long. If the Americans take us to war it will be within weeks [And it was].

As of two days ago, according to *The New York Times*, the Americans had mobilised in the Gulf region and the Mediterranean, 24,500 troops, 300 combat aircraft, 16 warships—half of them equipped with cruise missiles—and

13 support vessels, all ready to be brought into operation in a series of bombing strikes on Iraqi targets. Australia's proposed contribution is less formidable: a maximum 250 military personnel, including units of the Special Air Service (SAS), and two clapped-out Boeing 707 aircraft from the RAAF's VIP fleet.

Obviously we'll only be there for show. Thus when Clinton phones to thank our Prime Minister, his gratitude clearly has nothing to do with our material contribution. We are there for moral support only. And when the White House calls, that's all the President ever wants. Thank you.

The melancholy reality remains that Australia is the only country that said yes each time to the Americans on Vietnam, the Gulf and now Iraq. The real question is why? Why does an Australian prime minister, any Australian prime minister, find he cannot say no whenever the phone rings from Washington?

With Britain, until its empire began to disintegrate after World War II, we at least had the excuse of bending to what many Australians knew as the mother country. Now it seems, for all our feel-good rhetoric about Asia, our insecurity remains such that our political leaders believe the national interest demands we must forever be in thrall to a great and powerful friend. If so, we now hold 30 years of Washington's IOUs.

Howard's caution in his presentation of the decision is obvious. It contrasts with the flamboyance and bellicose nature of Hawke's announcement in 1990. Howard is anxious to keep the decision low-key. It's almost as if the Prime Minister is apprehensive about what it is his Government has done.

In a series of five television interviews on Tuesday, including one with the international broadcaster CNN, Howard repeatedly emphasised his Government's hope that the issue be settled without force and by negotiation just as he stressed the token nature of Australia's proposed commitment. He was anything but aggressive about the decision. But the die is cast.

It always is when Washington phones.

Alan Ramsey

# An Offer George Couldn't Refuse

**SEPTEMBER 15, 2001**

JOHN HOWARD appeared on the lawns of the Australian Embassy in Washington two days ago to make war, if necessary, with George Bush [the son] on whomever the US Administration can pin the blame for this week's terrorist atrocities. The blank cheque the Prime Minister said he'd offered the White House was: 'I've indicated Australia will provide all support that might be requested of us by the United States in relation to any action that might be taken.'

Unsurprisingly, given the suffocating parochialism of the travelling Australian media, the first question asked after this startling admission had nothing to do with going to war at all. It sought the 'latest information' on how many Australians might have died in the suicide attacks in New York and Washington. When Howard got through telling his questioner of the 'three confirmed dead' Australians among the estimated 'more than 4,000' dead Americans, the more relevant question was asked: 'When you say Australia will give its full support, what do you mean?'

'Well,' replied Howard, 'I'm talking diplomatically and otherwise. We haven't been requested to provide any military assistance, but obviously, if we were asked, we would. It is very important at this time that America knows she's got friends.'

He continued: 'But let me stress, I haven't been requested, and I'm not suggesting we will be, but we have to accept that this is an occasion where we should stand shoulder to shoulder with the Americans, because this is not just an assault on America, it's an assault on the way of life we hold dear in common.'

Offered the slow full toss of what he thought about the 'very extended applause' given his brief appearance at that day's meeting of Congress, Howard opened his shoulders. 'I was very touched. It was a demonstration to me of the closeness of the relationship (between Australia and the United States). I think the Americans appreciated the fact that I went there very deliberately. I mean, obviously

because of what has happened the arrangements for my address to the joint sitting were naturally cancelled.

'But I indicated I wanted to go there and demonstrate, by my presence, the compassion we felt for the American people and the closeness we felt and the identification with the values for which America stands. I mean, this is a time when you have to stand by people who have the same view on life as you have. You can't cherry pick a close relationship.'

And finally: 'I think it is important countries like Australia play a role in identifying ourselves with the Americans. I mean, just because you are big and strong doesn't mean you can't feel lonely and you can't feel your heart has been ripped out.' It's comforting to know George W. is in charge and Little John is there to help.

Alan Ramsey

# . . . And He Didn't

**OCTOBER 10, 2001**

GEORGE W. Bush made war on Afghanistan's Taliban rulers on Sunday, October 7, US time. In Sydney, wakened by phone from Washington at Kirribilli House, John Howard got the news in his pyjamas at 1 o'clock Monday morning, Australian eastern time. The irony of events lay in the anniversary everyone forgot. Sixty years earlier, on October 7, 1941, exactly two months before Japan's sneak attack on Pearl Harbour unleashed total war in the Pacific, John Curtin became Labor's fifth and Australia's 14th Prime Minister and one of its most revered.

Later that same day, Curtin drove to Sydney and, in his first speech as Prime Minister, spoke at a Sydney Town Hall war bonds rally. David

Black, in *In His Own Words: John Curtin's speeches and writings*, quotes Curtin as gravely telling an enthusiastic audience: '. . . The immediate obligation [as prime minister] is to wage war with the maximum of Australia's capacity . . . There is no man so humble who cannot contribute or do something; there is no woman so weak but that there is not available some act of service in the greatest crisis that has ever come to free men in any period of human history . . .'

Three weeks after Pearl Harbour, Curtin would make his most famous 'speech', which was no speech at all but a New Year's message written, by invitation, for Sir Keith Murdoch's afternoon newspaper, *The Herald*, in Melbourne.

Published on December 27, 1941, Curtin's 1,500-word article, according to biographer David Day 58 years later, created outrage in Britain and consternation in Washington and 'has since come to be regarded, popularly, as marking the point at which Australia came of age, breaking free of the historic bonds of Empire to seek its salvation with the Americans'.

The article's most enduring paragraph: '. . . The Australian Government regards the Pacific struggle as primarily one in which the United States and Australia must have the fullest say in [strategy]. Without any inhibitions of any kind, I make it quite clear that Australia looks to America, free of any pangs as to our traditional links or kinship with the United Kingdom . . . We are determined Australia shall not go [under], and we shall exert all our energies towards the shaping of a plan, with the United States as its keystone, which will give our country some confidence of being able to hold out until the tide of battle swings against the enemy . . .'

Sixty years later and those fateful words, which bound Australia and the United States in the Pacific in World War II and which would later found the ANZUS treaty exactly half a century ago, in September 1951, resonate yet again. Yet the irony of the 60th anniversary, to the very day, of their author's ascension to political power at the outset of this country's greatest peril, is ignored or forgotten.

If anyone was ever the political father of Australia's security ties with Washington, however much they were formalised by the Menzies Government's negotiation of ANZUS in 1951, it was, without question, Labor's John Curtin. And yet Labor these days has so little sense of history it does not realise the irony of last weekend.

I thought of this melancholy circumstance after John Howard took his Monday 1am phone call from Washington then went back to bed without letting Kim Beazley know what had happened. Last week, when Howard announced, with prime-time political gravitas, the military 'assets' his Government had decided Australia was 'making available', if needed, in the pursuit of Osama bin Laden, he solemnly undertook to keep Beazley 'fully informed' of developments. 'I want to pay all the courtesies that are due the Opposition leader,' Howard said. It was, obviously, one of his non-core undertakings.

Howard can be a thoroughly ungenerous twerp when he puts his mind to it, and clearly he sees the election campaign in terms of giving Beazley no quarter, no matter what the circumstance. Paul Keating used to treat Howard like a piece of political rubbish when it suited. Howard has not forgotten or forgiven. You wonder why they think it has to be so bloody-minded all the time.

John Curtin never was, so the books say.

Alan Ramsey

# The Two Ronnies

**OCTOBER 20, 2001**

AFGHANISTAN IS three-quarters the size of NSW which, in turn, is just one-tenth of the Australian land mass. It is a landlocked nation of goatherds and farmers and opium poppy growers. It has 25.8 million people, not counting 2.7 million nomads. As many as 4 million Afghans live as refugees among its six neighbours, mainly Pakistan. Its birth and death rates are among the world's highest, its per capita wealth among the lowest. Almost

half its population is aged under 15. What on earth is Australia doing making war with the world's richest, greatest military power on such an impoverished, inhospitable, godforsaken piece of dirt in the middle of nowhere?

Surely some other strategy to bring down Osama bin Laden and his Islamic fanatics was possible other than pounding this feudal, mud-brick nation to rubble with day and night air raids from US mainland bases half a world away and from four US carrier battle groups in the Indian Ocean?

Alexander the Great conquered the area in the 4th century BC. Genghis Khan invaded in 1219. So did the Soviets in 1979. None subdued, totally, the tribes of this mountain region of the Hindu Kush. All eventually died or left. Moscow bled 50,000 casualties in 10 years before withdrawing 100,000 troops in 1989. American CIA money and arms financed the opposing Afghan mujahideen ('holy warrior') forces. Now Washington's George Bush and London's Tony Blair seek to do what Moscow gave up trying, and Genghis Khan must have wondered why he ever bothered. But the Mongols never had John Howard and Kim Beazley.

George and Tony do. The triumphalism of the two Australian political leaders this week in seeking to outdo each other in the proud rhetoric of Washington's little helpers has been remarkable, if not nauseating. And the Parliament? It has no say.

What is happening is happening on the hustings, not in Parliament. The House of Representatives was dissolved when John Howard called the election two weeks ago. Thus the House cannot sit again until the Governor-General re-opens Parliament after the election. The Senate has not been dissolved. This is not a double-dissolution election. Only half the Senate's 76 members are up for re-election.

And while the Democrats and the Greens' Bob Brown believe Parliament should debate the Government's decision to join the US destruction of Afghanistan and its Taliban rulers in their pursuit of bin Laden's terrorist network and its allies, they don't have the numbers to test the disputed right to recall the Senate. Not without Labor, they don't.

And with Beazley as enthusiastic as the Prime Minister about answering the US call to arms, the Opposition will not be supporting any move to go back to Parliament in the midst of an election campaign. With no Parliament and no representative voice of the people, that left each political leader to stage-manage his own interpretation of what 'the people' might think of Australia's entry into 'war', as the Murdoch tabloids shrieked next day, but which is really no more than a token presence in another American military adventure. Bush phoned Howard on Tuesday night for the second time in a week. The timing could not have been better for the Prime Minister.

What Howard had to announce next morning instantly smothered all the Labor chortling about the so-called Great Debate three nights earlier, an event in which the Democrats' Natasha Stott Despoja crushingly dismissed Howard and Beazley as the Two Ronnies. It remains the cleverest quip of the campaign. It didn't stop Howard putting on his grave face on Wednesday and, flanked by the obligatory Australian flags, telling a Melbourne press conference in his most reverential voice: 'Well,

ladies and gentlemen, last night President Bush phoned me to discuss the progress of the coalition campaign against terror . . .

'And in the course of that discussion he indicated the United States would like to activate the commitment Australia had made to join the coalition force. I indicated Australia would respond. He then expressed his appreciation for for the way in which Australia had responded, (and) he requested us to make available (those forces) in circumstances and at times to be agreed between the respective military authorities in Australia and the US . . .'

The Australian contingent overall is bigger than Howard had announced 10 days earlier. There are now four ships going and six aircraft, including two refuelling tankers and four F/A-18 fighters, plus some helicopters. The force of 1,550 men and women includes only 150 combat troops, men of the SAS way short of the 1,000 fighting troops Australia first sent to Vietnam in June 1965, the last time we put ground forces to war as a client ally of Washington.

Our fighter planes won't operate in Afghanistan and the four ships will be stationed in the Indian Ocean and the Persian Gulf. Only the 150 SAS troops are likely, at some time, to be involved in hostilities. All this was just the nuts and bolts. And, of course, 'as circumstances permit', Howard and Beazley would be on hand to 'farewell our forces' as they leave 'on behalf of the Australian people'. Howard did not leave it at a simple announcement.

What followed was a gross trowel job to impress voters with, presumably, how important this Prime Minister is in Washington.

He said, utterly unblushingly: 'I should advise you that after I spoke to President Bush last night, and during the conversation, we generally traversed the course of events since September 11. It is the second time I've spoken to him since then. We in fact recalled the extraordinary change that had come over the world, and the challenges for both of us, since that very positive day we spent together, or a large part of the day spent together; indeed, on September 10, when I spent some three hours with the President and met many senior members of his Administration, having previously, at the (Australian) Ambassador's residence, entertained almost the entirety of the senior people within his Administration.

'And both of us reflected rather sombrely just how much the world had changed since that very positive and upbeat encounter between the leadership of the Australian Government and the leadership of the United States. But he remains very grateful. He made the remark during our conversation that the way in which the people of Australia and the people of the United States had interacted on this issue was something of a template for the behaviour of free peoples towards each other in the earlier years of the 21st century.

'There is no doubt he feels greatly indebted to the Australian people and very warm towards the people of our country because of the spontaneity of (our) response and the willingness with which Australia has aligned herself with the cause of freedom and the fight against terrorism . . .' And on and on and on.

Truly one of the great loads of self-aggrandising tosh. And similar dollops went on being gushed by Howard all week, our 'very significant and important contribution' being repeated up and down the country as campaign fodder. Excuse the cynicism, but why do they feel they must make a meal of it all? No less so his opponent.

Not to be overshadowed, and within an hour of that first Howard press conference, Beazley, back in Perth, rushed out his podium and his Australian flag, too, and told his assembled media, looking straight down the barrel of the TV cameras: 'As I said on Sunday night, we in the Australian Labor Party stand shoulder to shoulder with George Bush, Tony Blair and all the members of the international coalition in our determination that the scourge of international terrorism should be sought out and destroyed . . .

'Over the weekend I spoke to Tony Blair, and spoke to him about the operation generally, the situation of the international community in this troubled time. He was appreciative, too, of the strength of the Australian commitment . . . (and) . . . I believe the international leadership appreciates the fact we, in our terms, are making a significant commitment . . .

'It is particularly important for me to say, as the alternative Prime Minister, that all these operations and involvement of our personnel have the full support of the Opposition. We stand shoulder to shoulder with Tony Blair and George Bush and all the others who have committed themselves so steadfastly . . .' blah, blah, blah '. . . and it is important the Australian people, and those in the armed services, understand our resolution . . .' And on and on and on. Blah, blah, blah.

Five more times Beazley told us about 'George Bush and Tony Blair' and 'Tony Blair and George Bush'. And while Beazley emphasised that his call to Blair 'should remain private' he hastened to say: 'I think what's important for me to convey about that conversation with Tony Blair was my appreciation, firstly, of his gratitude of the steadfastness of the Australian people . . . and also his concern, which is my concern, too, that our people who have to sustain support for this effort for the long term, that they understand the character of the conflict . . .'

Like competing schoolboys. Howard anxious to impress with his phone conversation with Bush, and Beazley his call to Blair. What a hoot. All in the name of the election, each boasting of a 'big and powerful friend'. And these are our political leaders.

Alan Ramsey

# Chapter 18

# The Invasion of Iraq

## Do not Mention Israel

SEPTEMBER 19, 2001

THEY QUOTED the Bible, Tennyson's Ulysses, broadcaster Alistair Cooke, Robert Kennedy, Lincoln's Gettysburg Address, *The New York Times* and the ANZUS Treaty. One MP read a poem by his daughter. Another quoted himself. In 10 hours of speeches, 99 politicians in all, including 40 senators, spoke of evil, love, fear, anger, outrage, terrorism, humanity, decency, courage, cowardice, atrocities, obscenities, sacrifice, the dead, the living and justice. Kim Beazley said: 'I think we all knew that things were changing forever.'

Well, not in the Australian Parliament they haven't. And, given time, more likely nowhere else, either.

Twenty-four hours after the House and the Senate each unanimously adopted a condolence motion expressing Australia's 'horror of the terrorist attacks' in New York and Washington and committing Australia to militarily support US retaliation, not a thing had changed in national political life. Question Time in the Parliament yesterday was the usual bedlam as domestic politics, primarily the collapse of Ansett Airlines, resumed normal programming.

We presume support for the condolence motion was unanimous. Tasmania's very independent Independent, Bob Brown, tried to amend it in the Senate by scrapping the two clauses referring to the invoking of ANZUS.

Brown wanted to replace them with a form of words handing responsibility to the United Nations for tracking down those responsible for the two attacks. But he couldn't get a seconder and his amendment didn't even get to a vote, so we have to assume Brown was still in the chamber when the original motion was passed on the voices.

It was the speeches that most intrigued.

John Howard spoke only from notes and probably has not made a better speech since he became Prime Minister. That is, so long as you accept that not once did he mention the phrase 'the Middle East', just as he very carefully did not mention either Israel or the Palestinians, whose leadership Ariel Sharon's Government appears hell-bent on exterminating.

That a national Parliament at such a time could debate, for 10 hours, the terrorism visited upon New York and Washington without discussing Israel or the Middle East generally is like debating the failure of Ansett Airlines by ignoring the role of Air New Zealand. Yet that is what the Australian Parliament managed to do on Monday. Labor's Michael Danby, a zealous supporter of Israel, even insisted in his speech: 'This is not a fight over this or that policy. This (the suicide missions) is no justifiable response to American policy in the Middle East.'

What happened in New York and Washington last week could not, by any measure, be

a 'justifiable response' in any circumstances. But those who think Washington's absolute support, military and diplomatic, for Israeli interests and behaviour had nothing whatever to do with the terrorism of a week ago do not live in the real world. Yet no Australian politician had the courage to say so.

Well, not quite. Labor's Laurie Brereton would be Australia's foreign minister should Labor win the coming election. Brereton told the Parliament at one point: '. . . Terrible economic and political problems abound in the present context, which includes the hatreds of the Middle East. They will not be solved by military action either on the scale of the [1991] Gulf War or in the nature of a so-called surgical strike against the backers of last Tuesday's attacks.

'In this regard, I think it timely to reiterate remarks I made in this House more than three years ago. Back at that time, in March 1998, I observed that, given the trend in Arab public opinion and its perception of Western double standards, it was incumbent on the international community, including Australia, to do everything to encourage the Israeli-Palestinian peace process and to resolve other outstanding Middle East issues.

'A Middle East policy perceived, rightly or wrongly, as one focused just on Western interests will ultimately fail . . . It would be a pyrrhic victory indeed if we were to hunt down those immediately responsible for these atrocities but fail to find a lasting solution to the wider problems (of the Middle East). Last year the Middle East peace process collapsed. Violence has followed on a weekly and daily basis ever since. Terrorism will not disappear until (we) eliminate not only the terrorists but the roots of terrorism . . .'

The pity is neither Howard nor Beazley said anything as pertinent, despite their fine rhetoric. Nor did anyone else in the Parliament. What Monday's affair was all about was an emotional outpouring for 'our American friends'. The election is too close and Labor has made too much of a hash lately of the politics of other policy sensitivities. There was never a chance Beazley would let Howard blindside him on this one of high patriotism and powerful friends.

Alan Ramsey

# America's Chickens Come Home to Roost

**SEPTEMBER 15, 2001**

'*BAA, baa Moscow/Your troops are in Kabul/ You cannot have our athletes/But you can certainly have our wool*.' Remember it? Maybe not. The Soviet invasion of Afghanistan in December 1979 and the Fraser Government's uncritical support, in an election year, for the Carter doctrine of US support for the Islamic mujahideen ('holy warriors') guerilla groups, in their US proxy war against the Soviet-backed Afghan regime of Babrak Karmal, was a long time ago.

Twenty-two years later the Americans are reaping the consequences of a monster they helped create but could not control; and Australia, again, is 'shoulder to shoulder' with Washington, just as Bob Hawke was in February 1991 when he went to war in the Gulf with the father, and now John Howard, in an election year, is pledging to go to war with the son. Things change only to stay the same.

And if the terrorism in New York and Washington put most everything else into perspective, then recent history also says nobody should be blind as to why the United States is now counting the cost, in the unthinkable thousands, in the lives of its own citizens cut down on home soil in their very place of work.

Go back to February 1980. Australia's Malcolm Fraser, Prime Minister, had just come home from visits to Washington and London. A year earlier, in January 1979, the US-supported Shah of Iran had fled into exile after Iran's Islamic revolution brought to power the Ayatollah Khomeini and with it the ransacking of the US embassy.

The Soviet invasion of Afghanistan, on Iran's western border in the last week of December 1979, began what became Moscow's Vietnam as well as the last surrogate war dragging on for 12 years between the two superpowers.

On February 19, 1980, Fraser strode into the Australian Parliament, fresh from his talks in Washington, and in a speech lasting an hour, declared in terms very similar to some pronouncements this week: 'In the first weeks of 1980, the world is facing probably its most dangerous international crisis since World War II . . .

'The situation really is extremely serious and it does no service to this country, or to the cause of international peace, to try to dismiss or trivialise it in terms of domestic election politics . . . The Soviet Union is engaged in propping up an unstable and unpopular Marxist regime, internally divided and bitterly opposed by (its) people . . .

'There are already 500,000 refugees in Pakistan . . . Immediate short-term policies to meet the crisis (including sanctions) on Soviet access to Western grain, technology and credit . . . The other immediate means available to impose a cost is a boycott of the Moscow Olympics [later that year] if Soviet troops are not withdrawn . . .

'The case for a firm, measured and sustained response, the case for giving effective support to the US whose resolve is crucial, is essential to avoid another unnecessary war.'

Opposition leader Bill Hayden scorned: '. . . After two weeks as some sort of international messenger boy for great and powerful friends, the Prime Minister comes into this House believing the Parliament is as gullible as many of the journalists who travelled with him . . . I have no hesitation in saying the Government has every justification to regard the Soviet invasion with disgust. The Opposition shares those feelings. What is in dispute is the appropriate response Australia should make . . .

'On 8 January the Foreign Minister [Andrew Peacock] said: "I am not moved by suggestions of boycotting the Moscow Olympics". On 21 January he said: "Boycotting the Games is clearly the greatest rebuff one could serve to Moscow". He succumbed to the Prime Minister's view in just 13 days, a posture aptly summarised in the *Melbourne Herald* headline, "Peacock up the Khyber Pass".'

Labor backed Australia's athletes, ignoring its Prime Minister and refusing to join the US-proposed boycott. A week later Hayden told Parliament: 'The Prime Minister this morning referred to barnyard politics. We concede he knows about barnyard politics. That is where he gets the hides he sells to Poland to shoe the Russian army. It is right next to the sheep paddock where he gets the wool keeping the Russian soldiers warm in the Afghan winter.'

It was that sort of debate and that sort of political year.

Australia went to the Olympics. The Americans did not. Fraser won his third election but Carter lost his presidency to Ronald Reagan. Neither the Soviet invasion of Afghanistan nor the Olympics boycott could overcome American voter perceptions of the Carter administration's incompetence. Twenty-one years later and very few of us give a passing thought to events in Afghanistan all those years ago.

Nor do many recognise the forces set loose by Washington's clandestine intervention in those events. Khomeini, in time, became just another passed over US bogyman, as did Libya's Gaddafi, despite Reagan's attempts to bomb him into the next world, and as will, eventually, Iraq's Saddam. Now it is the turn of Saudi Arabia's exiled Osama bin Laden.

The proxy war in Afghanistan between the Soviets and the United States lasted until nine years ago. Soviet troops actually withdrew in February 1989, but each side went on supplying arms to their surrogates. That ended, by agreement, on January 1, 1992.

Three months later, the last of a string of Moscow-backed governments over the years fell, finally, to the mujahideen. By 1995 the Taliban, one of the hardline fundamentalist Islamic factions, had wrested nominal power among the often violent coalition of mujahideen groups. They have held it ever since.

Osama bin Laden remains one of the Taliban's wealthiest backers, as well as head of his radical Al-Qaeda ('the Base') group.

And who financed the growth of these various Islamic groups? Of course, the Americans. The Carter administration, using the CIA, began channelling tens of millions of dollars to various mujahideen factions in 1979.

The Reagan and Bush governments went on doing so right through the 1980s. To Reagan they weren't 'terrorist' groups, but 'freedom fighters'. And among the seven identified mujahideen parties operating out of Pakistan in opposition to the Afghan regime and its Soviet army supporters by the end of 1982 was the radical fundamentalist Islamic Union for the Liberation of Afghanistan, whose financial backers included bin Laden.

There is no evidence US funds over the years went to this group, though according to the public record, five of the other six mujahideen groups of the period were financed by US, Saudi, Pakistan and Iranian money dispersed by the Pakistan Army's Inter-Services Intelligence (ISI) directorate, the official distributor of American 'aid' based on Pakistani political preferences. It is Pakistan, more than any Islamic country, that Washington must now deal with in its hunt for those behind this week's cataclysmic violence, whoever they are.

Yet the irony of American aid and comfort over two decades to militant Islamic nationalism, in the name of 'freedom fighters' opposing communism, should escape nobody.

As one mid-1990s briefing paper for Australian MPs put it after the basement bomb explosion in 1993 in New York's now obliterated World Trade Centre: 'With regard to the international and regional impact of the Afghan conflict, there is, in the words of Jack Blum, a former special counsel to the US Senate Foreign Relations Committee, a "disposal problem". Said Blum: "What used to be containable because it was local and tribal now gets on a plane and heads for New York."

It is to the US's incalculable shame that Blum's words were not given greater attention.

Eight years later it remains a 'disposal problem', just as some group or other of fanatics willing to give their lives and those of several thousand others for a political cause have indeed got on a plane and headed for New York—and Washington, too.

And all the fine rhetoric as well as the wrenching grief cannot obscure the simple fact that it is the United States' own behaviour, as well as past official Washington foreign policy, that is, in large part, likely responsible for what has happened.

At no time, ever, has Washington given legitimacy to Islamic interests, be it in Afghanistan, Pakistan, Saudi Arabia, Iraq, Iran, or wherever. Or, of course, in what the Israelis have made their country, by whatever means, at the expense of what used to be Palestine and its dispossessed people.

Kim Beazley's father, Kim Snr, a Cabinet minister in the Whitlam Government of the 1970s, was one of the Australian Parliament's more clear-sighted observers of international affairs, as well as one of its finest speakers. In September 1968, when the Cold War was very much a cornerstone of Australia's view of world affairs, Beazley Snr told the House: 'We get very stirred up about communist atrocities. An atrocity is wrong because it is an atrocity, not merely because a communist did it. We need to face the fact that in the modern world there is an Islamic fanaticism which is very often not convenient of us to discuss.'

And eight months later, in May 1969, speaking about foreign policy in the context of Prime Minister John Gorton's visit to Washington that year, Beazley told Parliament: 'All this Government wants to talk about is communism. Let us look at Islam as a political force. What is it engaged in? It is engaged in many places in a total policy of massacre.' He went on to describe an Islamic tribal massacre of Nigeria's Ibo people, where people were 'skinned alive with broken bottles'.

It was a hardline view of Islamic fundamentalism by a politician who, all his life, has been a member of the Moral Rearmament movement. But his peers paid no more heed to what Beazley was saying than the US Senate Foreign Relations Committee seemed to with Jack Blum.

Now another US president is under immense pressure to exact 'just' revenge in the name of American outrage, and another Australian prime minister is only too willing to line up, 'shoulder to shoulder,' with an Administration that has done nothing since it came to office to try to bring reason, let alone peace, to the killing ground of what is Middle East politics.

Alan Ramsey

# Never Let Facts Spoil a War

**SEPTEMBER 14, 2002**

ROBERT FISK writes from Beirut about the cauldron of the Middle East. He has been doing so for 25 years. Nobody writes with greater authority or standing. His newspaper these days is *The Independent* of London, one of the great newspapers of the English language. One other point: Fisk is reviled by the Israeli Government and its extremists. Three days ago, in a week of excess and manipulation, Fisk wrote an article that was the sanest, most rational thing said, that I saw, about one of—but not the only, by any means—the more insane events of recent time.

It began like this: 'September 11 did not change the world. Indeed, for months afterwards, no-one was allowed even to question the motives of the mass murderers. To point out they were all Arabs and Muslims was fair enough. But any attempt to connect these facts to the region they came from—the Middle East —was treated as a form of subversion; because, of course, to look too closely at the Middle East would raise disturbing questions about the region, about Western policies in those tragic lands, and about America's relationships with Israel. Yet now, at last, President Bush's increasing manic administration has spotted the connection and is drawing all the wrong conclusions . . .'

Fisk does not overstate reality. His article appeared the same day our Prime Minister spoke to the National Press Club in Canberra. That day, of course, was September 11. John Howard rarely appears at the Press Club now that he is Prime Minister unless he is campaigning for votes. That he did so this week underscores the significance he gives the need to campaign for Bush. But it was one of the better questions asked of Howard that echoed the very same 'disturbing questions' raised by Fisk.

Q: 'Analysts have observed that a war in Iraq might stoke more Arab discontent and therefore terrorism. What do you say to those in the Arab world who have been saying there's been UN resolutions against Israel that have been ignored for decades, (and) why go after Iraq but not Israel?'

Howard: 'Well, you're not dealing with a similar situation. I mean, Israel, for all that many people will criticise it—like any other nation it is not beyond reproach—Israel is the one full, truly functioning democracy in the Middle East. The rule of law, even at the height of the most difficult situations between the Palestinians and the Israelis, still prevails there. I'm not aware Israel has a stockpile [or has] used chemical agents. I don't think the

sort of things of which Saddam Hussein has been guilty can be said of Israel.

'I think it's also fair to say it has been the policy of the Australian Government—and I'm very pleased there's been a more open expression of it from the United States in recent months—that the long-term solution in the Middle East is a home state for the Palestinians as well as the protection of the right of Israel to exist behind secure and internationally recognised boundaries.'

Delicately worded and disingenuous waffle. Howard ignored the question's central point: the clear double standard of Israel's 35-year defiance, with impunity, of UN Security Council resolutions urging its withdrawal from those Palestinian territories seized by Israeli military forces in the 1967 Six-Day War, among them the West Bank, Gaza and East Jerusalem. And how, pray, does 'the rule of law' fit the atrocity of missiles, tanks and helicopter gunships responding to the atrocity of suicide bombers?

Labor's new leader, Simon Crean, is no more immune where US and/or Israeli embarrassments are involved. On Melbourne talkback radio two days ago, a caller asked if Crean was aware of a recent report in *The New York*

*Times*, quoting leaked Pentagon documents, that the United States supplied Iraq with the wherewithal for chemical weapons during the Iraq/Iran war in the 1980s? Why, therefore, should Australia now become involved 'in trying to destroy the Frankenstein monster the United States created in the first place?'

Crean's reply was extraordinary.

'Well, I am aware of that report,' he said. 'I think it's important that if evidence is established that someone like Saddam Hussein has built the capacity (for mass destruction) and is prepared to threaten, then that is a threat to all. And that's why I've consistently said, if the case can be made, the evidence produced, the coalition built, (then) we will support (military) action (against Iraq). But what I'm sick and tired of hearing is the Prime Minister saying, 'We've got the evidence but I'm not going to tell you what it is.' And I'm sick and tired of hearing the Government saying simply, 'Because they (Iraq) haven't complied (with UN resolutions), that's all you need to know.' If that's the case, we've known that for two years. I think we've got a government that's playing with the circumstances rather than confiding in the Australian people . . .'

We've got an Opposition leader 'playing with the circumstances', too. Just as Howard had done, Crean ignored the question. He skewed what he'd been asked, to fit the only matter he wanted to talk about, which was to criticise Howard. He did not want to get drawn into criticism of past US policy of arming Iraq against an earlier Arab 'bogyman' of the Reagan years. And Crean's caller never got the chance to protest. The obliging talkback host cut him off.

The irony of US military support for Iraq in the '80s is no less aching than the grim reality of the view of a good part of the rest of the world to exactly what is meant by September 11.

As Robert Fisk wrote three days ago: 'If you talk to a Palestinian in Lebanon about the September massacre, he will assume you are referring to the slaughter, at the hands of Israel's militia allies, of 1700 Palestinians in Beirut in September of 1982. Just as Chileans, when hearing the phrase 'September 11', will think of 11 September 1973, when an American-supported coup d'etat led to the overthrow of the Allende Government and the deaths of thousands of Chileans.

'Talk to Syrians about a massacre and they will think first of all of the killing of up to 20,000 Syrians in the Islamist uprising at Hama. Talk about massacres to the Kurds and they will tell you about Halabja; to the Iranians and they will tell you about Khorramshahr; to the Algerians and they will think of Bentalha and a whole series of other village atrocities that have cost the lives of 150,000 Algerians.

'The truth is that the Arabs, like Chileans and other people far from the new centre of total world power, are used to mass killing. They know what war is like, and quite a number of Lebanese asked me in the days after September 11—our September 11, that is—if George Bush really did think America was at war.

'They weren't doubting the nature of the (aircraft suicide) attacks. They were just wondering if the US President knew what a real war was like. In Lebanon, you have to remember, 150,000 men, women and children were killed in 16 years; 17,500 of them—almost six times the total of US dead of September 11—and almost all civilians, were killed in just the summer of 1982, during Israel's bloody invasion of their little country, an invasion to which the US had given a green light.

'And in many cases, of course, the dead particularly in Lebanon, and ever more frequently in the Israeli-occupied territories, are being killed by American weapons. In the

Palestinian town of Beit Jala, for example, almost all the missiles fired into Palestinian houses [in recent reprisals] were made by the Boeing company. Only in the Arab world has the terrible irony been noted that the very same company that made those weapons also produced the airliners used to attack the US [a year ago] . . .'

Perhaps now you understand why much of official Israel detests Fisk. Nobody could fail to be moved by the power and grim elegance of what he writes. Nor could you not admire the unblinkered perspective he brings to what is happening in the Middle East. His essays are a far cry from the careful pap we get from so many political leaders in this country.

But even the pap is mild fare alongside the malevolent moans to be heard from the obsessed in this country's Jewish lobby when they put their mind to it. They will have no truck with criticism of Israel and its policies. And they will write letters, send emails and insinuate any voice of influence they can reach to make their displeasure known.

I had a political friend of 25 years who took sneering objection to a Saturday column dealing with US policy on Afghanistan post-September 11 last year. We had a sharp, expletive-laden exchange by phone. We have not spoken since. You have either to be Jewish or wholly uncritical, apparently, to voice an opinion on such issues.

Two days ago, after writing about the double standards that do not seem to trouble either our Prime Minister or the US President in what they see as the 'responsibilities' of the UN Security Council, I was accused, along with ignorance, of 'knee-jerk anti-Americanism'.

I am not anti-American and I am not anti-Semitic. I am anti-bullshit. And what I do resent, deeply, is that so many Americans think and behave as if nothing ever happens unless it happens to their country, and then, when it does happen to them, they think that somehow it is uniquely their experience.

That, to me, is the true lesson of September 11, 2001.

Alan Ramsey

# Little Men in a Coward's Castle

**FEBRUARY 22, 2003**

A WEEK ago the Australian Parliament closed down. It had sat for just seven days, four of them with the Prime Minister absent abroad with great and powerful friends. It resumes on Monday week to sit only 11 days in March before going into recess until budget day on May 13. Our national Parliament does not over-exert itself for the $500 million it costs taxpayers annually. For that you get a government, an opposition and 226 MPs. A week ago you also got one of the more shameful acts of bipartisan political cowardice.

First, go back five months.

Last September, 115 MPs debated Iraq; 84 MHRs and 31 senators. But that was all they did—talked. They didn't vote on anything. John Howard did not even speak. He shunned the debate after the opening speech by his Foreign Minister, Alexander Downer. Two days later the Government closed the debate. The only MPs to protest were Peter Andren and Tony Windsor, the two independents in NSW country seats.

Andren had proposed amending the Government's purely procedural motion that the House 'note' Downer's speech. What he wanted was an unambiguous declaration that Parliament opposed Australian military forces being involved 'in any action in Iraq' without a UN mandate. But the Government and Labor would have none of it.

Each squibbed a formal vote on Andren's amendment. Neither Howard nor Simon Crean wanted to circumscribe their options to support Washington. At the same time neither leader wanted Australian voters to see them hedging their support of the United Nations. So the Government simply shut the debate down, with Labor acquiescing, leaving Andren and Windsor isolated when the House of 150 MPs divided on the closure motion.

That was act of rank cowardice No.1.

Two weeks ago, in the second Iraq debate, 159 MPs spoke; 39 senators and 120 MHRs. In the Senate, Labor, the Democrats, the Greens and Meg Lees ganged up for some easy publicity by endorsing the meaningless proposal of 'no confidence' in Howard's handling 'of this grave matter'. But Labor went missing again when the Greens' Bob Brown urged the Senate to vote opposition to Australia's involvement in any attack on Iraq. This time Labor sided with the Government to defeat the two Greens, the seven Democrats and the now-Independent Lees, the former Democrat leader, 56 votes to 10.

The major parties were just as shameless in the House. Having avoided Andren's proposal five months earlier of unqualified Australian support for a UN mandate, now, with the opinion polls showing most Australians strongly supportive of UN backing, Howard and Crean competed furiously to be seen as the UN's champion. But Andren confronted them again.

This time his formal motion called on the House to 'insist that, in the absence of specific, unambiguous and unanimous support of the UN Security Council, Australian defence forces not be involved in any military action in Iraq'. And again the Government and Labor refused to be drawn. Again they squibbed it by closing off the debate. Their joint cowardice was not in opposing Andren. It was, as five months earlier, that both wanted to avoid saying so in a formal vote.

Ironically, on the very day this second Iraq debate ended so humiliatingly in our Parliament, US senator Robert Byrd, former Senate Democrat leader and now its longest-serving member (45 years), made a speech in the US Senate that puts to shame the pap of so many of our politicians. Byrd said, in part: 'On this February day, as this nation stands at the brink of battle, every American on some level must be contemplating the horrors of war. Yet this chamber is, for the most part, silent.

'Ominously, dreadfully silent. There is no debate, no discussion, no attempt to lay out for the nation the pros and cons. There is nothing. We stand passively mute in the US Senate, paralysed by our own uncertainty, seemingly stunned by the sheer turmoil of events. And this is no small conflagration we contemplate. This is no simple attempt to defang a villain. This coming battle, if it materialises, represents a turning point in US foreign policy and possibly a turning point in the recent history of the world.

'This nation is about to embark upon the first test of a revolutionary doctrine applied in an extraordinary way at an unfortunate time. The doctrine of pre-emption, the idea that the United States or any other nation can legitimately attack a nation not imminently threatening but may be threatening in the future, is a radical new twist on traditional self-defence. It appears to be in contravention of international law and the UN Charter. And it is being tested at a time of worldwide terrorism, making many countries wonder if they will soon be on our hit list or someone else's.

'High-level [US] figures recently refused to take nuclear weapons off the table when discussing a possible attack against Iraq. What could be more destabilising and unwise? US intentions are suddenly subject to worldwide speculation. Anti-Americanism based on mistrust, misinformation, suspicion and alarming rhetoric from US leaders is fracturing the once solid alliance against terrorism which existed after September 11.

'Here at home the mood is grim. The economy is stumbling. Fuel prices are rising. This Administration, now in power two years, must be judged on its record. I believe that record is dismal. In that scant two years, this Administration has squandered a projected surplus of some $US5.6 trillion over the next decade and taken us to projected deficits as far as the eye can see. [Its] domestic policy has put many of our states in dire financial condition. [It] has fostered policies which have slowed economic growth . . .

'In foreign policy, this Administration has failed to find Osama bin Laden. [It] has split traditional alliances, possibly crippling for all time international order-keeping entities like the UN and NATO. [It] has called into question the perception of the US as well-intentioned peacekeeper. [It] has turned the patient art of diplomacy into threats and name calling of the sort that reflects poorly on the intelligence of our leaders and which will have consequences for years to come.

'Calling heads of state pygmies, labelling whole countries as evil, denigrating powerful European allies as irrelevant, these types of crude insensitivities can do our great nation no good. We may have massive military might, but we cannot fight global terrorism on our own. Our awesome military machine can do us little good if we suffer another devastating attack which severely damages our economy. Our military manpower is already stretched thin and we will need nations who can supply troop strength, not just sign letters cheering us on.

'The war in Afghanistan has cost us $US37 billion so far, yet there is evidence terrorism may already be starting to regain its hold in the region. This Administration has not finished the first war yet it is eager to embark on another conflict with perils much greater. Is our attention span that short? Have we not learned that after winning the war one must always secure the peace? And yet we hear little about the aftermath of war in Iraq. In the absence of plans, speculation abroad is rife.

'Will we seize Iraq's oil fields, becoming an occupying power which controls price and supply? To whom do we propose to hand power after Saddam Hussein? Will our war inflame the Muslim world, resulting in devastating attacks on Israel? Will Israel retaliate with its own nuclear arsenal? Will the Jordanian and Saudi governments be toppled by radicals, bolstered by Iran which has much closer ties to terrorism than Iraq? Could a disruption of oil supply lead to worldwide recession?

'Has our senselessly bellicose language and our callous disregard of the interests and opinions of other nations increased the global race to join the nuclear club? In only two short years this reckless and arrogant Administration has initiated policies which may reap disastrous consequences for years. One can understand the shock and anger of any president after September 11. But to turn frustration and anger into the destabilising and dangerous foreign policy the world is witnessing is inexcusable. Frankly, many of the pronouncements by this Administration are outrageous.

'Yet this chamber is hauntingly silent. On what is possibly the eve of horrific infliction of death and destruction on Iraq this chamber is silent. On the eve of what could be vicious terrorist retaliation for our attack on Iraq, it is business as usual in the US Senate. We are sleepwalking through history. I truly question any president who can say that a massive, unprovoked military attack on a nation which is over 50 per cent children is 'in the highest moral traditions of our country'. Our challenge is to find a graceful way out of a box of our own making.'

This was a veteran American politician, not some eloquent Australian peacenik. If John Howard or Simon Crean ever said anything similar we'd embrace them for their wise, expansive leadership. Instead, by comparison, we have pygmies.

Alan Ramsey

# Enough to Make you Vomit

MARCH 19, 2003

FINALLY, WE'VE reached the pits. A sickening humbug of a prime minister genuflects to George Bush rather than the anger and foreboding of the Australian people. A pathetic Opposition leader is desperate enough to think war with Iraq could save his political career. The sanctimony in Canberra yesterday was vomit-making. Is there nothing politicians won't say or do in defence of deceit or ambition?

At least the charade is over. No more word games. No more denying the obvious. No more lies. It is a hard business trying to be objective about wilful men who invoke the Almighty and the prayers of the rest of us to justify unconscionable behaviour.

And now that it is done, watch our Government hide behind those symbolic military forces it has committed to the conflict to try to rebuild national unity from the odium and disgrace of its decision.

There is nothing uplifting in making war on a country of which 53 per cent of its people are under the age of 16, no matter how appalling its leader. There isn't a lot that's uplifting, either, in listening to our national Parliament harangue its way through what purported to be a 'debate' on the Government's decision, which is what was going on yesterday as these words made their way onto paper.

Far better to tell you about Dick Woolcott and his book.

I say this because the coming war and the political bastardry responsible for it will be around for months, and none of it will be pleasant. There is no light relief in the dark behaviour of small men and political pissants, particularly if they are one and the same. But there is much good humour in Woolcott's marvellously insightful book, a memoir of his life and times as a professional Australian diplomat, which was just about half a century.

I met him when I came to Canberra in February 1966. All these years later it's a delight to share some of the cracking stories Woolcott has been part of during what has been a memorable journey of influence and interest in the national life of this country.

A good line is worth a lot these days. In August 1988, when Woolcott was appointed head of Foreign Affairs the same day Labor's Gareth Evans became its new minister, they were walking together into the department for the first time when Evans asked: 'How many work here?'

'About half,' replied Woolcott, 'but we can change all that.'

Woolcott's visit to the United States as a member of then Prime Minister Billy McMahon's official entourage in November 1971 produced an equally memorable line. McMahon liked to play squash. He chose Woolcott as his opponent on this trip. And twice, in New York and London, Woolcott whacked his Prime Minister with his racquet, the second time cutting McMahon's nose.

The incident was widely reported back home. Woolcott writes: 'The situation was compounded by the humourist Alan Fitzgerald sending me a telegram that read: "Congratulations on second attack on PM. Hope third attack completely successful. Suggest you dump body in Channel." Unfortunately, McMahon was an early riser and went through all the cables. He read Fitzgerald's telegram and was so angry he hardly spoke to me for two days.'

Nothing in the book quite matches the rich if incorrect humour of what became known as Woolcott's 'Liberian dispatch' as Australian Ambassador to West Africa in 1968. Paul Hasluck, then Foreign Minister, banned its circulation after Woolcott wrote the report, largely as a joke, following the 'reinauguration' of Liberia's president William Tubman. Woolcott includes the infamous dispatch in his book and it needs to be read in its hilarious entirety.

An extract: 'President Tubman is a shortish, plump, cigar-smoking, vain, omnipresent character. He is solid and stiff-necked and resembles an ebony puppet or a golliwog in horn-rimmed glasses. He carries a black stick and wears morning dress to the office.

'To an even greater extent than de Gaulle was said to be the embodiment of modern France or Prince Sihanouk the embodiment of Cambodia, President Tubman is Liberia. A current anecdote is that he had asked his vice-president in the lift at the executive mansion if he had broken wind. The vice-president, who could be described as something of a hole in the political air, is said to have replied: "No, Shad, but I will if you want me to."

'The inaugural banquet was the climax of the celebrations [but] once seated it was difficult to move, a problem emphasised by the Asantehene (king) of the Ashantis from Ghana. The Asantehene was upset by one course. What to do? With regal sangfroid he simply stayed where he was and vomited into his soup plate. To leave, he later explained, might have been taken as an insult to the President.'

There is much more to Woolcott's book than such anecdotes. But in the mood of yesterday, with all those grey people whining at each other in Parliament, you can understand why I prefer them.

Alan Ramsey

# The Joke is on the Kelly Gang

**OCTOBER 22, 2003**

GEORGE BUSH 'tells jokes'. That is not my discovery. *The Australian's* editor-at-large, Paul Kelly, uncovered this breathless revelation after he flew to Washington from Sydney last week. Kelly got in to see the US President after the Americans arranged for six newspaper journalists, one from each of the six Pacific countries Bush is visiting in seven days, to attend a White House group massage ('Kelly, fourth from left') before Bush began his tour in Tokyo last Thursday.

Australia is sixth in the schedule, after Thailand, the Philippines, Singapore and Indonesia. Bush arrives in Canberra early this evening. He'll be gone 19 hours later. First, he addresses a tightly closed Parliament and national television late tomorrow morning, the only way Australians other than politicians and their invited guests will see him.

However, the day after last week's selective White House press conference Kelly wrote a front page 'analysis' of what he says we can expect: 'George W. is tanned and fit. He wears a light blue-grey suit, light-blue shirt with red tie. He is businesslike and friendly, looks you in the eye and engages like all good US politicians do. But wait for it he's funny, he tells jokes and his body language is relaxed and confident. A long way from the wooden wonder of the silver screen.'

Kelly meant television, of course. George Jnr was made for television. But Kelly didn't reveal any of the 'jokes' he says Bush tells. The Nine Network's Laurie Oakes did. Oakes, too, got in to see Bush for a Washington interview last week, one separate from Kelly's group therapy.

Nine ran a news clip last Thursday night and the full interview at the weekend. The 'joke' came after Oakes asked his ninth of 10 questions. Oakes: 'The polls show you dropping in popularity. I was going to ask why do you think you and Tony Blair seem to have lost support (over the invasion of Iraq), but John Howard hasn't?'

Bush: 'Well, it must be his charisma!'

Even Bush laughed, which shows he can't be a complete dill. But then he added: 'I don't know. Actually, I'm in pretty good shape politically, I really am. I don't mean to sound defensive. Politicians, by the way, who pay attention to polls are doomed, if you're trying to chase opinion . . . So, I'm up-beat about it. As to why Howard is maintaining his popularity, and his, you know he married well. And he's smart.'

Maybe that's another joke.

I'm sorry, but after the pretentious smarm by respected journalists you'd think should know better, I'm entitled to some tasteless levity. The Murdoch papers in this country, as elsewhere in the world, are unashamed boosters of the Bush presidency and its invasion of Iraq. When somebody like Paul Kelly goes to the United States to write a critique on the President's clothes, his tan and his supposed sense of humour, you really do wonder if there is nothing the Murdoch communications giant won't do.

Yet this is the Government, if we're to believe the unlamented former Communications Minister Richard Alston, that wants to get rid of cross-media laws and make it possible for groups such as Murdoch, and the one or two other big players, to screw media ownership down even more tightly.

I prefer Geoffrey Barker's elegant essay in Monday's *The Australian Financial Review*. Barker, like Kelly and Oakes, has been in Australian journalism for many years. His pen is as erudite as any and his prose the envy of most. His Monday piece, entitled 'Playing at Patriot Games', said in part: 'The demands of Australian patriotism are becoming too onerous. Loyal Australians are now expected, on demand, to join uncritically in simultaneous shows of mass grief and triumphal nationalism.

'Those uneasy about emotion-charged spectacles, or who find them banal and undignified, are seen as uncaring or cynical towards their fellow Australians . . . Once it was enough to love a sunburnt country, to enjoy and to appreciate the uncomplicated Australian lifestyle. Political, intellectual, artistic and even religious life was rich, diverse, vigorous and not averse to risk-tasking. Australians could argue politics, economics, religion and sport, remember their honoured dead with reverence, and get on with life with all its pleasures and pains, loves and hates. Not any more.

'In a potentially sinister evolution, bloated and seemingly interminable spectacles of grief and glory have become authoritarian politics continued by other means . . . Opposition or even scepticism is unseemly and unpatriotic, an affront to Team Australia . . .'

Now that is real journalism.

Alan Ramsey

# The One Death we Noticed

**FEBRUARY 5, 2005**

SEAN MAHER, an American marine, was due home from Iraq on Friday. He died in an ambush on Wednesday, the 687th day of the US–British occupation. Maher was shot driving a Humvee near Falluja, in Iraq's north. He was 19. He was the 1442nd American soldier killed in Iraq and the 1613th to die among all forces, cajoled or coerced, of what politicians in Washington, London and Canberra insist on parroting as the coalition of the willing, like some April Fool's Day joke.

The additional dead since the invasion 22 months ago, according to Pentagon figures, are 86 Brits and 85 'others' from 14 countries, among them 20 Italians, 17 Ukrainians, 16 Poles, 11 Spaniards, seven Bulgarians and three Slovaks. Other client countries with troop deaths are Denmark, the Netherlands, Estonia, Hungary, Latvia, Kazakhstan, El Salvador and Thailand.

You rarely read in Australia of this growing toll. You never read an official figure of how many Iraqis have died. The Americans insist they do not keep tally, though deaths among Iraqi civilians since the March 20 invasion almost two years ago were estimated last November [2004], by an Anglo–American science group, to be 100,000. Confirmed US 'wounded' now exceed 15,600—another figure US newspapers report is continually fudged, understated or suppressed.

What we did read this week was news of the first Australian killed in action there.

Americans have died, on average, in multiples every day of Iraq's occupation. However, our media lost interest a long time ago. So did most Australians. Either we're inured or totally indifferent. One Australian changed that. One dead Australian—particularly the first—out-rates, in news value, 1442 dead Americans, 1613 Coalition dead and certainly 100,000 dead Iraqis, even if they are civilians.

Either we don't care about the others or we don't want to know. We do care about Flight Lieutenant Paul Pardoel. At least, our media's judgement was we care. News of his death dominated Tuesday's front pages before slipping inside on Wednesday and vanishing on Thursday, no doubt to our Government's relief. We want no body bags from Iraq, thank you.

Pardoel wasn't part of Australia's risible military commitment in Iraq, half of whom aren't even based there. That didn't matter. It was enough his parents live in Victoria, that he was an RAAF officer until three years ago and that, with dual Australian/British citizenship, he was serving in the RAF when he died. Alexander Downer, our clot of a Foreign Minister, distinguished himself in London by mouthing that most cringing of political banalities about senseless death: 'I want his

family to know, and his friends to know, that he certainly did not die in vain.'

Rats. Pardoel's mother said so, too.

In a brave interview, given our Government's hubris about Iraq, Margaret Pardoel told ABC radio *AM*'s Rachel Carbonell in Melbourne this week: 'He said, "Mum, it's very risky in Baghdad. There's nowhere to hide. It's very, very dangerous." [His wife] Kelly [in London] was getting very nervous, but he told her, "Well, it's coming to an end, it'll be all over and we'll be back in Canberra and we'll start our new life."'

Carbonell: 'So what do you think, then, of the security situation in Iraq?'

Margaret Pardoel: 'Well, it's very American. He even stayed at the American base. Very disturbing.'

'Why is that?'

'Because I don't like Mr Bush. I don't think this should have gone on. I think it's just cold-blooded murder. Look at all those young American boys that have been slaughtered, and there's more and more happening. I don't like the man, what he's doing.'

Slaughtered, indeed. Two-thirds of all 1442 US deaths in Iraq have been troops aged under 28, a full third 23 or less. John Howard, in Singapore, wasn't as crass as his Foreign Minister in London in reacting to Pardoel's death. 'I extend to his parents, and to his wife and other members of family, my personal sympathy and that of the Australian people,' was all he said. It was more than enough.

Why does Howard think he speaks for the rest of us when somebody dies in a senseless war about which he lied, quite blatantly, in committing Australia while pandering to that dangerous twerp in Washington? How about an apology rather than condolences? What about a bit of grovelling to all of us for that fabricated twaddle he fed the country—and went on feeding it—about weapons of mass destruction? Even the Americans have given up trying to sustain that one.

Then there is Mamdouh Habib. He arrived home a week ago after three years of military detention in Egypt and Guantanamo Bay, Cuba. The Americans in the end charged him with nothing and let him go. Our Attorney-General, Philip Ruddock, one of the Government's hard men, had to concede the day Habib got back here that 'it does not appear likely Mr Habib can be prosecuted for his alleged activities' under Australian law.

Which raises the question, if the Americans would not charge him and Australia cannot charge him, why persist in verbally slagging Habib with 'alleged activities'? Instead, all we get from Ruddock is the slur, as sinister as it is sly: 'Mr Habib remains of interest in a security context because of his former associations and activities. It would be inappropriate to elaborate on those issues. Relevant agencies will undertake appropriate measures. Consistent with long-standing practice, the Government does not intend to detail the nature of these measures.'

What this means, of course, is ASIO and the Federal Police will bug Habib's phone, watch him day and night and generally hound him until they lose interest or lose office.

That is what Australia has become under the Howard Government's foreclosure on the rights and civil liberties of individuals and minorities who come under suspicion and 'remain of interest in a security context'.

And what does our recycled Opposition leader think of Habib's freedom after being held by the American military for three years without charge?

Kim Beazley told reporters last weekend: 'Understand this, we have no truck with terrorism and we are firm in our resolve to ensure Australia is free of that threat, under any circumstances. But we also have principles we believe is [sic] important for us to uphold if we're going to win this conflict long term. It may produce different views on the situation of this gentleman.

'On the one hand, if there is any association between a person and a terrorist organisation they must expect to be surveilled, and we would expect that to happen. On the other hand, if a decision has been taken that a person must be incarcerated, then charges should be laid. I mean, these are simple propositions. You don't have to have all of one view or all of another view in connection with a particular case.'

What on earth is he saying?

Beazley always was an on-the-one-hand, on-the-other kind of politician when you sorted through his forest of words. Nothing has changed. Principles? Neither Habib in his freedom nor David Hicks, still in the hands of the Americans who continue to lose in the civil courts in their illegal attempts to try him before a closed military tribunal, can expect much 'lustre or clarity' from the 'new' Beazley Opposition.

However, when it comes to political and public indifference, the story of the deportation of a Pakistani who sought and was denied political asylum should shame us all. Reporter Andra Jackson wrote the story in Melbourne's *The Age* newspaper eight days ago. She told of a woman passenger, Sonia Chirgwin, who saw two 'burly men' drag the struggling man through a flight's rear door in Sydney. The aircraft was on its way to Melbourne before returning to Bangkok.

The man was handcuffed, and chained from the handcuffs to a harness around his waist, with another chain from the harness to shackles around his legs. 'Gaffer tape was wound around his head, covering his mouth, so tightly as to distort the shape of his face,' the woman passenger was quoted as saying. 'He appeared to be in a state of terror. He was shaking his head a lot. They put a blanket over

him and an eye mask on him during take-off. What I saw was brute force.' She was speaking out, she said, 'to increase awareness that this is how people leave Australia'.

The National Party's Peter McGauran, as acting Immigration Minister, confirmed the story. He told *The Age* the restraint had been used after the man had tried to 'bite his escorts'. The paper published the story in 12 paragraphs on page two. It got minimal publicity anywhere else. Nobody seemed to get upset. The Opposition said nothing. Indifference everywhere seemed monumental.

What are we doing with Australia?

Alan Ramsey

**Postscript:** *US military deaths in Iraq as at May 1, 2009 were officially recorded as 4284, including 3441 combat deaths, since the US-led invasion on March 1, 2003. US wounded were put at 31,230 with an unofficial estimate of 100,000. Civilian deaths were unofficially estimated at having exceeded 1.2 million in six years, including 650,000 women and children.*

# . . . and the One Million we Didn't

**FEBRUARY 19, 2005**

KIM JONES, a career diplomat, used to be director-general of the Office of National Assessments (ONA), the intelligence analysis agency Malcolm Fraser set up in 1977. Fraser didn't trust military intelligence. He wanted an independent civilian agency reporting directly to the Prime Minister—and only to the Prime Minister. Although ONA operates under its own act of Parliament it does not report to Parliament. Fourteen months ago, after immense political flack over ONA analysis and

how John Howard either used, abused and/or influenced its reports, Jones, then 63, ended his five-year appointment and retired.

A month later, in January last year, Howard appointed Kenyan-born Peter Joseph Varghese, 48, who at the time was senior adviser (international) on Howard's 41-member personal staff. This week, immediately after lunch on Monday, 48 bureaucrats of the Department of Prime Minister and Cabinet fronted Senate estimates. Varghese was one.

But he had to wait seven hours until ONA's interrogation—or was it a debriefing, even an interview?—began precisely at 8.52pm.

The questioning lasted 33 minutes. Apart from some gentle opening feints on ONA's protected status—even ASIO reports annually to Parliament—all the questions were about one issue only. That issue was why Australia does nothing, and seeks to know nothing, about the extent of civilian deaths caused by the invasion and occupation of Iraq to which Howard has lent, slyly and mendaciously, this country's name and political weight in alliance with George Bush's Washington.

Labor's John Faulkner did all the asking.

Faulkner has been little seen or heard since Labor's 2004 election defeat, other than to stand down after almost nine years as Senate Opposition leader. He is, however, appalled by the Government's callous indifference to what is being done to the Iraqi people in the name of democracy, and sought to prove his point this week. Varghese, coldly hostile, or so it seemed, could see it coming, however polite each was to the other.

Faulkner: 'I would like to ask you about civilian deaths, civilian casualties, in the Iraq war. Can you indicate in general terms to the committee what the situation is?'

Varghese: 'ONA do not have an assessment of the numbers of civilian deaths in Iraq. We do not have access to any source of information that would shed any particular light on that. There are a number of assessments around, including those by non-government organisations. We are obviously aware of those. But we do not have any independent information which would provide anything approaching an accurate number, or a number based on a well-grounded source of information.'

'Are you saying no agency or organisation from whom you might ordinarily source your reports has actually been involved in trying to establish what these figures might be?'

'That is correct, to the best of my knowledge.'

'Is it an issue ONA has raised at any stage? Have you made any attempts to see if you could establish what the situation is? Or is it just considered not important enough to even worry about?'

'We draw on whatever sources are available when we put our (assessment) material together. And, as I explained, we do not have a reputable source that would give us a firm number.'

'Isn't the Government of the United States of America, and its agencies, one of the sources you draw on?'

'It is. We do not have a number from it.'

'Are we aware of any work the US Government or any of its agencies might be undertaking in trying to establish these figures?'

'No, I am not. As I said, they have not shared a number with us.' 'Do you have any reason to believe they have a number to share?'

'No, I do not. The (Pentagon) does release numbers in terms of US defence personnel, but nothing has been released in relation to civilian casualities.'

'What about Iraqi police and military casualties?'

'I do not have a number for those. I would have to check.'

'Are you aware of any request from the Australian Government to try to establish what the level of civilian casualties is in Iraq?'

'No.'

'No tasking of ONA?'

'No. The matter would have been discussed within ONA, and more broadly, at the time that the British Medical Association publication, *The Lancet*, had a figure of 100,000.'

'What was the outcome of that discussion?'

'Our sense was that the methodology for it was not particularly transparent. Our guess—and it would be no more than a guess—was that the number may have been exaggerated.'

On October 29, 2004—just four days before polling in the US election—*The Lancet* published, on the internet, the result of a study carried out by a research team from Johns Hopkins University in Baltimore in association with researchers at Baghdad's Al-Mustansiriya University. The study was based on a door-to-door survey in September of 8000 people in 33 randomly selected locations across Iraq and it concluded that a minimum 98,000 civilians had died in the violence, and its aftermath, since the US-led invasion 18 months earlier, in March 2003.

The research's reported key finding: the risk of death in Iraq from violence had increased 58 times since the invasion, and more than half the people who had died, in excess of the death rate over the 15 months before the invasion, had been women and children. *The Lancet*'s editor, Richard Horton, wrote in an editorial accompanying the study's conclusions that the research had been 'extensively peer-reviewed, revised and edited' before publication.

Here in John Howard's Australia, as in official Washington, the study cut no ice whatever. Our newspapers barely mentioned it. And all it got from Peter Varghese and his ONA colleagues was 'a discussion'. He told John Faulkner this week: 'I am giving you a common language usage of the word 'discussion', as in a group of people sitting around a table having a discussion.' What the Liberals' George Brandis interjected to brand, 'Tearoom gossip, Senator Faulkner.'

Labor's new Senate leader, Chris Evans (WA): 'The US defence department does not actually keep a death toll of the Iraqi military they are there supporting?'

Varghese: 'The US figures relate to US casualties.'

Evans: 'I am asking you the question—does the US keep a tally of Iraqi military and police casualties?'

Varghese: 'I'd have to take advice on that.'

Faulkner: 'So, to your knowledge there has not been any work by ONA on civilian casuality numbers.'

Varghese: 'No.'

'That is it?'

'That is it.'

'No one from the Government has asked ONA to brief them on civilian casualities?'

'That is correct.'

'No department or agency has asked?'

'That is correct.'

'And ONA cannot assist this committee and say what the number of civilian casualities is?'

'No.'

'You have no idea?'

'I cannot give you a reliable number.'

A few minutes later, with the Varghese well as dry and barren as the Australian outback, he was thanked and let go. Faulkner then turned his attention to officials from the Prime Minister's department. Could anyone from the department's international division assist?

Official: 'I cannot add anything to what Mr Varghese said.'

Faulkner: 'Has the issue ever been raised with the international division?'

Official: 'No, not to my knowledge.'

And then Faulkner got cranky.

He said, with some heat: 'Australia is involved in a war in Iraq. It seems perfectly reasonable for senators around this table to ask, what I have certainly been trying to do for the best part of an hour, what the civilian casualties are as a result of that war. What I'm told is nobody knows, nobody has asked, nobody even tries to establish what the casualties might be. That's true, isn't it?'

Senator Robert Hill, Defence Minister, lamely: 'At the moment I don't know how you would determine it.'

'Is anyone trying?'

'There is no point in information that may be misleading or unhelpful. How do you collect it?'

'Who is trying?'

'There is no point, if you concede you are not going to be able to produce a meaningful figure.'

'Has anyone bothered to ask?'

'Ask who?'

Faulkner: 'Has anyone asked the Americans? Given the number of people they have in Iraq, given their role in the military intervention there, given our relationship with them and our involvement, that would not be a bad place to start. Has anybody bothered to ask them?'

Hill, evading the question: 'We have certainly had dialogue with the Americans on efforts to minimise civilian casualties.'

And after a bit more round and round in circles, Faulkner nailed the obvious truth. 'I happen to think it does not suit people to find out these statistics,' he told Hill, sitting across from him, arms folded. 'That is what I believe. Of course it does not suit! But I do think some effort ought to be made by responsible governments to try to establish the impact on civilians. But governments avoid the embarrassment. I am merely asking, what efforts have been made? The answer is none.'

The answer is we don't want to know.

Alan Ramsey

## Two Gallipolis



LES CARLYON once wrote a luminous story about a dead horse its owner buried standing up. You would know Carlyon, most likely, as the bloke who wrote *Gallipoli*. What made Gallipoli such an epic was the detail of Carlyon's superb story-telling. It was the detail of the dead horse story that got me. The horse was Sir Tristram, the great stallion who stood at stud in New Zealand's Waikato. Carlyon had been to the stud before Sir Tristram was put down after an accident in 1997.

In early 1999, Carlyon was writing about Sir Tristram's champion son, Zabeel, and he wanted to fly to New Zealand to see the dead stallion's grave, to be there, to feel its presence, its might and power, if you like, and to let his imagination run. His editor, Paul Bailey, didn't blink.

If you think Carlyon's writing in *Gallipoli* makes you weep, you should read his empathy with horses. Like this, from *The Bulletin* in March 1999: '[Studmaster Patrick] Hogan, the flint-hard dealer in horseflesh, takes you outside to Sir Tristram's grave, walking, as he always does, with the brisk authority of a sergeant-major.

'He leans over the headstone, and it's as though he isn't really talking to you so much as reassuring himself that the old horse is at peace and properly cared for. "His head's

here, pointing this way, towards the sun, and his tail goes back that way. He's in there like this—see?" And he extends an arm to indicate the direction of the horse.

'When Sir Tristram broke a shoulder and was put down, Hogan had him buried standing up. A friend told him that in some ancient civilisations a great and noble person was always buried that way. Hogan liked the poetry. So a dozen men slid into the grave and somehow stood up the leaden body as earth was packed underneath to hold it steady. Then a priest conducted a 40-minute service for the horse they called "Paddy." A wonderful story, surely.

Two nights ago I thought of that great horse buried upright and Carlyon flying to New Zealand just to feel its presence. Only now, in the theatrette of the Australian War Memorial, Les Carlyon was at a lectern giving the memorial's anniversary ovation, and his story was one of mythology and how, at times, we don't remember what we should never forget, yet too easily romanticise folklore. In no way did he put down the Anzac legend and the 100,000 dead of all our wars. He simply put both into context, just as we should always do with our politicians.

Here is some of what he said, and it, too, will raise the hackles if not the hair: 'What was to become one of the strongest strands of our folklore began with falsehoods. The papers [on April 30, 1915] ran a British War Office announcement saying the Allies were advancing steadily up the [Gallipoli] peninsula. According to the press, the Australian death toll had crept up to 41. Then Ellis Ashmead-Bartlett's story appeared.

'Ashmead-Bartlett worked for the London *Daily Telegraph*. He was an experienced and intelligent war correspondent and a stylish writer occasionally careless with facts. But the best thing about him, as far as Australian editors were concerned, was that he was English, and here he was writing admiring words about Australians. England was the mother country and the child craved approval.

'Ashmead-Bartlett had the Australians jumping out of their boats and rushing trenches with bayonets. He had men, 'shot to bits', lying on the beach and cheering throughout that first night. Clergymen quoted Ashmead-Bartlett in their Sunday sermons.

People cut out his words for scrapbooks. Enlistments soared, reaching heights in July and August of 1915 never again reached. Ashmead-Bartlett, without meaning to, had started the Anzac legend.

'The trouble was, there was also an Anzac reality. It, too, was something to be proud of, but it was not the same story Ashmead-Bartlett had created. Censorship is inevitable in war and Ashmead-Bartlett had to leave things out. (His) omissions, plus (his) enthusiasm, meant Australians became captivated by a story that wasn't accurate and sounded like an adventure written by Kipling.

'Ashmead-Bartlett made Gallipoli sound romantic, and it wasn't. Rather than fleeing, the Turks were fighting bravely. In military terms, the [Anzac Cove] landing was nearer a failure than a success. The Australians were clinging to about 400 acres [162 hectares] above the beach, in the rough shape of a triangle.

'After that first day they could not advance. The casualties were not the 'few hundred' the newspapers were suggesting. By the time Ashmead-Bartlett's report appeared, the Australian and New Zealand casualties were approaching 8000, of whom more than 2000 were dead . . . As a result of all this, young men were lining up at the recruitment centres with a fraudulent picture of the war in their heads. And families with husbands and sons at Gallipoli were living with false hopes.

'And soon the Gallipoli campaign had a hero. Simpson, the Christ-like figure. Simpson the one-man epic with the donkey. Simpson the man who didn't carry a gun. In death he enjoyed a grace he had never enjoyed in life. He became Everyman at the Gallipoli front. He was beatified, then canonised. He was described as a six-foot Australian when in truth he was a Geordie who wanted to go home and stood five-foot-nine. He lodged in

Australia's collective mind and grew bigger and bigger. And he was a brave man who performed selfless acts. But—and I hope this doesn't sound unkind, because it isn't meant to be—there were larger heroes on Gallipoli, dozens and dozens of them.

'Men like Harry Murray, who became the most decorated Australian of the war. His mate, Percy Black, who died at Bullecourt. Alfred Shout, who won the VC at Lone Pine and talked cheerfully as they carted him off to die. Walter Cass, one of the heroes of Fromelles in French Flanders the following year.

'Fred Tubb, who won the VC at Lone Pine and died two years later trying to win another during the battle of Menin Road. The irrepressible Pompey Elliott. Bert Jacka, who won the VC on Gallipoli and should have received another at Pozieres. And William Malone, the New Zealander who should have won the VC on Chunuk Bair.

'Gallipoli was also a fine training ground for future Australian generals: Monash, Glasgow, Gellibrand, Rosenthal, Hobbs, Holmes, Blamey and Morshead. All these were on Gallipoli, but for reasons unclear, we remember Simpson best of all.

'In some ways the mould for the Gallipoli story was cast back then, when the Great War was still going on. The story, so the legend had it, was essentially about the beach and the rushing of the hills. It was essentially romantic. And, as time passed and the Allies had to evacuate the peninsula, it became a sort of romantic tragedy, eventually the best remembered tragedy in Australia's military history, which surely sells short what happened to us at Singapore in 1942.

'Gallipoli was about Simpson and the beach.'

Which, of course, it never was, except in folklore. Carlyon told the story of a Sydney couple some years ago who'd wanted 'a guide around the Gallipoli battlefield'. They flew from Istanbul in a chartered helicopter, insisted they go straight to the beach at Anzac Cove, spent 20 minutes there, took photographs, said it was 'very moving', thanked their guide, and flew back to Istanbul.

Said Carlyon: 'I like to think the man was a rich Sydney property developer. Whoever he was, he missed the real story, which was up on the escarpment. He missed seeing the scenes of true heroics. He missed seeing the sheer improbability of the Australian positions. He missed seeing Lone Pine where, in the grottoes, Australians did things so brave and so brutal they beggar description. He missed seeing Chunuk Bair, where the New Zealanders fought a battle as frightful as Lone Pine. In short, he missed the grander story of Gallipoli, which was about the hanging on (for eight months) rather than the rush across the beach.'

And in an essay of 5000 words of eloquence lasting 50 minutes but which seemed like five, Carlyon concluded: 'I don't think it matters if there are two Gallipolis, one that belongs mostly to folklore and mythology and another to facts and reality. But I do think the factual story is the more affecting, the more worthy if you like.

'The story of what happened to the infantrymen, the volunteers from Ballarat and Bathurst, stands the scrutiny of 90 years. Getting ashore was not that hard. Hanging on, up on that ridge, for eight months—that was hard. The Australians defended absurd positions. They looked after each other. They kept their good humour.

'There is a cheerfulness in soldiers' letters from Gallipoli one seldom comes upon in letters from France. The food was unspeakable, the flies a plague. [So were] dysentery and lice . . . The miracle is simply these men didn't lose heart. And they didn't, not even when they knew all was lost and they were creeping away by night, leaving so many dead.

'That, to me, is why we are right to remember Gallipoli. We are surely right to honour them. We are surely right to walk past the political intrigues and the blunders and say Gallipoli says something good about the Australian people and the Australian spirit.'

And, you could say, they all deserved, like noble warriors, to be buried standing up.

Alan Ramsey

# Valour is More than a Slouch Hat

AUGUST 17, 2002

YOU WILL likely have never heard of Dr Geoffrey Vernon. Nor of Herb Kienzle. John Howard obviously knows nothing of them, either. The military knows, though. And had the Prime Minister read or been told of either man he must have acknowledged them three days ago. He could not have failed to. Vernon and Kienzle made possible what happened on the iconic Kokoda Trail 60 years ago. They are that significant to this country's recent history. Surely our national memory should honour valour and sacrifice symbolised not only by the slouch hat.

This was never more true of eight civilians, among them two women and a six-year-old boy, captured by invading Japanese troops in Papua in the last week of July 1942. What happened to this small group is told, in all its grimness, in *Retreat from Kokoda*, the celebrated account of the Kokoda campaign written by ABC war correspondent Raymond Paull and acknowledged as 'a classic military history' by *The Oxford Companion to Australian Literature*. Paull died in 1972. His book was published in 1958.

In it he wrote of the missionary group:

'The rapid [Japanese] advance inland trapped many of the Europeans at the hospitals, missions and plantations on the Buna coast [of east Papua]. Few succeeded in eluding the enemy and crossing the [Owen Stanley] mountains to the south coast. Lieut Louis Austin and an Anglican mission party travelling from Ioma to Tufi were betrayed to the Japanese by the natives of Perembata village. [The group consisted of] Miss Margaret Branchley, Miss Lillian Lashman, the Rev Henry Holland, the Rev Vivian Hedlich, Mr John Duffill, two half-caste mission workers, Louise Artango and Anthony Gore, and Gore's six-year-old son.

'At Buna, on 12th August, 1942, outside the headquarters of the Sasebo No 5 Special Naval Landing Party, the entire group was beheaded one by one with the sword, the boy last of all. The self-appointed executioner was Sub-Lieut Komai, a company commander. Komai was identified also as the 'Bushido' executioner of Flight-Lieutenant William Ellis Newton, VC, at Salamaua [in Papua] on 29th March, 1943. An Australian War Crimes investigation team traced Komai to the point where his death was established beyond doubt. The natives responsible for the betrayal of the mission party were hanged.'

Our Prime Minister spoke this week at the dedication, high in the Owen Stanleys, of a memorial to the Kokoda campaign. The timing was exquisite. The date was Wednesday, August 14, just two days after the 60th anniversary of the execution of the mission workers. Howard in his speech remembered

'the courage, the commitment, the professionalism and the raw love of country of the Australian Army'. He honoured the Australian dead of the campaign. 'We also honour those people of Papua New Guinea who, at great risk, assisted Australian soldiers,' he intoned, gravely.

But there was no mention of honour for civilian courage and sacrifice. No word of the nine beheaded at Buna. No reference to the two missionary nurses, May Hayman and Mavis Parker, also 'betrayed by a traitorous guide' and captured at Popondetta in the first weeks of the Japanese invasion, then 'taken to a spot where graves had been dug and repeatedly bayoneted'. No mention of betrayal, either.

That brings us back to Vernon and Kienzle.

Vernon was an extraordinary man. Paull wrote, without qualification: 'The legendary figure of the Kokoda Trail was Dr Geoffrey Hamden Vernon. A tall, elderly Australian, Vernon cheerfully took upon himself the care of the native carriers toiling over the trail beneath the loads of supplies and equipment and returning with stretcher casualties. The Australian people, who generously extolled the praises of the 'Fuzzy Wuzzy Angels' in the months ahead, failed to realise that the carriers' patience, tenderness and fortitude with wounded Australians rewarded, in part, Vernon's unsparing services on their behalf.

'Son of a Sydney architect, Vernon graduated in medicine and surgery to a practice in the distant Queensland town of Winton. He relinquished this to serve in the First AIF as regimental medical officer with the Light Horse, and returned to Australia with the Military Cross and a deafness caused by a bursting shell on Gallipoli in 1915. The outbreak of World War II found him [as a planter] in Misima [in the Owen Stanleys]. Knowing his age (56) and disability excluded him from active service, he volunteered to substitute anywhere in [Papua] for a younger man.

'A walker on a marathon scale, he combined duty with enjoyment for the next two years on medical patrols. When the Australian Government evacuated [600 white] women, children and older men in December 1941, Vernon refused to go. Authorities threatened him with arrest. He ignored them, determined to find his own niche. In June 1942, after serving in a native hospital at Sapphire Creek, he transferred to Ilola [in the foothills of the Owen Stanleys] and there became responsible for the carrier lines on the Kokoda Trail.'

A Japanese invasion force landed at Gona on the Papuan north coast, without incident, on the afternoon of July 21, 1942. Their advance inland was rapid. Japanese troops reached Kokoda by July 28 after fierce clashes with retreating Australian forces. The Australians withdrew from Kokoda the next day. Vernon was with them. He had walked from Ilola, arriving at the village of Deniki, overlooking Kokoda, on the morning of July 28.

Peter Brune, an Adelaide school teacher, in his 1991 book *Those Ragged Bloody Heroes*, quotes Warrant Officer John Wilkinson, of the 39th Battalion: 'Vernon arrived out of the fog. Very pleased to see him. He had some

instruments and dressings in two triangular bandages. He nearly got shot owing to his unregimental dress. Shorts, which were really strides rolled up; a blue pullover tied around his neck; a felt army hat worn as no hat should ever be worn, and a long newspaper cigarette in his mouth. A small dillybag, and some army biscuits and tobacco in it. He saw me and spoke, "Jack, I heard there was some action here and thought you may need some assistance. Where do I start?" What a man!'

Brune writes: 'Vernon was responsible for maintaining the health of the native porters. His compassion and skill were also of immeasurable value to the young Australian militiamen of the 39th Battalion. He was to die in 1946 at the age of 63, with scant recognition from authorities. A native hospital at Maipani in a remote part of Papua serves as his only memorial.'

Paull's epitaph in *Retreat from Kokoda* concurs. He writes of the tiny, ill-equipped, under-trained garrison in Port Moresby at the time of Japan's attack on Pearl Harbour in December 1941, which opened the war in the Pacific. The 49th Battalion was a militia (civilian) unit from Queensland. Two more militia units, the 39th (from Victoria) and the 53rd (from NSW), raised the garrison to brigade strength in January 1942.

The 39th was aged between 18 and 21. One draft of 100 troops, mostly only 18-year-olds, which was added to the 53rd Battalion just before it sailed to Port Moresby, had never seen or handled a rifle. It was the 39th Battalion (460 men), the first troops sent to Kokoda in June 1942, that took the brunt of the Japanese invasion (3000 combat troops) of Papua.

Of Vernon and Kienzle, Paull says: 'Major-General Basil Morris [commander of Australian troops in Papua at the outbreak of war] fortunately possessed two men of unusual ability. The first, Dr Vernon, kept the supply line moving when Australian troops needed it most desperately in the months ahead. The Australian Government gave him no tangible recognition. His only memorial is a native hospital in Papua's muddy deltas.

'The other man, Herbert Kienzle, a planter, commissioned as a lieutenant in ANGAU (Australian New Guinea Administrative Unit), was responsible for organising and maintaining communications across the Owen Stanleys to Kokoda. The Government rewarded him with the MBE for his not inconsiderable part in the success of the campaign.'

Years later, Major Noel Symington, of the 39th Battalion, would be unrestrained in his contempt of authority for its treatment of Kienzle. Symington told Brune: 'I do not consider sufficient recognition was given this gallant officer by the army commander or by his country. They gave him an MBE, or something. A bloody insult.'

Nothing has changed. Neither the army nor the Government publicly recognised either man this week. Nobody not wearing a slouch hat or a Papuan beehive got a mention. Yet, how John Howard larded it on for the diggers! What had happened in the Kokoda campaign had 'turned around the course of World War II', he asserted modestly in paying homage to 'a heroic and great generation of Australians, one that might never be matched in future'.

Yet 60 years ago at least one politician thought differently.

On the day the Japanese overran Kokoda, July 28, 1942, Billy Hughes, one of the more despised rats of Australian political history, railed in Federal Parliament against what he saw as the ease of the Japanese invasion of Papua and their rapid advance inland. 'The Japanese ought not to have got there,' he insisted. 'Every day they are creeping nearer and nearer.'

Two months later, despite the desperate fighting in the Owen Stanleys, Hughes was still fear-mongering. 'The Government must be ruthless,' he ranted on September 23. 'The war in New Guinea cannot be won by Allied troops holding their own. The Japanese must be driven back . . .' Always, somewhere, a politician is having a moan.

Kokoda was retaken on November 2. Another two months of jungle attrition, in combined operations with US forces, drove the Japanese out of Papua in January 1943. Geoffrey Vernon's and Bert Kienzle's contributions should never be forgotten.

Alan Ramsey

# The 27 Executions we Ignore

APRIL 26, 2003

ALEX BELL, 29, of Ballarat, in country Victoria, was executed at Thanbyuzayat, Burma, on March 16, 1943. Bell was a sapper in the Australian Army. He'd been working in Malaya as a metallurgist when Japanese forces landed, following Tokyo's sneak attack on Pearl Harbour that brought World War II to the Pacific on December 7, 1941. Bell enlisted on January 27, as Japanese troops were sweeping down the Malay Peninsula to Singapore, pushing 19,000 raw troops of the Australian 8th Division (among others) ahead of them. Bell was a soldier only three weeks before he became a prisoner of war for 13 months.

And the day he died at the end of that 13 months Alex Bell would shake hands with the

Japanese officer of the firing squad about to kill him. He thanked the officer for unexplained 'courtesies and privileges'. Although wounded, Bell declined to kneel or sit, his hands bound. He would die on his feet, Bell said, and he asked that his commanding officer, Brigadier Arthur Leslie Varley, an Inverell stock and station agent with 'keen blue eyes and a sparse frame', be told. Then they shot him.

Varley, a Military Cross winner, at 24, from the trench warfare in France and Belgium of 1914–18, was afterwards taken to Bell's execution ground. There the Japanese firing squad 'presented arms' to honour the dead Australian's courage. Varley would write in his diary: 'The whole of Bell's behaviour has been most gallant.' And for what?

Bell's 'crime' had been a simple one.

He attempted escape from one of the Japanese POW work camps established to build the 420 kilometres of the infamous Thai–Burma railway from May 1942 to November 1943. There were three in the escape attempt, all Australians. They'd become prisoners, with 17,000 other Australian troops, all ranks, including 1300 wounded, after the British surrender of Singapore, in February, 1942.

That capitulation, after a Japanese campaign by 80,000 troops advanced 1100 kilometres in just 70 days, delivered 130,000 military forces—British, Australian, Indian and 'local volunteers'—into Japanese POW camps, many never to leave alive.

A quarter of a million Australian troops were funnelled into the four years of war in the Pacific. A total 21,600 became prisoners. More than one in three, or 7800 (36 per cent), died in captivity.

A total 13,870 survived to return home. Only 'about eight' successfully escaped in the four years. Twenty-seven others variously tried, were caught and executed. The official war history records that 193 others were 'known' to have been executed for 'other reasons' and a further 375 'believed' executed for 'other reasons'.

Bell was one of the 27 who died trying to do 'his duty'. That is, escape, as all Australian servicemen were ordered to attempt if they became prisoners. The two men with him were, like Bell, citizen soldiers. Major Alan Mull, 46, a sales traveller, of Strathfield, NSW, had enlisted in Sydney on May 3, 1940. Gunner Keith Dickinson, 39, a West Australian living in Bendigo, Victoria, enlisted a year later on June 4, 1941. In February 1943 they escaped from the Thetkaw railway work camp, 15 kilometres south of Thanbyuzayat. Their goal: to walk to India.

They got 80 kilometres before Dickinson, exhausted, could go no further. The others went on, as agreed in camp. The Japanese recaptured Dickinson. He was taken back to Thanbyuzayat and shot, on March 2, without trial. On March 10, a further 160 kilometres north, Mull and Bell clashed with a pro-Japanese 'native patrol'. Mull was killed and Bell 'badly wounded'. Like Dickinson, Bell was returned to Thanbyuzayat. He was shot six days later, as recorded in Varley's diary.

We know this because it is there in the official war histories. There is even more in the files of the Australian War Memorial. The service records of the dead leave you catching your breath. So can the prose and detail of the war histories. There are 22 official volumes covering World War II. Volume four of the seven-volume series on the army, entitled *The Japanese Thrust*, was written by Lionel Wigmore, a Sydney journalist and Canberra public servant who was in Singapore until just before its fall. He died, aged 90, in 1989.

But Wigmore did not chronicle the terrible ordeal of Australia's prisoners of war. That was done by A. J. (Bill) Sweeting, the last survivor of the war history unit set up in 1944 by the

Curtin Labor Government under Gavin Long, a former journalist with *The Sydney Morning Herald*. Sweeting, now 84, was with the unit its entire life, until the last volume was published in 1977.

His harrowing, meticulously recorded 200-page chapter on Australian POWs, including appendices, is entitled, simply, *Prisoners of the Japanese*. It will stay in the memory and this country's heritage long after he, and the rest of us, are forgotten.

Varley, the dead Bell's CO, saw more than two of his men executed. He was there at the deaths of the Australians known as the Tavoy Eight, one of the more poignant of group 'murders' (as the deaths are recorded on some of their individual army records).

All eight were Victorians. All eight were members of the same anti-tank unit, the 2nd/4th Regiment. Two even came from the same country town, Ouyen. One was a grocer's assistant. Another was a fireman. There was a truck driver and a railway worker and a farmer from a place called Fish Creek. Four were aged between 21 and 27. One man, Lance-Bombardier Aubrey Emmett, came from a family in Ouyen which already had lost two uncles, brothers (one a father of six children), in the trenches of World War I. Now the same grim outcome was replaying.

Aubrey Emmett enlisted just three months after he turned 21 on May 16, 1940. His brother Frank, two years older, had enlisted 15 days earlier. Aubrey was barely 23 when a Japanese firing squad executed him and his seven mates, all in a line, at Tavoy, on Burma's north coast, on June 6, 1942, just a month after they'd been shipped there as POWs from Singapore. Brother Frank was in the same anti-tank unit. And he, too, was a POW in Burma, and later in Japan. But, unlike his young brother, Frank never attempted escape. He went on to survive 3 1/2 years depravity in captivity to return home to Ouyen in September 1945.

Of the eight diggers shot that June day in Tavoy, Varley, a witness to their execution, noted in his diary: 'The spirit of these eight Australians was wonderful. They all spoke cheerio and good luck to one another and never showed any sign of fear. A truly courageous end.'

There is a terrible irony about Varley's captivity. He survived Changi and 18 months in the death camps along the Thai-Burma railway, having returned home an honoured hero, at 25, from World War I 20 years earlier. Then, on September 6, 1944, a bit less than a year before Japan's surrender ended World War II, Varley was senior officer in a group of 1200 POWs, including 650 Australians, shipped out of Singapore for the Japanese port of Nagasaki.

They never got there. Six days later, off the island of Hainan, in the South China Sea, their ship, the *Rokyo Maru*, was torpedoed by an American submarine. More than 150 Australians survived. Brigadier Arthur Leslie Varley, with the 'keen blue eyes and sparse frame', did not. He was last seen drifting, with a number of his men, in a lifeboat. His death is recorded as 'drowned at sea'. He was 50 years old.

I have written here of only 10 of the 27 'known' cases, officially recorded, of Australian servicemen executed during World War II for abortive escape attempts from the Japanese. The others involve similar extraordinary stories, including two diggers (a corporal and a private) who rowed 320 kilometres, only to be caught, starving, weeks later and returned to Singapore where they were shot.

It is to military authorities' everlasting shame that Australia has always refused to acknowledge the valour of such incidents. None of the 27 men received posthumous recognition, unlike those in some similar failed escape attempts from German captivity in Europe which ended in executions of both British and Australian servicemen, mostly air crew.

It is as if some sort of pariah status attaches to soldiers who surrender rather than 'fighting to the death'. Military authority seems embarrassed by them. So much so that official British war history ignores altogether their POWs, dead or surviving. In this country there seems a fear they might tarnish the bronzed Anzac image, irrespective of the years of starvation and bestiality in POW camps and the courage of those who survived them and those who gave their lives trying to escape.

John Bradford, an Adelaide amateur naval historian, has been researching military archives since 1994 to build a case to get the Howard Government to review the issue. But a series of letters in the last three years to two junior defence ministers has failed to get even a twitch from the dead hand (no intended pun) of political and military bureaucracy. The most recent letter advised Bradford the 'matter is closed'.

Twenty-seven dead soldiers deserve better.

Alan Ramsey

# Postcard from Changi

**AUGUST 10, 2005**

JEAN WHYTE, from Leura, NSW, married her soldier sweetheart, a private, five weeks before he sailed to Singapore, eventually to become a prisoner of war of the Japanese. That was 64 years ago. She would sit at night in the Blue Mountains with her short-wave radio, bought with wedding money, and search the airwaves for any news of him. He would sit in Changi prison and write poetry for her.

Four years, six months and two weeks would pass before they would hold each other again, on September 22, 1945. That was the day he arrived home by flying boat at Rose Bay. A newspaper photo of the pair embracing is the centrepiece of Jean's album of memories. He is wearing the jumper she knitted when they thought he was being sent to the Middle East. He kept it in his kitbag all the years he was a POW, vowing to survive to wear it the day he returned home to his young bride.

David Griffin, also from Leura, married Jean on Saturday, March 8, 1941. He was 25. She was 22. He had enlisted, at his third try, in the AIF's new 8th Division 24 hours earlier. The army put him in a unit that looked after ambulances. The convoy of ships that took him overseas, and into captivity 11 months later, sailed from Sydney Harbour on April 11, 1941—Good Friday. He died on March 25 last year, aged 88.

Two years before his death, Griffin published a book of poems, *Changi Days*, under the dedication: 'To Jean, my wife of over 60 years who saw me go, waited long years for my return and was there when I came back.' She is now 86 and still drives her ride-on mower, his 80th birthday gift, at their property near Mittagong.

Theirs is a great love story.

In 1944 Japanese headquarters in Singapore sent a motorcycle rider to Changi with a radio message which had been monitored overnight. It was addressed: 'NX69235, Sgt (Charles) David Griffin, 2/3 motor ambulance convoy. From wife. Message: 'Dearest David. Well, happy. Hope together soon. July radio received. Family, aunts, daddy, Ted and Chris send greetings. Love kisses sweetheart. Jeannie.'

She recalls: 'I'd got this radio message which was picked up by a woman on short-wave in Western Australia, and she sent it on to me. It was very stilted, from the Japanese, saying David was well, which he didn't even know had been sent. I replied, of course, and the Japanese picked it up in Singapore and sent it out by motorbike to the gaol, because they were so thrilled I'd responded to their message.'

It was the only radio message that got through to David Griffin in 3 1/2 years of captivity. His wife got three of his. One of these, sent 61 years ago tomorrow, read: 'Dearest Jeannie. Very well and cheerful. Still in [prison] library [at Changi]. My thoughts are flying to our reunion. David. 11 Aug, '44.'

What Jean remembers with the greatest joy is the day early in 1944, before the radio message was picked up in Western Australia, that she got a handwritten postcard from Changi prison.

After the fall of Singapore in February 1942 and the surrender of all British and Allied forces, including 23,000 Australians, David Griffin had been posted 'missing, believed a POW'. It was another nine months before she officially learnt he was alive.

The postcard came 15 months later. 'Daddy and I were eating our lunch at home in Leura and I could hear postie blowing his whistle. I said, "I think he must have something," so I ran down to the gate and there was postie sitting on his horse, holding up this card. He had a lot of cards, and mine was from David saying "God bless". The Japanese allowed a maximum 30 words. I got four of David's cards all together, I think, and I used to carry them with me. Near the end of the war somebody pinched my wallet, so they were gone.'

Griffin would become Sydney's lord mayor years later and be knighted by the NSW Askin Government. His 'Jeannie' was with him in their sunroom the morning he had a stroke 17 months ago. He died without regaining consciousness. It was the same room in which she learnt last week she'd won a $1000 award for a piece of her sculpture, currently on exhibition at the Darling Park offices in Sydney. National wartime anniversaries tend to remember only the servicemen, and not the wives and widows.

Alan Ramsey

# Windows to the Soul

**APRIL 30, 2005**

LYNETTE SILVER is an extraordinary woman. She researched for five years how the Imperial Japanese Army murdered 1787 Australian and 641 British prisoners of war in what was then British North Borneo—now the Malaysian state of Sabah—in 1942–45. Then she wrote a book, *Sandakan: A Conspiracy of Silence.* It was published in 1998 and reprinted four times. Silver first rang me in August 2003.

I met her, and her husband, Neil, at Sandakan airport a week ago. In between, more than 700 *Herald* readers donated almost $100,000 to a trust fund for their 'windows from the heart' stained-glass memorial in Sandakan's 1890s Anglican stone church.

The reason why the church, is simple.

The first group of Australian 8th Division POWs—numbering 1496, including 145 officers—sent to Sandakan after Singapore's infamous surrender, were shipped from Changi camp on July 8, 1942. They arrived at the port town, on Borneo's north coast, 10 days later and, so popular story says, marched up the hill overlooking the port, singing *Waltzing Matilda*, and spent their first night in and around St Michael's Church. Next day they marched to what was called the eight-mile, now to become the infamous Sandakan POW camp.

Two further POW groups, including 750 Brits and 500 Australians, arrived in April and June, 1943. All were put to work building a nearby military airstrip. The cemetery where dead POWs were buried was on the edge of the airfield, 500 metres from the camp. There is a housing estate built over it today. So, too, medium-density housing has buried the site of all the Australian POW huts in the camp. And just down the road is the Sandakan Golf and Country Club.

All the dead Australians—more than 1000 were buried at Sandakan—were retrieved, many unidentified, and reburied at Labuan War Cemetery in the late 1940s. The others died during a series of death marches from Sandakan to Ranau, in Borneo's interior, in January–February and May–June, 1945. The Japanese executed the last prisoners—'only 32 were then alive, six of them unconscious', record the Australian official war histories—12 days after the war ended on August 15 that year. The Japanese High Command ordered their deaths to cover up the Sandakan atrocities.

Only six of Sandakan's 2434 POWs survived. All six were Australians. All six escaped in the early months of 1945. None is alive today.

Keith Botterill, a Katoomba textile worker when he enlisted, aged 19, in August 1941, was one of them. At the Australian War Memorial in Canberra you'll find a sombre, black-walled room in the building's basement. One wall is spotlit. It is this wall that is covered in row after row after row of small military photos of all 1787 Australian troops who died at Sandakan. It is just the most dramatic, wrenching presentation.

Botterill died of emphysema in January, 1997. In front of the War Memorial's Sandakan wall is a black couch on which you sit, in the quiet gloom, and think of all those dead men and what they went through. A Roll of Honour carrying every name is alongside on the couch. And behind you, suddenly, Keith Botterill's voice can be heard, telling the terrible stories of what happened in Sandakan 60 years ago. You leave the room shaking.

Sandakan is one of the least known—and commemorated—wartime atrocities. Politicians rarely go there. The former colonial coastal town, now a small city of 300,000 people, is in the middle of nowhere. So is the POW Memorial Park that embraces only a sliver of what was the infamous Sandakan camp. There were 69 of us there this Anzac Day from various parts of Australia, some even from Britain. They came for the dedication of the remembrance windows on the Sunday and the Anzac Day service on Monday.

There wasn't a politician anywhere. Only family of 36 of the dead POWs, including three Brits, plus pilgrims and family friends commemorating them all.

At the church on the hill is a leather-bound honour roll of the names and units of all 2428 Sandakan dead, as well as an honour roll of the names of the 700-plus donors to Lynette Silver's windows appeal. Not a cent of public money went into it. Not a politician's name attaches to it. All of it from the heart of family and friends and old diggers, and a couple of generous corporate sponsors.

What we did get was an honour guard of five Australian soldiers who came from Darwin. The Australian High Commission in Kuala Lumpur organised their presence, heads bowed, at the Sandakan Park's stark, black granite memorial plinth, three metres tall, with its only inscription: 'In remembrance of all those who suffered and died here, on the death marches and at Ranau.' It is a very moving memorial. It's beauty is enhanced because no politician's plaque sullies it.

We put wreaths and cards and flowers at its base. We burnt gum leaves—because that's what the Australian POWs apparently did to remind them of home. We honoured the roll call of family members who came forward, one by one, in their 60s, 70s and 80s, to get their Rising Sun army badge in memory of their dead loved one. And we listened to Lynette Silver make a speech to leave any politician, John Howard most of all, discomfited.

I have edited what she said. Her words should reach more than just our small Anzac Day gathering so far off in the stifling jungle green of that hallowed yet terrible place.

'I am honoured to join you at this very special Anzac commemoration. Nothing has ever stopped Australians remembering our country's young men who gave their lives for the rest of us, not even war itself. Throughout capitivity in Sandakan, our POWs kept up the tradition, begun in 1916 on the battlefields of France, by holding their Anzac services beneath the Big Tree, right here, on the very spot where we are now standing.

'Traditionally on Anzac Day we focus on gallantry and sacrifice. The heroism I want to talk about does not earn medals. It is not glorious. It does not inspire poets. It does inspire me. It is long-term heroism— relentless, unflinching, and unyielding. The kind exhibited by those we honour today— your fathers and grandfathers, your brothers, uncles, cousins and friends. The kind of heroism which sustained POWs through years of unspeakable depravity and deprivation.

'The 'don't-let-the-bastards-grind-us-down' kind of heroism. The heroism which enabled emaciated, starving men to march 250 kilometres across some of the most inhospitable terrain anywhere. The heroism which saw those who could not keep up shake hands with their mates, knowing the killing squad was on its way. The heroism which sustained those still at Sandakan, and those in the Ranau jungle camps, until the very last of them faced, with great valour, their executions 12 days after the war had ended.

'It is hard for us, in the year 2005, to imagine what it must have been like 60 years ago for those men forced to endure circumstances so dreadful as to defy the scope of normal human experience. This simple, granite memorial, close to where the Big Tree stood, is like the men it commemorates—unpretentious and undeniably tough. The words inscribed on it are minimal. They remind those who seek self-glorification that memorials celebrate the dead, not immortalise the living.

'Yet we do not need a memorial to remind us of our loss.

'For many, today may be your first chance to really express your grief; the memorial service you never held, the funeral you never attended, the personal act of remembrance you never took part in. You may have come here with heavy hearts, but do not let sorrow overwhelm you. Be inspired by their gallantry and determination. Remember, all of you, these men never gave up. They may have been forced to surrender their bodies, but never their will, never their indomitable spirit. All were heroes. Honour them with pride. They deserve no less.'

Knocks you over, doesn't it?

Lest we forget.

Alan Ramsey

# The Desecration of Anzac Cove

**APRIL 16, 2005**

AUSTRALIA FED 331,781 young men into the World War I mincer of France, Belgium, Gallipoli and the Middle East. Almost 60,000 never came home. Of those who did, 213,000 returned wounded, either in body or mind. Another 85,000 Australians enlisted but did not serve overseas. In a nation of just 4 million, 416,809 of its men—all volunteers—were in uniform at some time during the years 1914–18. Only three are still alive. Two are Victorians. They are both 105. The other is a West Australian. He is 106. Just the three of them. They are all that is left of that terrible time in history that gave us Anzac Day.

Gary John Beck, AO, is a man of today.

Beck, 63, is a former air vice-marshal and commandant of the Australian Defence Force Academy, Duntroon. He retired in 1997. The following January the Howard Government appointed Beck director of the Office of Australian War Graves. It has twice reappointed him. His third term ends next January [2006]. Two years ago, in the annual, 106-page *War Graves Journal*, Beck wrote in his review of 2003: 'Gallipoli is a rewarding exercise each year, though it remains a frustrating experience, knowing we will receive complaints about the lack of adequate amenities and services.

'We continue to introduce improvements as we are able, given that the [Gallipoli] peninsula

is a Peace Park where development has long been suspended in order to preserve the cultural heritage of the area. But there is an urgent need for Turkish authorities to recognise that growth in services and facilities is far outstripped by the growing number of visitors all year round. More and more Turkish people are visiting the memorials, seemingly in response to the growing number of foreign visitors . . .

'I know our services [at the Office of Australian War Graves] are gratefully received by the hundreds of lctters we receive. But that is no reason to rest on our laurels. The very highest standard is required in all we do to demonstrate that Australians are grateful for the service and sacrifice of our veterans and the wartime heritage they bequeathed us.'

Ah yes, our 'wartime heritage'.

That's the one at Gallipoli going backwards hand over fist, in what used to be the best preserved of all the World War I battlefields, in the name of more 'amenities and services' for the tourists. All we need now is a McDonald's at Lone Pine.

Journalist and author Les Carlyon had something to say about what is being done at Gallipoli after we learned that bulldozers have been ripping up the landscape above Anzac Cove since last year to widen, by 20 metres, the road to new car parks, would you believe, in time for Monday week's 90th anniversary Anzac Day ceremonies. To be attended, no less, by John and Janette Howard, who are taking the Opposition leader, Kim Beazley, with them.

'Who decided?' asked Carlyon, in Melbourne's *The Age* newspaper a few weeks ago. 'I've spoken to hundreds of people at the Anzac Day service [at Gallipoli], and I've never heard anyone say, 'This is terrible that we've got to walk all this way to get here', which you do. Because of the [old] road, they pull the buses up well before Anzac Cove. You see 70-year-olds and 75-year-olds walking up there, because they've obviously made the decision they want to go and, if that involves a little bit of hardship, then so be it. Why are we doing it?'

Because the Office of Australian War Graves wants 'adequate amenities and services' at Gallipoli and, with the Howard Government's full approval, asked Turkey's Government, diplomatically, to get its finger out and provide them. And although the public rumpus about Anzac Cove's degradation only broke out six weeks ago, the official letter, from Beck's minister—at the time, Sydney's twittering Danna Vale, since replaced—went to the Turks more than a year ago.

Our Government just didn't tell us.

However, it has known for two years that, where the Turks have since been bulldozing the wider road along Anzac Cove and extending nearby car parks, is the site of human bones. Beck has known, too. So, too, Australia's former ambassador to Turkey. An

Australian archeologist, Dr David Cameron, told them back in March/April 2003. That is, at the very time Howard's Government was taking Australia into war in Iraq, here was this bloke, a visiting archeological fellow at Sydney University, making a nuisance of himself over the site of our most iconic battlefield 90 years ago.

And 'they' wouldn't listen, no matter how much he prodded.

There are those of us convinced the reason Cameron was ignored two years ago—and went on being ignored—is because what the improved 'amenities and services' for the expected 20,000 Australians at this year's 90th Anzac Day anniversary at Gallipoli is really all about is the visit of just two tourists—John and Janette Howard. That is, all the whizzbang of a giant media spectacular, thank you, for the Howards in the second (they were first there in Australia's Olympic year, 2000) and last Anzac Day at Anzac Cove of his prime ministership.

Whatever, our Prime Minister shouldn't think Cameron intends letting go of what he believes is the wilful desecration of Anzac Cove.

The last time Howard was confronted by niggling queries was on March 17 [2005], the day Parliament adjourned until the Budget on May 10. Labor asked four parliamentary questions but Howard oozed his way around all four without conceding anything. Two days later Cameron, angered by the Government's slippery behaviour, sent Howard an angry email. Howard did not reply. This week Cameron tried again.

Although he has declined all media approaches, Cameron on Monday wrote a 2000-word letter to Beazley, and sent a copy to Howard. The letter sets out Cameron's attempts since January two years ago, through personal dealings with Beck, to make the Howard Government aware of the physical and cultural vandalism of Anzac Cove and to urge the end of the roadworks. Now Cameron wants further work proposed after Anzac Day to be abandoned. Neither Howard nor Beazley has replied. Beazley, however, apparently intends releasing the letter this weekend.

The day before Parliament adjourned for seven weeks on March 17, Labor's Anthony Albanese, Beazley's spokesman for environment and heritage, sought to embarrass the Government by calling for public disclosure of all documents on heritage assessment and correspondence with Turkey relating to 'excavation work at Anzac Cove'. Twice Albanese moved the proposal in the House. Twice the Government used its numbers to gag all debate.

Next day, in Parliament, Howard stonewalled a series of questions. He would 'check' various documents and 'look at' various 'records', to see if there was anything he could say, 'keeping in mind the obligations we have in relation to dealings with a foreign government'. All Howard would concede was: 'We made certain requests in relation to a road in one part of the area which was, as I understand, a little away from Anzac Cove. They were made in the context of providing easier movement of people, given the large number of people who go to Anzac Cove, not only on Anzac Day but throughout the year. If there is anything further I can make available, I will make that available.'

There wasn't, and there hasn't been.

And when Albanese asked if Howard was aware 'that a respected Australian archeologist, Dr David Cameron, conducted a survey of the Gallipoli battlefields in 2003' and that Cameron 'had held talks' with a range of Australian officials, including Beck and his Office of War Graves, Environment Australia, and our ambassador to Turkey, Howard replied he was 'not aware' of either Cameron's report or of 'those discussions'. Like Manuel of Barcelona, our Prime Minister knew nothing.

Ten days earlier, on March 7, when Labor's Mark Bishop first raised the issue in the Senate, Howard's Defence Minister, Robert Hill, sought to suggest it was really a matter for the Turkish Government and, goodness gracious, Australia simply wasn't involved. Reading from a prepared answer, which the Foreign Minister, Alex Downer, repeated in the House the next day, Hill told Bishop: 'The Turkish Government has, over the decades, taken very good care of Anzac Cove, and the Australian Government wants to place on record its appreciation of their interest in preserving the military heritage of the (Gallipoli) peninsula.

'Over the past several years there has been erosion of both the (Anzac Cove) beach (where the Australian landings took place on April 25, 1915) and the road above the cove, resulting in hazardous coach access for visitors. Australia's ambassador has had very positive meetings. The road requires urgent reinforcing in advance of the 90th anniversary of the Gallipoli landings. Turkish authorities responsible for the work are well aware of the historical significance of the site . . .

'The director of the Office of Australian War Graves returned recently from Gallipoli and reported some delay to roadworks due to weather. He will be visiting Turkey later this month in connection with Anzac Day services and will report further on his return . . .'

Yes, but not to Parliament or anyone else outside the Prime Minister's office. Beck, the Government's man driving whatever it is that is going on at Anzac Cove, has been as silent as he has been publicly invisible. What, I wonder, would those 416,809 Australian World War I diggers think of it all?

*Alan Ramsey*

# One of Us Being One of Them



NINETY YEARS ago a youngish, beautiful man—no other way adequately describes him—wrote in his diary: 'It appears we're going to the Dardanells and I am determined not to be left behind. There seems a chance of my getting into Hood battalion, which would suit me very well, as I should find myself with Denis Browne, Rupert Brooke and 'Ock' Asquith.' The date was Monday, February 22, 1915. The man who wrote those words was Fred Kelly, Australian.

Or, as history would prefer, Frederick Septimus 'Sep' Kelly, Sydney-born and Eton-educated pianist and composer, Oxford scholar, brilliant sculler and Edwardian man about London, who lived most of his life, from the age of 12, in England and rarely visited the country of his birth.

And in February 1915 he got his wish. His impeccable connections got him into the Royal Navy's Hood battalion to join his three friends. In less than two years three of the four would be dead, Kelly one of them.

The only one to survive the Great War would be 'Ock' Asquith, younger son of the British Prime Minister, Herbert Asquith, who had taken Britain into the war, though 'Ock' would lose a leg on the Western Front in 1917. Rupert Brooke ('If I should die, think only this of me: that there's some corner of a foreign field that is forever England') would die two months later, on April 23, 1915, from blood poisoning, without hearing a shot fired, and Kelly would be one of those who buried him on the Greek island of Skyros. Brooke was 28.

William Charles Denis Browne, composer and critic who wrote for *The Times* of London, would died a further two months on, killed at Achibaba, on Gallipoli, on June 4, 1915. He was

27. Kelly would survive the Gallipoli slaughter, winning the Distinguished Service Cross for 'conspicuous gallantry' during the evacuation from Gallipoli, only to die in the Somme trenches in November 1916. He was 35.

I know all this because of two people.

One is Dr Therese Radic, of Melbourne University, whose book, *Race Against Time*, edits and introduces Kelly's diaries, held by the National Library, for the period October 1907 until four days after the Gallipoli landings. Kelly's last entry, as published, is dated April 29, 1915. The final two lines read: 'Both the [British] 29th Division and the Australians seem to have behaved heroically and won a footing, though suffering heavy casualties. He [a British staff officer] warned us against the Turkish use of the white flag.'

The other is Peter McCallum, of Sydney University, the *Herald*'s classical music critic. It was McCallum's letter published in the *Herald* on Monday which argued: 'I make no comment about Johnny Farnham, but the obvious choice for the Gallipoli concert is the Elegy for String Orchestra, in memory of Rupert Brooke, written at Gallipoli by a young Australian pianist and composer, Frederick Septimus Kelly . . .'

McCallum writes of Radic's book: 'The diaries provide a rare portrait of an extraordinary life—that of a wealthy Australian living overseas before World War I in the company of some of Europe's most influential people . . . Their publication restores a remarkable Australian to the national roll of honour.'

An extraordinary life indeed.

But 'Australian'? For all his talent, being born in Sydney was about the only Australian thing Fred Kelly ever did. His father's money educated him and financed his lifestyle in England and, at the age of just 20, he shared a large inheritance when his father, Thomas Hussey Kelly, died in 1901.

It had been Tom Kelly, an Irish emigrant, aged 30, who began as a clerk in Sydney 'about 1860' and who quickly amassed a fortune as a wool buyer and mining investor. He sent all three sons to Eton, but only Fred didn't come back. Even his sister Mary became Fred's housekeeper in Buckinghamshire until she married a British naval officer, also named Kelly, who would later be knighted and become Admiral of the Fleet.

The Kelly son who was the 'real' Australian was William Kelly, Fred's older brother by four years, who married a British actress, came home and went into federal politics for 16 years in what is now Malcolm Turnbull's seat of Wentworth, and who lived to the ripe old age of 83 before moving into Waverley Cemetery in 1960.

However, the diaries are wonderful.

The day after the Australian landings at Anzac Cove in 1915, and the night before the Hood Battalion went ashore on April 27, Sep Kelly would write: 'I got in an hour's sleep before lunch and another hour before tea. Before dinner I played Scarlatti's C Minor sonata and Chopin's I Minor Ballade. We all expect to be in action tomorrow.'

Only a Pom would do that.

Alan Ramsey

# I'm Sorry, Ivan

**AUGUST 17, 2005**

BOB GOLLAN was a schoolteacher. Then World War II engulfed Australia and in September 1942 Flight Lieutenant Robin Allenby Gollan became an RAAF navigator in Beaufort reconnaissance bombers. In early 1944, while based near Sydney, Gollan and Ivan Barber, his closest friend, were due a weekend's leave before again being sent north. And because Barber, a West Australian, had no family close by, Gollan, with a young wife and baby son, invited him home in Sydney.

But Gollan's leave was cancelled at the last minute and he was ordered on a weekend operation. Barber offered to take his place. The RAAF agreed. Gollan went home to his wife and baby. Barber went off on flying operations. Over the weekend two of the Beauforts collided, killing both four-man crews. Flying Officer Cedric Ivan Barber, 29, was among the dead.

Bob Gollan, then 26, never forgot it should have been him. He said yesterday: 'Ivan and I were a bit older than most of the kids in No. 1 squadron, so we'd become close friends. We'd already collected our week's grog at the time—two bottles of beer each—when the order came down for me to replace someone. I remember us looking at each other, and him saying, 'Look, you've got your family to see. I'll go in your place.' And he did. Obviously I remember him—vividly. We lost a lot of mates, but if he'd not taken my place I'd have been the one who died that weekend.'

The date was February 2, 1944.

After the war Gollan lectured at Sydney Teachers College until, in 1953, he began a distinguished career of almost 30 years at the new

Australian National University in Canberra. Among his appointments was as Manning Clark professor of history until 1982, the year he retired as emeritus professor. It was the year I met him. Bob Gollan loved the Australian bush—'the bush' was the only recreation ever listed in his Who's Who entry—and he and Anne bought an isolated, unspoiled lump of bush and beach near Bermagui, on the South Coast, where camping out was the closest thing I knew to paradise.

Last week Gollan, now 87, got a letter. It came with a commemorative medallion marking the 60th anniversary of the end of his war. The letter rekindled memories of his dead friend. It fired up a lot else, too. 'I've been boiling for so long,' Gollan said yesterday. So he sat down and wrote a letter of his own.

This is what it said:

'A few days ago, like thousands of other old men and women, I received a shiny medallion and a letter signed by John Howard and De-Anne Kelly. They thanked me for my part in protecting 'the Australian way of life in times of conflict' and for helping to build 'our community in times of peace'. It made me think of Ivan Barber, a West Australian wheat farmer who substituted for me on an operation, so I could take a few days' leave, and who died in my place.

'I wondered what he and the more than 40,000 men and boys who died defending our country in World War II would feel about John Howard's Australia. Certainly most people are materially better off. We have shared in the bounty of the one-fifth of the world which has become rich. But we have become a country governed by lies and fear.

'John Howard has surrendered the self-reliance, for which we fought, to curry favour with the most dangerous military power in history. He has stoked the fear of terrorists who may target us because of his fawning subservience to US President George Bush. He boasts he stands for mateship and egalitarianism at the same time he attempts, by his industrial relations 'reforms', to destroy the institutions on which those qualities have been nurtured.

'The chief law officer [Philip Ruddock] seems not to understand the principles of the rule of law and calls those who do 'armchair critics'. He and Howard undermine the very principles of democracy in the name of defending them. The Foreign Minister rails against those who don't accept his opinion as fools. He supports his stand by some weird interpretations of history.

'Yes. We would not have survived without the American alliance. But the Americans I served with believed, correctly, we were defending a great democracy. Today the alliance, for which Howard and his coterie are prepared to sell our soul, is a militaristic plutocracy.

'I'm sorry, Ivan.'

Gollan sent his letter to his local paper, *The Canberra Times*, which, to its immense credit, published it prominently. It deserves to be read by the entire country. Bob Gollan will never write anything so powerful as his very personal defence of the Australia John Howard is killing.

Alan Ramsey

**Postscript:** *Bob Gollan went into hospital two years later, on October 10, 2007. He told an old academic friend, Pat Troy: 'I'm going to walk out of here or leave in a wheelchair, then I'm going to hang in there long enough to vote that bastard out of office.' John Howard called his last election the following day. Twenty-four hours later, at 6am, Bob Gollan died. He would have been 90 in December. He could not quite 'hang in there' to keep his impassioned vow. Others did it for him . . .*

# Chapter 20

# Six (and a Half) PMs

## Howard and Peacock

**AUGUST 10, 1996**

IT WAS the most destructive political feud in memory. It lasted more than 10 full years and, for all that time, it fouled the electoral legitimacy of the Liberal Party. It began the day after Bob Hawke steamrolled Malcolm Fraser on March 5, 1983. It embraced four election losses, five changes of leadership, and

it was still as corrosive as ever of the Coalition the day after Paul Keating thumped John Hewson on March 13, 1993.

Then it consumed John Hewson, too, and condemned the Liberals to the fleeting political absurdity of Alexander Downer. Finally, just under two years ago, Andrew Peacock felt enough was enough. He quit politics in September, 1994. Four months later, in January 1995, John Howard regained the leadership the pair had been tearing at each other over for the better part of 12 years.

Peacock went off to become very wealthy and Howard went on to become Prime Minister. And that was that. Now, at last, it's really over.

The poison has been purged. Fittingly, the end of the beginning occurred in a cemetery in early June. The end of the end was sealed five weeks later in John Howard's office suite in Sydney. That was three weeks ago, on Monday, July 22. The two of them talked for an hour and a half, a couple of old political tarts finally at ease with one another. And why wouldn't they be?

Although neither was to know at the time, two days later, Janette Howard was to learn she must undergo major surgery in the week that followed, news that would overshadow the family occasion of Howard's 57th birthday on the Friday. For the moment though, in Howard's city office that Monday, he and Peacock were closing off old enmities and settling unfinished business. Mostly they talked, just the two of them.

And when it was over and Peacock had left to return to Melbourne, he went with Howard's anointment as Australia's 15th ambassador to Washington, an appointment yet to be announced but which Peacock will take up next February. John has giveth and Andrew has accepteth. The deal has been done. The irony of it all will escape no-one, least of all John Howard.

After all that had gone on between them over, all those years—the turmoil, bitterness, recrimination, back-biting, blackguarding, distrust, disloyalty, disunity, dislike and sheer bloodymindedness—that, in the end, it should be Dull John from Earlwood who finished up in The Lodge, with Flash Andrew from Kooyong accepting his patronage of the most prestigious diplomatic appointment available, is the stuff of fiction. A moment to savour.

Yet Peacock said no when first approached. He'd called Howard to wish him well the day Paul Keating announced the election on January 27, 1996. They spoke briefly by phone the day after the result on March 2. Then, some weeks later, when a go-between, acting on Howard's behalf, got in touch to ask if he might be interested in Washington, a surprised Peacock declined, saying he was too committed by business interests for at least a year.

The intermediary returned a month later. Would Peacock consider it if Washington was held open until the end of the year? This time he said yes. The next contact was Friday, June 7. Howard was in Melbourne for, of all things, the dedication of a memorial garden for prime ministers in the city's general cemetery. Menzies' ashes were to be interred in a marble monument as the garden's centrepiece.

And there, during a ceremony marking the final rites over the Liberal Party's founder and first Prime Minister, its sixth Prime Minister took his old adversary aside to say they must get together to discuss Washington. It was the first time they'd actually met since well before the election. And it was those few words in a cemetery that set up the July 22 meeting in Howard's Sydney office.

It couldn't have been more appropriate.

Nor could Peacock's appointment. When you think about it, he was born to be Ambassador to Washington. Twenty-eight years in politics were preparing Peacock all his public life for the appointment now handed him by the very man he spent almost half his political career trying to keep out of the prime ministership.

That isn't just a glib line. Their shared record over the years is a political nightmare.

It went on and on, one disaster after another, all of them, unsurprisingly, in the wasteland of opposition, a reality their mutual behaviour ensured.

They were leaders to each other's deputy and deputy to each other's leader. Each held the top job twice. Howard was deputy to Fraser and Peacock. Peacock was deputy only to Howard. Howard never forgave Malcolm Fraser for bypassing him, as his deputy, when Fraser stood down after his 1983 election defeat and, in doing so, immediately pledged support for Peacock.

In 1985, Howard replaced Peacock after Peacock quit, in pique, when the Liberal party room wouldn't remove Howard as his deputy for Peacock's preferred alternative, John Moore. In 1987 Howard sacked Peacock from his shadow ministry over the notorious Kennett car phone conversation; but then, following Hawke's third election victory a few months later, after Peacock lost to Howard in another leadership ballot, his Liberal colleagues perversely made the defeated Peacock Howard's deputy over the incumbent, Neil Brown.

Two years further on, in 1989, Peacock ousted Howard to regain the leadership he'd publicly asserted, with a smile, in 1985, he was never sure he'd really wanted. It took two more election defeats, two more changes of leader and another six years before Howard got it back again.

And throughout the greater part of that six years, Peacock used all his considerable influence with his colleagues to ensure John Howard's political career was dead. He backed John Hewson over Howard in 1990, he persuaded Hewson to run again as leader to stop Howard after Hewson lost to Keating in 1993, and when he walked away from Hewson in early 1994, with Hewson's leadership terminal, Peacock still wouldn't lift his blackball on Howard.

Only after Peacock had taken himself out of politics did the whole political equation change. His decision was as crucial to John Howard's future as it was the distant sounding of the end of the Keating Government. Labor couldn't see it at the time and neither could many others. Yet, in retrospect, it was the seminal move that made all that followed possible.

So you see, you could argue John owes Andrew, after all. Whatever, Peacock will not be the first ex-politician to go to Washington, nor the first former Cabinet minister. Not by a long chalk. Indeed, only politicians filled the post in its first 18 years, not all of them Liberals.

The Chifley Labor Government appointed one of its own, Norman Makin, Australia's first fully credentialled ambassador to the United States in 1946. Menzies replaced Makin with his Foreign Minister, Percy Spender, in 1951. Another knighted Liberal, Howard Beale, also a Cabinet minister, replaced Spender in 1958. Beale had the job six years.

Malcolm Fraser sent Bob Cotton from his Cabinet in 1982. Labor, under Hawke, let Cotton stay until 1985. All the 10 other incumbents over the years have been professional diplomats, with the exception of Paul Keating's appointment in 1983 of his senior staff adviser, Don Russell. In our embassy's 50th year, therefore, given those who've gone before, it's far from inappropriate to send Andrew Peacock.

There is no more experienced politician, nor one with the exceptional range of international and American contacts. Only Gareth Evans, in recent years, served longer as Foreign Minister, and only Evans, among today's politicians, has the polish. Fraser probably would have killed for the job, but it was never going to be his, even without Memphis.

As it is, Howard, in rewarding an old adversary, has buried the poison of their shared past. It is a magnanimous and politically skilful gesture that will do much for his standing and authority right across the Liberal Party. News of the pending appointment has been bobbing around for months. When Howard's July 22 meeting with Peacock was reported in *The Australian* 12 days ago, the reaction was all good. The Prime Minister's office, while saying nothing officially, is delighted.

Eight years ago this month Bob Hawke made his former rival Governor-General. Perhaps the only real difference is John Howard didn't have to be asked.

Alan Ramsey

# The Night the Air Turned Blue

**AUGUST 10, 1996**

LATE ON the night of Saturday, March 21, 1987, Jeff Kennett, then Victoria's Liberal Opposition leader, rang his old mate, Andrew Peacock, at home in Melbourne. It was 11.30pm. Peacock was already in bed. Kennett was on his way home after a strong Liberal victory in a State Upper House by-election that day. Yet Kennett was fuming. He'd just had a robust exchange by phone with John Howard in Sydney. Now he wanted to tell someone about it. So he used his car phone to ring Peacock.

Kennett: 'I've had the biggest run-in with your little mate tonight.'

Peacock: 'Why?'

Kennett: 'Oh, he got on the phone and said, "Are you happy with the result?" And I said, "No, I am not." And he said, "Why?" And I said, "Because without your front pages and total disunity, I would have got another four (per cent) and you f---ed it up for me!" And he went off his brain.'

Peacock: 'God, did he?'

Kennett: 'He said, "I didn't like the way you kept me out of the campaign." I said, "I wouldn't have you in it. I didn't have any Federal people in it." And I said to him, 'Tomorrow, I'm going to bucket the whole lot of you."

Peacock: 'No, don't do that, Jeffrey.'

Kennett: 'I said, "Tomorrow, John." He said, "I know where your sympathies lie." I said, "I couldn't give a f---, I've got no sympathies any more. You're all a pack of s---s, and tomorrow I'm going berserk." Well, he went off his brain, and at the end of it I said to him, "Howard, you're a c---. You haven't got my support, you never will have, and I'm not going to rubbish you or the party tomorrow, but I feel a lot better having told you you're a c---.'"

Peacock: 'Oh, s---!'

Kennett: 'And the poor little fella didn't know whether he was Arthur or Martha.'

Peacock: 'Oh, s---!'

Kennett: 'I just thought I should let you know . . .'

Peacock: 'Well, f--- him. I'm not worried . . .'

There was much more, just as explicit and all later reproduced in the newspapers, including the *Herald*. The transcript was from a tape recording of the conversation illegally picked up, on an electronic scanner, by a group of randomly eavesdropping enthusiasts who, by accident, tuned in to Kennett's car phone. Two days later, the same day the transcript lit up the media, Howard, as Federal leader, sacked Peacock from his frontbench for what he quaintly called 'a clear impression of disloyalty'.

That was nine years and four months ago. Howard's leadership at the time was in utter turmoil, his public standing at a record low 13 per cent. Three months later he lost his first election as leader in a campaign he always felt was sabotaged. And two years after that Peacock ousted him—and promptly lost another election to Bob Hawke. Kennett meantime went on losing to John Cain in Victoria before also losing the State Liberal leadership [and later regaining it].

Now Howard is Prime Minister and Kennett is Premier and Peacock is going to Washington as our next ambassador. And in March 1987, on the day that car phone conversation galvanised national politics, who would have picked it?

Alan Ramsey

# Gorton and Fraser

**AUGUST 22, 2002**

JOHN GORTON was stubborn, wilful, erratic, open, sharp-minded, rubber-tongued, self-destructive, immensely charming (when it suited), immensely natural, just as immensely rude (when it suited), hugely likable (mostly) and, while ever there was breath in his body, intensely and passionately Australian. What he was not was a great prime minister, or even a very good one.

Only death has made him either in the extravagance of language as much a part of the rites of passage as humbug and hypocrisy.

It is 31 years since Gorton's Liberal Party colleagues dispossessed him and gave the prime ministership to Billy McMahon, a vastly lesser man but an infinitely more accomplished and sly politician. (Do not be misled by the political mythology of Gorton having done himself in by voting himself out; Gorton was destroyed by his own wilful flaunting, throughout his leadership, of conventional policies and attitudes so long embraced by the Menzies era of Liberal rule, particularly by two of Gorton's most poisonous internal opponents, NSW's Bob Askin and Victoria's Henry Bolte. The ultimate tied vote of confidence in Gorton's leadership on March 10, 1971 was only the catalyst. His party would have eaten him, even more noisily, had Gorton not accepted defeat and gone.)

It is 27 years tomorrow since Gorton, appalled by the Liberals' election of Malcolm Fraser as leader two months earlier, resigned from the Liberal Party in disgust. Seven months later, in the 1975 election that confirmed the death of the Whitlam Government, Gorton's quixotic bid to regain a Senate seat as an independent was just as easily swept aside.

He'd even advocated a vote for Labor.

For all of the next 16 years the Liberal Party shunned Gorton, and it was John Hewson, himself a political pariah with his colleagues after his leadership collapsed in 1994, who began the process of drawing Gorton back into the fold a decade ago.

Yet most of those brave Liberal souls who've been making so much of Gorton's 'greatness' since his death on Sunday went absolutely missing for two decades, and longer. I can't ever remember John Howard, for instance, in his first 20 years of political life, having a good word for the man he now tells us was a 'very distinguished Australian'.

However, it wasn't only the politicians.

Unlike the overblown coverage of the past two days, by a generation that mostly knows little of him except what they're fed, the press gave Gorton an absolute pizzling for much of the time he was Prime Minister. My recollection is he was forever being monstered or lampooned by some journalist or editorial or other, while the cartoonists had a picnic.

And the papers made pigs of themselves on the gossip, joyously stoked by Labor, around Gorton and his fondness for a drink and the company of women. Later, in the main, there was bugger all media sympathy once McMahon turfed him out of his ministry in August, 1971 and after Gorton—who ran as a Senate Independent in the ACT—dropped out of sight altogether following Fraser's 1975 election rout.

Yet Gorton was, in his singular way, exactly what Howard says he was: a distinguished Australian, even if his ambivalent attitude to Aborigines and immigration wouldn't bear too great a scrutiny. But it was mostly his highly interventionist manner of getting things done, trampling over colleagues and across the bureaucracy if necessary, that could be so chaotic.

He was never a respecter of process or of human nature, let alone political egos. Yet for all that, in those three years of his prime ministership, he was a blast of fresh air too many poe-faced Liberals (and too many of us in the press) never really understood.

I once made a clown of myself by shouting at Gorton in Parliament. It just about destroyed me. It didn't help Gorton much, either. Although I apologised abjectly at the time, and meant it, mainly to save my own skin, I forever regretted my behaviour.

Yet when Malcolm Fraser, someone whom Gorton, quite wrongly, never forgave, acknowledged him unreservedly two days ago as 'a great nationalist passionate about Australia', I thought it an honest tribute to a party leader and Prime Minister who, as Fraser told Parliament at the time, had been disloyal to him, one of his senior ministers, and yet, across the next 30 years, right up to his death, never conceded fault.

The pity is Gorton should have gone to his grave without any resolution between them.

Alan Ramsey

# The Day the Air Turned Rancid

**JUNE 5, 2002**

TOM HUGHES has become hugely wealthy from a lifetime of dismantling people in front of others. Five days ago his charmless, graceless eloquence in memory of John Gorton, his political mentor and friend of thirtysomething years, was served up to Malcolm Fraser for free. How bitter the words for having stewed all those years.

And how ironic that Hughes, a Catholic, should use a Protestant pulpit so grossly in defence of his dead friend to humiliate their once Liberal colleague before a church full of people. So courageous, too. Yet there was one remarkable instance of redemption.

In the congregation of Sydney's St Andrew's Cathedral for Gorton's memorial service were three former prime ministers, not just one. Fraser and his wife, Tamie, were flanked by Margaret and Gough Whitlam and Blanche and Bob Hawke. And at some point after Hughes had finished his 'eulogy', Gough Whitlam reached an arm around Tamie Fraser and, tapping her husband on the shoulder, was heard to say, gently but distinctly: 'Let not your heart be troubled, comrade.'

That it was a line borrowed from earlier in the service is beside the point.

Whitlam's compassion for an old political foe, and one who'd done him in so spectacularly in 1975, was class of the highest order. So, too, Fraser's dignity in sitting there, a captive listener, the congregation's several hundred eyes boring into him, as Hughes intoned: 'I realise what I'm about to say is said in the distinguished presence of a former parliamentary colleague. (But) I have to speak the truth, and I will.'

And he did, as Hughes saw it.

Yet why he felt the 'truth' about his old friend was not enough, but should include, too, the necessity for the 'truth' about a man he posed as one of Gorton's 'political assassins' 31 years after the event, only Hughes would know. Funeral rites are supposedly about resolution. Hughes ensured this one included revenge. There is no more enduring bitterness than political bitterness.

Hughes, like Ainsley Gotto and Jim Killen, has been a loyal keeper of the Gorton flame for 33 years. He came into politics in December 1963 and was there six years while the making of five Coalition ministries passed him by, the last three years of which he was a member of what was irreverently known as the Mushroom Club, a group of Liberal backbenchers, mostly Gorton supporters, who enjoyed a good dinner and a convivial drink,

until Gorton's third ministry, in November 1969, made Hughes Attorney-General. He survived just 15 months.

When Gorton's prime ministership ended in the turbulent events of March 1971, Hughes's ministerial career ended, too, not because he wasn't any good but because he was politically dispensable as a Gorton ally.

McMahon dumped Hughes, along with Killen, who'd been Navy Minister, and Dame Annabelle Rankin, a junior minister from Queensland who burst into tears when McMahon told her she was out and, as a result, McMahon sent her to New Zealand as high commissioner. All Hughes and Killen got was relegation to the back bench.

A year later, after the satisfaction of comfortably defeating a preselection challenge for his safe Liberal seat of Berowra, Hughes announced enough was enough and that he'd be leaving politics at the subsequent election, the one in December 1972 that would make Whitlam Prime Minister for an equally turbulent three years. And leave Parliament Hughes did, to make a fortune as a barrister, mostly in libel law.

Thus all these years later you can understand if curmudgeonly people like me were to suggest that when Hughes stood at last Friday's memorial service and felt it incumbent to publicly square the ledger by dumping on one of the purported 'assassins' of Gorton's prime ministership, he also squared the ledger for the 'assassination' of his own political career, too.

Was Fraser disloyal to Gorton?

It was a very long time ago and most people these days know little of what happened and care even less. But if you take the time to read the public record, in detail, of Gorton's last months as Prime Minister and of the bizarre events of March 1971 that brought him down, any fair assessment would judge Gorton as having acted at least as disloyally to Fraser as Hughes and others assert Fraser was to Gorton.

Whatever, consider Whitlam's magnanimity last Friday rather than Hughes's bitterness. It is far more rewarding of the human spirit.

Alan Ramsey

# Working for Mr Curtin

JULY 5, 2008

JOHN CURTIN is 63 years dead today. On Thursday, July 5, 1945, Australians woke on a wartime winter morning to learn their Prime Minister had died overnight. In his biography *John Curtin: a life*, David Day recalls that a storm had swept across Canberra's 'surrounding sheep paddocks' that night as the inspirational Labor leader died in his bed behind the blacked-out windows of The Lodge.

Curtin, a journalist and reformed drunk, was Australia's 14th Prime Minister and Labor's fifth. He'd been in public life 17 years and in office just three years, eight months and 29 days, under the crushing burden of World War II. He was only 60 the night he died of an abused, worn-out heart.

The following morning Curtin's body lay in state, in an open coffin, 'surrounded by wreaths of wattle and native flowers, among the marbled columns' in Old Parliament House, Day would later write, while colleagues filed past, including a weeping Ben Chifley. After a funeral service, broadcast by national radio, the coffin was taken on a gun carriage to Canberra airport. There it was put aboard a military DC3 for the flight to Perth, Curtin's home city, after circling over Parliament, its roof crowded with mourners.

Endree Hay, 22 at the time, remembers the day clearly.

Endree's grandfather was an Irish immigrant farmer who settled in country Victoria. Her father, from a family of seven, had begun his working life, at 16, as a telegraph messenger in the Commonwealth public service. The family history is all there in the *Australian Dictionary of Biography*, written some years back by the man now Australia's Inspector-General of Intelligence and Security.

Endree Hay thinks her father, Patrick McGovern—whom the Chifley Labor Government would appoint commissioner of taxation in 1946 and whom the Menzies Coalition Government knighted in 1959—was at Canberra airport the day after Curtin's death. What she 'remembers clearly' is standing with her mother in the garden at home, both of them weeping, as they watched the Curtin funeral plane circle over Parliament House, with an escort of Kittyhawk and Boomerang fighters, before flying away to the west.

Endree is now 85, a little bird of a woman. She still lives in Canberra, near her children and grandchildren. These days she drives a small Japanese imported car. Sixty-six years ago, as Japanese forces fought Australian troops in New Guinea, she cycled to and from Parliament to work for 'Mr Curtin'. That's how I met her, through a mutual friend. He was as taken with her link to Curtin's wartime prime ministership as I was.

The McGoverns and their two teenage daughters moved to Canberra from Melbourne in late 1939. In early 1941 Endree sat the public service entrance exam and went to work as a typist at Census and later the new War Memorial, still being built. Then she was transferred to the typing pool 'of about 10 or 12 girls' in the Prime Minister's department. One day, the head typist, Bea Aldred, told her she was going to 'Mr Curtin's office' at Parliament House. She was 18.

'I was just plucked out of the typing pool,' she says. 'Everything was exciting. I was very young, very starry-eyed, and I was very lucky, of course I was.' She admired 'Mr Curtin' as 'very clever, compassionate and courageous'. And he was 'very considerate' to work for.

'There were three of us girls. Gladys Joyce was the senior [Curtin's personal secretary] and there was Mary Maguire [who later married Jim Scholtens, for many years head of the Office of Government Hospitality and Ceremonial and who would be knighted in 1977].'

In April 1944 Endree ('Mother had a very old friend with a French husband and she became my godmother. I think that was the connection') married a young Australian Army officer, Bob Hay, the day before his 24th birthday. She was 21. 'And that meant I had to leave my job. I was upset but those were the public service rules. People these days cannot believe that's the way things were. So I had to retire when I married. And I didn't ever work again, outside the home. Why? Because nothing else I could have done could possibly have matched working for Mr Curtin. I was so lucky.'

She was indeed. Her 'soldier boy', in time, became Major-General Robert Hay, CB, MBE, deputy chief of the Australian General Staff, commander of Australian military forces in Vietnam in 1969–70 and commandant of Duntroon military college. He died in 1998. His widow, a decade later, counts the myriad good fortune in a fortunate life, not least her two years as a staffer with 'Mr Curtin'.

Alan Ramsey

# The Best PM we Never had

**APRIL 5, 2008**

TEN YEARS ago I wrote about John Button. I've been doing that for more than 30 years, 21 of them in this space. The computer tells me my *Herald* tally exceeds 40 Button articles. An edited version of the August 1998 piece says why. He lit up political journalism in the same way he illuminated political life.

To quote: 'This story has nothing to do with anything really, except good-humoured normalcy, and when political life is so despairing and national leadership, here and overseas, so awash with squalid conduct and buffoonery, normalcy is welcome wherever found. I discovered it in John Button's memoir, *As It Happened*, a book as seamlessly good-humoured as it is a light in the window of the Australia that was.'

Button was Industry Minister in the Hawke/Keating Labor governments for 10 years in a political career that lasted 19 years; but back in the late 1950s, fresh from Melbourne University with a law degree and a ticket to Italy, he left Australia to seek life, love and adventure in Europe any way he could find it. In London, working night shift in a sausage factory, he got rent-free lodgings with an Australian dentist friend on the understanding that when the friend hosted dinner parties Button would act as his manservant, 'Skinner'.

Wrote Button: "In the late summer a French girl, Monique, came to stay. She was beautiful, petulant, moody, neurotic. One afternoon I returned to the flat to find Monique lying naked, except for a pair of knickers, on the lounge room floor. She was unconscious and had an empty pill bottle in her left hand. Panic-stricken, I rang for an ambulance, and paced the floor for what seemed an interminable time.

'Then I heard the distant sound of a siren. Delay, I thought, might be fatal. So I picked Monique up and carried her down two flights of stairs and into the bustling Edgeware Road.

'People looked at me strangely. The siren grew louder. Then an ambulance flashed past, its wail receding. I stood on the footpath with my strange burden, hoping the earth would swallow me. I couldn't carry Monique back up two flights of stairs. I couldn't stay where I was. For a moment I contemplated the cowardly solution of putting her down on the footpath and catching the next plane out of London. Then a second ambulance arrived.'

The story ended happily. Monique recovered, more quickly than did Button, a small if perfectly formed man unused to lugging unconscious young women up or down flights of stairs. For much of the 1980s he was one of those who carried the Hawke Government. He got out in 1993, three years before Labor's defeat. The concluding chapter of his memoir is entitled 'The Road To Geelong'.

Button often drove it, down from Melbourne, to see his beloved Geelong football team, and he used the journey as a metaphor for much of his life and what is happening to Australia. He concludes: 'In politics and football there are small triumphs and sometimes big prizes. It's the same in most people's lives. You have to persevere, to take sides and, win or lose, accept the consequences. I keep the faith my team will make it, and Australia, too. It may take time.'

Both took nine years. Button saw Geelong win its first grand final in 44 years, on September 29, 2007, then Rudd Labor swept into power seven weeks later, on November 24. But, in between, Button learnt he had pancreatic cancer. The five months since have been diabolical.

On Tuesday this week, Button's partner, Joan Grant, emailed a group of us: 'Dear Friends, we brought John home today. He hated the hospital routine, although we all agree the care and help of all kinds was wonderful. We are aiming to keep him here as long as we can, with the assistance of daily visits from nurses. He sat out in the sun this afternoon. His sister Muriel's partner Frank has constructed a stunning wooden ramp (for the walker or wheelchair) from the courtyard to the cottage, where John will sleep, as the bedrooms in the house are up too many stairs. We hope he can have enough peace and love to keep him going for a long time. Thank you, all who have sent such beautiful, heartfelt and encouraging messages. Joan'.

The best Prime Minister we never had.

Alan Ramsey

**Postscript:** *John Button died overnight, aged 74, at his Richmond terrace in Melbourne three days later. His partner, Joan Grant, emailed at 8.10am on April 8: 'Dear friends, John died in his sleep. After the last few weeks I know it's what he wanted. We are relieved he didn't have to go on with the misery any longer. I know you sorrow with us. Much love, Joan.'*

# Chapter 21

# The Dark Side

## Palestinians Unclean

OCTOBER 25, 2003

DR HANAN Mikhail Ashrawi is a woman, a professor of English, an international human rights activist, and a politician. A year ago she was chosen, unanimously, to receive the 2003 Sydney Peace Prize. The Premier, Bob Carr, will present Ashrawi with her award at State Parliament in 12 days. The first four recipients of the annual prize were honoured at functions in the Great Hall of Sydney University. They included South Africa's Archbishop Desmond Tutu (1999), East Timor's President Xanana Gusmao (2000) and Australia's Sir William Deane (2001).

For Hanan Ashrawi, the Great Hall is out of bounds.

This is not because Ashrawi is either a woman, an academic or a political activist. It is because she is a Palestinian. That is enough to ensure a virulent campaign of distortion and ridicule by Jewish critics to brutalise her image and try to have Carr renege on Ashrawi's presentation and the award taken from her. So far Carr has refused to buckle. Not so Sydney University.

Earlier this year the university's chancellor, Justice Kim Santow of the NSW Supreme Court, made it known to Professor Stuart Rees, director of the Sydney Peace Foundation, and to Kathryn Greiner, the foundation's chairwoman at the time, that the Great Hall would be closed to Ashrawi. Rees and an academic colleague, Ken McNabb, took the matter to Sydney's vice-chancellor, Gavin Brown. In what was called a 'difficult and shameful' meeting, Brown confirmed the decision. The campaign now is about maximum political pressure for other corporate and civic sponsors to abandon Ashrawi and intimidate Carr.

Lucy Turnbull, Sydney's Lord Mayor since Frank Sartor joined Carr's ministry after the NSW elections in March, is the latest to fold her tent and take flight. Sartor, as Lord Mayor, had earlier arranged for the City of Sydney to be a $30,000 annual sponsor, for five years, of the Peace Foundation lecture, which is always given, in a separate function, by the peace prize winner the night before the award ceremony on the first Thursday in November.

On Tuesday this week, in a brief 'Dear Professor Rees' letter dated October 20, Turnbull told Rees the Sydney City Council 'will be unable to participate in this year's Peace Prize events'. That is, the council was blackballing both the lecture and the award ceremony. Turnbull's reasons for doing so were a travesty: the usual ignorant mishmash of allegations forever trotted out by the usual suspects against any Palestinian with international credibility and standing in the peace process.

Lucy Turnbull should read the letter from a Jewish academic at Oxford University published in the *Herald* yesterday. Then she should go hide her head in shame. The letter responded to Tony Stephens' story in the *Herald* two days earlier about Turnbull's craven cave-in to the anti-Ashrawi campaign. It said: 'Opposition to awarding the Sydney Peace Prize to Dr Hanan Ashrawi has so far been based on historical ignorance, ideological blindness, wilful malevolence or provincial political opportunism.' (Are you listening, Malcolm?)

The letter continued: 'Dr Ashrawi has been a rare and precious voice of reason in the peace process and her commitment to a just solution has been exemplary. She has consistently encouraged Palestinians to reject violence, despite continuing Israeli territorial expansion and systemic political oppression.' (signed) Ben Saul, Tutor in International Law, Magdalen College, University of Oxford, England.

And what does Rees think of Lucy's white feather? He said yesterday: 'When I negotiated the sponsorship contract with the City of Sydney, I did so with Frank Sartor, not Lucy Turnbull. She's an interesting person. I've had face-to-face communications with all the major corporate sponsors who support us over this issue. I even flew down to Melbourne to talk to Rio Tinto. But Lucy Turnbull and co are like the Medicis of the Town Hall. She never talks to me. All I got was this summary note a couple of days ago in which, for her own purposes, she completely misinterprets Ashrawi's public statements and says she won't publicly support us this year.

'In other words, she won't be seen in the same company as Ashrawi. She doesn't even want to be seen in the lecture theatre. Apparently it's more than her husband's political life is worth.'

Ah, yes, of course Malcolm Turnbull's much publicised stalking of the Liberals' Peter King in his pursuit of the eastern suburbs' federal seat of Wentworth. Lucy Turnbull has gone to ground since her 'Dear John' letter to Rees this week. But a senior business figure phoned Rees on Tuesday to tell him of a conversation he'd overheard at a function the previous night. It apparently included Lucy being told something like: 'That wretched King is going around saying you support the Palestinians because you're a party to this peace prize.'

Rees commented: 'So Hanan Ashrawi gets her name sullied and ridiculed because the Turnbulls want to be more important that they already are.'

And Kathryn Greiner? Greiner was chairwoman of the Sydney Peace Foundation for four years until her resignation this year over an issue of solidarity involving her husband, Nick, against the Senate of Sydney University and unconnected with the peace prize bitchiness. She was one of the jury of six who selected Ashrawi unanimously in September

last year as this year's recipient (the other five: Rees; social researcher Hugh Mackay; Dr Jane Fulton from University management; Stella Cornelius, Sydney's 83-year-old grand dame of conflict mediation; James McLachlan, a director of Kerry Packer's PBL).

Greiner remains a non-voting member in support of Rees. But two weeks ago, on October 9, she phoned Rees to talk frankly about her concerns with an accelerating campaign against Ashrawi.

A file note of their conversation reads: Greiner: 'I have to speak logically. It is either Hanan Ashrawi or the Peace Foundation. That's our choice, Stuart. My distinct impression is that if you persist in having her here, they'll destroy you. Rob Thomas of City Group is in trouble for supporting us. I think he must have had a phone call from New York. And you know Danny Gilbert [partner in the law firm, Gilbert and Tobin] has already been warned off.'

Rees: 'You must be joking. We've been over this a hundred times. We consulted widely. We agreed the jury's decision, made over a year ago, was not only unanimous but that we would support it, together.'

Greiner: 'But listen, I'm trying to present the logic of this. They'll destroy what you've worked for. They are determined to show we made a bad choice. I think it's Frank Lowy's money. You don't understand just how much opposition there is. We cannot go ahead. If only there was progress in the Middle East, this would not be such a bad time.'

Rees: 'I won't be subject to bullying and intimidation. We are being threatened by members of a powerful group who think they have an entitlement to tell others what to do. This opposition is orchestrated. The arguments are all the same that Hanan Ashrawi has not condemned violence sufficiently, that she was highly critical of Israel in her address to the UN's Johannesburg Conference on racism, and wilder accusations that do not bear repetition.'

Greiner: 'But you're not listening to the logic. The Commonwealth Bank, I was at a reception last night, is highly critical. We could not approach them for financial help for the Schools Peace Prize. We'll get no support from them. The business world will close ranks. They're saying we are being one-sided, that we've only supported Palestine.'

Rees: 'Kathryn, we need to avoid the trap of even using the language of 'one side'. That's not the issue. We are being bullied and intimidated and you are asking that we give way to it. The letter writers and the phone callers who this group encourage have spent weeks bullying a 25-year-old colleague of mine who handles the foundation's administration. You are asking me to collude with bullying.'

Greiner: 'I'll tell you how serious this is. Bob Carr won't come to the dinner. He'll flick the responsibility to [his deputy, Andrew] Refshauge at the last minute. And you won't get the Town Hall. It is more than Lucy's life is worth. They will desert us as well.'

Rees: 'I've never given way to bullying. Public life is too much characterised by cowardice. If we give way I'd be so ashamed I couldn't face myself. The image of the Peace Foundation would be shameful. Our reputation would count for nothing.'

Greiner: 'My friend, I am telling you what the reality is. The foundation will be destroyed. I'd hate to see its work come to nothing over this. Our critics are saying it's an awful choice.'

Rees: 'These critics are 'they' and 'them', invisible but powerful people. They stay powerful because they are invisible. They bully and intimidate in the same breath they behave as unblemished pillars of the community. Do you mean to say that in cautious, often gutless Australia we are not going to follow through on this? No. I remain completely committed to our decision.'

Alan Ramsey

**Postscript:** *Dr Ashrawi came to Australia and got her peace prize. Bob Carr, like Stuart Rees, stood his ground and officiated at a crowded award ceremony at NSW State Parliament. Frank Lowy emerged to write a letter to the* Herald *and make a phone call to Carr. Neither action changed anything. The shrill and the malevolent remained shrill. Ashrawi graced her cause. Mark Leibler shamed his. Hanan Ashrawi addressed the National Press Club eight days after the ABC advised the club it would not televise the function.*

# Nowhere to Hide

**FEBRUARY 9, 2002**

PETER JOHN Hollingworth spent all his working life in the service of the Anglican Church until John Howard made him Governor-General 10 months ago. Hollingworth was a bishop, then an archbishop, before ever he was the Queen's man. His church, like any church, is nothing if it does not offer faith and moral leadership. And on the eve of his 67th birthday (in April) faith and moral leadership are what Hollingworth has represented for the better part of half a century.

Now that image is grievously tainted. The squalid revelations of a squalid court case that ended, ironically, just before Christmas say so. Yet few seem to realise how grave the issue is for the Governor-General and his political benefactor, the Prime Minister.

Here was an Anglican Church school, the prestigious Toowoomba Preparatory School, accused during four weeks of evidence by former students, staff and parents of having sought to cover up the paedophile behaviour of a teacher, Kevin George Guy, who preyed on adolescent girls for at least six months before he gassed himself in his car the day he was due to appear in court on December 18, 1990, to answer sexual abuse charges against one of his victims.

And not just covered up by school authorities.

By the church itself. 1990 was the very year Hollingworth was appointed, from Melbourne, where he was director of the Brotherhood of St Laurence, to be the Most Rev. Anglican Archbishop of Brisbane. As such, he became head of the church in Queensland. Hollingworth has three daughters. In 1987, three years before he became archbishop, he was named Father of the Year in Victoria. The award is recorded in *Who's Who*. So is Hollingworth's nomination as Australian of the Year in 1992. *Who's Who* says nothing about what happened in the three months between November 30, 1990, and the end of February, 1991.

That is the period Hollingworth became complicit in events mishandled by the Toowoomba school authorities and the Anglican diocese of Brisbane in hushing up, for legal reasons and the school's reputation, Guy's suicide and the detail of his predatory behaviour.

A single man, Guy had been appointed boarding master at the co-educational school in 1987. He was responsible for all student boarders. It was the adolescent girls he 'lured', surrounding himself with what were later described in court as well-developed, pretty year 7 girls who would sit on his knee during

the school day, rub sunscreen on him at the school swimming pool, 'tussle' with him on the school oval, and spend time in his room.

Guy repeatedly abused one of his victims for almost seven months, from Anzac Day weekend in 1990 until the night of November 9, when the girl was discovered missing from her dormitory bed. She had kept a tryst with him in the form 7 common room where, over the months, they committed sex acts on 30 separate occasions, sometimes for up to hours at a time. They would, a jury was told 11 years later, 'undress, fondle each other, have oral sex and lie naked on each other'.

The girl was 12 years old.

Kevin Guy was 39.

The day police charged Guy, on November 30, 1990, was the day Hollingworth was first told of the scandal. He had been archbishop only a matter of months. And although the 12-year-old girl's anguished parents later wrote to him, as did a school nurse on Christmas Day 1990 horrified that school authorities were seeking to 'cover up' the reasons for Guy's suicide, Hollingworth, to his later professed regret, did nothing that conflicted with church legal advice that the school admit nothing, apologise to nobody and inform only the parents of the 20 girls named in Guy's suicide note ('I was in love with so many girls'. Guy listed 20 names, whatever he might have meant by 'love'. 'Why is it our education system has to sophisticate children and take away their naivety? It seems cruel to make them into adults. Why do puppies have to become dogs . . .'), but not inform the parents of the school student body as a whole.

And the church, the school and its archbishop never did. Guy's suicide and the reasons for it remained, in general, their secret. The headmaster of the time even wrote to parents six days after Guy's suicide, referring to it only as 'the tragic death of senior resident master Kevin Guy whose love and great effort for this school will be sadly missed'. It was an extraordinary letter by a school determined to protect its name and the church's purse.

And that is where matters stayed for 11 years.

Even then, after the whole sorry business went into open court on November 13 last year, three days after the federal election, and Hollingworth's name was publicly linked in questioning terms to what had happened 11 years earlier, still the story, for some bizarre reason, never made it into the light of day, except fairly modestly in Brisbane.

Not until December 19 last year, after the 12-year-old plaything of the dead teacher, now 24, had sued the school and the Anglican Church and had won an $834,800 damages verdict from a jury of two women and two men after a four-week trial, did Hollingworth end his long silence with a 2 1/2-page statement vetted by the church's legal advisers.

Such was the dreadful bind in which Hollingworth found himself. Apparently neither he nor Howard had known the court case in Toowoomba was coming until it arrived, or so it is now suggested. Certainly it is difficult to imagine Howard would have gone ahead with Hollingworth's appointment to Yarralumla had he been aware of the pending civil court action and the squalid, tragic detail it would set loose around the archbishop's name and behaviour 11 years ago.

Yet now Hollingworth was Governor-General and all the official advice being pressed on him was to leave it to the church to deal with and for him to stay silent and not involve his vice-regal office, despite the political and media clamour that insisted Hollingworth explain himself for his inaction and lack of moral courage 11 years earlier. There were some shrill calls for his resignation. There was more measured questioning of the damage done to his own standing and the escalating damage he was doing the office of Governor-General.

In the end, Hollingworth insisted on defending himself. Enough was enough. What he told Howard, I have no idea. Neither does anyone else. The two men spoke at length. It is most likely that Howard would have agreed he could not continue to say nothing. Hollingworth's apparent spineless silence was only inciting hostility. It was the action of a man with something to hide and no real explanation to excuse his behaviour.

Yet that is exactly what his statement suggests. It alluded to the pressures he was under. He had felt it 'inappropriate' to comment after the court decision 'because of my position as Governor-General'. However, it had 'become clear some people would use my silence not only to draw into controversy the standing of the office of Governor-General, but also to make completely unfounded allegations against me personally. I cannot stand by and allow this to continue'.

Yet in defending himself, Hollingworth could only fall back on legalisms and grubby matters of money. 'I accepted it was imperative that insurance coverage not be jeopardised,' he said, acknowledging the real world but grievously wounding his moral authority. As he later added, so lamely yet damningly: 'I am sorry that legal and insurance considerations to some extent inhibited our taking a more active role and more overtly expressing the church's concern for the physical, emotional and spiritual welfare of those affected by the actions of Mr Guy.'

There is a great deal of unhappy detail unearthed by the court case that will bedevil Hollingworth for a long time to come. Almost two months after Guy's suicide, Hollingworth met for three hours with the then school headmaster who, at one point, offered to resign. Hollingworth rejected the offer. From that point of direct personal involvement, irrespective of his moral obligations to the school's students, there was no way from there

Hollingworth could ever argue the affair had nothing to do with him. None at all.

A week ago an ABC television crew for the *Australian Story* program flew to Canberra to interview Hollingworth, his wife, Anne, and one of his daughters. Hollingworth imposed no restrictions. He did not ask to vet the questions beforehand. The interviews are scheduled to be broadcast on Monday, February 18. Hollingworth will speak to no-one else.

Yet the story will not die.

One interview on the ABC will not kill it. Not by a long chalk. The Anglican Church and its servants grossly mishandled the repercussions of one predatory teacher's rampant paedophilia 11 years ago. Yet they have only just begun to reap the whirlwind. It is inconceivable that Hollingworth can survive, however long it may be before he inevitably resigns as Governor-General.

Alan Ramsey

# Defending the Indefensible

**MAY 7, 2003**

WHEN JOHN Howard spoke to reporters at Sydney Airport last Thursday before leaving to see George Bush for the third time in 20 months, he said categorically he would not 'sack the Governor-General', Peter Hollingworth. Three days later, in New York, Howard was asked by Australian reporters: 'Should the Governor-General resign?' He ignored the question.

Instead, the Prime Minister replied: 'Let me simply say this, repeating what I have previously said, that there is nothing in his conduct, as Governor-General, and indeed no proper basis in relation to other matters, for me to recommend to the Queen his commission be terminated. Beyond that I don't intend to comment.'

Howard is a political artiste in answering questions he's not asked by ignoring those he is. He is at his most shameless when the issue is most sensitive. Hollingworth's strangely know-nothing, do-nothing attitude as Anglican archbishop of Brisbane for 11 years, while several gross sexual predators preyed on students, both girls and boys, under the church's care in Hollingworth's Brisbane diocese, is one such issue.

The assertion of 'nothing' in Hollingworth's 'conduct' as Governor-General to warrant dismissal 'and no proper basis in relation to other matters' is sophistry. Constitutionally, appointment and dismissal is purely at the Prime Minister's discretion. There is no written protocol on termination. A governor-general's appointment can simply be withdrawn by the British monarch on the recommendation of the Australian Prime Minister, which he or she is bound to accept. It is just that it has never happened in a century of federation.

So Howard is throwing up a straw man when he talks about 'no proper basis' for dismissal. That is for him alone to determine. It is just as specious to say, as Howard told reporters the day he left Australia, 'I'm told there's no finding in the report of any deliberate misconduct' by Hollingworth in his previous role as archbishop of Brisbane.

What does that mean? That 'accidental' misconduct is OK? It is a nonsense. Howard is just engaging in tosh by dressing up the gravity of his language to excuse his embarrassment that his choice as Governor-General has turned out such an awful dud. And when he returns to Australia at the weekend Howard should read the report so shaming of the Anglican Church's appalling behaviour on the issue of child abuse within the church in Brisbane under Hollingworth's term as archbishop.

It is 471 pages in length and is entitled *Report of the Board of Inquiry into Past Handling of Complaints of Sexual Abuse in the Anglican Church Diocese of Brisbane*. The board of inquiry instigated by the church itself was just two people: Peter O'Callaghan, a Melbourne QC, as chairman, and Professor Freda Briggs, of Adelaide, an eminent authority on child development. They were appointed in March last year and conducted the inquiry in private. Their report, completed on April 22, was tabled in the Queensland Parliament last week to give it parliamentary privilege after John Howard declined the church's request to table it in the Federal Parliament.

Hollingworth did not speak to the board. instead, the board, 'through his solicitors, received lengthy statements of facts and submissions' on Hollingworth's behalf. Remarkably, given Howard's public whitewash of his Governor-General, one of Hollingworth's statutory declarations concerning a priest who buggered a student for four years was found by the board to be a concoction.

The report stated: 'The board is satisfied Dr Hollingworth was told by the complainant on 30 August 1993 that the sexual abuse was not an isolated occurrence [as Hollingworth claimed he was told after he allowed the priest to continue in his ministry] but consisted of repeated criminal acts.

'The board finds Dr Hollingworth's recollections are faulty, and that he has apparently reconstructed what he believed he was told rather than recalled what in fact was said. Dr Hollingworth made a statutory declaration he believed the abuse was an isolated occurrence. The board is satisfied he was told the details of [repeated] abuse. There was nothing that could have entitled Dr Hollingworth to believe otherwise. The board considers no bishop acting reasonably could have reached the decision to continue a known pedophile in the ministry. There were no extenuating circumstances, nor can the board imagine any . . .'

And while this is the most serious finding against Hollingworth, one he acknowledges was a major lapse of judgement, it is hard to understand how the Prime Minister can excuse his Governor-General making a sworn declaration which was dismissed by the board of inquiry as utterly false.

That is not all. There are a number of dreadful serial abuses of teenage children cited that raise questions about the then archbishop's responsibility in the church's flawed behaviour, irrespective what he knew or did not know. He was the head of the church for 11 years. He should have ensured it was his business to know. The ultimate duty of care was his.

Alan Ramsey

# Read the Report, PM!

MAY 10, 2003

IT WAS about protecting the Anglican Church's money and reputation, much less about protecting abused children. You only have to go back to how the whole dreadful business began 13 years ago. Read the letters two mothers went on writing, seemingly endlessly, on behalf of their grossly abused daughters, one aged 13, the other 12.

Yet all the church and its fashionable prep school in Toowoomba did was hush up the scandal around a dead paedophile teacher, while Peter Hollingworth, Brisbane's new archbishop at the time, knew what had happened but asked little and did nothing for 11 years until it became a sordid court case 18 months ago. And then the archbishop, by then Governor-General, was on the phone to the lawyers to get them to protect him in the newspapers. It really makes you spit.

In the 471-page independent report on sexual abuse commissioned by Hollingworth's Brisbane successor, Archbishop Phillip Aspinall, one of the genuinely admirable people involved, there is a damning summary of legal advice and associated correspondence in the lead-up to the Toowoomba court case that began on November 15, 2001 (which, if you recall, just happened, fortunately, to be five days after the last federal election).

Some excerpts:

**August, 2000**: The concluding paragraph of a letter by the legal firm Minter Ellison to the church's insurer, New Zealand Insurance: 'We have spoken to Mr Bernie Yorke [registrar and general manager] of the Anglican diocese and [solicitors] Flower and Hart and they have both expressed the desire that AB's [the 12-year-old's] claim be settled with as little publicity as possible. Apparently the TPS [school] has a new headmaster and has put the incident of Mr Guy [the dead pedophile, who preyed on 'blonde, blue-eyed, tanned girls' aged between eight and 13] behind it. The Anglican diocese is anxious not to raise the matter of Mr Guy in the public arena, lest bad publicity affect the [school].'

**November 8, 2001:** After a telephone conference call between the church's legal people: '$50,000 was the best offer made by the insurer at mediation. The other side indicated $250,000 was wanted. Insurer put formal offer of $80,000 plus costs. [Their solicitor] indicated defendant might go to $100,000. [Plaintiff's solicitors] said they would recommend AB accept $200,000.'

**November 12, 2001:** 'A call to Mr Yorke informs him the matter will be going to trial. He says the school council has had a meeting and will not be paying a cent. It was over 10 years ago and the perpetrator is deceased.'

**November 15, 2001**: The day AB's lawsuit goes before a jury in Toowoomba: 'The plaintiff won't settle for $250,000. There has been complete support from the parents [of children at the school]. The school council says we won't put any money in. They will wear the publicity likely to attend the evidence of the nurse.'

Later the same day: Extract from correspondence between [law firms] Minter Ellison and Flower and Hart [solicitor]: 'First thing in the morning I made application to exclude evidence of a highly prejudicial kind that the psychologist, Joy Connolly, had attempted to speak to Archbishop Hollingworth about

this matter [in December 1990, the month the teacher suicided] but he was leaving on vacation [in Victoria] and refused to see her. The matter was resolved with the trial judge [a woman] indicating, provisionally, it was inadmissible. In conjunction, I sought the suicide note of [the dead teacher, which named up to 20 girls] be ruled inadmissable. [It was.] Jury was empanelled— four rather elderly but quite attentive citizens who appear to be taking an active and considered part in trial.'

**November 22, 2001:** The day Hollingworth's name is first mentioned at the trial: 'Call from Mr Yorke. The Governor-General is very concerned. He wants it known he was not told of anything until after the suicide. He wants me to speak to the *Toowoomba Chronicle* tonight.' Later the same day: 'Call to Mr Yorke. Told him we should not be arguing the evidence outside the court. The archbishop (Hollingworth) is adamant he knew nothing about it. Perhaps [the barrister] can make a statement about it in court.'

**November 23, 2001:** 'Call from [solicitor at court]. The letter from archbishop of 25 February, 1991, has been admitted to evidence. The archbishop will be mentioned today in the context of the AB letters.' Later the same morning: 'Call from [solicitor]. Evidence was adduced as to letters this morning. They rang for the archbishop and he failed to return the calls. One juror has been gasping and sobbing during the evidence. The other side [AB's solicitors] has withdrawn its offer of $350,000. There will be more publicity adverse to the archbishop.'

The four-week trial ended on December 19, 2001, with a record $834,000 verdict in favour of the schoolgirl, who was sexually abused for up to five months, often twice a week. The church did not appeal.

The subsequent board of inquiry called the verdict a 'financial catastrophe' for the Brisbane diocese. The second girl, the 13-year-old referred to as CD, settled out of court for 'a large sum' after the success of AB's suit. This older girl's mother had tried for nine months to get the Toowoomba school to pay for counselling for her daughter. It refused. Hollingworth, who was drawn into the argument, declined to intervene.

The board of inquiry would comment 11 years later: 'The pervasive theme in the conduct of [the school's headmaster, his deputy and staff, and the school council] was reserve or scepticism in accepting the girls' [accusations against the dead 39-year-old teacher who killed himself the morning he was due to face court] and the desire to keep the matters 'in house' to protect the reputation of the school. Briefly put, the welfare of the abused students was subordinated to considerations as to what was seen as best for the school. It seems this was perceived by the jury and reflected its large award of exemplary damages.'

Of the long and abortive fight to get the school to pay for counselling, as well as the school's and the church's refusal for 11 years to apologise to either girl for fear of jeopardising the church's insurers, the board noted: 'AB and CD and their parents confirm there was no attempt on the part of the headmaster, the school council or any other person in authority to manifest an interest and concern about how these two young girls were faring [in the months and years after the pedophile's suicide].

'There was never any expression of concern by school persons in authority at what had happened. This required those girls to pass through adolescence to adulthood with the perception they were not believed, and had it not been for them taking action many years later, that would have remained the position. The irony for the diocese and its insurers is that had solicitude and concern been shown, apologies proffered and counselling costs met, the reputation of the diocese would not have been blighted and a million-plus dollars might have been saved.'

And Peter Hollingworth?

At least four parents wrote to him. So did the counsellor, Joy Connolly. And so did the school nurse, Sister Christine Munro, who told Hollingworth in a letter dated December 25, 1990: 'My reason for writing is to voice my deep concern at the manner in which the headmaster and the school council are handling the current crisis [of the paedophile house master's suicide]. I attended the meeting where the headmaster addressed staff, I believe, to the point they are being deceived . . . At this stage it appears there could be a cover-up. I simply ask, could you please see that the truth is made known to us all as soon as possible . . .'

CD's mother wrote to Hollingworth on January 15, 1991: 'I am hoping you can bring your sensible, down-to-earth approach to the school's current situation, where a web of silence is being woven at our daughter's expense . . . Why wasn't Mr Guy immediately stood down to safeguard the welfare of all children? Why did the school not adopt an open attitude and inform all parents of the manner of his death and the reason for same? After enduring weeks of sexual abuse, my daughter had the courage and maturity to break free from that awful web of secrecy. Why should she perhaps be forced to go through an even worse hell?'

AB's parents wrote to Hollingworth: 'Enclosed please find copies of letters to Mr Brewster [headmaster], the school council . . . and to Bishop Charles. As you can imagine, we are appalled by the huge cover-up that seems to have taken place . . .'

The board of inquiry would find 12 years later: 'The letters from the mothers of AB and CD do them credit. Their attitude is epitomised by what AB's mother wrote to the board: "If there had been unconditional recognition of the abuse and an apology for it, that may well have been the end of the matter" . . .'

Hollingworth wrote to Sister Munro and to the parents of AB and CD only after he returned from leave. His cowardly letter was dated February 25, 1991. It said: 'I have received your letter of concern and want to assure you I have been in close consultation with the headmaster, the chairman of the school council and Bishop Charles. I understand you will now have received a second letter [from the school] that the matter is in hand and appropriate action has been taken . . . Please be assured I am monitoring things closely and I believe your concerns are being met.'

Monitoring things closely?

Another four serial sex abusers, including two priests, would prey on victims in Hollingworth's Brisbane diocese over the next 10 years. All were hushed up, excused or rationalised for the same venal reasons. It is an appalling record during Hollingworth's archbishopric. And now he and his political benefactor pretend he has nothing to answer for.

Just read the report, Prime Minister.

Alan Ramsey

**Postscript:** *Peter Hollingworth resigned three weeks later, on May 29, 2003, having served just 23 months of his five-year term . . . And, in going, under public odium greater probably, because of the manner of his leaving, than the political outrage against John Kerr's self-serving treachery in 1975, Hollingworth went with indexed superannuation of $185,000 a year plus various other publicly funded perks that prime ministers, whoever they be, give each other and their appointees when they are put out to grass. The entire episode was one of the most odious and shameful of Howard's prime ministership.*

# The Day Politicians Lost their Voice

OCTOBER 17, 1998

A DISEASE of extreme virulence swept the crowded ranks of the nation's politicians this week. It was the one that rendered them mute the instant the tax affairs of Kerry Packer, Australia's wealthiest citizen, and his Consolidated Press group became news.

The media was almost as tongue-tied, particularly the Murdoch press. On the very day Rupert Murdoch's 65 per cent of the country's metropolitan papers were reporting, at length, their executive chairman's remarks to his News Corporation's annual general meeting in Adelaide, Murdoch's fellow media owner's tax obscenity barely rated in any of them.

The courage of the politicians was profound.

Here was a tax case that had gone on for seven years and which, in a Federal Court judgment on Tuesday, delivered to Packer personal and corporate tax savings totalling $258 million because of the highly complex way a man of his wealth can minimise tax liability.

And while an election has just been fought in which so many 'courageous' politicians of various stripes verbally battered voters for seven weeks on the necessity or otherwise of a 'bold' new tax regime for a new century, did any one of them volunteer a single word this week on what Packer was able to achieve by his legal advisers' manipulation of the Tax Act?

The whole of the re-elected Government was in Canberra the same day the court decision was in that morning's papers. Did the Treasurer, Peter Costello, issue a statement reassuring taxpayers of the Government's determination to close tax loopholes? Did he call down the television cameras to say anything about anything, with or without his Teddy Bear? Did John Howard initiate a statement? Did Kim Beazley weigh in with Labor's point of view? Did anybody say anything?

Well, yes. A Labor backbencher, Anthony Albanese, turned up on ABC morning radio to offer the opinion that most Australians would 'choke on their breakfast' when they read the Packer story. And, later in the day, the Democrats' Meg Lees released a statement in which she delicately avoided any reference to Kerry Packer by name but talked of 'today's episode' and the need for Parliament 'to legislate to ensure wealthy Australians and corporations pay their fair share' of tax. The Prime Minister subsequently got involved only under sufferance.

At his press conference the same day to announce what a superb election victory the Government had achieved and how he would now be 'a different Prime Minister', three times John Howard was asked about the Packer case. Three times he refused 'to comment on an individual, whether it's Mr Packer's position or, indeed, anybody else's'. But he did restate his 'well-known view' about 'people paying their fair share' of tax, and emphasised that 'some of the anti-avoidance measures' in the Government's GST package 'will make the use of those sorts of (avoidance) devices a lot more difficult in future'.

Next day, in Brisbane, Kim Beazley, like John Howard, was drawn into the issue only by reporters' questions. His response echoed the Prime Minister. 'I wouldn't want to comment on an individual tax case like Mr Packer's,' he told radio 4QR's Carolyn Tucker. 'I don't know the full circumstances.' But Beazley, too, pledged Labor's 'full support' in Parliament if the Prime Minister 'wants to make wealthy Australians who are avoiding tax pay their fair share'.

The political courage of all concerned was truly uplifting.

The same could be said of much of the press. Only *The Australian Financial Review* led its front page with the Federal Court decision. Only the *Review* spelt out the detail and complexity of what had happened and how Packer had defeated the Tax Office. The only other paper that thought the story significant enough for its front page was this one. Every Murdoch paper across the country buried it well inside. One, the *Mercury* in Hobart, did not report it until two days later.

By yesterday four capital city papers had editorialised on the outrage of legal tax avoidance. The *Herald* was one. Two of the four, including the *Herald,* were careful to suggest no 'blame' should attach to the media magnate. Kerry Packer's wealth and corporate power earn him more than a risible tax bill.

Alan Ramsey

# Celebration of the Obscene

FEBRUARY 18, 2006

PETRINA SLAYTOR lives in Sydney's Greenwich. She has worked all her life in community programs and plays the bassoon. Frank Leverett lives in Canberra and works for the Prime Minister. Whatever he might play, it is never the fool. He is a serious man. Seven weeks ago an affronted Petrina Slaytor wrote to John Howard. He did not write back.

Instead she got a letter three weeks later from Frank Leverett.He wrote in his capacity as head of the Ceremonial and Hospitality Branch of the Department of the Prime Minister and Cabinet. His letter, dated January 19, said: 'Dear M/s Slaytor. Thank you for your letter of January 2 to the Prime Minister about the State Memorial Service for the late Mr Kerry Packer, AC. I have been asked to respond.

'It has been the policy of successive Australian Governments to offer state funerals and/or memorial services to distinguished Australians from a wide range of backgrounds and professions who have made significant contributions to Australia. Such services are offered as a mark of respect and in recognition of the particular contribution they have made.

'In addition to holders of relevant public office, such acknowledgement has been offered in the past to scientists, entertainers, sports people, members of the medical professions, indigenous leaders and [military people]. The State Memorial Service for the late Mr Packer will be conducted in accordance with past practice and the relevant guidelines.

'Thank you for your interest.

'Yours sincerely . . .' etc.

Petrina Slaytor was neither mollified nor amused. She showed Leverett's letter to an old friend, Dr John Carmody, a writer, former music critic and longtime *Herald* reader. So annoyed was Carmody that he took up his pen and laid into the Prime Minister's man in Canberra. 'Dear Mr Leverett,' he wrote on January 24.

'You recently wrote in response to a friend's letter to the Prime Minister which protested the Government's decision to provide a state memorial service for the late tycoon, Mr Kerry Packer. Having read your letter, I am moved to write my own. I am, of course, conscious your letter was simply to explain a decision of government, not of your department or yourself. Nevertheless, I believe you should be conscious of the significance of the words you choose to write.

'You referred to a policy whereby 'distinguished Australians' (or their families) are offered such occasions. No reasonable person could consider Mr Packer 'distinguished'. 'Conspicuous' certainly, notably in his appalling wealth and the power he so blatantly abused. But certainly not distinguished, in any undegraded sense of the word. You also referred to persons who had made a 'significant contribution to Australia'. The word 'contribution' connotes something positive or worthy or beneficial.

'None of these remotely applies to Mr Packer . . .

'I consider that many families with truly distinguished, deceased loved ones would be entitled to feel affronted. For example, when the great priest and worker for Aboriginal Australians Father Ted Kennedy died last year—the nearest person to a saint I ever met—he was given no such public honour. Nor, a few years ago, was Sir John Eccles, the Nobel Prize-winning medical scientist. The list of such great but neglected Australians is long . . .

'It is appallingly inappropriate that a man who so brazenly ordered his affairs so as to avoid paying tax should have taxpayers' money spent on him in this way . . . One is forced to the conclusion timidity and fear have driven this decision. The Government is afraid [of] attack by the media which his family and companies control. This is a sad day for Australia, but for all the wrong reasons. 'Yours sincerely . . .' etc.

Carmody has heard nothing. Neither have the rest of us.

A great many Australians would know of Packer's 'significant contribution' to self-interest and to his family's immense wealth, just as they'd have been aware of his contempt for income tax. What they've not been told, by the Government that now honours him, is what it thinks his 'significant contribution to Australia' might have been.

Howard has been asked about the issue only once. On the day, coincidentally, Carmody wrote to Leverett a month after Packer's death, Melbourne radio's Neil Mitchell asked Howard on air: 'There's been some criticism today of the state funeral for Kerry Packer. What's your reaction?'

Howard replied: 'It was my decision alone. And I made the offer to the Packer family as a mark of respect for the enormous contribution he's made to the country. I mean, it obviously wasn't to provide the family with financial assistance. And the basic cost, to the taxpayer, is not very high. But I think it appropriate on occasions that people other than former ministers be honoured with state funerals.

'The Federal Government, in the time I've been Prime Minister, we gave Nugget Coombs a state funeral (in November 1997), we gave Charlie Perkins a state funeral (in October 2000), I gave B.A. Santamaria a state funeral (in March 1998). We co-operated with the South Australian Government in giving Don Bradman a state funeral (in 2001). And a number of State governments have given figures, outside the normal ambit of people, state funerals.

'I think Kerry Packer, like him or not—and a lot of people liked him and a lot of people didn't—was a remarkable business and media figure. And if we are to have a broad view of the life of this country, we ought to honour business figures, from time to time, as well as sporting, political and military figures.'

Mitchell let the matter drop. He'd asked his one Packer question. No other reporter, before or since, has raised it with Howard. Some have written about it, occasionally unflatteringly. None has confronted our Prime Minister. Nor any other member of his Government. The Opposition has been just as silent, just as acquiescent.

Instead, unlike Leverett—whom Carmody pressed even though he was ignored—Howard has been allowed to skate past with a mouthful of words that explain nothing to give substance to the phantom legacy of Packer's 'enormous contribution' to the country that has gone on making three generations of the family immensely wealthy.

In doing so, Howard nominated four others—'outside the normal ambit', as he put it—as qualifying, by his lights, for national recognition of a state funeral/memorial service. The 'contribution' of those four—to public life (Coombs), Aboriginal leadership (Perkins), sport (Bradman), even to national political affairs (Santamaria)—is obvious. Not so Kerry Packer's.

What Packer excelled at was making money, of building on the fortune his father left him. He bought loyalty as ruthlessly as his mere presence intimidated politicians. His mercenaries—in sport, the media, his casinos and across the business world—saw him as God and behaved accordingly. He was a crude, rude, ruthless bully, however charming when it suited, and woe betide, by all accounts, those who crossed him.

But he was a very rich bully, and it made all the difference. As for political life, he was utterly contemptuous of it, other than for what his minions could bend from its practitioners on behalf of his business interests. Anyone who saw Packer's appearance at the 1991 parliamentary committee hearing on the Australian print media has not forgotten his sneering, boorish behaviour. Some delighted in it. Most were shocked by his oafishness and his arrogance.

Yet all bent the knee to it. They were still doing so yesterday inside the Opera House, the nation's most splendid piece of architecture, our most internationally admired building. The irony is damning. The Packer family television network and its masthead magazines, *The Bulletin* and *The Australian Women's Weekly*, have been polishing the mythology since Boxing Day. All our newspapers—all of them—joined the queue.

John Howard's Australia. A celebration of an obscene tycoon and his obscene wealth. John Carmody is right. A sad day, indeed.

And let's get the patronage of state funerals/memorial services into perspective. In the past 20 years—inclusive of the 1986 funerals of Dame Annabelle Rankin, Leslie Bury, Lionel Murphy and ballet's Sir Robert Helpmann, up to the pomp and ceremony in Brisbane of Reg Swartz's departure last week—there have been 'about' 60 state funerals/memorial services hosted by various governments, not all of them federal.

The majority of these—about 45—have been to honour politicians, not all of them all that honourable. Federal Cabinet ministers of all colours get the offer of a State funeral as a matter of course. Anyone else is determined solely by the Prime Minister or Premier of the day.

Thus Labor's Peter Beattie gave one of Queensland State politics' great villains, Johannes Bjelke-Petersen, a state funeral last year, just as Paul Keating honoured Sir Edward 'Weary' Dunlop and Professor Fred Hollows in 1993, and Menzies' widow, Dame Pattie, in 1995, and Bob Carr gave country music's Slim Dusty a state funeral in September 2003.

There is no protocol, no hard and fast guidelines, no matter what bureaucrats might say in correspondence with questioning voters. It is purely and simply whatever any prime minister or premier thinks he can get away with politically. John Howard put his money on the Packer family. And its power is such that any other prime minister would have done the same. The deferential Labor line-up at the Opera House says so.

Alan Ramsey

# Chapter 22

# This Wide Brown Land

## The Banjo Man

SEPTEMBER 6, 2003

'BANJO' PATERSON was born on February 17, 1864. He died in 1941, 12 days before he would have been 77. Yet by 30 he'd already written the three ballads that immortalise him in Australian life. His *Clancy of the Overflow* and *The Man from Snowy River* were completed by age 26. Paterson was 30 when he wrote the words to *Waltzing Matilda* in Dagworth, Queensland, in 1894.

A lifetime later an Australian Prime Minister travelled to Winton in the far west to celebrate Matilda's centenary performance. On April 6, 1995, Paul Keating told a section of Winton's joyous 10,000 crowd that weekend why 'The Banjo' was the pulse of this nation.

His speech remains as fresh as a Paterson couplet.

Speaking from notes, Keating began: 'This is one to tell our grandchildren about; we were in the North Gregory Hotel when Australia celebrated the first performance of *Waltzing Matilda* 100 years before. And we were all in evening dress, which is something the swagman would have found amusing, but maybe the squatter, the troopers and Banjo Paterson would have appreciated. All would have liked the irony in it.

'I was in Bourke yesterday, another place in the romance of the swag, and another place suffering the drought. Yesterday in Bourke the town was gathered for an extraordinary event, a marathon race from Bourke to Parramatta to raise money for the Fred Hollows Foundation.

'Fred is buried in Bourke, and they celebrate his memory as a man who loved the bush and the values of the people who live there. Here in Winton these celebrations remind us of the same things. They are reminding us of the spirit of the bush and commemorating a song which has lifted our spirits for 100 years. There are no limits to the power of a good song. In times like this, music is not as good as rain, but it may well be the next best thing.

'*Waltzing Matilda* was born in a drought era, of course, and it is not hard to imagine this might have had some effect on its melancholy theme. And there is equally no doubt that, in all the varieties of hard times, *Waltzing Matilda* has galvanised the spirit of countless Australians. If culture is that which defines people, if it is the expression of their collective sentiment, Waltzing Matilda sits at the centre of our culture a wellspring of the national sentiment, a pool, a billabong.

'I suspect there is no one here who has not, at some time, somewhere in the world, heard or remembered the tune and felt deeply affected by it. I'm sure it has brought Australians home before they intended, and given others the strength to stay away a bit longer. For a century it has caused Australian hearts to beat faster. I venture to say it has caused more smiles and tears, and more hairs to stand up on the back of more Australian necks, than any other thing of three minutes' duration in Australia's history . . .'

There is a point to this beyond enjoying a simple story elegantly told from the heart. The power of simple, sincere language is seemingly foreign to a generation of politicians who seem only to understand the political necessity of the snappy 10-second TV and radio grab. To read a Keating speech is to be reminded of a skill not heard since he and Gareth Evans and John Button quit political life and Jim Killen went home to Brisbane and Mick Young and Fred Daly died.

Name any one of the current lot you'd cross the street for.

Mark Latham? On a good day, sure. Peter Costello, sometimes. John Howard drowns us in monotonal banalities. Simon Crean drones listeners into a stupor. Neither understands the simplicity or rhythm of language. Each is incapable of being even interesting, let alone inspiring. Howard is a competent parliamentary debater, nothing more. Crean is simply indescribable.

It was Crean's craven speech to Melbourne's Jewish community last Sunday that sent me in despair to Mark Ryan's *Advancing Australia*, a 1995 collection of Keating speeches no longer in print. His 'Ghost of the Swagman' speech in celebration of *Waltzing Matilda* in Winton eight years ago is but one example of passion creatively offered in everyday language. It is not just a skill but a gift.

You think I gild the lily for a prime minister I bagged for much of his last two years in office? One has nothing to do with the other. Twenty-five years ago I wrote speeches for Bill Hayden. I've worked in journalism or with the written political word all my life. Most of us recognise quality. I rarely got within a bull's roar of what Keating was so often capable of in his speech craft.

Here's some more from his *Matilda* speech:

'I have no doubt that all through these celebrations people will be talking about why *Waltzing Matilda* endures. Why it means so much to us. Who the swagman was and what, therefore, the song was meant to signify. I won't be buying into the historical debate. But there is no question it is easy to take from the lyrics an affirmation of the idea of the fair go which still strikes a powerful chord in Australians. And may it always do so.

'Paterson's story describes a class struggle, and if ever there was a class struggle in Australia it was in the 1890s. His sympathy is with the battler the swagman against the squatter. So we can see it as an egalitarian song. We can think of the swagman's jump into the billabong as the Australian statement of liberty or death.

'But the truth is, none of these things come into my mind when I hear it sung. They didn't come into my mind when the entire crowd at Croke Park in Dublin sang it before the Gaelic football final when I was there [in 1993]. I don't know what came into my mind then; I think the experience emptied it of all rational thought. But afterwards I was aware of the enormous power of the song on an Australian's senses. All sorts of music can move us, but to hear *Waltzing Matilda* sung so fervently and beautifully by the people of another country 12,000 miles from home is to know that nothing can move us like our own song.

'When you hear it, you don't think about a political position, or social and psychological issues. Nor do you think about the historical context of droughts and strikes a century ago. What *Waltzing Matilda* tells us in an entirely uncomplicated way is that we are Australian. And it tells us in a way I think is equally Australian. It tells us without beating drums or waving flags or pounding our chests. It tells us with a simple melody and a story, and a highly ironic story at that . . .'

There was nothing ironic about John Howard's Tuesday speech to an Australian–American Association lunch in Melbourne. He had nothing to say and said it in his usual self-satisfied way to the servants and acolytes of George Bush's Washington.

On Wednesday and Thursday there were radio talkback appearances, with Melbourne and Canberra ABC, in which Howard was unusually ragged. He got a hard time from three Melbourne listeners and both announcers were no less insistent with their questions. There was a snide crack, by inference, at Keating's taxpayer-funded perks as a former prime minister ('I think somebody like Mr Hawke or Mr Fraser who's held the position for a long period, I don't think that is unreasonable, I really don't') but the announcer didn't pick up Howard's obvious failure to anoint Keating.

Perhaps this was because Keating had upstaged Howard that same morning.

Where the papers had pretty much ignored Howard's Tuesday speech to the Americans, Keating's Wednesday book launch in

Melbourne of Stuart Macintyre and Anna Clark's *The History Wars* got half a page in the opinion section of *The Age* with Keating's blast at the 'reactionary' Howard and 'the babble of lickspittles and tintookies [puppets]' around him in their 'rancorous' view of Australian history and identity.

And Keating, of course, did not hide his delight that the book describes him as 'Mr Howard's chief tormentor'. Which brings us back to *Waltzing Matilda*.

Keating concluded that 1995 speech: 'There is no national song I know of quite like it in the world. I think what happened with Banjo Paterson and *Waltzing Matilda* happened in the realm of the spirit. I think he wrote a story to a tune which quite mysteriously, in ways we'll never know, picked up the spirit of [Australia] as it was then. And, like the ghost of the swagman, it never died. And it touches us as a ghost might, as the spirit of the bush might.

'When we were kids, that was the other line I think we used to wonder about, the one which says, 'His ghost may be heard as you pass by the billabong.' I confess to wondering what you would hear. What sort of noise would the old swagman make? What does it sound like when you stuff a jumbuck in a tucker bag? It took me ages to realise this was Banjo Paterson's whole trick: the song is the ghost of the swagman, and 100 years later we are hearing it as loud as ever.'

It's a wonderful punchline to a speech which, if it doesn't move you, you've got a heart like the Moruya granite in the Harbour Bridge. But think about it: the ghost Howard is now hearing again as his prime ministership passes by the accumulating years, is no less than his 'chief tormentor' of the past two decades, old PJK himself.

The thought would tickle Keating hugely.

Alan Ramsey

# How He Loved to Reel 'em in

**MAY 13, 2006**

OVER THE hills south of Canberra is Brindabella Valley. It is a magic place. I first saw it, at its best, when the *Herald*'s Peter Bowers took me there to fish for trout in the Goodradigbee River 40 years ago. Two historic properties dominated at the time, the largest owned by the Dowling family. The other, Koorabri, is at the far end, where the Goodradigbee rises in the high country behind Kosciuszko National Park before it runs the length of the valley, then on through gorges and precipitous bush country to the Murrumbidgee, near Wee Jasper.

It is Koorabri that has Gwen Meredith's log cabin.

This remarkable woman, in her 99th year, lives in NSW's Southern Highlands. Australians everywhere still revere her as the author of two beloved ABC radio serials of another time. One, *The Lawsons*, ran for five years and 1299 episodes until February 5, 1949. Its sequel, *Blue Hills*, a family saga of Australian country life, went to air three weeks later, on February 28, and lasted until its record 5795th episode on September 30, 1976.

And the log cabin?

It was built by Koorabri's owners in the early 1950s, for Gwenyth Valmai Meredith and her husband, Ainsworth Harrison, an engineer. Both were fly-fishers and bushwalkers, and when I rang this week Gwen Meredith recalled happy memories of 'long holidays' at Koorabri. *Blue Hills* disciples with long memories would recognise the valley's influence on the long-running serial.

And the point of this history lesson?

Well, Richard Carleton.

Carleton, at age 26, came to Canberra in 1970. He replaced Mike Willesee as federal political reporter for ABC television's *This Day Tonight* after Willessee, the show's founding Canberra man in 1967, moved on to anchor *Four Corners*. Two years later, in 1972, four journalists negotiated with Koorabri to jointly lease the old Meredith cabin on a year-to-year basis. Carleton was one. Peter Luck and Gerry Stone, *TDT* colleagues in Sydney, were two others. The fourth was Richard Walsh, publisher at the time of *Nation Review*—'the ferret'—and later a Packer executive.

The arrangement lasted a decade. They were 10 great years, for the quartet and their families and friends. Luck and Carleton were the fishing obsessives. Luck still travels to the valley from Sydney when he can, more than 30 years later, to sketch and write poetry. The others have dropped away, one by one. Carleton was the last, a few years back.

Luck emailed this week: 'Attached is a bushfire pic [from Christmas 2003]. Still terrifying 100 digital generations removed! Peter and Fran said the noise was even more terrifying, like a thousand locomotives. Incredibly, they saved every building on the property, including our little log cabin. I have a theory that the huge pine, which went up like a roman candle, acted as a sort of sacrificial anode. As it was, cinders found their way through the roof and burnt holes in the sofa cushions, but everything else remained pristine. The hut is still magic, and there are lots of memories of Richard there. Love to Laura and Tosca . . .'

Carleton was my friend for 35 years. We 'met' out the front of Old Parliament House in the early evening of March 9, 1971 not all that long after he arrived in the press gallery. He was on one side of a TV camera and I was on the other. That was the day I'd yelled, from the gallery, at the Prime Minister, John

Gorton, that he was a 'liar', while Gorton was recounting to Parliament a conversation between us in his office a week earlier concerning Malcolm Fraser.

I got foolishly sensitive to what Gorton was saying, and now I was trying to explain to Carleton and his viewers why I'd made such a clown of myself. (Carleton would tell the *National Times*'s Sally Loane six years later: 'I've still got saliva in my right ear from Alan Ramsey when he yelled, "You liar!" to Gorton. I was standing right next to him. Arthur Calwell said something like, "Deal with the animal" as he looked up into the gallery, and I remember hoping they didn't think it was me.')

We became firm friends ever after, bonded by profession, by support for our personal relationships with others, and by the exhilaration of fishing the streams and rivers of the Brindabella Mountains as well as the waters of the South Coast. What I learned about my friend was that he was a very private person behind all that flamboyant bombast at times, and, while he could behave outrageously, he was loyal and generous with his time to those who had his trust, which seemed few.

Since his death, some silly, ignorant things have been written, as they were throughout his career, by people who knew him only as difficult or for his celebrity with the *60 Minutes* machine. For example, in *The Australian* this week: 'Carleton was not part of the almost incestuous press gallery push. Rather than living within a kilometre of Parliament House, he lived almost isolated in Brindabella Valley.'

Absolute bunkum. Across the 14 years, in two stints, that Carleton worked in the Canberra press gallery, he lived the entire time within a few kilometres of Parliament House in four splendid locations, none of them 'isolated'. Depending on family circumstances, often in some tumult in those years, Brindabella Valley was his retreat at weekends, never his home.

Thirteen of those 14 Canberra years were with the ABC, not the '25 years' often reported this week. But those 13 years were what established Carleton as a journalist of substance and significance—particularly his second stint from 1979 until he delivered himself, for $250,000 a year, into the showbiz maw of the Nine network and moved back to Sydney, in August 1987, from where he'd come 17 years earlier. Along the way he'd had a bad year (1976) with Macquarie radio, when it was still owned by Fairfax, and two good years (1977–78) with BBC television in London.

His marriage to Susie had gone by the time he returned to Australia, driving a Land Rover the length of Africa on the way here, bringing Margaret with him. This was long before he married Sharon on a memorable Saturday afternoon in the Brindabellas in 1983. Last Sunday afternoon, 23 years later, Sharon was driving to Melbourne with their teenage son, Oliver, when a mobile phone call shattered them both by telling them Richard was dead.

The second eight years with the ABC were, to me, the high point of Carleton's professional life. Those were the years he set the standard in political scrutiny for television journalists, forever baiting politicians on his nightly program with his oh-so-polite, at-the-throat questions, which a livid Bob Hawke famously depicted as Carleton's 'perverted reasons' and 'stupidity' behind 'your silly quizzical face'. The incomparable Jack Waterford, of *The Canberra Times*, one of the very few of us around for all 14 years Carleton was in the gallery, this week nailed him as 'master of the mongrel question'.

It is a wonderful line.

Waterford wrote: '[Carleton] had a tremendous capacity to disconcert, unnerve and surprise the person he was interviewing, in a way virtually guaranteed to make [his questions] unpredictable, and to shift [his victim] away from prepared responses, meaningless blather, or a simple refusal to address the question. There are good political television journalists today, but few are as fearless as Carleton was by, say, 1980, or more prepared to ask "the mongrel question", or to tell a politician, bluntly, he was evading the point.'

Amen. Carleton was all that, and more.

And then he joined the Nine network.

He'd have done so years earlier had it been possible. It wasn't. But when Alan Bond seduced Kerry Packer with $1 billion for his Sydney/Melbourne network in January 1987, the door opened. Nine announced in August that year Carleton's decision to join the network (I'd argued he was selling himself short and I was in Dublin when he sent me a telegram that said simply, 'Tick, tick, tick').

In November, Nine announced he was replacing Jana Wendt at *60 Minutes*, where his log-cabin mate from earlier years, Stone, was executive producer. Wendt went to *A Current Affair*. And that was that. Carleton had quit journalism for the money and celebrity of Nine's entertainment machine. We all make our choices. Nineteen years later and *60 Minutes*'s titillation formula, a straight pinch from its American parent, still rates strongly. Carleton, at 62, stayed to the end.

Last Sunday he walked up a hill in Tasmania, turned around and dropped dead. He was cremated on Thursday and the Nine family orchestrated his public farewell early last evening. I never quite made it.

Next week, sometime, Richard's real family will travel to Brindabella Valley and scatter my dear friend's ashes in the Goodradigbee. Gwen Meredith couldn't have written a more fitting ending.

Alan Ramsey

**Postscript:** *Gwen Meredith closed the circle on the Brindabella cottage only a few months after Carleton's death when she died, in her sleep, at her home in the NSW Southern Highlands on October 3, 2006, aged 98.*

# A Sun Burnt Country

NOVEMBER 15, 2008

DOROTHEA MACKELLAR died in Sydney on January 14, 1968. She was 82. Her ashes are interred in the family vault in Waverley Cemetery, with its 50,000 graves and 80,000 internments, including those of literature's Henry Lawson, poetry's Henry Kendall, *The Bulletin's* founder, J.F. Archibald, cricket's Victor Trumper and swimming's Sarah 'Fanny' Durack, iconic Australians, all six.

A week ago a note arrived inside a book, saying: 'Dear Alan and Laura, here is my latest book I thought you might enjoy, particularly since it is heavily weighted with Brindabella shots. I've taken them over 30 years. I used to be a bit snooty about Dorothea's *My Country*, but it has continued to embed itself in the core of my heart.

'Love, Peter Luck.'

This is the centenary year of the publication in 1908 of *My Country*. It first appeared in the London magazine *The Spectator* four years after the teenage Mackellar, born in Sydney and 'barely 18', began 'dreaming up her little masterpiece' after travelling with her parents to England in 1903. Titled originally *Core Of My Heart*, Mackellar completed the 48-line work back in Sydney, after 'several drafts over four or five years', and, following its debut in London, it was first published in Australia in October 1908 in *The Sydney Morning Mail*.

A century later, Luck has combined the iconic last five stanzas, line by line, of the 'simple, evocative poem that has become Australia's unofficial spoken national anthem', with three decades, page by page, of his photography of 'this wide, brown land' in a stylish book he calls *Dorothea Mackellar's My Country: A Centenary Celebration 1908–2008.*

I've known Peter Luck forever, it seems. More than 40 years ago the ABC's Ken Watts recruited him, in a current affairs program staff of 50, from *The Canberra Times* to join Bill Peach, Mike Willesee, Caroline Jones, Sam Lipski, Gerald Stone, David Salter and Frank Bennett, among others (including a very young researcher, Bob Ellis), for the launch on Monday, April 10, 1967, of television's hugely successful *This Day Tonight.*

*TDT* lasted the better part of 12 years, until December 5, 1978. The program infuriated politicians and ABC management alike; introduced us over the years to Mike Carlton, Richard Carleton, Stuart Littlemore, Tim Bowden, Tony Joyce, Paul Murphy, Paul Lyneham and Tony Ferguson, among others; spawned anaemic commercial rivals *A Current Affair* and *Today Tonight*; and began, for Luck, a career in television current affairs journalism that well exceeded three decades.

But photography, like fly fishing in the Brindabellas, south of Canberra, was always Peter's passion.

And it is his photography he matches with Isobel Marion Dorothea Mackellar's sublime words to illustrate his great love of Australia, and hers too. Luck writes in his new book: 'Over the years millions of Australian schoolkids have recited the words 'I love a sunburnt country', and the phrase 'wide, brown land' is as familiar as Donald Horne's 'the Lucky Country'. As with other anthems, there's a verse that's rarely recited. The first stanza is a description of the British landscape, in stark contrast to the country yearned for by a patriotic young dreamer beguiled by the character of the Australian bush.

'*The love of field and coppice/Of green and shaded lanes/Of ordered woods and gardens/Is running in your veins/Strong love of grey-blue distance/Brown streams and soft dim skies/I know but cannot share it/ My love is otherwise.*

'Dorothea did not share that love for the green and scepter'd isle that was England. She loved a 'land of sweeping plains, of ragged mountain ranges, of droughts and flooding rains'. A wilful, lavish land whose inhabitants were mesmerised by both its beauty and its terror. It seems paradoxical that Australia's most famous poem, set far from the city, was penned by a delicate, young socialite, the daughter of a wealthy doctor and politician who owned homes in Sydney's most affluent suburbs as well as a string of country properties.

'To me it feels as though *My Country* might have been written by Banjo Paterson, a flinty bush horseman and war correspondent, or by Henry Lawson, a hardened, world-weary journo with a drinking problem. But it was the aristocratic Dorothea Mackellar who so perfectly captured the ambivalence of the Australian ecosystem and its capricious climate.'

Another irony in the life of this intense Australian was her British gong, an OBE, awarded in the 1968 New Year's honours list, one of the last administrative acts endorsed by the Holt Government before its Prime Minister drowned a fortnight earlier. And two weeks after her OBE was announced, Luck relates, Mackellar—twice engaged but never married—died in her sleep 'a wealthy but essentially lonely old woman'. Her great love affair was with Australia.

Alan Ramsey

# A Sort of Financial Person

**APRIL 7, 2007**

GROWING UP near Taree, Ken Henry would wade out, with his father and brothers, in the river estuaries of the NSW North Coast and stand there, up to his armpits, to catch flathead late at night on the turn of the tide. That was 35 years and more ago. He learnt early to move with stealth among predators. Henry still risks deep water. He still lives with sharks. And he still stalks flathead fish and, at times, boofhead ministers.

This week was one such time.

The Howard Government appointed Henry head of the Commonwealth Treasury on April 27, 2001. At 43 he was already one of our most respected bureaucrats. He has an honours degree in commerce and a doctorate in economics. For five years in the late '80s and early '90s he was Treasury adviser to Paul Keating. Now, at 49, he has 22 years in Treasury. Peter Costello is his sixth Treasurer. Last Australia

Day, the Government made him a Companion of the Order of Australia, our highest gong. The award jointly acknowledged his 'care of native wildlife'. (It meant the real thing, not the politicians!)

Nothing better explains Henry than one of his speeches. And no, I don't mean the behind-closed-doors speech leaked to *The Australian Financial Review* this week that hugely embarrassed the Government and its Treasurer over water and climate policy. That speech saw Costello respond: 'Treasury is no water expert. Treasury is good at Treasury.' The minister known as The Smirk was at a school for circus performers at the time. It seemed appropriate.

Malcolm Turnbull made an even bigger dill of himself.

Turnbull is John Howard's 'water boy' and behaves as such. He told ABC radio loftily on Wednesday: 'Treasury don't know anything about water . . . This is really a political issue. All that's required is political leadership.' And when the ABC persisted, Turnbull said: 'You've got to make judgments, but they are not judgments, frankly, that a, you know, that someone who is only a sort of financial person can make . . . It involves dealing with practical people, people who've got a lot of dirt under their fingernails, who work all day in the bush and know how things work.'

What an arrogant twit he can be.

Turnbull should read Henry's speech to the Australian National University in Canberra on September 21, 2001. Maybe he might learn more than sneering banalities about 'people who work all day in the bush and know how things work'. Henry dedicated that speech to 'my father, John Henry, timber worker'. It was the year the timber worker's son became the most senior economic bureaucrat in the country.

Here is what Ken Henry said, in part: 'At the age of 13 I didn't know what economics was. But I had already had my first lesson in economic policy. It is, quite plausibly, a lesson that may well explain why I am where I am today.

'Some 38 years ago, my parents walked off the dairy farm they had been leasing and my father returned to cutting railway sleepers and, later, logs for local sawmills. For all but a few years of the remainder of his working life, my father worked in the timber industry, mostly felling logs in state forests. He worked long hours, leaving at dawn and returning after sunset.

'One day, about 30 years ago, he arrived home in the late afternoon. He had something he wanted to show his three young sons. He bundled us in the car and took us down to the sawmill. There, on the ground was the biggest log we had ever seen. When our father stood at its base it was apparent it measured some two metres in diameter. And it was 12 metres in length, as long a log as a truck could carry. All up, about 7000 super feet of timber.

'He was very proud of his achievement: to have taken out a log of that immense girth, single-handedly, with nothing more than his chainsaw. And we were very proud of him.

'Then the questions started. "Dad, how old do you reckon that tree must have been?" "Oh, very old. At least 100 years. Anywhere up to 500 years." "Where did you find it?" "It came out of the Lansdowne State Forest." "How many houses do you reckon you could build out of it?" "The framing for at least three houses." "So how much would that log be worth?" "I'm not sure, but certainly thousands of dollars."

'When I think about it now, it seems to me it could have been at that instant that my future career was set. The continuing questions and answers went something like this: "How much do you get?" "Not much, only a couple of hours' wages." "So the sawmill gets the rest?' 'Not all of it. The State government charges royalties on all timber taken out of state forests. Royalties are like a tax." "So what would the royalties be on that log?" "A few dollars I guess, perhaps not that much."

'Our father told us he had cut down hundreds of trees just like the one from which this log had come, but he'd had to leave them lying in the bush. He explained that old hardwoods typically had hollow cores—'pipes' he called them—and the sawmill didn't consider it economic to pay the transport costs to bring in a log with less than one foot of solid timber around the hollow core.

'The problem was you couldn't tell how hollow a tree was until you cut it down. That didn't trouble the sawmill, because it paid royalties only on what it took out of the forest. The Forestry Department didn't get a cent for what was left behind on the forest floor. So hundreds of trees, hundreds of years old, were torn down, their carcasses left to rot where they fell. The memory of that afternoon has troubled me ever since.

'I don't know if I managed, at the age of 13, to discover the source of the sense of unease I felt at the time. But if I did, I hope that as I looked at that enormous hardwood log, that I found entirely unacceptable the fact that somebody could legally appropriate, for only a few dollars, this extraordinary asset of the people of NSW that would take perhaps hundreds of years to replace.

'I hope this smacked to me of highway robbery. I hope I was less than impressed that the elected representatives of the people of NSW appeared to be demonstrating such disregard for the protection of their citizens' property. I hope I wondered about the ability of governments— and not just the venal—to redistribute wealth so arbitrarily, and to disenfranchise future generations. And I hope I vowed that one day I would do something about it . . .

'Growing up on the NSW mid-North Coast, I was reminded, constantly it now seems, of the failure of economic policy. I recall my disquiet on learning that ancestors on both sides of my family were "cedar getters". "What's a cedar getter, Dad?" What I heard him say was something like: "Well, that's why we don't have cedar trees anymore."

'I remember being concerned when I learned that every generation of Australians caught fewer and smaller fish than the preceding generation. I remember learning that weeds were not native plants, and that rabbits that destroyed river banks and foxes that killed chooks were not native animals. I remember learning that soil erosion was caused by humans. I remember being horrified by the apparently wanton destruction wrought by the rutile miners who ripped through the sand dunes where I used to surf, leaving a moonscape devoid of the stunning Christmas bells that used to grow there in profusion.

'I remember being perplexed when the Killabakh Creek that tumbled down through the rainforests of the Comboyne Mountain and then swept around the periphery of my maternal grandmother's dairy farm simply dried up.

'I remember being absolutely staggered to learn that one of the conditions of my paternal grandfather's retaining possession of his 600-acre 'soldier settler' block of rainforest timber was that he clear a certain number of acres each year, and watching over the years as the trees were replaced by bracken fern and lantana, and as the soil washed into the creeks and gullies, replacing the native fish that had long since been exploited to extinction.

'And I remember, too, that as the weeds spread and farming became too difficult, my grandfather turned to more facile means of making a quid, stripping the native orchids out of what was left of his rainforest property. And if I didn't understand the 'how' or 'why' of these things at the time, I did at least develop a deep conviction that something was horribly wrong . . .

'When I asked my father the other day why the Killabakh Creek dried up when I was a schoolkid, I suggested that unpriced access to irrigation water was surely the culprit. He thought that might have had something to do with it. "But don't forget," he added, "we fell timber all over the Comboyne Mountain, pushing in dozer and snigger tracks and roads for the log trucks. That's where the water would have gone. You can see it from the erosion left behind." My question for policy advisers, then, is this: how much erosion are we going to leave behind?'

How's that, Malcolm Turnbull, for 'someone who is only a sort of financial person'?

Alan Ramsey

# From Darwin to Alice with Dick

**SEPTEMBER 7, 2002**

A HUNDRED years and $1 billion later and, suddenly, the Darwin to Alice Springs railway isn't just a politician's promise. What is likely the world's last great transcontinental rail project is going like the clappers. They started building in April last year. They're scheduled to finish in April 2004. It took six years from 1911 to go west to east, from Kalgoorlie to Adelaide, in constructing the great southern line.

It will now take just half that to go north to south to complete the great northern line. This time it's actually happening. Believe it.

Alfred Deakin's second Government (1905–08) first promised the Darwin to Adelaide railway in 1907. After two world wars sandwiched the Great Depression of the 1930s, the Labor Party pledged to complete its construction in its 1965 platform 'as a matter of urgency'.

Gough Whitlam repeated the pledge in his 1972 policy speech. Malcolm Fraser promised in 1980 to build it for the 1988 bicentenary of white settlement. Bob Hawke promised in 1983 to match Fraser's promise but welshed two years later.

John Howard pledged in 1998 to build it to celebrate 100 years of Federation. He used his Federation slush fund of $1 billion of Telstra sale

money to keep his promise. Financial closure was signed off by the Commonwealth, the governments of South Australia and the Northern Territory and a private consortium in April 2001.

Howard did not spend all his (our) $1 billion on the railway. The three governments—each one, at the time, non-Labor—committed between them $480 million of up-front public money in October 1999. Fifteen months later, in January last year, the governments put in another $80 million when haggling with the private tenderer, Asia Pacific Transport (APT), came close to fracture. Total public funds: $560 million of a $1.1 billion construction project. Another $200 million is committed to buy rolling stock and 'ancillary' items. Cost all-up: $1.3 billion. The private consortium is committed to $740 million of this.

For its money the consortium builds, owns and operates the railway for 50 years. For our money the public gets to use the railway, for freight and passenger travel, over the 50 years, after which it's supposed to revert to public ownership. This is called, apparently, a BOOT concession: Build, Own, Operate and Transfer back. We shall see. (Well, some of us will, anyway! And by then it will be much too late.)

And who makes up the APT consortium?

A bunch of six partners, some Australian, of which the major shareholder (50 per cent) is Halliburton KBR, an arm of the US multinational, Halliburton, based in Houston, Texas. The K stands for Kellog, an engineering subsidiary, and the BR for Brown and Root, also part of the Halliburton group. A few years ago, when Halliburton was considering a bid for the Darwin to Alice BOOT concession, its chief executive travelled to Australia from Houston several times.

Dick Cheney was still Halliburton's CEO when the company lodged its successful bid with the AustralAsiaRailway Corporation, a statutory agency established by legislation in 1997 by the SA and NT governments and supported by the Commonwealth.

Next time you see or hear the man who is George W. Bush's Vice-President and one of those most rabid in wanting to make war on Iraq, remember he's also the bloke instrumental in a US giant getting the nod to build our last great railway. It is a small, strange world (and bound to get smaller if ever Cheney were to prevail in the White House).

From Darwin to Adelaide is a bit over 3000 kilometres. By the time the Commonwealth formally assumed control of the Northern Territory on New Year's Day, 1911—it had been 'the Northern Territory of South Australia' before Federation—the SA railway system already had built 240 kilometres of line south from Darwin (or Palmerston, as it then was) to Pine Creek, and roughly 1000 kilometres of line north from Adelaide to Oodnadatta. Two pieces of legislation formalised the transfer of authority: SA's *Northern Territory Surrender Act* of 1907 and the Commonwealth's responding *Northern Territory Acceptance Act* of 1910.

This is not just arcane detail.

It was the argy-bargy between Adelaide and the new Commonwealth over the terms of transfer that became responsible for most of the debate, false political promises and outright lies of the next 90 years. South Australia ceded away control of the Northern Territory on the absolute guarantee the Commonwealth would complete the north–south railway to Adelaide. This guarantee was written into the 1910 Acceptance Act, the Commonwealth's own bill. The catch was the legislation did not say when it would be built. This allowed a succession of federal governments to prevaricate and delay for the whole of the 20th century.

As Patsy Adam Smith writes in her marvellous 1969 history of Australian railways, *The Rails Go Westward*: 'By 1929 the northern end of the railway had been extended from Pine Creek [south] to Birdum, 316 miles [about 500 kilometres] from Darwin, leaving a gap of 600 miles [almost 1000 kilometres] to Alice Springs. And here, in 1969, it remains, a gap that is called by some a "shame and a scandal". Supporters for closing the gap claim the Commonwealth should honour its written pledge. They point out that Alice Springs had a population of only 40 white people before the railway [north from Adelaide] came in 1926 and is now a thriving town.'

Fifteen years later, in 1984, after the Hawke Government insisted it would only complete the railway if the NT government paid 40 per cent of the then estimated $540 million cost, the territory's Chief Minister, Paul 'Porky' Everingham, refused. He accused Hawke of dishonouring his 1983 promise as well as the original 1910 legislated Commonwealth pledge. Nobody had ever said the territory's small, highly-subsidised population should have to pay even a cent to build the railway, Everingham insisted. And he was right.

Eighteen years later, after Labor went on prevaricating and obfuscating right through the 1980s and the first half of the 1990s, including two 'independent' reviews on the economics of the project, one by David Hill and the second by Neville Wran, Everingham is still right, even though he's now long gone from politics. But the Howard Government has accepted reality.

So have the governments of South Australia and the Northern Territory. That reality is that the railway was never going to be built by any one government or any group of private investors not supported by public money. So now it is a partnership of all three governments, plus private money. Or so we're told.

The website of the AustralAsia Railway Corporation tends to blur the financial responsibilities. It explains: 'The Corporation was established in 1997 by the NT and SA governments to manage the awarding of a BOOT concession and to enter into contractual arrangements with the successful consortium. The governments jointly guarantee the corporation's obligations specified in contractual arrangements covered by the project documents. The respective rights and obligations of the two governments and the project are regulated by an inter-governmental agreement.

'The corporation has negotiated a detailed concession deed which seeks to deal with all risks identified as having the potential to arise during the project, and balance those risks by apportioning appropriate responsibility . . .'

You feel that could mean anything if the project ever runs into financial strife somewhere in the years ahead. A stack of governments in Canberra over the years insisted the railway could never pay for itself and would simply eat public money. Whatever the fine print between the three governments and the Halliburton KBR joint venture, we'll no doubt learn in time.

For the moment the railway's construction, by contract to yet another joint venture involving four of the APT consortium partners and driven by its Texan project director, Al Volpe, from Halliburton KBR, is going gang busters. They started from scratch on the entire 1420 kilometres from Darwin to Alice Springs. Four construction crews totalling some 800 men are working at four different sites. The figures are mind-boggling. Almost 400 kilometres of track had been laid by the end of last month, with another 740 kilometres cleared, 2 million tonnes of ballast put down and 30 bridges built. In some places, the project is three months ahead of schedule.

One freight train a day will run each way when the line is completed. These massive freighters will be an extraordinary 1600 metres long. They will be the lifeblood of the railway. If they don't pay, the railway fails, simple as that. As for passenger services, two tourist trains a week are scheduled for Adelaide to Alice Springs. A weekly, 47-hour Darwin service will leave Adelaide on Sunday, arriving in Darwin on Tuesday afternoon. It will leave to return to Adelaide on Wednesday morning, arriving on Friday morning. Public interest is enormous.

The services will be operated by Great Southern Railways, the present operator of the popular Ghan train that runs from Adelaide to Alice Springs, and has done for 70 years. You can already book right through, from April 2004, and price schedules are available.

Prices start at $198 one-way Darwin to Adelaide. The deluxe accommodation won't be cheap. It wasn't ever going to be after waiting 100 years for the train to arrive. It has been a long time coming.

Alan Ramsey

**Postscript:** *The rail link was completed in September 2003. The first freight train completed the trip from Adelaide to Darwin in January 2004 as John Howard officially opened the line in a Darwin ceremony on January 17. The first passenger train arrived in Darwin on February 4. But that was the best of the good news. In November 2008 the company running the freight line went into voluntary administration.*

# Railroading the Outback

NOVEMBER 19, 2005

DO YOU recall the 10,000 drums of 'low-level radioactive waste' the Keating Government trucked from Sydney to Woomera in 1994 for 'interim storage'? The waste was several thousand tonnes of contaminated soil. It had come from CSIRO research carried out on radioactive ores in the 1940s and '50s at Melbourne's Fishermans Bend. The Defence Department discovered the toxic soil in 1989 when it took over the old research site. How did it get rid of the soil?

It simply dug it up, stuck it in 44-gallon drums and trucked it north across the border to Sydney's Lucas Heights, headquarters of the Australian Nuclear Science and Technology Organisation, and said: 'Here—it's your problem.' Five years later, in December 1994, the Keating Government trucked 'the problem' west across the border to a defence site at Woomera, South Australia, after anxious Sydney locals took legal action to get it moved. Eleven years later, so I'm told, the 10,000 drums are still in 'interim storage' at Woomera.

So is 'the problem'.

Nobody wants It. Nobody ever wants radioactive waste. In July 1992, the Keating Government set about trying to find two national storage sites for the relatively small amount of waste Australia creates from 'nuclear materials' in medicine, industry and scientific research. Thirteen years later and the Commonwealth is still looking.

Every time the Feds, whoever they be, get anywhere near a decision, the local, self-serving shrieks are deafening. 'Not in my backyard', or nimby, as it's known, is the agonised cry from the states.

The parochial fearmongering is sickening.

Originally, one of the sites—an 'engineered, near-surface underground facility'—was to be for 'low-level' waste (soil, discarded protective clothing, laboratory equipment, wrapping materials, etc). The second site—'an interim, purpose-built, above-ground store', designed to operate 'for up to 50 years'—was for 'intermediate-level' waste, mostly industrial (radioactive residues from 'mineral sands processing, industrial gauges, reactor components, irradiated fuel cladding, disused seal sources', etc).

In 1992, the first politician given the impossible job of nuclear waste disposal tsar was Simon Crean, Minister for Primary Industries and Energy at the time. Crean got nowhere. In the years that followed, neither did anybody else, Labor or Coalition.

When, finally, the Howard Government's Nick Minchin named Woomera for both 'facilities' three years ago, SA's new Labor Government, under Mike Rann, rushed off to the Federal Court—and succeeded. That effectively killed the Woomera proposal. The incongruity—and hypocrisy—of South Australia having the world's largest uranium deposit, at the huge Olympic Dam/Roxby Downs mine, was conveniently ignored.

The moans from State Labor elsewhere have been no less shameless.

In July last year, the Howard Government decided 12 years of political dithering and gamesmanship was enough. It was abandoning the search for a 'national waste repository', it said, and would go it alone with a 'storage facility' on Commonwealth land for 'radioactive waste produced by Commonwealth agencies'. The states and territories could 'make their own arrangements' to get rid of their own waste.

Four months ago, Canberra upped the ante by announcing a federal storage 'facility' for both low- and medium-level radioactive waste would be constructed at one of three sites, on Commonwealth land, in the NT. Two are just north of Alice Springs. The third is near Katherine, south of Darwin. The Commonwealth has absolute legislative authority. John Howard has parliamentary control to enforce that authority.

Ten days ago, the enabling legislation, the Commonwealth Radioactive Waste Management Bill 2005, went through the House of Representatives. The debate was predictable. The Government wanted to establish a 'safe and secure facility' for the 'management of radioactive waste produced by Commonwealth agencies'. The Opposition wanted to stop 'arrogant and heavy-handed' legislation that set up a 'radioactive waste dump' in Territorians' 'backyards'.

So, does the Howard Government have an eye on the future when it starts building federal nuclear waste 'facilities' in the NT? After all, it does have that spanking new $1.3 billion Darwin to Alice Springs railway line nobody felt could ever be economic.

Think about it. And think about the giant American corporation Halliburton, and its engineering subsidiary that built the railway. Think, too, of the then Halliburton chief executive, Dick Cheney, who came to Australia in the second half of the 1990s to negotiate the railway deal with the Howard Government and the South Australian Liberal Government of John Olsen, who Howard would later send to a cushy diplomatic post on the US West Coast.

Imagine a railway line from a new high-security port in Darwin down to Alice Springs and right past each of the three potential sites to a new nuclear waste facility. How useful that could be if ever we got into the nuclear power cycle or began taking high-level waste, at a price, from overseas. It isn't all that fanciful. Bob Hawke is only one who thinks it's a good idea.

As Hawke told ABC TV's Maxine McKew in September [2005]: 'We have a real issue in the world of nuclear waste being stored in unsafe places. The bonus for Australia is we would revolutionise the economics of (this country). Forget the current account deficit problem. Australia would be earning billions making the world safer. We are talking about billions and billions of dollars a year.'

Don't think it couldn't happen.

Alan Ramsey

# Chapter 23

# Celebration, Renovation, Capitulation

# A Night to Remember

MAY 12, 2001

GUSTAVUS THEODORE von Holst died 67 years ago this month. A frail, bespectacled man, he was a composer who made his living as a trombonist and teacher for half his life at a London girls' school. His best-known work, the orchestral suite *The Planets*, he began composing the year the Great War of 1914–18 engulfed Europe. The suite consists of seven movements, each named after one of the seven planets known at the time. Fifty-four years after Holst's death in May 1934, the ABC began telecasting an eight-part miniseries on June 28, 1988. That was *The True Believers,* a dramatised account of Ben Chifley's 1940s Labor Government and his death in 1951.

Four nights ago, at the Melbourne Park Function Centre, just across from the great cavern of the MCG, 1600 people each paid $110 for a four-hour gala dinner to celebrate the centenary of the Federal Caucus—the Federal Parliamentary Labor Party. Past and present included five national Labor leaders, three Labor prime ministers, five serving Labor premiers and about 260 Labor MPs, Federal and State, including 40 ministers. It was, in all respects, a hugely emotional reprise of the True Believers self-image.

And there was no greater irony on this night of Labor nights than that Gustav Holst, an Englishman born in Cheltenham, London, wrote what is now embraced as the anthem of

Australia's oldest (and most stridently republican) political party: the Jupiter movement of Holst's *Planets* suite, one of the enduring standards of English orchestral literature. And the seductive imagery all began with that television series 13 years ago.

Because of its stirring symbolism, Paul Keating adopted the Jupiter theme when he launched Labor's 'impossible' 1993 election campaign. And the night his Government completed its stunning victory over John Hewson's Coalition that year, Holst's haunting music dominated as Keating fronted a jampacked Bankstown Sports Club to announce to a national TV audience: 'This is the sweetest victory of all.'

It was the same heartfelt line Neville Wran had used the night of his fourth and last NSW State election win nine years earlier. This time, with the crowd roaring, Keating, washed by adulation, added his own famous line: 'This is a victory for the True Believers.'

But which True Believers?

Three weeks later, in late-March 1993, with Labor's fifth term in the bank, Keating hosted his True Believers' victory bash in the Great Hall of the Parliament. Yet from there it was all downhill.

Four years later, in 1997, with Keating gone and Labor struggling in Opposition, the Jupiter theme was haunting television audiences again, this time internationally during the Westminster Abbey funeral of Diana, Princess of Wales. It had been her favourite hymn, adapted and retitled *I vow to thee my Country*. And two years after that, the rugger buggers borrowed it as their True Believers' anthem for the 1999 rugby World Cup.

Everybody's been having a piece of it since a near-anonymous Australian composer discovered Holst's lyricism for a television political soap 13 years ago. And there it was again, in all its glory, at Labor's Melbourne blast on Tuesday.

It was no coincidence. Labor's Senate leader, John Faulkner, and his Victorian mate, the redoubtable Robert Ray, had been organising the dinner for months, just as Faulkner personally drove the *True Believers* book project with publishers Allen & Unwin for more than two years.

That Federal Labor's Caucus centenary should fall a single day earlier than the Parliament's centenary, allowed its Senate schemers to gazump the Howard Government's very own $4 million Federation extravaganza (thank you, taxpayers), an event

of excruciating mediocrity in all but cost and banality. Faulkner and Ray chortled all week while the Prime Minister fumed and fizzed. It was a nice change to hear the Government whingeing rather than Kim Beazley.

Given the Coalition's worsening staggers since Christmas, Labor's centenary dinner was always going to be a celebration of great tribal intensity and expectation. Yet two of the speeches from among the string of Labor luminaries who spoke reminded us that, despite their flawed years of political decline, Gough Whitlam and Paul Keating were the very pinnacle of national leadership in this country in the past half-century.

Each had 10 minutes. Whitlam, two months short of his 85th birthday, spoke first. He was, quite simply, sensational. Ignoring Faulkner's offered presence, he climbed the stairs of the dais, unaided, and walked to the podium. And there, putting down the script he'd written, he looked up and out and, pausing just enough, that still-firm voice repeated his electrifying 1972 campaign launch opening: 'Men and women of Australia.' The roar from his 1600 audience all but lifted the roof.

And I doubt there was a dry eye after he'd told us, in wonderful cadence: 'For once, Shakespeare got it wrong. His Henry V said, "Old men forget." My problem is the multitude of vivid memories brought about by the grandeur of (this) occasion, the association with my birthplace, the presence of so many colleagues, and your warm and enthusiastic welcome. Maintain your zeal and your enthusiasm through the coming campaign . . .'

What followed was speech-making of immense quality. The coming election would be no contest if Beazley's political will and command of simple, unadorned language was anything of the order demonstrated by the predecessor now midway through his ninth decade.

And Whitlam, like Keating would, deplored the Howard Government's slavish support for the dangerous irrationalities of the new Bush White House. 'It is pitiable for Australia to follow the United States in spurning international organisations and arrangements on disarmament and environment because it cannot control them.' Neither Howard nor Beazley has been so unambiguous with the new Washington Administration.

Keating spoke third, behind Hawke and ahead of Beazley. He was the only one of the four—Bill Hayden was not invited to speak— who did not provide a transcript beforehand. Instead, while Hawke was haranguing us with one of his old-style ACTU rants, full of podium thumping and finger pointing, that was so awful it was good, or at least vintage Hawke, Keating sat at his table, still scratching away with his fountain pen, amending a word here or there, polishing his script right up until Faulkner, the night's MC, introduced him to a storm of applause that exceeded even Whitlam's welcome.

Keating is a true political spiv, although, at his best, one that is all class.

He was the last of the Big Five to arrive, alone, at the dinner, a good half-hour behind the others, and therefore, with us all seated, he got everyone's attention. And when it came time to speak, he walked, languidly, to the podium, stuck his left hand in his trouser pocket and, before he said a word, imperceptibly moved the flexible microphones upwards, just as Hawke, the smaller man, had moved them down. Later, a woman with shining eyes, who'd told Keating she wished he was still in politics, said he'd replied, without rancour, that 'the light has gone out'.

You'd never have thought so from his performance this night. Nor, like Whitlam, from the quality of what he had to say. It was a cogent, precise mix of sentiment, Labor tribalism, review, clear-sighted vision and, above all, unambiguous language. If there was one thing he pressed above all it was for this century to be an Australian century, not an American century, like our first 100 years of Federation had been a British century.

For instance, after sticking it to 'the forelock tuggers' of Australia's founding fathers, he said, in part: '. . . But apart from free trade between the States and a limited defence and currency function, there was no plan for a national economy, no economic tools, no uniform taxation, a corporations power which a conservative court pushed to one side, a deadly second chamber, the Senate, and kingly powers for the intended British representative, the Governor-General. It was a mass of compromise; and along with the strategic guarantees from the old country, it gave Australia a British century, save for the last 25 years. And Anzac, and all that came with it, was part of it . . .

'This election may well decide whether we have an Australian century in the 21st century, or an American century, as America resists multilateralism and a multipolar world and tries to go in with an introspective attitude and tries to soak up its allies.

'The conservatives, you can bet on this, will forelock-tug their way to Washington, and our future as an independent country, as a republic in Asia, in our neighbourhood, will be lost . . . For Australia's sake, I hope we can consign Howard to the scrapheap of history, to that pile of people who never really believed in us, who had no abiding faith in us, and who would rob us of our destiny . . .'

Like it or lump it, you could have no doubt where Keating stands, where he thinks the Labor Party must take Australia if it gets the chance. There was no windbaggery, no blah, no talking up a confected storm yet committing to nothing. Like Whitlam, he kept precisely to his 10 minutes, and when he ended, wishing 'Kim and the party well', his audience didn't want to let him go. Keating still has the touch and the light is not out.

Later, as rivers of people jostled around the five leaders' tables, queuing for autographs in their *True Believers* books, selling at $50 a copy, Ray and Faulkner reviewed the day and the dinner and their two years of organisation, and were well satisfied. Faulkner said, dryly: 'Not bad for two old factional hacks.'

Not bad at all.

Alan Ramsey

# Up and Down the Stairs

**MARCH 1, 2003**

JOHN DAWKINS is a business consultant these days who lives in the Adelaide Hills with Maggie and Alice and grows grapes and thinks how fortunate his life has been. He used to be Paul Keating's Treasurer. Before that, when Hawke Labor first came to power 20 years ago, Dawkins, at 36, was its youngest member of Cabinet. He remained a minister almost 11 years. Then, just before Christmas

1993, Joe Dawkins, as most of us knew him, got up one day in the Parliament and said he'd had enough, he'd never intended to 'grow old in this place' and he was going home to Maggie and his new baby daughter to lead a new and sane life again. Dawkins was 46 years old and escaping after 20 years in public life.

His resignation is a great story.

Dawkins tells it with style and ribaldry and huge whoops of laughter, and a few days ago, over the phone and a glass of wine, he told it again. 'It was supposed to happen on the Thursday,' he recounted. 'I mean, the Parliament was supposed to get up on the Thursday for Christmas recess, but we didn't becaue, you'll remember, it was all about the Mabo legislation, and the Democrats were dicking us around, so the Senate got stuck sitting for all of Friday and Saturday, too, I think, so it turned out the Christmas valedictories in the house were switched from Thursday to Friday, so I had to wait the extra day.

'Why did this matter? Well, I actully didn't tell Keating I was going until an hour before I announced it in the House, and I'd waited to tell him until I knew exactly when I'd get the chance. You see, I didn't want his spin doctors, mainly Geoff Walsh at the time, to get even a sniff of what I was doing, otherwise they'd have turned it around. Keating himself wouldn't have but I didn't want them to get the chance to muddy things with the press gallery as to why I was going.

'Anyhow, we had this cabinet metting on the Friday afternoon, and Paul, with his mind on Mabo in the Senate, was kind of disengaged from this really serious policy issue about health funding. Graham Richardson was health minister and he was trying to rejig the Commonwealth–State financial arrangements so that instead of health funding being part of the agreement, it would be a separatc agreement that he would run. And I fought him and beat him in the Cabinet. Then when Cabinet finished in late afternoon, I said to Keating as we walked out, "Mate, there's something I want to tell you. Can I have five minutes?"

'So I walked with him back to his office and sat down and told him I was going, and just then Geoff Walsh [Keating staff adviser] comes in and says they'd knocked up some speacking notes for the valedictories, and

Keating said, "Well, Dawkins is announcing his retirement." And Walshie said, "Then these won't be any [expletive] good," and threw the notes down and left. When Richardson heard, he was absolutely furious. "Why the [expletive] did you spend all that time doing me over in Cabinet if you were going?" And I just looked at him and said, "Precisely!"'

This coming Wednesday night, at Canberra's Boat House By The Lake, 175 people, all Labor MPs or former MPs and their partners, will celebrate, with Bob (73) and Blanche Hawke, the 20th anniversary of Labor's election, on March 5, 1983, to what became 13 unbroken years of national government. Richardson will be there. So will John Button (70) and Don Grimes (65) and John Kerin (65) and Susan Ryan (60) and Kim Beazley (54) and Brian Howe (67) and Michael Duffy (65) and Neal Blewett (69) and Chris Hurford (71) and John Brown (71) and Stewart West (68) and various other old soldiers from that first Hawke government.

We were ministers once, and young.

Dawkins won't be there. Neither will Keating (59) or Bill Hayden (70) or Lionel Bowen (80) or Tom Uren (81) or Ralph Willis (64) or Peter Walsh (68) or Barry Jones (71) or Arthur Gietzelt (82) or Gordon Scholes (71 or Barry Cohen (67). A bag of others will be missing, too. Keating will be in London, and phoned his apologies. Hayden sent Hawke a genuinely warm message. For the others, the night was organised on a first-in/best-dressed basis. Seating is limited.

A lot of unhappy old politicians are on a long waiting list. Only 12 members of that first Hawke ministry have made it. The biblical metaphor is a nice irony. It is old Labor warriors' night and, for a number of them, probably their last.

But not for Joe Dawkins.

It is Dawkins's birthday tomorrow, his 56th (a date he shares with Michael Duffy, Carmen

Lawrence and Jeff Kennett). Only Beazley, 34 when he became a junior minister in that first Hawke government, was younger than Dawkins. The difference was that Dawkins was a member of the '74 political class, an election that produced Button, Walsh, Grimes, the late Mick Young and the Liberals' Fred Chaney and John Howard. Beazley was elected in 1980, Hayden's only election campaign as leader. Dawkins recalls the events of 1983 with mixed feelings.

'When Hayden resigned the leadership for Hawke, and Fraser called the election, I was with Beazley in London on a parliamentary study tour. I remember telling Hayden by phone he shouldn't go, he shouldn't give in to Hawke, but even I knew it was kind of inevitable. So Beazley and I got on the next plane, and Kim was anxious all the way back he'd lose his seat, and I told him not to be an idiot, that he was going to be a minister in a few weeks' time, so shut up.'

'So we got back to Australia and the first thing that happened was the election of Brian Burke's Labor government in WA [on February 19, 1983]. We had this strange overlap in the West where the federal campaign didn't really start until the State campaign ended, so for us it was really only a two-week campaign federally and we just built on the euphoria of the Burke victory.

'And as Maggie reminds me, everyone in Labor was so pissed celebrating the State victory it was hard to get people to focus on our campaign. Fortunately, it didn't matter. We got this State Labor landslide for Burke and people just went back two weeks later and voted Labor again against Fraser and Little Johnny.

'It was very much just Hawke versus Fraser, and all of Fraser's body language said he knew he was rooted from day one. And he was. People had had enough of him and Howard and all the others and, really, Hawkie didn't have to do much. Neither did the rest of us, except not make mistakes. And we didn't.

'As for the election itself, the most important thing for me was the disappointing seven lost years under Fraser. I think Fraser was probably a decent enough person, but the only way he could govern was by dividing people, which is how he became Prime Minister in the first place.

'And people forget how enormously ineffectual Howard was as Treasurer for five years, how there was no substantial economic reform. And for those of us younger and politically alive, and I was only 36, for us it was a life goal, as they say now—something I'd been thinking about since my early 20s and the political struggle against the Vietnam War and coscription, to get into a Labor government. To actually become a Cabinet minister at 36 was an extraordinary feeling.

'I remember after the election, the first day back in Canberra, I went skipping up the front steps of Old Parliament House, feeling a million dollars, and there, coming out of the place, as a Fraser minister for the last time, was Fred Chaney. And really, Fred looked so delighted coming down the stairs, so pleased, I thought, to be relieved of the burdens of office, and there was me, so delighted to be going up the stairs and so delighted to be taking them on.

'I've never forgotten the moment. We'd know each other for years, both of us elected to Parliament the same year, both flying back and forth across the country from Perth, usually on the same places. Now he was skipping down, saying, very cheerily, "Oh well, good luck," and I was skipping up, saying "Thanks, Fred." A great memory.

So is Dawkins' debt to Hayden.

'When Hayden gave up the leadership, he negotiated with Hawke that people like Blewett and Walsh and me had to be looked after. We were part of Hayden's frontbench and Hawke had political debts. But he honoured his word to Hayden. What we ended up with in 1983 was Hayden's frontbench, all 22 members of it, all genuinely elected by the whole of the

Caucus instead of just factional alliances, and that whole Hayden frontbench ushered into office as the Hawke Government, basically with policies Hayden and the rest of us put together over the five years before Hawke became leader a month before he became Prime Minister.

'So if you want my key message, it was the end of the years of waste and divisiveness Fraser fostered and relied on to stay in office. Reconciliation was Hawke's one big policy idea, some say his only idea. He tacked his third R onto Hayden's Recovery and Reconstruction platform. It helped produce, in my view, easily our best government in living memory.'

Thus Labor on Wednesday celebrates 20 years since the start of the long Hawke/Keating run in 1983. What it will try to ignore a week later is the 10th anniversay—and the ensuing 10 years' hard Labor—since its last election victory in 1993.

Alan Ramsey

# The Hearse Does its Job

NOVEMBER 29, 2003

SIMON CREAN left his self-respect at home yesterday. Otherwise he could not have made that gagging resignation speech he delivered to end one of the sorriest, most self-destructive periods of major party political leadership in recent memory. Crean even had the hide to advise his successor: 'Don't let your personal ambition cripple the Labor Party.'

Personal ambition is all that kept Crean in the leadership far beyond the point he should have excused himself, with some dignity, and left of his own volition.

I cannot remember a politician less suited to lead the Labor Party, nor one who went on so relentlessly doing himself in, day after day, by his own leadership inadequacies, and yet who, when the inevitable end came, sought to suggest he was being cut down not by his own flaws and failures but by 'political and media decision-makers'. Such self-delusion explains why his colleagues had no option but to elbow Crean out the door.

Even this he could not admit.

Crean tried to pretend: 'It has become obvious I no longer have the confidence of the leadership group and a majority of my shadow ministers'.

The reason it had 'become obvious' was two of the key people who propped up his leadership, the Labor Left's John Faulkner and Martin Ferguson, went to Crean's Canberra digs three nights ago and told him his eroding support in Caucus was now such he would be thrown out by a party vote if he did not resign before next Tuesday's last Caucus meeting of the year.

One day an unwanted political leader will stand in front of the cameras and say, honestly, that he/she now realises he/she has been a complete leadership fraud and, having recognised he/she is out of his/her depth, has decided, without having to be nudged/shoved/cajoled/leaned on or shot, to get out of both the leadership and elected politics, and 'thank you for putting up with me and I apologise to all those rank-and-file party members who've long known, as I now recognise, I should never have taken on the job in the first place'.

It would be novel indeed, an expression a friend used yesterday when he emailed it was time to 'junk' the hearse I put in Crean's driveway in December last year. Well, now the hearse, finally, has been able to do its job, its unwilling corpse battered, bagged, borne away and buried. Only John Howard will weep. But for despairing voters, it has been a long year.

As for the instant revisionism going on among the more thick-headed, not to mention the chief political writer who only 10 days ago was confidently asserting that, under Crean's leadership, the Government and Labor were ending the political year 'evenly poised', just remember that when Labor dumped Hawke for Keating in December 1991, even after winning four elections and though he was still Prime Minister, it did so only after Caucus members realised, following a month of bad opinion polls, that their individual careers were threatened, not just the Government's.

Crean's leadership was never going to survive the nearer the election got and the longer those relentless opinion polls kept turning up every fortnight. As Paul Keating used to say, with monotonous regularity, self-interest wins every time.

And Crean's successor? A generational change that skipped recycling Kim Beazley would be the choice for the future. Beazley can't lead Labor to victory, but he can hold the line. And, for Labor, that's probably enough for now. But really, it should be Mark Latham or Kevin Rudd, preferably both.

Labor lost three elections in a bit less than six years. It has now burned another two years. Eight years blown away. Howard is beatable but never by Crean's rabble.

Has Labor learnt anything?

Alan Ramsey

# Mark Latham Arrives

**DECEMBER 3, 2003**

IT WAS the ultimate accolade. The instant Parliament sat yesterday the Howard Government got stuck into the new bloke. Simon Crean was Opposition leader for almost two years and the Government hardly ever said boo to or about him. The ineffectual Crean was John Howard's security blanket. And if Labor ever found the backbone to get rid him, Howard was looking forward to Kim Beazley coming back as the next best booby. Howard got it wrong. Instead Labor got it right.

It jumped forwards, not backwards, however slim the margin between recycling WA's Beazley, at age 55 (in nine days' time) and twice an election loser, and opting for NSW's Mark Latham, at 42 the youngest federal Labor leader in a century after a mere 10 years an MP. Only Labor's first leader, John Watson, another New South Welshman, was younger, at 34, when his Caucus of 22 MPs (two others were absent) chose him over Queensland's Andrew Fisher in May, 1901.

Those with doubts must surely have known Labor had got it right politically as soon as the House got down to business after lunch yesterday. Latham by then had been leader a mere four hours. Yet from the moment the Speaker opened proceedings, some of the Government's most senior ministers, with Howard leading, were railing away at Latham as if the devil himself had suddenly appeared in their midst.

And, of course, for them he had.

Even before this, Howard and the Nationals' John Anderson, a nice man but another political dunce, made soothing noises about poor Simon and dear Kim and their wives and families in a too-cute show of

Government concern for their former punching bags' welfare and future. It was all such a charade.

The Government's obvious strategy to paint the two Labor losers as good men and true, both of them experienced ministers and parliamentarians, whom their party has turned its back on for this dreadful tyro with the foul mouth, is just a blind for what is, suddenly, all their nightmares possibly come true.

Despite the bravado, Latham scares the bejesus out of the Coalition. He is not another Labor leadership patsy and the Government knows it. Whatever you've heard and whatever self-serving hysteria the Government goes on beating up, Latham is the real thing. He is not Simon the dead or Kim the wimp. He might well crash and burn one day, but if he does it will be because he's trying like blazes and not because he's sitting there, like a rabbit in the headlights, waiting to get run over.

An old political friend phoned to say yesterday that Paul Keating of the late 1980s/early '90s, as the daredevil Treasurer cum Prime Minister hurtling down the slope on one ski, well, if Latham gets up to speed, 'he'll make the Paul of old look like the soft option'.

No bets yet.

But I also noticed, among the mass of words before yesterday's ballot, *The Australian's* Phillip Adams going on about the choice between 'the Bomber' (Beazley's old nickname) and 'the Bomb', an unflattering reference to Latham, that ''Tis truly said, when you're standing beside him and hear ticking, it's not his wristwatch.'

Adams did not source the remark. I heard it, first-hand, 15 months ago. It comes from Labor's former national secretary, Gary Gray, who resigned from head office in early 2000 rather than go on tolerating the internal party bastardry of Beazley's dithering leadership. But two months ago Gray phoned to say he felt he'd been wrong about Latham's political discipline, that now 'he could be the hope of the side'.

Gray is not easy either to please or intimidate. Ask Paul Keating, who made a rare political appearance yesterday to support Latham's leadership, for the first time publicly. 'It was a victory for a new beginning and a defeat for the bankrupt factional system and its operatives,' he said succinctly.

Last weekend, at a Labor fundraiser in Sydney, Keating added for party loyalists: 'Only two factions matter: the smart people and the dills.' He has never hidden his opinion of where he thinks Beazley resides.

Keating, of course, is a Latham political mentor—they lunch together every month or so—as is Gough Whitlam, whom Latham once worked for, just as he did Bob Carr. Whitlam is a huge Latham fan. And while both Whitlam and Keating are Labor heroes, they also led Labor to two of its worst electoral defeats. John Howard would not be the only one to think it a wonderful irony if Latham were to complete the treble.

A couple more points.

Laurie Brereton, another old NSW Labor general, was Latham's chief numbers organiser.

Latham owes him hugely. It is a matter of history that in the 103 years (minus a month) since Federation, NSW has had a voice in Labor's federal leadership (either leader or deputy, sometimes both) for just over 80 of those years. It is an extraordinary accomplishment. And it means NSW Labor has never been used to being excluded from the national leadership.

Yet Victoria and WA have filled both leadership posts since the Keating Government's defeat in March 1996. It was Brereton's personal crusade, before he leaves political life, to end the sequence. Latham's election achieves this, to Brereton's great satisfaction. If Labor were to upset the odds, terrify Howard and win next year's election, watch what happens to Brereton's career in public life.

As for all the hooey before yesterday's ballot about what a close result would mean for a 'divided' Labor Party, forget it. As Latham said afterwards, John Curtin became leader by 11 votes to 10 over Queensland's Frank Forde in October 1935 and went on to become one of Australia's most revered prime ministers. Keating won by only five votes in December 1991 and Whitlam turned back Jim Cairns in 1968 by three votes.

The margin can mean nothing. It depends on who has done the winning. And Mark Latham has it in him to be anything.

Alan Ramsey

# How to Kill a Country
## THE VERDICT: ELECTION 2004

**OCTOBER 11, 2004**

A SMALL book turned up last week entitled *How to Kill a Country*. It was written by three Sydney academics about our 'free trade' deal with the United States. They could as easily

have been writing about what, spare us, happened on Saturday.

How on earth could we have put this scheming, mendacious little man and his miserable claque back in office for another three years? Worse, how could we have brought them to the very brink of absolute control of the nation's entire parliamentary process and authority? Very easily, as things turned out, to the cost of the rest of us and our national self-respect.

For almost nine years this Government, incompetent in most everything except mediocrity, debauched its word and the people's trust, along with voters' gullibility, their ignorance, their taxes and, in the end, their greedy self-interest.

It deceived and dissembled about joining us with Washington's military adventurism in Iraq, and it went on deceiving and dissembling, irrespective of the heightened threat to our national interest, to keep our minuscule presence there purely for the political pleasure of George Bush and his cronies.

Then when we reached the one time every three years of a people's audit, 4.6 in every 10 of us turned round and said, thank you, gimme the money and flog us for another three years.

Most times, despite the thick and the avaricious and those who feel it's just all beyond them, we get it right as a nation. Not this time. This time we've really buggered things. A politically immoral man who, by any civilised measure, disqualified himself from public life, has been given a pat on the back and even more power. This time the people's will has got it dreadfully wrong. Now we all have to pay for the comfortable idiocy of the manipulated minority.

And it is a minority: the 46 per cent who voted for the Coalition, or 4.6 in every 10. The other 5.4, in the main, wanted something better, and were denied by a lowest common denominator system in which all the spoils go to a degraded 50 per cent plus one.

I thought we had more brains, more self-respect. I was wrong in thinking enough voters 'just might' see through the confidence trickery of John Howard, master illusionist

and toad of a human being. I apologise for nothing.

However, don't get snowed by the spin merchants about the size of the Government's win. Howard's real achievement is the Coalition's Senate victory. In the House of Representatives, Labor went into the election with 63 seats (after a redistribution of boundaries turned two marginal ALP seats into two marginal Liberal seats), the Government 83, with three independents and one Green MHR. By midday yesterday, with a bit over 10 million votes counted in an electorate of 13 million, the most likely result, after the doubtfuls are finally sorted, is that Labor will have a net loss of between one and three seats.

Labor's loss was great in votes, not seats. It's primary vote (38.3 per cent) is only marginally better than under Kim Beazley's losing leadership three years ago (37.8 per cent). What is different this time is the Liberal Party (40.3 per cent) out-polling Labor in primary votes (as distinct from a joint Coalition vote of 46 per cent).

That happens rarely: twice only in the Liberals' 60-year history, the last time, ironically, in the Fraser victory of 1975 that buried the Government of Latham's political father figure, Gough Whitlam. Still, Latham's time will come. Believe it.

Alan Ramsey

**Postscript:** *The 2004 final count saw Labor's primary vote (37.64 per cent) slip below the 37.8 per cent Labor recorded under Beazley three years earlier. It was Labor's worst national vote in 80 years. Yet Labor still picked up five seats—four from the Liberals and the NSW seat of Cunningham it had lost to the Greens in a by-election the previous year—while losing eight seats to the Coalition, a net loss of three. And 'Latham's time' was never going to come, as events evolved three months later.*

# Mark Latham Leaves

**JANUARY 29, 2005**

IT WAS a public execution, not a resignation. A year ago Mark Latham gave the Labor Party heart and its voters hope. He was the political heretic who brought life to a dead opposition. A year later, after he'd failed to deliver in 12 months the electoral gratification that the fumblings of Kim Beazley and Simon Crean had been allowed to bury, ever deeper, across almost eight years, Labor did to Latham what in a more primitive age was done to heretics.

It burnt him at the stake, in front of us all, to the applause of a mostly accommodating media and those interests, internal and institutional, that Latham's confronting leadership style had so offended. Now we have Beazley again, the first time in Labor's 104-year history of 17 Federal leaders it has felt desperate enough to revive one of them.

Going backwards seems a perverse way to go forwards, particularly by re-embracing a leader whom John Howard has already twice done over so thoroughly. But refashioning old rope worked, of course, for non-Labor under Menzies in 1949 and again for Howard nine years ago, and this Labor Caucus has no shame in trying anything. Thus we have the Jolly Green Giant back with us, that chubby face and beaming smile as chubby and beamingly beckoning as ever.

And the casualty?

A political friend, appalled by the internal manoeuvring to get rid of Latham, observed on Thursday: 'When it happened, I thought: "You dopey buggers, you have abrogated Federal parliamentary leadership to a bunch of low-rent State leaders, and the implications of that you are just too stupid even to think about, let alone understand." To think the Peter Beatties [Queensland Premier] and Mike

Ranns [SA Premier] of this world were out there offering gratuitous thoughts and views about who should grace the national leadership of the Labor Party, and why, is just too bizarre. And yet the so-called faction leaders obviously were orchestrating it.'

He was even more explicit about Beazley's resuscitation. 'Just imagine all those Caucus members who had to get on a plane to Canberra today to go to one of those dreadful f---ing faction meetings of the usual vacuous bunch of pricks before they all march off to tomorrow's ritual anointing of yesterday's man. It's no laughing matter. I'm afraid our political fortunes have fallen, at a national level, on very hard times.'

Of Latham's demise, he said: 'The oldest political party in the country, committed since its formation to political investment in decent public administration at a national level, cannot afford to trash its people of potential the way this bloke was chewed up and spat out. You can argue Latham got there too quickly and that he made some mistakes. Yet the reality is Latham is no longer in public life simply because of the way the Labor Party failed to respect talent and the necessity of having quality people in Parliament. Instead, they just trashed him.

'Nor was there any doubt that the people behind it, along with those insidious interests encouraging them, were not going to stop until they got him. I mean, all those garrulous Labor premiers tricked out by their State political machines, all with their own agendas, all given 48 hours' notice of the general direction events were likely to take. [NSW's Bob] Carr even sought to diminish the impact of Michael Egan's resignation from his Government by having Egan fortuitously announce

it an hour before Latham's resignation press conference—and on the same day, of course, that Carr had to deal with that damning report on the Waterfall rail disaster.

'[Darwin's] Clare Martin and [the ACT's] Jon Stanhope were the only two [state or territory Labor leaders] who didn't see some personal benefit in tap dancing on Latham's grave.'

My friend concluded: 'Latham's illness left him a very sick bloke. In the end he had no will to fight. Any senior politician needs key colleagues he can rely on absolutely as sounding boards, people unafraid to say what is going wrong, and why. But when all this went pear-shape for Latham after the election, there was nobody. [John] Faulkner had gone and so had [Laurie] Brereton. And that was it. There was no one else.

'And instead of him, as some had suggested, building a praetorian guard who could fire political bullets for him and generally keep an eye out for trouble and those creating it, Latham went the other way. He withdrew even more—a decision, I think, made while he was extremely ill and debilitated and in consultation only with Janine, his wife.

'Then there were the low-lifes, never admitting the axes they had to grind, who were out there being so pure, so bloody sanctimonious. It made you want to vomit. And remember this: as we contemplate the brave new world of Beazley renewed, reflect on the fact that the blokes who convinced Kim, when he first became leader in 1996, to run a million miles from Labor's history, not least the reality of its economic management as well as the myths, they're the same spineless lot now responsible for defining and selling Labor's economic message, whatever it might be.'

Indeed they are.

And the delight of the umbrella lobbying organisations that speak for big business in Canberra was palpable in welcoming the return of the comforting Beazley good cheer. Heather Ridout, chief executive of the Australian Industry Group, reflected the broad corporate attitude when she trilled glowingly in one of the first reaction statements released in the Canberra press gallery: 'Mr Beazley is well known and respected by the business community and he brings to the Opposition leadership an understanding of the challenges faced by business and industry.

'As part of the Labor governments that led the economic changes in the 1980s he understands the imperatives of reform and the critical need for that process to be ongoing. The period ahead promises the possibility of extraordinary reform, extending from the known agendas of Telstra and workplace relations to other areas including the possibility of further changes to the tax regime.

'An effective opposition is fundamental to our system of government and the Opposition has the potential to play a most important role, especially with a reform agenda that is shaping to be so extensive and challenging.'

Come into our parlour, cooed the spider.

The Government, predictably, did not waste time seeking to seduce Beazley's trusting goodwill. Typical of the usual political tripe both sides employ in abusing one another was the statement in the name of Queensland's Ian Macdonald, junior Minister for Fisheries, Forestry and Conservation. 'The Labor Party has again turned its back on country Australia by resurrecting Mr Boondoggle as its new leader,' said Macdonald's speechwriter, under the childish alliteration 'Beazley Back to Bash Bush.'

The more senior but no less silly Kevin Andrews, Howard's Minister for Employment, was no less subtle in 'challenging' Beazley 'in his third attempt at leadership' to 'recognise that Labor must abandon its disastrous industrial relations policies of the past and support the Howard Government's vital workplace relations reforms.'

Welcome back, Kim.

There is another three years of this tripe coming, all of it even more absurd now that the Government has the numbers in both houses of Parliament from August to do as it wants and when, whether or not Beazley accepts the blandishments of corporate lobbyists like Heather Ridout or the meaningless challenges of ministers like Kevin Andrews. Can't any of them, just once, argue an adult point of view? Fred Daly, were he alive, would say no.

Fred, who died almost a decade ago, was a Labor MP for 32 years. His political longevity embraced the governments of seven prime ministers, three of them Labor, from the Curtin Labor Government when Daly was elected in 1943 to the Whitlam Labor Government in which he was a minister and which infamously ended in 1975. No shrewder politician ever was elected. Daly was gone from political life five years before Kim Beazley ever got to Canberra.

Latham would have known Daly. They were both sons of NSW Labor, with safe Sydney seats, even though almost two decades stood between the end of Daly's parliamentary career (1975) and the beginning of Latham's (1994). Some years ago Daly wrote admiringly of Arthur Calwell's political savvy in thwarting an ambitious Gough Whitlam, Latham's political father figure, in the early 1960s. Quipped Daly, in putting down Whitlam: 'Old dogs for the hard road, puppies for the footpath.'

Latham sorely missed someone like Fred this past year.

Alan Ramsey

# Chapter 24

# An Honourable Craft

## 'Feel Free to Fuck Off'

APRIL 5, 2003

NOT ALL the atrocities happen in Iraq. You should see what the Howard Government's security hysteria has done to your national Parliament. And 12 days ago the ABC's online news produced this breathless paragraph of gagging schlock: 'Hollywood was tremorous ahead of a war-muted Academy Awards ceremony, with police marksmen on standby as early, low-key guests began arriving to the cheers of a small group of die-hard fans.'

Oh, 'tremorous' indeed.

Tim Bowden reminds us what our eight cents a day used to get, along with plain, unmangled English. Bowden was 30 years an ABC staffer or, as he reports with old-time ABC respect for accuracy, 29 years and 11 months. Radio, television, overseas postings he did the lot. Bowden cut his journalistic teeth on Hobart's *The Mercury* newspaper in the 1950s and he learnt the art of radio with the BBC in London in the early '60s. He's still going, of course, that cheerful, open-faced presence now heavily into writing, and his irreverent memoir, *Spooling Through* (Allen & Unwin), is a wonderful rollick across half a century of Australian life.

His description of school dances circa 1952 in Tasmania, and his discovery of girls, is, for me, exquisite nostalgia ('Have you got a cordial bottle in your pocket?'), along with the attendant unrequited passion ('Virginity in the early '50s was a ferociously guarded condition. If chastity belts had been available, they would have been worn.') My memory of Gosford, NSW, in the same era, is that they were, or might just as well have been.

Bowden was no more successful with dogs. BBC radio in 1961 sent him one day to interview a man who trained guard dogs. 'Mr Derbyshire was as savage as his Alsatians. I introduced myself as being from the BBC. "I'm fed up with you poncy, wet-behind-the-ears reporters thinking you're going to interview me and then just stuffing off back to the office," he said. "Have you any idea what it's like to be attacked by a vicious dog?" I said I hadn't, and hoped I never would. "Well, you can piss off right now. The only way you'll get an interview with me is if you let me demonstrate what it's like to be bitten by one of my dogs."'

So Bowden did, to his cost. But he got his story.

Alastair Cooke, the eminent British journalist and broadcaster based in Washington, was just as ferocious. 'When I heard he was in London I arranged an appointment. My first question was something like, "Mr Cooke, at this moment in Australian history we seem to be torn between the old ties with Britain and the new realities of American influence. How do you think Australia should resolve this dilemma?" He snapped back: "I don't know. What do you think?"

'I stopped the recorder in dismay and confusion. Cooke told me to start again. I ground out the same question. Again, he asked what I thought. I mumbled something about, with luck, getting the best of both worlds. "Yes, well that's the kind of confused and muddled thinking that will almost certainly lead to utter disaster. And furthermore . . ."'

Bowden's interview died on the cutting-room floor.

In Singapore in 1965 for ABC radio, Bowden met Arthur Cook, of London's *Daily Mail*, who'd previously worked for the London *Daily Express* in Iran until Cook 'miswrote' a story about the trial of a failed coup leader in which he wrongly sentenced the unfortunate to immediate death. Cook's foreign editor cabled ominously next day: "WHY YOUR EXCLUSIVE STILL EXCLUSIVE?" This was followed 24 hours later by: "IT'S MOSSA-DEGH'S NECK OR YOURS." At this point Cook switched to the *Daily Mail*.

That same year, in Vietnam, Melbourne's Creighton Burns, later editor of *The Age*, ran headlong into the Australian military's dislike of journalists. A PR major invited Burns and Donald Wise, of London's *Daily Mirror*, to dinner in the Australian officers' mess tent. Bowden writes: 'As they sat down, all the officers moved away down the table. Wise smiled and said loudly, "What did you say the motto of this battalion was, dear boy: Feel free to f--- off ?" Donald's description became the catchcry of journalists trying to do business with the Australians.'

Nothing has changed.

Alan Ramsey

# Thanksa Million

**JULY 14, 2007**

ANYONE SERIOUS about politics knows the name. Fifty years ago he was a brash, aggressive police rounds reporter for Sydney's brash, aggressive *Daily Mirror* afternoon newspaper. That's when I first knew Max Walsh. He was 20 years old. I next saw him nine years later, as a brash, aggressive political writer in Canberra for the Fairfax family's *Australian Financial Review,* the country's first national newspaper. The date was February 1966.

Only by then the tearaway Max Walsh of the 1957 *Daily Mirror* was the upmarket Maximilian Walsh, the Canberra bureau chief of the upmarket *Review*, even though colleagues knew him ever after—and most particularly in the national press gallery—as 'Thanksa', as in the rhyming slang of 'thanks a million'. By 1974 he was his paper's editor, then its managing editor, and when he quit in 1981 to join the Nine Network's new *Sunday* program, then later to jointly anchor ABC television's nightly *Carleton/Walsh Program* with Richard Carleton, Maximilian Walsh was established as one of the foremost Australian journalists of the past half-century.

This is no hyperbole. Walsh's influence on national economic/political writing in the nine years he was in the Canberra gallery was immense. All this from a bloke who began working life as an 'aggressive and argumentative junior assistant proofreader' on the *Herald* in 1955, as Gavin Souter would record in his superb 1980 history of Australia's oldest newspaper, *Company of Heralds.*

Walsh would never change. Even the Fairfax executive who interviewed him in 1962, when Walsh joined the *Financial Review*, would note: 'He is intelligent, somewhat bellicose and urgently in need of leadership.' Yet Walsh, while working for the *Daily Mirror* at the time, was 'halfway through a part-time economics degree at Sydney University and had just topped his year in government'.

His career surged, despite all. In September 1971, assigned to do a major piece on the then Prime Minister, Sydney's Billy McMahon, for the Fairfax group's new weekly, *The National Times,* Walsh's forensically blunt article— 'Public McMahon and Private Billy, the facts and the myths'—drew a terse memo from the company chairman, Sir Warwick Fairfax, to Walsh's managing editor, V.J.Carroll: 'The article gives the impression Mr McMahon is a bit of a lightweight who has got to the top by a lot of smooth-talking without much achieve-ment. This view is superficial and unfair . . . I look to you to deal with [Walsh] with a very firm hand . . .'

Whatever Carroll did or did not do, voters agreed with Walsh. Fifteen months later they dumped the McMahon Government after 23 years of Coalition rule and Labor under Gough Whitlam swept into power. Within Fairfax, redemption, like victory, was sweet. Walsh became editor of the *Financial Review* two years later and Carroll editor of the *Herald* in 1980. Sir Warwick was gone by 1977.

Years later, after Nine's *Sunday* and the ABC's 'car wash' program and a long stint of mixing both with regular commentary in the *Herald*, Walsh became editor-in-chief of the Packer group's *The Bulletin.* That was in December 1998. And this week's issue, when it appeared on Wednesday, carried the tease on its cover: 'Max Walsh, farewell column: "Keating was right".'

Read it. His last *Bulletin* piece, perhaps his last for anybody, is a real snorter. And like Billy McMahon and Sir Warwick Fairfax 36 years earlier, John Howard will hate this one, too.

Measured but devastating in its economic analysis of why another Sydney Liberal Prime Minister is in deep trouble, Walsh, now 70, concludes: 'Perhaps I'm getting ahead of myself in suggesting not only a Liberal loss but also an extended sojourn in the wilderness. But Paul Keating was right when he said: "When you change the Government, you change the country." This year's election could be a bigger watershed than most imagine. Business and investors take note.'

A few weeks ago Max and Geraldine Walsh celebrated at their Mosman home, with its stunning views straight out through Sydney Heads, with family, friends and colleagues drawn from half a century of political and economic journalism. His professional life has been good to him, no doubt.

But Thanksa's been very good to it, too.

Alan Ramsey

# Bless you, Patricia Rolfe

**SEPTEMBER 13, 2008**

WHEN PATRICIA Rolfe died, aged 87, in a Sydney hospital three weeks ago, another of the lights went out in what it seems fashionable these days to call the death throes of 'old media'. Rolfe spent all her working life in the maw of the former Packer publishing empire, except for a brief stint with *The Sydney Morning Herald* after she returned to Australia from London in 1960. What set Rolfe apart was her more than two decades as deputy editor and/or literary editor of *The Bulletin,* our oldest and most iconic magazine until its 'new media' private equity owners killed it off last January after 128 years of existence.

To Denis O'Brien, Pat Rolfe was one of two great influences (the other was Donald Horne) in his career. O'Brien is old media. He migrated to Australia from London in 1950, at the age of 21, and after learning his journalism on country papers in Toowoomba and Launceston, and seven years with Brisbane's *Courier Mail,* he ultimately became one of *The Bulletin*'s stable of writers in the late 1960s and early '70s, during Horne's second stint as editor.

I got to know O'Brien by chance. *The Bulletin* had sent him to Canberra to write 'colour' pieces about the political turbulence of March 1971, when the Liberals changed prime ministers, and he was silly enough to be standing behind me in the press gallery the day I disgraced myself by shouting 'You Liar!' at Prime Minister John Gorton on the floor of the house before bolting out the door and across the roof of Old Parliament.

'They were all looking up at me,' O'Brien recalls, 'because you'd fled and I'm standing there and they were saying, "Who the bloody hell was that?"'

I was off crook when Pat Rolfe died. The obituaries had been published and her funeral mass long said before I got back to work. But Pat was such a significant marker in Australian journalism, in an era that's all but gone, that I felt a sketch of the career of somebody like O'Brien, now rising 80, would get into context a period many of us in the print business at the time remember as 'the best'.

In 1962 David McNicoll, editor-in-chief of Sydney's *Daily Telegraph*, then owned by Frank Packer, Kerry's father and iron-fisted guardian of a grateful Menzies Government, which would later knight him for his paper's years of thugging the Labor Party, offered O'Brien a job as theatre critic for *The Sunday Telegraph* but forgot to tell the paper's editor, Johnny Moyes. When O'Brien lined up on his first day, with Wally Crouch, the paper's 'gun' reporter, nobody knew what to do with him.

Eventually O'Brien got two pages (later four) at the back of the paper called Leisure, which for four years he wrote, edited and laid out, including the back page, which carried his television column. He recalls: 'In 1966 I was going on holidays, it was December, and in my last TV column I did this piece about the way in which, at Christmas time, there's nothing decent to watch, and I gave it a headline saying, 'The dull thud of an Old Year'. I got into all the stations, but when Packer [who owned Channel 9] saw it, it became the dull thud of my career.

'He'd come in from the races this Saturday afternoon, as he always did, pissed to the eyeballs, and when the first edition came up, with its "dull thud of an Old Year" on the back page, well, hey, "What the hell's this?" Then, "Tear that out", and he ordered McNicoll to write a substitute piece. I knew nothing until 5 o'clock the next morning when the phone rang at home at Manly and John Iredale, who did the Veritas column in the rival *Sunday Mirror*, said: "Have you read your paper yet? They've done you over proper." It was humiliating, about "critics and who needs them?" No names, but I thought, well, that's the end of that.'

And it was.

O'Brien took over the Ray Castle column from Allan Barnes in *The Daily Telegraph* and Barnes a year later would come to Canberra to distinguish himself writing politics for *The Age* in Melbourne. Two years on, in 1968, O'Brien moved up one floor to join *The Bulletin* under Horne and Rolfe. The next four years were the best of O'Brien's career and included a Walkley Award for feature writing. O'Brien's colleagues included Ron Saw and Ross Campbell, and eventually a young Malcolm Turnbull, whom Pat Rolfe years later would recall as a 'beautiful young man'.

Remembers O'Brien: 'Pat was there long before I got there and long after I left. She was an institution, the arbiter of journalism values I believe no longer exist.'

Vale old media.

Alan Ramsey

# Malcolm and the Mogul

**SEPTEMBER 20, 2008**

MALCOLM TURNBULL has been dogged by cats for three decades. Almost five years ago, during Turnbull's bitter stoush in February 2004 to wrest (by 88 votes to 70) Liberal Party pre-selection for the Sydney seat of Wentworth from the unfortunate incumbent, Peter King, my artist colleague Ward O'Neill did a wonderful drawing of Turnbull for the *Herald*'s sister paper, *The Australian Financial Review*. It showed Turnbull with a coffee mug bearing the image of a cat, and a cat rubbing affectionately against his leg.

Political aficionados with long memories understood.

So would the fallen Canadian newspaper mogul Conrad Black, now doing six years in a Florida pokey for defrauding shareholders of $US6.1 million in illegal bonuses from his former company, Hollinger International, once the world's third largest publisher of English language newspapers, including those of the Fairfax group. Black is still fighting on appeal from his gaol cell, having already lost one appeal this year.

Fifteen years ago, with Keating's Labor having just won the 'unwinnable' 1993 election, Random House published Black's autobiography, a rollicking read entitled *Conrad Black: A Life In Progress*. The jacket blurbed breathlessly: 'He pulls no punches in describing the people with whom he has dealt with over the years—ranging from Paul Keating and Kerry Packer to Malcolm Turnbull and the [then] Fairfax management, to Margaret Thatcher and Bill Clinton.'

Not until page 412 did readers get to you-know-who.

Describing events in 1991 involving Black duly becoming Fairfax's principal shareholder after the calamitous attempt by young Warwick Fairfax to buy the Fairfax empire, Black wrote in part: 'It emerged that a proposal had been

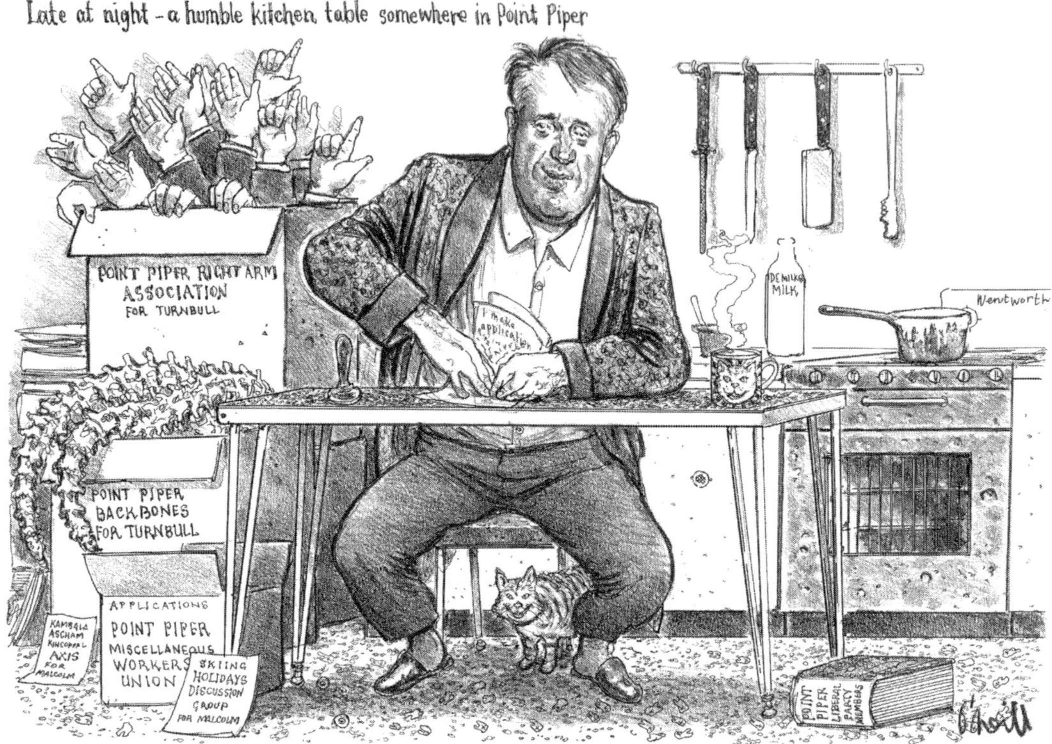


assembled in Sydney by a stockbroker, Neville Miles, and by a merchant banker, Malcolm Turnbull, wrapping up the (mainly) US junk bondholders who were in litigation with the Fairfax banking group and had a paper value of $450 million to defend . . . Turnbull and Miles could scarcely have been less alike personally. Where Neville Miles is a rather deferential, quiet, and serenely courteous South African, Malcolm Turnbull is mercurial and volcanic.

'He is an intelligent and attractive and articulate man, who sometimes has considerable difficulty maintaining his self-control against an onslaught of unimaginable compulsive inner tensions and ineluctable ambitions. Malcolm had immense agility at composing scenarios whose common feature was the happy ending of his ruling the world, or whatever part of it was currently under consideration. Malcolm's

fugues were notorious; such as the time [as a young single man] he allegedly punctuated an altercation with a friend by disposing of her cat. He became uncommonly belligerent and histrionic, threatening vengeance on people, including occasionally himself.

'Malcolm had risen to prominence in Australia as a lawyer, especially in his examination of one of Margaret Thatcher's senior civil servants in the Spycatcher affair, when the British Government set out to stop publication of the memoirs of a retired intelligence officer in violation of his pledge to secrecy. Malcolm performed his task brilliantly and won the case.

'In his intense and urbane pugnacity, Malcolm Turnbull is sometimes the personification of modern Australia, justly seeking recognition of his country's status as a maturing entity in the world. This is generally the aspect of him that is to the forefront in his ceaseless crusade for republican government in Australia . . .'

Black had much more to write about the Australian political and corporate players with whom he dealt. Among them: Bob Hawke ('a charming old political roue'), Malcolm Fraser ('as I put it in *The Sydney Morning Herald,* "a sanctimonious balloon in need of a puncture"') and Paul Keating ('a more capable leader than any other current English-speaking head of government' and 'as I came to realise, an extraordinary powerful combination of Bankstown cunning, Irish political ward-heeler, cultural autodidact happy to discuss antique clocks with the Queen and constantly listening to classical music, and a great comic talent splendidly aware of the absurdity of much activity, including much of his own'.)

Black's relationship with Turnbull did not conclude well. His caustic final reference in his book to the man who is now Australia's alternative Prime Minister is brutally adversarial. You'll have to read the book for the detail, however. Better still, ask Turnbull.

Just don't mention cats and urban myths.

Alan Ramsey

# Death in the Afternoon

**JULY 17, 2002**

IAN 'STORKY' Arnold was editor of the now defunct Sydney afternoon Fairfax screamer, *The Sun,* for three years until 1977. On November 11, 1975, a Tuesday, a breathless Neil O'Reilly, forever known to his newspaper contemporaries as Seamus, rang Arnold from Canberra at 1.50pm with the stunning news of the Whitlam Labor Government's sacking. O'Reilly had just sprinted across the Old Parliament and up the stairs. He could barely get the words out, he was sucking air so hard.

The point of this story is what happened next.

O'Reilly, in between gasping for breath, rattled out his story over the phone to a copy-taker who typed it two sentences to a page. The slips of paper were run individually to Arnold and the paper's chief sub-editor, who were remaking the paper's front page and an inside page at the same time as the production staff downstairs were alerted that a special edition was coming.

'It was the fastest turnaround at *The Sun* ever,' Arnold recalls. 'From the time Seamus rang to the time one of our 'zebra' vans dropped a bundle of the new edition, with poster, at the Town Hall at 2.15pm, was 25 to 26 minutes. And we couldn't print enough, we sold so many.'

O'Reilly died six weeks ago. *The Sun* newspaper he worked on for most of his working life died in 1987, killed off by television. Most people don't realise how the death of afternoon newspapers in this country—everywhere, for that matter—reflects the remorseless change in mass communications, most particularly in our reading habits and in how we get our information. Nothing has been the same since.

I met O'Reilly when I joined *The Sun* from Darwin in late 1956, the same year Australia got TV and its population reached 9 million. Tall, thin, laconic, a cigarette always in his mouth, Seamus reminded me of the Bluey character in Alec Gurney's 'Bluey and Curly' newspaper comic strip of the time.

And when I got to Canberra from the Vietnam War 10 years later, Seamus was here, too, still on *The Sun* which he'd joined in the late 1940s as a copy boy who, the *Herald*'s Tony Stephens tells us, used to deliver crime paperbacks to Ben Chifley, the Labor Prime Minister of the day.

You'd be surprised by the journalists who came through the helter-skelter of the afternoon tabloids. People like Lou d'Alpuget, Tess van Sommers, Ron Saw, Tony Ferguson, Derryn Hinch, Mike Willesee, Merton Woods, Zel Rabin, and Blanche 'Fifi' d'Alpuget, who got her start writing about television for *The Sun*. None ever regretted it, especially if they experienced the cut-throat mayhem of the Sydney rivalry between *The Sun*, bought by Fairfax in 1953, and the Norton family's *The Daily Mirror*, later sold to a young Rupert Murdoch in 1960.

There was no newspaper rivalry like it, ever, in this country.

Many later turned up in Canberra, among them Max Walsh, Laurie Oakes, Eric Walsh and Rob Chalmers, all spawned by the *Mirror*; Mike Willesee, originally off Perth's *Daily News*; Glen Milne, from Brisbane's *The Telegraph* and recruited to Canberra in 1985 by *The Sun*; Kerry O'Brien, Peter Barron, Colin Parks, Ken Begg, Tony O'Leary, Elwyn Spratt, Jack Alsop, Les Love, and Kevin Power for *The Sun*; and, of course, Alan Reid, who made his name reporting politics for *The Sun* before Frank Packer, Kerry's father, bought Reid for his *Daily Telegraph* in the late 1950s.

A lot were memorable characters, few more so than the *Mirror*'s Jim Quirk, or Brother Quirk as we knew him, a man of great appetites who drank like a fish but couldn't swim like one and who, eventually, fell off his boat in Queensland one night and drowned. Quirk's pots and pans samba, as he called it, a very blokey party stunt he performed in the nude, will not be forgotten by those who witnessed it in the '60s.

All of which means, what?

Not a lot to anyone who wasn't around at the time, I suppose. But Seamus's death got me thinking about them all again and how journalism has become so different with the afternoon screamers gone. They were brash and they were loud but they taught their reporters skills they never lost and they encouraged and fed newspaper reading habits, with their seven editions a day, often six days a week, year in and year out, now forever changed by the insidious sponge of television.

Vale Seamus and the tabloids.

Alan Ramsey

# George's Gone and Granny's Dying

**FEBRUARY 4, 2004**

GEORGE RICHARDS left the *Herald* for the last time last Friday. He thought he could just walk away after 45 years. Not so. When the lift doors opened on the ground floor at Sydney head office that afternoon, his colleagues were waiting. 'We all stood in the foyer, rattling steel trays and shaking jars filled with paper clips,' Julia Baird, the then Opinion page editor, said later. 'There must have been 200 of us.' It was, it seems, an emotional moment.

Richards, a Sydney High old boy, joined the *Herald* in September 1958. Nobody had been at the paper longer when he left his office on the 26th floor that last time. He was, I think, just about the last significant link with the old Fairfax family-run *The Sydney Morning Herald*, with the possible exception of Valerie Lawson and Tony Stephens.

*Herald* readers will know George Richards, without ever knowing his name, as the bloke who, for the last 15 1/2 years, anonymously put together Column 8, just as a string of unidentified predecessors had done for more than 40 years, among them the column's founding editor Sid Deamer, Duncan Thompson, Bill Fitter, Col Allison, Jim Cunningham, and even, for brief stints so I'm told, Peter Bowers and Lenore Nicklin.

In all the column's 57 years, since it first appeared, signed Granny, down the right-hand side of the *Herald's* frontpage on Saturday, January 11, 1947, nobody edited Column 8 longer than did Richards, not even the legendary Deamer (whose departure the *Herald* gracelessly declined to acknowledge, even with a single paragraph, when he stood down from the Granny column, after 14 years, and retired in 1961).

And yet, when Richards' last column appeared last Saturday, he thought he could slide away into retirement with a brief item which concluded simply: '"Granny" Richards thanks the thousands of readers who have contributed items and who, we know, will continue to do so. He also thanks This Paper's readers who look for it each day.'

I thought Richards (and Column 8) deserved a bit more, even though the *Herald* gave him a grand send-off, the day before he actually left, at a function attended by staff, past and present, and *Herald* luminaries from the 'old' years, among them David Bowman and Vic Carroll (both former editors), Gavin Souter, Alan Dobbyn and Ian Hicks.

Very many years ago, when Richards was a cadet journalist at Frank Packer's *Daily Telegraph*, which he joined as a copy boy in 1950, he edited an issue of an in-house 'junior' training paper called Telegus. An issue of August 1953 is locked in my memory because the second item in a Column 8-type front-page column read: 'Copy boy Alan Ramsey comes to work in the Turf Room each day from Gosford. He gets up at 5.30am and home at 8.30pm 30 hours a week travelling.'

My first byline. Thirty-five years later, after I joined the *Herald* in May 1987, George, quite out of the blue, sent me a copy of the relevant Telegus from all those years earlier. Oddly, we've never met, even though we've worked on the same newspaper (if in different cities) for almost 17 years. Yet that umbilical link stretches back half a century.

As for Column 8, some of us weep it was ever abolished from the front page, a piece of vandalism in August 2000 that swept, after 53 years, one of the most widely read and best-loved features of the paper out of sight to a nasty tabloid format deep inside. I mean, it's *The Sydney Morning Herald* we're talking about, for God's sake, even if after becoming the 'new' *Herald*. What did they think they were doing?

You really wonder, sometimes. Yet three years later and the bloke responsible for the paper's redesign at the time has been redesigned, too, right out of the company. Too late, too late, they cried. Thanks for nothing. Column 8 has survived, in a fashion, despite the best efforts of some over the years. The Granny signature was killed in 1967 but not Granny herself. And now her loving disciple, George Richards, has gone. Nothing stays the same.

*Alan Ramsey*

# Goodbye, Les Tanner

**AUGUST 1, 2001**

BACK IN the late 1970s/early '80s, when Bob Hawke's political ambition was forever threatening Bill Hayden's leadership of the Labor Party, Hayden once asked me why it was some cartoonists always drew Hawke taller than him when, in fact, the reverse was true. Those sorts of things really niggle politicians, who we mostly forget are human too, but I don't recall having had the courage to say it wasn't Hayden's height relative to Hawke's the cartoonists were seeking to illustrate.

Hayden's angst came rushing out of the past after Les Tanner died in his sleep at his Melbourne home 10 days ago. Many years earlier, Tanner and Peter Coleman co-edited a selection of cartoons from across 180 years of the rich tradition of Australian political cartooning. It was the introduction to their book, *Cartoons of Australia's History*, I wished I'd known about and been able to quote to Hayden all those years ago.

It eloquently answers his question.

Tanner, the cartoonist, and Coleman, the journalist, editor and, later, politician and father-in-law of Peter Costello, wrote: 'A cartoonist has no right to be fair. If you are a fair-minded, sober kind of artist, you should not be a cartoonist. Cartoonists are satirists, not magistrates. They seize on one important aspect of a situation for the purposes of ridicule or dramatisation and hammer at it as unfairly or righteously as possible.

'A censor of books is not, for the cartoonist, a servant of the public trying conscientiously to strike a balance between the freedom of literature and the need to protect the morals of the Commonwealth. He is usually a drooling, idiotic pervert who finds secret, dirty meanings where none exist or viciously wants to impose his own narrowness on everyone else.

'A politician is not an overworked citizen doing his modest best. He is a weed, a parasite, a corrupt party hack, unable to distinguish truth from advantage. These images may be, to one degree or another, unfair, but—and this is their value—by their unfairness and often their crudeness, the cartoonists [catch] the attitudes, prejudices and hopes of the Australian people of the time . . . usually [far better] than journalists' reports, let alone government documents.'

I knew Les through his extended family.

His sister, Gwen, was the wife of the late Adrian Deamer, a distinguished editor of *The Australian* and a man a good many of us who worked for him both admired and loved. Dinner at the Deamers in Sydney, as they say, was an experience if either Jim McClelland or Les Tanner was at the table, too. All three greatly enjoyed a drink and an argument.

Gwen told a rollicking wake for her brother at his favourite Melbourne pub, the Pump House, last Friday that these arguments could be so willing that her husband once ordered his brother-in-law out of the house. Next morning, when Adrian came down for breakfast, there was a note from Les on the table: 'Can't we stay together for the sake of the children?'

It was this wit that put Tanner's talent up there with the pre-eminent political cartoonists. He spent the first 40 years of his life in Sydney and his last 34 in Melbourne. He made his name with Frank Packer's *Daily Telegraph* and *The Bulletin* in the 1950s and '60s and his reputation during the next 30 years with *The Age*. Tanner's close friend Bruce Petty wrote of him last week: 'I am surprised I feel so shaken at his not being about.'

For all the years of his superb pen—and he wrote as astringently and as wittily as he drew—Tanner's name will forever be remembered in Australian journalism as the cartoonist who jointly caused Kerry Packer's father, Frank, an uncompromising Liberal acolyte, to pulp an entire edition of *The Bulletin*. The incident was as forthright a demonstration of Packer's authority and politics as anything later enforced by his younger son.

Peter Coleman, *The Bulletin*'s editor at the time, upset Frank Packer with an editorial in February 1967 critical of the contentious hanging, in Victoria, of Peter Ryan, the last person legally executed in this country. Tanner enraged him with an accompanying cartoon showing Victoria's then Liberal Party Premier, Henry Bolte, a ruthless, cunning and immensely successful country hick, holding a noose. The caption underneath read: 'I do not bow to mob protest, only mob support.'

Coleman and Tanner were gone from *The Bulletin* within weeks, Coleman into law and later NSW Liberal Party politics and Tanner to Melbourne to join *The Age*. Last Friday, colleagues and family farewelled Les at the Pump House to the strains of Jimmy Durante creaking through *I'll be Seeing You*. Here in Canberra, in an election year, the older among us will be remembering him.

Alan Ramsey

# Chapter 25

# End of the Line

## Spineless Leadership of the Liberal Kind

**SEPTEMBER 3, 2005**

PARTY LEADERSHIP. One bloke had it and trashed it by sheer stupidity. The other bloke wants it, desperately, and could go the same way. John Brogden and Peter Costello. One State, one Federal. Both with everything to gain. But no discipline, either of them. No patience either. And no spine. In politics a dangerous, self-defeating mix. How did it come to this?

The Liberal Party's John Brogden pinches a woman journalist's bum at a Hilton Hotel party and refers to Malaysian-born Helena Carr, wife of the NSW Premier, as a 'mail-order bride'. The Labor Party's Bob Hawke tells a hotel dinner audience of 600 to 700 people a 'joke' in which the 'humour' is keyed to the penultimate remark, 'f--- Mrs Gandhi!', India's then Prime Minister.

And what happens? Brogden's behaviour incites shrieking newspaper headlines, his resignation as NSW Opposition leader, and a failed attempt at suicide. Hawke's behaviour, utterly muffled by the press, does nothing whatever to slow him becoming Prime Minister 20 months later. Why the double standard?

Why is Brogden pilloried and his career destroyed amid media frenzy over 'sexist' and 'racist' behaviour in August 2005, yet Hawke's outrageous 'sexist' and 'racist' ridicule of the Prime Minister of the world's most populous democracy attracts neither media lynch mob nor any hint of political 'disgrace' in July 1981? Simple. Ignorant, racist indifference and a very protective press corps, is why.

You know of Brogden's admitted indiscretions. Let me tell you about Hawke's.

In July 1981 Federal Labor held a special national conference at Melbourne's Southern Cross Hotel. Bill Hayden was Opposition leader. Hawke, a notorious womaniser but the political press's hero, was just nine months an MP. Ironically, the conference was about Labor women's political rights. A highlight was a fundraising dinner where politicians stood and told jokes. The winner, by acclamation, was Labor's deputy leader of the time, the wonderfully droll Lionel Bowen.

Hawke's joke died in the blocks.

It concerned an Indian lottery in which, when the winning tickets are drawn, third prize is a round-the-world trip, and second prize, won by 'Mr Mukerjee', is a fruit cake. Mr Mukerjee complains bitterly. Ah, explains the lottery MC, but the cake is baked by 'our great and glorious leader, Mrs Gandhi.' 'F--- Mrs Gandhi,' says Mr Mukerjee. 'No, no,' says the MC, 'you will be wanting first prize.' All this told, at ridiculous length, in Hawke's sing-song mimickry of an Indian accent.

Audience response, apart from mixed guffaws and groans, was mostly an uncomfortable silence. Yet, although the function was taped and reporters were present, the Hawke 'joke' never made it into the press. Not a word. Four weeks later, the Indian High Commissioner complained in writing to Hayden and called to see him in Canberra. Niki Savva, then with Melbourne's mass-circulation *Sun News-Pictorial* newspaper (and, many years later, Peter Costello's press secretary), broke the story on September 3, 1981.

But Savva's paper deleted the Hawke 'joke'. It even expunged her reference to it as 'ribald'. It ran the article well inside. Other newspapers later picked up on it briefly after Hawke went on ABC radio the same morning to apologise, admitting the 'joke' was inappropriate and in poor taste, but insisting it was not racist. He blamed political opponents for spreading it. In that, at least, he was right.

Only a Fairfax weekly, the now deceased *National Times*, printed Hawke's Gandhi 'joke' three days after Savva's story appeared. *The Sydney Morning Herald*, under Jenni Hewett's byline, reported the Indian diplomat's complaint in nine gentle paragraphs. The press, by and large, didn't want to know. It treated the story as inconsequential. One pundit dismissed it as 'a hopelessly old joke, badly told' by Hawke, and he informed readers: 'It won't be repeated here.'

John Brogden has not been so lucky. What he has been is spineless.

Three weeks after the Hilton Hotel drinks, *The Sunday Telegraph*, in a story written out of the Canberra press gallery, unearthed Brogden's indiscretions last weekend. That same night Brogden was advised, in the strongest terms, to wear the flak, admit he'd been a fool and tough it out, once he'd squared his idiocy with his family. The advice came from within his parliamentary party and from the broader Liberal organisation.

One of those who phoned to tell him 'not to panic' and to hang in there was former NSW Liberal Party president Bill Heffernan, later the target of some poisonous misreporting. Yet Brogden had no stomach for a fight. He caved in the next morning, with little more than a blubber, amid the most excruciating political press conference imaginable.

That doesn't excuse Brogden's behaviour, whether in his cups at the time or not. It simply dismisses him as painfully weak. Anyone can make a mistake. Anyone can make a fool of him or herself. And everybody does, at sometime, despite the acres of sanctimony when the media so chooses. But Brogden, a young man with everything to fight for, couldn't find the courage to fight for his leadership. Instead, overwhelmed with shame and self-pity, he quit. He'd shown himself up as a fool. The Liberals, you'd have to say, are well shot of his 'leadership'.

Take heed, Peter Costello.

Our Treasurer has been in public life 15 1/2 years. He's been his party's deputy Federal leader for 11 years (since May 1994) and his Government's Treasurer since the Coalition regained office in March 1996. For a politician who turned a mere 48 three weeks ago he has done very nicely. He should keep in mind that the man whose job he craves was 22 years in Parliament—and 13 years in Opposition—before ever he became Prime Minister (at age 56).

And if Costello really believes life is being mean to him, he should not forget that Harold Holt, the Liberals' longest-serving Treasurer (7 1/2 years) until Costello, was 30 years and five months (elected August 1935) in Parliament before, finally, he grasped the holy grail of the prime ministership on Australia Day, 1966, only to lose it—and his life—in a wild surf off Victoria's Portsea 23 months later.

Holt's patience was immense, if only because it had to be. Menzies was a leader who'd earned the right to determine his departure at a time of his own choosing. He'd formed the Liberal Party, in 1944, from a rabble of various non-Labor groups, and after his coalition took Government from Chifley Labor in December 1949, it went on to hold it through another six elections before Ming opted, at age 71, to hand over to his deputy, the loyal and patient Holt, 16 years and two months later, in January 1966.

Only two prime ministers before Menzies retired undefeated, both more than half a century earlier. No Prime Minister has done so since. Howard is set on being the next. And Menzies, with that benchmark retirement age of 71, has laid down the precedent, should Howard, who turned 66 just a few weeks ago, choose to follow it. That is, another five years. It depends entirely on him. Like Menzies, Howard, too, has earned the right, you'd have to think.

Yet Costello, the boy-deputy Howard inherited in January 1995, thinks he can decide when that time should be. Costello is, like Keating was, bored with being Treasurer. He wants the king's castle. Unlike Keating and Hawke, Costello has no agreement with Howard on a retirement date, and never did have. And unlike Keating, he has neither the balls nor the votes to force the issue to a party room challenge.

Instead, we get these childish word games Costello has been playing this week, trailing his coat around the radio and TV stations, dumping on his colleagues, Malcolm Turnbull in particular, rabbiting on about leadership, pretending he is 'leading' when all he's doing is being a political pain in the Government's collective rectum, and causing his own supporters to tear their hair at what the Treasurer thinks he's doing. They've no idea, I assure you. Is all the advice coming from Michael Kroger, Andrew Peacock's son-in-law?

You have to wonder, really.

I mean, there seem to be increasingly heroic stories, attributed to anonymous 'Costello backers', of the sort that Howard should tell poor Peter what he intends doing on the basis that 'tension over the leadership is damaging the Government'. What utter bunkum. The only people pushing that sort of tosh is the Labor Opposition and its wallowing leader, Kim Beazley. The only bloke causing 'tension over the Government's leadership' is Costello himself. And very deliberately, too. What his 'backers' would most like is for Costello to discipline his undisciplined mouth.

Instead we get this sort of twaddle: Melbourne radio's Neil Mitchell, on Thursday: 'What did you mean yesterday when you said, "I lead this country"?'

Costello: 'Well, actually, Neil, let's be precise, it is all there on the record, but expect (it) to be misrepresented. I said, as Treasurer and deputy leader in a sense I lead, and I have to lead in relation to economic policy. That is what I said. I mean, you can't blame the journalist who wants to sell a newspaper for turning that round into a headline. What else would you expect me to do . . . ?'

That isn't quite what he said at all. And what others 'expect him to do', in his own best interests, is just shut up. Instead, this weekend the Treasurer flies to Indonesia with a planeload of invited journalists. Guess what they're all going to be writing about?

Peter Costello, like John Brogden, will yet talk his leadership to death.

Alan Ramsey

# Up the Road with Bill

**NOVEMBER 3, 2007**

FROM THE potato grower on the Murray to the waterless hamlet just inside the Queensland border and the wheat farmers, with their failed crops, in between, exactly 2600 kilometres straight up the guts of NSW. Up and back, that is, in three days and three hours. The election is irrelevant by comparison. Water is now Australia's absolutely critical issue, not the campaign games of John Howard and Kevin Rudd. 'There's the real world,' said Bill Heffernan, nodding to the conveyor belt and the thin stream of wheat making a pyramid in the grain holding centre we were passing near Walgett in the state's far north. 'That's where the loaf of bread in the supermarket starts.'

Heffernan is the NSW Liberal senator some people think, quite wrongly, is just another dinosaur. He knows more about country people and what is happening in the bush— and what needs to be done—than all those bone-headed Nationals in John Howard's Government put together.

And while Heffernan won't thank me for saying so, Howard's lousy judgment, as well as his lack of courage, failed him and his Government when he didn't move outside the envelope and make the outspoken farmer politician from Junee Minister for Primary Industries after the 2004 election. Instead, Howard took the easy Coalition option and continued elevating National dunces like Warren Truss and Peter McGauran and John Cobb, and he left Heffernan to rot on the back bench because he wouldn't trust his friend and ally after Heffernan had said what he thought, under parliamentary privilege, in March five years ago about the High Court's Michael Kirby, a darling of the Labor Party.

Howard cared more what the judiciary thought of him personally, a former suburban solicitor, than he did about the political wellbeing of his Government.

Which brings us back to two grumpy old men in a four-wheel drive.

As always, Heffernan went to look for himself. He had a wad of letters and emails from NSW farmers here and there across the State, most of them desperate for help for the same reason. Water.

If Howard wouldn't make him a minister, he did make Heffernan chairman of a taskforce looking into how Australia might develop its waterlogged north as our next great food bowl after the ailing Murray–Darling Basin.

The job has become Heffernan's passion. Locking up Australia's food security, he calls it.

He tells a great story about a young farmer from Gilgandra who moved to the NT five years ago, bought 2000 acres of bush at $10 an acre south of Darwin, and then, joined by his brother, last year cleared $1 million growing watermelons for city buyers in the south. Heffernan tells the story as he likens the opportunities for agriculture in the north to having bought a house in Sydney and Melbourne in the 1960s.

Whatever, when he left Canberra at lunchtime last Sunday, he drove south to Mulwala on the Murray, opposite Yarrawonga, first to talk to a potato grower in trouble buying water at soaring prices after his licence allocation was reduced; then on to see Doug and Bronwyn Thomas, a couple with four school-age children, who've spent $470,000 on the family farm in the last six years on the latest, most efficient irrigation technology to grow feed to fatten lambs, only to have the NSW bureaucracy cripple their water allocation by an arbitrary 84 per cent reduction in their licensed entitlement of 600 megalitres a year.

Now they have to buy bore water at prices that have gone crazy.

Brian Peadon is chief executive of the National Water Exchange, the stock exchange of the exploding water trading market in NSW and Victoria. Last year, he says, was dreadful for farmers in both states. The water licensing system is out of control.

'The stress farmers are under this year is even more intense,' Peadon said by phone yesterday. 'And there's all sorts of awful political games going on at the moment which don't help. The message we're trying to get across is that last year was a disaster socially in country areas, and this year is going to be worse because (governments are) still fiddling. In fact, what is going on within the government bureaucracies is just putting the most enormous strain on farm families.

'My short-term objective is to alleviate that strain. The long-term policies, we're fighting those out, but diabolic things are happening at the moment (within State government agencies). To put things in perspective, a normal temporary transfer of water takes three or four days by the time you get [the water]. This year it's taking 36 days, and counting.

'So even though people have made the decision, "Well, I'll sell the scrap of water I've got, here's my income for the year, I'll save the farm", given the record prices, they're not being paid because the governments just won't approve the transfers. Approve or deny them or do anything. It's even worse in Victoria because they won't let anything go and [are] putting the pressure back on NSW farmers.

'We're seeing State governments, or State bureaucracies, playing with people's lives. We have people desperately wanting the water, paying the money, it's held in trust accounts, the (sellers) desperately wanting the income, yet neither is happening. People are just watching their crops die while these guys are playing bureacracies.

'It's the national water plan and, you know, there's the State thing too, and the poor old farmer is being held as the ammunition in the fight. It's really very serious. In the data last year, in our customer base—we have 22,000 customers—we had eight identifiable suicides in the Murray region, with the majority in northern Victoria. Now the pressures are even greater. I can't stress enough what's happening is absolutely appalling.

'My part, in NSW, is just getting somebody (within the bureaucracy) to try and take some ownership and responsibility with Victoria. Again, to put it in perspective, in the Murray–Darling Basin we deliver the same document to 17 separate government agencies. You know, doing the same thing with 17 of them. You get held up at that mid-bureaucratic level and you can't get anything done.

'And you just don't know who to grab and shake to solve these problems, whether it's policy or just incompetence, or whatever. But at the end of the day the system doesn't work. It's been going on for years, but this year is crisis year.'

Heffernan knows exactly what Peadon means.

He tells an awful story about a farm family south of Gundagai when cattle prices plunged in the 1980s. The father went to the station to pick up his kids on their arrival home from boarding school. One wasn't on the train. The others he drove home. There he shot the family, including his wife, and hanged himself on a shed hoist.

He has another piece of horror involving a family dispute among siblings over division of the farm. The father settled by later going to the shearing shed and plunging a pair of electric shears into his throat. They found his body at the bottom of the shute where the sheep are dropped outside.

'People in the cities don't understand the pressures on farm people,' Heffernan said, as we drove north from Mulwala through Griffith and West Wyalong, Forbes, Parkes, Dubbo, Walgett and on up to Lightning Ridge and Angledool, near the Queensland border. 'When I wanted to get into politics some years ago, an old State Liberal colleague told me that so long as the bread, the milk, and the meat and veg were in the supermarket, city people didn't give a rat's arse about where it all came from. They just looked on farmers who complained as whingeing cockies.

'Nothing has changed.'

Alan Ramsey

# The End of the Line

**NOVEMBER 24, 2007**

THE END of the line. Remember that heading in the *Herald* a few weeks back, after one of the opinion polls bumped up the Government's lousy standing a point or two? 'Lazarus stirs', it said optimistically of John Howard. Wrong. It was just the flies moving. Yesterday, in the nation's Parliament, with hardly a politician to be seen anywhere, we got some election realism. Three rows of recycling bins, whacking big green ones with yellow lids. More than 300 of them.

Where? In the basement corridor of the ministerial wing. The bins seemed a more apt commentary than all the desperate, last-minute Coalition windbaggery going on around the nation on what is about to descend on the Prime Minister after 33 years in public life and almost 12 years remaking Australia in his own miserable, disfigured image. They arrived two days ago. And whoever they're for, 48 hours before a single vote is cast today, you felt somebody, somewhere, finally got it right.

The end of the line.

Howard doesn't think so, obviously.

'Everybody at some point has to retire and depart the scene,' he told ABC radio's Chris Uhlmann yesterday, 'and what I'm doing is not to mislead the public, to lay out my plans (for a change of Liberal leaders), to say there will be

a transition well into the next term. It will be Peter Costello, the second most experienced person in public life and who's been at the centre of Australia's economic strength for the last 11 1/2 years. You see, we are a team . . .'

Uhlmann: 'But if you're not done after (almost) 12 years, when will you be done? When can Australians make a change?'

Howard: 'Well, it's a question of assessing what is good for the country. You keep focusing on the personalities. I just ask Australians, particularly those who haven't made up their mind, if they think our nation is fundamentally going in the right direction. I ask them not to change the Government, because when you change the Government, you do change the direction of the country.'

Indeed you do. And hallelujah!

Howard obviously does not understand this is exactly what voters seem intent on doing, irrespective of some heroic assessments in the final opinion polls. A clear majority remain heartily sick of the Prime Minister and his Coalition claque of tired mediocrities.

The 'it's time' factor has been driving political sentiment all year, just as the dominant policy issue in the cities has been the Government's hated Work Choices legislation. Clearly, it has not occurred to Howard that, for almost a year, ever since Kevin Rudd replaced

Kim Beazley as the Labor alternative, an overwhelming majority of voters agree it is, indeed, 'a question of assessing what is good' for Australia.

What voters have been 'assessing', in increasing numbers, is they prefer Rudd's 'fresh leadership' to Howard's 'same as usual' approach. And if Howard couldn't bring himself to get out of the way and allow an election choice between Rudd and Costello, then his 'fellow Australians', as he prefers to call them, rather than his 1996 appeals to 'Australia's battlers', will use the ballot box to get rid of his Government.

At Thursday's final National Press Club speech, ABC Television's Michael Brissenden confronted the issue of Howard's slippery behaviour in avoiding questions about what defeat for the Government says about his leadership.

Brissenden: 'It's been pointed out that Paul Keating also said in 1996 that obviously if you change the leader, you change the country, too. When he was defeated, many on your side said this was a rejection of the sorts of things [Keating] stood for: political correctness, those sorts of things. If you are rejected (this time), does that mean the Australian people have rejected the change you've brought (about)?'

Howard: 'I'm not going to hypothesise about defeat, OK? And I don't believe we are going to be defeated. I believe we're going to win. I'm therefore not going to hypothesise and start reflecting and eliminating and getting into all of that. I am conscious (of Keating's remark) and I believe in 1996 people did want to change the direction of the country.

'[But] one of the big differences I don't find, as I go about the country, is that people want a change in the fundamental direction of Australia. I find that people are broadly happy (with it). They have complaints. I mean, I understand that. A lot of people disagreed violently with everything I stand for, I understand that. And there are people unhappy with this or that. Some are saying we like your economic policies but we don't like other policies. I accept all that.

'But I've been in a lot of election campaigns (and) this is not an angry campaign. This is not. I don't actually think it's dirty, either. I mean, there's been some silly things done; I've talked about one of them [the fake terrorism pamphlet by Liberal Party goons in Sydney's outer western suburbs] a bit. There's been a few silly things said elsewhere on the other side. But overall it's not a dirty campaign. It's not been an acrimonious campaign . . . So I don't think people do want to change (Australia's) fundamental direction.'

This is what Howard is good at: sliding around responsibility, around accountability, for things that go wrong. Why should anyone be surprised when he says, 'No, of course Australians don't want to change the country's direction', however he defines it, just as he insists they really don't want to change any of his Government's policies. How then, you wonder, does he account for all those 'fellow Australians' who tell the opinion pollsters his Government stinks, his leadership most of all?

All that soothing tosh about 'no anger' among voters as he 'goes about the country', that it's not been a 'dirty' campaign, though some 'silly things' have been done, by both sides. He can't be serious. If he does believe such twaddle, it only emphasises how out of touch he's become. Howard's true 'genius', if you like, is forever talking to what he sees as his base constituency as if they are no more than sheep. In this he might well be right.

Monday of this week was a Howard anniversary of sorts. On November 19, 1977, John Kerr, as governor-general, swore Howard in as Malcolm Fraser's Treasurer when Melbourne's

Phillip Lynch was forced to resign after he got caught up in a nasty land scandal in a wondrously named outer-suburban development called Stumpy Gully.

Thirty years later, most Australians have little idea what a very ordinary Treasurer Howard turned out to be. Like Peter Costello, he was just another lawyer-politician salesman who knew bugger-all about economics. It is a nice irony that the 30th anniversary of Howard's first big heave-ho up the slippery pole—he was Treasurer for five years—should come on the first day of the last week of his last election campaign.

And, I continue to assert, his last week as Prime Minister. Two days ago, an old Labor friend, sometimes referred to as Whispering Death, the nickname of that wonderful West Indies fast bowler Michael Holding, phoned to say, very quietly: 'I think we might have got (him) this time.' I think he's right. The end of the line.

Alan Ramsey

**Postscript:** *The 'old Labor friend' was John Faulkner, whom my 'old colleague', Mike Carlton, outed a week later by 'borrowing' the quote for his* Herald *column. Know, too, the* Herald *declined to publish Faulkner's actual words, insisting it would not be party to calling the Prime Minister 'the little c . . .', which is the childish code used for sexually explicit profanity in a 'family newspaper'.*

# Finally, we get it Right

**NOVEMBER 26, 2007**

WE HAVE our country back. John Howard's Australia died with his Government on Saturday night. So did the political careers of a whole raft of Coalition MPs. It couldn't be more exquisite than that the Labor iceberg should take our outgoing Prime Minister down, too.

And where was the carnage greatest, despite all that Howard blarney in the campaign's dying days that 'I can still win'? Labor made gains everywhere, but the Liberal bloodbath in NSW and Queensland alone gave Kevin Rudd the 16 Coalition seats (and more) he needed to put Labor into office federally and complete the ALP sweep in every State and Territory.

Nine Labor governments in total. We've not seen its like before.

There was a lot of confected guff yesterday from Coalition colleagues who survived about what a 'great' Prime Minister Howard had been, even the 'greatest' after Menzies, the Liberals' deified founder. Yet the reality is that Howard's enduring legacy is the utter destruction of the party to which he professed, on election night, to 'owe' everything.

All those State and Territory Labor governments now in office, with the exception of NSW, came to power under Howard's watch as Prime Minister. That is, the Liberal Party's Federal leader oversaw the demise of every Liberal or Coalition government in every Australian capital, except Sydney, as he plunged onwards through four Coalition victories federally across the better part of 12 years. Now his Government joins them all in the cemetery.

Yet this, we're told, is a 'great' Prime Minister, the national head of the Liberal Party and the senior partner for almost 60 years in what remains of the conservative non-Labor coalition in Australian politics . . . Such is the reality of Howard's 'greatness'.

As for this last election, th-e one that kills Howard off politically, along with the meanest, most miserable, self-absorbed Federal Government to blight Australia in living memory, Rudd out-campaigned him, with discipline and immense energy, like Howard had not previously been thrashed in his 33 years in national political life.

And for many of us, as Howard and his strategists pulled on every ugly negative they could come up with, not just in these past six weeks but over the past year, it was a delight to see him flounder so badly and fail so completely. All that remains to sweep him out of sight is to get rid of the more obscene remnants of his governance.

Peter Costello, one of those who went through the ritual yesterday of 'talking up' the selfish little man who never understood when it was time to get out, has been smart enough to understand he is not going to hang about and try to resurrect the wreck Howard leaves behind. Who could blame him?

Now, while Costello honours, on the back bench, his commitment to voters in his Melbourne seat, those other political misfits like Alexander Downer, Philip Ruddock and Tony Abbott should think about another life outside politics. None are part of the Liberals' future. For God's sake go, and make our Christmas complete.

Alan Ramsey

Printed in Dunstable, United Kingdom

85050401R00211